The Scottsboro
Boys in Their
Own Words

The Scottsboro Boys in Their Own Words

Selected Letters, 1931–1950

Edited by
Kwando M. Kinshasa

McFarland & Company, Inc., Publishers
Jefferson, North Carolina

LIBRARY OF CONGRESS CATALOGUING-IN-PUBLICATION DATA

The Scottsboro boys in their own words : selected letters,
    1931–1950 / edited by Kwando M. Kinshasa.
        p.   cm.
    Includes bibliographical references and index.

    ISBN 978-0-7864-7204-8
    softcover : acid free paper ∞

    1. Scottsboro Trial, Scottsboro, Ala., 1931.   2. Trials
(Rape)—Alabama—Scottsboro.   3. African Americans—
Alabama—Scottsboro—Correspondence.   4. African
Americans—Civil rights—United States—History.
    I. Kinshasa, Kwando Mbiassi, editor.
    KF224.S34S35   2014
    345.761'02532092396073—dc23   2013037862

BRITISH LIBRARY CATALOGUING DATA ARE AVAILABLE

Front cover image: Clarence Norris, right, and Charlie Weems,
left, in Decatur, Alabama, July 16, 1937 (AP Photo)

Manufactured in the United States of America

McFarland & Company, Inc., Publishers
    Box 611, Jefferson, North Carolina 28640
    www.mcfarlandpub.com

To my wife, Imani Kinshasa,
and her uncompromising sense of justice

TABLE OF CONTENTS

ACKNOWLEDGMENTS

There are many individuals and institutions who contributed to this publication. However, it was the foresight of a close family friend many years ago, Ms. Willie Mae-Lacy, who put me in contact with a Scottsboro defendant, Clarence Norris, that eventually provided the basis for this volume. In similar fashion, my brief discussion with Attorney Mimi Rosenberg some years ago as to the value of letters written by the Scottsboro defendants is greatly appreciated. An immense appreciation is extended towards Dr. Ira Goldwasser and his wife Harriett Broekman in Amsterdam, who assisted me in researching and translating archival material related to the Scottsboro case written in Dutch at the Internationaal Instituut Voor Sociale Geschiedenis (International Institute for Social History). This material assisted me in better understanding Mrs. Ada Wright's (mother of two of the Scottsboro defendants) visit and presentation to the Dutch Scottsboro Defense Committee in 1933. Special thanks to colleague and scholar Dr. Patricia J. Gibson (John Jay College of Criminal Justice, CUNY) for sharing her thoughts on the relationship between written historical narratives and grammar. I am also extremely thankful for an invitation afforded me by Ms. Sheila Washington to visit the Scottsboro Boys Museum in Scottsboro, Alabama, and for affording me the opportunity to meet with community residents who remembered events surrounding the trials in both Scottsboro and Decatur, Alabama. Special gratitude and respect are expressed to the wisdom and knowledge of the late attorney Joseph Fleming. His awareness of the controversial legal aspects in the Scottsboro case was extremely instructive and insightful, as was his insistence that I get the job done.

I am indebted to the PSC-CUNY Research and Award Program at John Jay College of Criminal Justice's Sponsored Research Program Director, Mr. Jacob Marini, and his excellent staff, for providing me the necessary financial support to bring this project to fruition. Without this assistance, conducting my research at archival institutions throughout the nation and abroad would have been difficult at best.

    The following universities and archival institutions are acknowledged
for their support and providing me with access to both source and contextual
material related to the Scottsboro Boys. Specific gratitude is extended to: the
Manuscript, Archives and Rare Books Division, Schomburg Center for
Research in Black Culture, the New York Public Library, Astor, Lenox and
Tilden Foundations for providing me with the opportunity to examine and
include the International Labor Defense Records (Sc Micro R-981). Similarly,
I wish to thank the National Association for the Advancement of Colored
People (NAACP), for authorizing the use of their correspondence, documen-
tation and image also housed at the Schomburg Center for Research in Black
Culture; the Alabama Department of Archival History (ADAH) in Mont-
gomery, Alabama; the Harry Ransom Research Center at the University of
Texas in Austin; the Henry Wadsworth Longfellow Dana Collection's Scotts-
boro Boys Trial Collection, 1932–1938, in the Manuscript, Archives, and Rare
Book Library at Emory University (MARBL) in Atlanta, Georgia; the Allan
Knight Chalmers Center located in the Howard Gotlieb Archival Research
Center at Boston University, Massachusetts; the Beinecke Rare Book and
Manuscript Library at Yale University, Connecticut; and the Bobst Library's
Tamiment Library archival photo and documentation collection at New York
University. A special appreciation goes to Mr. Thomas Mills, Head of Col-
lections at the Cornell University Law Library, New York, for his assistance
in providing me with the opportunity to photograph the model freight train
used by Attorney Samuel Leibowitz during the 1933 trial in Decatur, Alabama.

    I must also acknowledge and honor the support of my parents who when
I was a child sat with me at the kitchen table and through countless conver-
sations over many years taught me the importance of the historical narrative.
Last, but not least, I thank my family for their understanding and patience
while I worked on this project. I salute their concern for my health and the
project, and applaud their appreciation of what I do.

PREFACE

Most Americans, particularly those who were black or white, explicitly knew in 1931 that for the foreseeable future their place under an American conception of democracy would be formulated by their race, class and gender, as was that of their father's father. One's ancestors were either enslaved, induced to feel that they were members of a suspect race or were valued citizens of a slave-owning society. Implicitly this meant that to challenge the rights of those anointed by social privilege and entitlement in 1931 was to defy tradition and a governing race's accepted wisdom on what constituted social order.

Hollace Ransdell, a young teacher, journalist and activist, found this to be the case when, as a reporter for the American Civil Liberties Union, she was sent to the American south and observed the tribulations of Alabama's Scottsboro rape trial. After a few months Ransdell reported, "Southern whites feel to their marrow bone only one thing about the Negro, and they say it over and over. Hundreds of thousands of them have been saying it for generations. They will continue to say it as long as anyone will listen. It is their only answer to the Negro problem. It is their reply to the questions of the Scottsboro case — the Nigger must be kept down" (Ransdell, 1931, p. 11).

And just who were these "Niggers [who] must be kept down?" What was their background? Why were they considered by some to be a threat to the social order, and to others an embarrassment, a problem they would like to whisk away? While an epigrammatic sketch of each defendant's background might assist in answering these inquires, as would possibly an understanding of the social context from which they emerged, neither could explicate or illuminate the inner core of each defendant's feelings. Only their personal words could assist in that task. However, with this said, the following profiles are helpful in orientating the reader to the minimum that was provided the public in 1931 about each African American youth, soon to be defined as the "Scottsboro Boys."

One overall characteristic that each of the defendants and their white female accusers shared was the harshness of their social backgrounds. For

1

example, both Charlie Weems 19, and Clarence Norris 18, for whom the "Scottsboro boys" indictment was named, *State of Alabama vs. Charley Weems, and Clarence Norris,* came from rural Georgia backgrounds. Though Charlie Weems's mother died when he was four, and only one of his seven siblings survived childhood, he managed to finish the fifth grade of school. Weems soon found a job as a stock boy in a pharmacy and worked as such until 1931, when he decided to try his luck by migrating by rail to Memphis, Tennessee. Clarence Norris was born in a little rural town in Georgia called Warm Springs. From the age of seven, Clarence worked on a little one-horse farm that his father had maintained in the nearby town of Molena. Toiling literally from sun-up to sundown, he missed school after the first grade. Not wanting to do sharecropping all of his life he left home at 17, and eventually began to ride the rails looking for work. After he was arrested in Paint Rock, Alabama, his mother, Mrs. Inez Norris, became a vocal advocate for her son's innocence and release. Similarly, Ozie Powell, 16, also born in rural Georgia, had but one year of school prior to "jumping" the train to find work in distant lumber camps. Court documents, mainly his psychiatric report, indicated that Powell had an extremely low IQ level, somewhere slightly above 64. This would cause him to suffer horrendous wounds and abuse throughout his imprisonment in Alabama.

Though Norris, Weems and Powell, as well as the rest of the Scottsboro defendants, were generally aware of the duplicity of the law as it pertained to black "hoboes" traveling the rails during the Depression, they were particularly aware of racist social mores upon which southern state laws were premised and the dangers that accrued from being, essentially, black vagrants.

Upon being arrested in Paint Rock, Alabama, on March 25, 1931, and subsequently tried in nearby Scottsboro for assault and rape of two white female hoboes, they were not prepared for a struggle for freedom that would take decades of trials and appeals, hinged on interpretations of Alabama and Federal law to secure their release from imprisonment. In these ensuing legal battles a number of critical life-saving constitutional rights precedents in both *Powell v. Alabama* (1932) and *Norris v. Alabama* (1935) not only prevented the execution of these nine black youths, but also established legal precedents for other imprisoned African Americans:

> In *Powell v. Alabama* the issue of equal protection under the 14th Amendment to the Federal Constitution was critical in that it challenged the failure of the State to provide effective assistance of counsel even though it sought to execute the defendants. It was also argued that this thereby jeopardized the defendants' chances for a "fair, impartial and deliberate trial" [en.wikipedia. org/wiki/Powell_v._Alabama].

In *Norris v. Alabama* it was also argued that the State of Alabama's purposeful exclusion of blacks from the jury service was a blatant circumvention of the 6th Amendment to the constitution (Ransdell, p. 102). However, many southern states' rights advocates declared that "extra legal methods" were being superimposed upon a people accustomed to self government, and that the U.S. Supreme Court's decisions in the Scottsboro case ran counter to what the "people" of the State so desired (Carter, 1979, p. 322). Nevertheless the *Norris* decision directly attacked the "long term absence of blacks from juries in jurisdictions with sizable black populations" and within twelve years set a precedent that allowed "the reversed convictions in five cases in which a black defendant had been sentenced to death by all white juries in counties where blacks had been absent as jurors for decades" (Ransdell, p. 177).

Two other arrested youths, Andy Wright, 19, and Roy Wright, 12, were brothers from Chattanooga, Tennessee. Andy attended school and was considered a good student until the sixth grade, when his father died and he quit school to assist his mother in supporting the family. He began driving a truck for a food producer at age twelve, a job he kept for seven years until the company's insurance company learned of his young age and raised their rates. In March 1931 Andy and his younger brother Roy, along with two friends, Haywood Patterson and Eugene Williams, decided to widen their horizons in search of work by traveling to Memphis, Tennessee, where it was rumored government jobs were available hauling logs on the Mississippi River. Jumping on a Southern Railroad freight train as hoboes they headed westward to Memphis, with no inkling that unanticipated events would soon change their lives forever.

Among these four migrants, Haywood Patterson, 18, was the most seasoned. Born and raised in Georgia, Patterson was the son of a sharecropping family. He left school after the third grade and worked as a delivery boy for a time, after which he left home at the age of fourteen and took to the rails as an itinerant worker, traveling back and forth from Ohio to Florida and then on to Arkansas. By early 1931 he was a veteran traveler who had left his family to obtain work as a steelworker in Chattanooga. Little is known about the background of Eugene Williams, 13, except that he worked as a dishwasher in a Chattanooga café and was friends with the Wright brothers and Haywood Patterson when they jumped aboard the western-bound freight train.

Of the nine Scottsboro Boys, 17-year-old Willie Roberson's physical health was most problematic. He had just left his job as a hotel busboy in Georgia and was also travelling to Chattanooga to find better work when events conspired against him. Years earlier he lived in a number of brothels, and unfortunately contracted syphilis, which left him with sores all over his genitals. Because this made it very difficult and painful for him to walk or have sexual intercourse, Roberson concluded that if he could eventually make it to Memphis, Tennessee, and then Chattanooga to earn some money he could eventually find a doctor to treat his serious illness. Hardly able to walk without a cane, he barely managed the fateful climb aboard the Southern Railroad freight train.

Another seriously handicapped youth on the Southern Railroad was seventeen-year-old Olen Montgomery. Born and raised in Monroe, Georgia, Olen suffered poor eyesight and a cataract; he was also literate, and a song writer. He too boarded the Southern Railroad freight train bound for Memphis, Tennessee, with the expectations of finding work to pay for new glasses and possibly an operation to remove his cataract, as he wrote to his lawyer, George Chamlee: "I was on my way to Memphis on a oil tank By My Self a lone and i was Not Worried With any one untell I Got to Paint Rock Alabama and they Just made a Frame up on uS Boys Just Cause they Cud" (Olen Montgomery Transcript: PBS *American Experience Scottsboro: An American Tragedy.* DVD. Goodman and Anker, 2005). Suffering greatly under both the psychological and physical torture of Alabama's Kilby State Prison, with its electric chair known as "Yellow Mama" and its convict farm labor system, Montgomery composed and expressed his feelings and thoughts in a ballad entitled "Lonesome Jailhouse Blues," where he exclaimed, "All last night I walked my cell and cried, Cause this old jailhouse done get-so lonesome I can't be satisfied" (PBS Goodman & Anker, 2005).

For these nine African American migrants life became treacherously complicated at Paint Rock, Alabama, when two white female hoboes cried rape. Not surprisingly, up to her death in 1982 the older of the two accusers, Victoria Price, 21 at the time of the arrests, maintained that she was "gang raped" by six of the nine black youths. On the other hand, within a year of the alleged rape, Price's traveling companion, Ruby Bates, 18, recanted her charge and admitted in a letter to a boyfriend in broken English, "...i know it was wrong too let those Negroes die on account of me ... i was jaze But those white Boys jazzed me i wish those Negroes are not burnt on account of me..."(Carter, p. 187). Important as this statement was to defendants and their attorneys during the early trials, it was also indicative of the differences between the two women, something that was readily apparent in spite of the social environment of which they were products.

Both women were cotton mill workers in the economically depressed northern town of Huntsville, Alabama. Though most of the mills in that part of the country were either short of work or simply not running during the early years of the Depression, one social service worker noted of this particular area, "under the strain of life in Huntsville, the institution of the family does not stand up very well. It is a rare mill family that is not touched in some form by prostitution, disease, prison, insane asylum, and drunkenness." Elaborating on this, social researcher Ransdell subjectively explained, "That's the kind of thing these mill workers are mixed up with all the time [and] I'm beginning to forget how decent people behave, I've been messing around with venereal disease and starvation and unemployment so long" (Ransdell, p. 7). More revealing of social structure, Ransdell adds, "There was no evidence of a functional father in either Price's or Bates' household."

One resident of Huntsville, Alabama, described Victoria Price as "a twenty-one year old spinner at the Margaret Cotton Mill in Huntsville, Alabama, making $1.20 a day. The Margaret Mill was old and dilapidated and fighting a losing battle against the depression, leaving Price with only five or six days of work a month." This denizen also claimed that "Price was the promiscuous, hard drinking, hard swearing daughter of a Huntsville widow who lived in the poor, racially mixed section of town. She made love in box cars and fields, slept in hobo jungles, and rode the rails in a pair of beaten overalls" (Scottsboro Trial Homepages: Victoria Price, p. 1). In fact, an affidavit by the defense team in the Scottsboro trial tended to support this profile of Price when it stated Price was "a common street prostitute of the lowest type," a woman who would "be out at all hours of the night and curse and swear, and be a general nuisance to the Negro population" (Scottsboro Trial Homepages: Victoria Price, p. 1).

However, seventeen-year-old Ruby Bates is described in another report as being "a large, fresh, good-looking girl, shy, but a fluent enough talker when encouraged. She spits snuff juice on the floor continually while talking, holding one finger over half her mouth to keep the stream from missing aim. After each spurt she carefully wipes her mouth with her arm and looks up again with soft, melancholy eyes, as resigned and moving as those of a handsome truck horse" (Ransdell, p. 8). And while these descriptions differ in pulling together a profile of each accuser, an interviewer of both Price and Bates noted that "neither one had the slightest notion of the seriousness of what they were saying. The only opinion they had run across so far was that which said the "Niggers" must get the death sentence at once or be lynched. Never having met any other attitude on the Negro question, they both assumed that this was my attitude, and therefore spoke to me as they thought all respectable white people speak" (Ransdell, p. 9). Lacking any social references except that established by two centuries of southern lore, racism, violence, class and gender oppression, the world for white southerners like Price and Bates was premised primarily upon the notion that "poor they be, but niggers they ain't!"

The racial struggle between African and European Americans for the lives of the Scottsboro youths was not limited to the defendants or their accusers, but was transferred to the legal battleground of courtrooms attended by attorneys of the ILD and the NAACP. On this battlefield, ideological struggles as to the proper strategies to be waged in defense of the Scottsboro youth were as intense and critical for the defendants as their physical proximity to the electric chair at Kilby Prison in Montgomery, Alabama. Not surprisingly, the next nineteen years of struggle converted these youths into men, particularly as their ongoing saga evolved into narratives of heroic proportions. Whether it was their revolt against the living conditions within Birmingham, Alabama's, city jail; their rejection of slave-like working conditions at the Kilby Prison's cotton mill; Atmore State Prison's notorious farm system; beatings by racist and opportunistic guards; Ozie Powell's stabbing of a deputy sheriff who cursed and slapped him; Haywood Patterson's dramatic escape from the Kilby Prison; or Clarence Norris's successful violation of his parole by fleeing Alabama and not returning until his pardon by Governor George Wallace on October 25, 1976, these years turned into decades while the Scottsboro defendants struggled to sustain a level of self respect that went far beyond the walls that entombed them. In this respect, the following selected letters of the Scottsboro defendants are a valuable resource for understanding the intensity of the African American struggle for survival and development in the face of intense repression.

INTRODUCTION

An examination of the Scottsboro, Alabama, rape case of 1931 must confront what noted attorney Haywood Burns observed as "an American story, at once tragic, and gripping, ultimately, perhaps ennobling" (Burns, 2003, p. 1). In an absorbing approach, Burns's observation not only addresses the historical and undeniable reality of American racial and judicial duplicity, but the heroic nature of those who, with relatively few weapons in their possession beyond an immense sense of personal dignity, challenged and dared to carve out for themselves a role as courageous survivors. And while the Scottsboro trial was indeed a judicial case of immense importance that touched the nerves and souls of people throughout the nation and world, it was also a saga of immense human proportions that is illuminated by the letters of its primary participants, the Scottsboro defendants.

With this in mind, a contemporary review and analysis of the Scottsboro case should not begin with the events that unfolded on a cold March 25, 1931, morning in central Alabama, where a group of black and white hoboes on a Southern Railroad freight train battled for seating space in one of the chert carry freight cars. Nor does it begin when the train was stopped and boarded by the local sheriff and his deputized residents in the little town of Paint Rock, Alabama, who were searching for blacks they suspected of earlier assaulting and throwing whites off the train. It does, however, begin with a realization that American mores and laws dating back to the earliest formation of the republic forbade or severely limited social relationships between the races. Within this social construct, any pursuit of justice that would permit a person of African heritage the right to physically resist provocations by European Americans was generally denounced as if in compliance with antebellum American law that demanded, "blacks of all types — the free, the enslaved, and those of disputed status — were [to be] discriminated against racially by the criminal law" (Kennedy, 1997, p. 81).

Though the penalty for violating deeply entrenched southern racial protocols was well established by centuries of de jure and de facto practice, why these nine black youths were not lynched forthright on March 25, 1931, may have more to do with happenstance than law. Clearly it could be deduced that the sudden discovery of two white female hoboes dressed as men and *their* fear of being arrested as vagrants may well be viewed as a fortuitous development for the nine black youths. Fearing the consequences of being sent to a convict labor camp for vagrancy, the two female hoboes, Victoria Price and Ruby Bates, upon questioning by the local sheriff, opportunistically claimed that while on the freight train they were gang raped by the nine black hoboes. This charge of rape by black men, particularly within the historical context of America, was enough of a catalyst to set in motion a series of events in the fertile soil of racial hatred and social economic stress that was Alabama. For the nine black migrant youths, gone were the earlier serious charges of being vagrants or useless miscreants. Minimized though not completely forgotten were the socially egregious charges of assaulting white men on the train. Facing them now in the halls of Alabama's judicial system was the clarion call of two women that they were gang raped and otherwise abused by "*niggers.*" This was not the rape of *any* two women, but that of two *white* women by black men.

In this and similar instances the important racial dissimilarity between the alleged white victims and their accused black perpetrators transformed the charge itself into a fact, and the sentencing of guilt into a mere formality before execution. Accordingly, in a society in which civil and human rights of non-whites had been continually and systematically abated by federal, state, and local laws since the end of Reconstruction in 1877, any semblance of respect for anyone with pronounced African physical features was rare. To expect that any testimony or social narrative by an American citizen of African heritage within a southern context would be given the same credence as that of a white person was ludicrous. Equally significant, any accusation of rape involving a white female trumped any other charges placed upon a black man, and when the charge was leveled, all immediately assumed guilt. The only other criminal charge that approached the seriousness of such an allegation was interracial violence in which the white person was viewed as being the victim.

While a racialized charge of "rape" in the Scottsboro case triggered an onslaught of national and international journalistic interest due to the infamous reputation of the American judicial system towards its black citizens, few legal pundits could have predicted the impact this case portended for the American judicial system. Fewer still who were aware of the events in Paint Rock, Alabama, anticipated a forty-five-year judicial battle that would galvanize both the legal ingenuity of the International Labor Defense (ILD) and the National Association for the Advancement of Colored People (NAACP) on behalf of the nine defendants. With this noted, though the nine Scottsboro defendants and some family members received international attention, public recognition or understanding of their personal courage, physical fortitude, psychological stamina, ingenuity and intelligence was scant throughout their ordeal. Such recognition would have required a review of their correspondence in the form of letters sent back and forth between the defendants and supporters, family members and attorneys over a period of two to four decades. The present volume collects and presents that correspondence.

The selected letters, memoranda and legal correspondence written by or to the nine defendants, their family members, supporters or attorneys from 1931 to 1950 provide unique insight into the personalities of incarcerated young men living on the precipice of psychological collapse and physical execution. Their letters are a journey into the torturous landscape of American judicial history as seen through the mind's eye of the Scottsboro defendants. As such these often poorly constructed written reflective narratives are but the beginning salvos of broader thoughts and feelings on incarceration, racial violence and often clashing difficulties between a client's demands and the concerns of their legal representation.

Notwithstanding the day-to-day psychological stress of incarceration, with its explicit violent surroundings and limitless array of violations, through these letters the reader can review how judicial precedents conceived to function within a specific official context may have devastating and unwanted repercussions upon a defendant in another context. And while living conditions for the Scottsboro defendants in Montgomery, Alabama's, death house, Kilby Prison and its State Farm were horrendous and akin to the violence in Birmingham's jail, they were sadly representative of conditions experienced by many other Alabama state prisoners (see Appendix B). However, it was only when these nine defendants captured the attention and support of millions of people throughout the nation and in foreign countries by describing in letters the level of penal brutality, torture and anguish they experienced that they emerged not only as prime examples of judicial injustice, but also as spokesmen against judicial brutality and penal torture.

With this in mind it is also imperative to understand that most of the Scottsboro defendants were not literate enough to write their own name or complete extensive letters without the assistance of others. In many instances this help came from Olen Montgomery or a reliable jailhouse trustee. As a result, letters by any one Scottsboro defendant tended to reflect different writing styles over a period of time as other inmates assisted. However, this was not true for Haywood Patterson. Though semi-literate when arrested at Paint

Rock, Alabama, he became an articulate, robust, self taught writer who was also considered by the prosecution as the "most guilty and the most defiant" of the Scottsboro Boys! Within a year of incarceration, Patterson was able to express himself in such a convincing manner that his correspondence to lawyers and supporters outside of prison was soon recognized by the ILD (International Labor Defense) as one of the most effective tools to propagate the case worldwide (Scottsboro Trial Homepage: Biography Page, pp. 1–2). In fact, the written "real time" thoughts of the Scottsboro defendants have become an extremely important part of the African American historical narrative, particularly when understanding that this case was one of the most significant judicial cases in American history.

*   *   *

Though over the past thirty years the editor's perspective concerning the Scottsboro defendants and their accusers was affected by numerous interviews with Mr. Clarence Norris — which resulted in the book *The Man from Scottsboro: Clarence Norris in His Own Words* — I am also cognizant of the problematic relationship between a researcher and the primary informants, and the difficulties therein with subjective historical narratives. However, after spending many years reading prison letters from Norris and the other eight defendants, I have come to understand these expository narratives, with their unique variations, as more than simply "letters from prison." They are instead indexed, real-time coherent responses by incarcerated black migrants to physical degradation, psychological coercion and racial repression. As such, we can appreciate the difficult choices that were made to survive, choices that had unforeseen consequences beyond the shadow of their own being, yet choices from which significant history was fashioned.

While thoughts expressed through the letter format can encapsulate the drama and stress experienced by the writer, understanding the essential aspects of a life through letters can be challenging for the reader. This is surely the case when the topic is life imprisonment or the expectation of execution and all of the accompanying connotations of guilt or innocence. With this said, the following selected letters provide the reader with an opportunity to delve into the world of condemned individuals. By describing the terrors of their incarceration, the Scottsboro defendants and supporters have prepared the reader to understand what the defendants certainly considered as their only existing alternatives to life-long incarceration: physical escape or acceptance of execution by the State of Alabama.

In this regard, I regret not having an opportunity to personally interview all of the Scottsboro defendants. What more could we have learned from Haywood Patterson about his dramatic escape from Kilby Prison Farm outside of Montgomery, Alabama? Similarly, one can only envision the anger of Ozie Powell, who cut the throat of an insulting deputy sheriff while being transported from prison to court.

Similarly, an opportunity to interview Victoria Price or Ruby Bates would have been intriguing, primarily because their now legendary charge of being raped or otherwise sexually violated by male blacks is very much a part of American judicial and social cultural mythology. This mythology was buttressed by the notorious comments of Scottsboro Judge Callahan, who in the third trial in 1933 charged the jury with the following infamous directive:

> Where the woman charged to have been raped as in this case, is a white woman, there is a very strong presumption under the law that she would not and did not yield voluntarily to intercourse with the defendant, a Negro; and this is true, whatever the station in life the prosecutrix may occupy, whether she be the most despised, ignorant and abandoned woman of the community, or the spotless virgin and daughter of a prominent home of luxury and learning [Randall, 1997, p. 101; *New York Times,* December 1, 1933].

* * *

Finally, it should be noted that probably the most amazing aspect of the nineteen-year legal ordeal, as well as the additional twenty-six-year struggle for Clarence Norris's pardon, was its extremely broad political and ideological appeal. In my effort to fully understand the totality of this historic case and the highly complex politics surrounding it, I decided to review the case through the archival microfilm files, writings and correspondence of the defense teams, meaning the International Labor Defense (ILD) and the National Association for the Advancement of Colored People (NAACP). A critical component of this research project was made possible by affording me the time and space to carefully review volumes of letters and correspondence from these two organizations through access to much of this material at the Schomburg Center for Research in Black Culture (SCRBC) in New York City.

This said, the reader is now offered a golden opportunity to review two organizations that (a) were politically opposed to each other's ideological thinking and philosophical approaches on how to confront racism and the American class structure, and (b) disagreed on the correct manner to fight racism within the United States and how best to inform the American populace about the Scottsboro case. The selected letters in this volume will assist the reader in recognizing that the NAACP in the 1930s primarily viewed its political mandate as one defined by judicial activism via the court system.

While the NAACP's primary constituency was national, the ILD openly propagated direct and politically radical approaches to resolving not only national and international issues, but doing so through processes that required the mass mobilization of people. Its political organizing efforts were able to draw upon support from international socialist and communist entities as well as national chapters of the ILD. With this in mind, one can begin to assess each organization's influential strength, relative to the Scottsboro defendants' negligible social awareness at the onset of their trial.

Though the defendants' political astuteness would apparently evolve over a period of 19 years, an analysis of letters written between the defendants and the NAACP and ILD suggests that over those years, until the last defendant was released from Kilby Prison, unforeseen and dangerous nuances of their lifestyles and personalities would emerge.

Because the Scottsboro trial attracted international attention and support, archival material in the form of letters and other correspondence has spread throughout the world, e.g., legal correspondence, pins, photos and political propaganda. Though archival institutions within the United States have acquired much of this correspondence, the process of obtaining access or even knowing where to look can be daunting. Personal papers related to a specific person(s) associated with the Scottsboro case might not appear in any general online indexing of the case, but instead will appear in a private paper collection in a distant city or country, such as with the Richard B. Moore Papers Collection, which can be reviewed at the Schomburg Center for Research in Black Culture (SCRBC) in New York City.

For example, I traveled up to Cornell University Law Library in upstate New York to review archival documents on the trial donated by the trial lead attorney, Samuel Leibowitz. Discovering that a model train exhibit utilized by attorney Leibowitz during the second Scottsboro trial in Decatur, Alabama, is part of the law library's permanent exhibit was a major and pleasant surprise. Archival research can be enhanced by a developing sense of the evaluation of your subject matter.

Significant letters related to the trial were obtained from Boston University's Howard Gotlieb Archival Research Center/Allan Knight Chalmers Papers. From this archival center I was fortunate to consult the actual letters and legal correspondence between Dr. Chalmers, Haywood Patterson, and ILD worker Miss Hester G. Huntington. Patterson, being one of the few defendants who became a proficient and literate writer while incarcerated, also became an extremely controversial individual, as is reflected in his letters. Dr. Chalmers and Hester G. Huntington became two of many important ILD contact persons for the Scottsboro defendants. Reading their letters and responses to the various problems faced by the defendants increased my understanding of their non-negotiable situation and the limitless tragic possibilities that existed throughout this case.

As a final example in stressing the unique network of writings that surrounds the Scottsboro case, I found it necessary to review letters and petitions from international political activists and concerned individuals such as Ezra Pound, Sinclair Lewis and Andre Gide. This material was discovered as part of the Nancy Cunard Collection at the Harry Ransom Center at the University of Texas at Austin. One particular aspect of Nancy Cunard's papers demonstrated the breadth of dynamic and explosive political activity in Europe on the Scottsboro case during the early 1930s and before the onslaught of World War Two. As the heiress of the Cunard shipping line, Nancy Cunard was quick to raise questions about class alliances and political organizing around the Scottsboro case, as well as to criticize aspects of the defense team's strategy. Her writings and correspondence with a Scottsboro mother, Mrs. Ida Norris, and defendant Haywood Patterson are important and symptomatic of the breadth and influence of the Scottsboro case and the defendants' search for justice.

1

LETTERS FROM 1931
Establishing the Legal Ground

March 30, 1931: The Grand Jury indicts all nine Scottsboro defendants for rape

April 6–7: Defendants *Clarence Norris* and *Charlie Weems* are tried before Judge A. E. Hawkins, are convicted, and sentenced to death by electrocution.

April 7–8: *Haywood Patterson* is tried, convicted and sentenced to death by electrocution (see Appendix D).

April 8–9: *Olen Montgomery, Ozie Powell, Willie Roberson, Eugene Williams* and *Andy Wright* are tried, convicted and sentenced to death by electrocution.

April 9: *Roy Wright*, the younger brother of Andy Wright, is 13 years old. The jury vote on Roy is 11 to 1, as one juror voted for a life sentence.

April–December: The International Labor Defense (ILD) and the National Association of Colored People (NAACP) begin to vie for the right to represent the Scottsboro defendants in court.

In April 1931, the International Labor Defense (ILD) issued reports highlighting their conflict with the National Association for the Advancement of Colored People (NAACP) over which organization would be the legal representation for the nine African American youths who were arrested in Alabama a few weeks earlier, on March 25. In this regard the ILD published the following:

> Nine boys were arrested in Paint Rock, Alabama, on March 25th, arraigned on the same day and committed to jail without bond on a charge of rape. Judge Hawkins immediately called a special term of the grand jury which convened on March 30th, immediately indicted the boys and committed them to jail, all in one day. Judge set the trial for April 6. In three days all of the boys were tried, convicted and sentenced to die in the electric chair, with the exception of Roy Wright, who is only 14 years old; one juror held out for life imprisonment for him, because of his youth, causing a mistrial. In two weeks,

15

without being given time to prepare their defense or take as their lawyer other than those appointed by the court itself and a thoroughly undependable lawyer sent from Chattanooga, the boys were sentenced to a legal lynching.

Met for First Time When Arrested

The facts as thus far gathered are: Andy Wright, Roy Wright, Haywood Patterson and Eugene Williams, are friends and from Chattanooga, boarded the freight train in their city on the way to Memphis in search of work. Olin Montgomery was traveling alone, Norris and Weems were traveling together, as were Willie Robinson and Ozie Powell. None of these groups knew each other; they met for the first time when they were taken off the train at Paint Rock. When taken off the train they were taken off in four different groups and from four different cars, widely separated on the train which consisted of about 45 cars. At about 12:30, near Stevenson, a fight started between white and colored boys in a gondola. The white boys evidently got the worst of the argument and hopped off the train at a point outside of Stevenson, which is about 18 miles from Paint Rock. About ten minutes after the white boys jumped off, the colored boys who had participated in the fight also hopped off the freight.

The train stopped at Paint Rock, where two groups of armed deputies on each side of the train combed the train from engine to caboose, and rounded up everybody they could find on the train. The round-up resulted in the nine boys and the two girls dressed in overall. None of the boys had seen the girls before or knew on what part of the train they were located.

Arrested for Hoboing

At the time of the arrest, the deputy, who had evidently deputized the others, stated that he was picking them all up for hoboing. The nine boys were confronted with the two girls at Paint Rock. The sheriff asked two girls if these boys had done anything to them, and the girls answered no. They were all taken to Scottsboro in autos. In the Scottsboro jail, the sheriff continued to confront the boys with the girls and kept yelling and insisting that the girls identify these boys as having attacked them. The girls refused on several occasions. Then made indefinite charges, but were finally bulldozed into making the rape charges.

It is reported that the white boys, who were forced off the train at Stevenson, had someone telephone ahead to stop the train and get the Negro boys who had forced them off. The deputy's posse stopped the train to arrest the Negro boys who had fought the white boys; instead they found the nine defendants, who remained on the train because they did not participate in any fight and had nothing to fear. When the two white girls were also found on the same train, the immediate lynch law cry of attacking a white woman was set up.

Accusers Are Irresponsible

The two girls, Victoria Price and Ruby Bates, are notorious prostitutes. Ruby Bates had previously been arrested for "hugging" a Negro on one of the main streets of Chattanooga.

Affidavits from local residents testify the irresponsibility and disreputable character of both women. The court physician who examined them stated that when they were first examined "they were not nervous or hysterical over it at all."

From the very day of the arrest everything was done to rouse lynch spirit, and to create the atmosphere for the lynching in the courthouse by the State of Alabama. On the day of the trial, 10,000 farmers were in the little town of Scottsboro (population 1500). Shouting by the mob, applause in the court-room, within the hearing of a second jury, and the music of a brass band, greeted the announcement of the first death verdict.

It was in such an atmosphere, within three days, that eight young boys were condemned to be electrocuted, on the unsubstantiated evidence of two irresponsible prostitutes. (Evidence recently come to light proves that one of the boys now doomed to die for rape is incapable of having sex rela-tions).

The trials were not only swift, but irregular. Stephen Roddy, hired by some ministers in Chattanooga (since then it is claimed he was hired by the NAACP), stated in court that he was "not employed counsel for the defen-dants." Neither he nor the other defense attorney, appointed by the State, even communicated with the parents of the boys, although they are all minors, and the death penalty could be — and is — asked for!

Roddy's entire character has come under suspicion since the trial. An obscure lawyer, who never had a case outside the police court up to this time, it is alleged that he has just been released from an asylum where he has been treated for habitual drunkenness.

His handling of the defense, either intentionally or because of incompe-tence, constitutes a betrayal of the eight youths — a betrayal to death. Although he knew the hopelessness of the case for the boys, and that their right of appeal would be based on his exceptions, Roddy permitted incompe-tent testimony throughout, without offering objections. Nor did he, at the end of the third trial, sum up his case, <u>nor make a plea to the jury to acquit,</u> although the prosecution exercised this right and took the opportunity to press for a death penalty.

The question of participation in this case by the National Association for the Advancement of Colored People has become a controversial one. The enclosed letter by William Pickens, Field Secretary of that organization, throws light on this subject. Mr. Pickens has endorsed the struggle being made by the International Labor Defense, which defense organization this Committee has pledged to assist.

The International Labor Defense took up this case immediately (when) it came to their attention. At the moment of writing it has secured a victory to this extent: a rehearing of a motion for new trials for all nine children has been allowed. The attorneys handling the case are General George W. Cham-lee of Chattanooga, and Joseph Bronsky, of New York, backed by a staff of attorneys in New York City. They are the only attorneys in the case, having been hired by the International Labor Defense with the consent of the chil-dren and their parents. It is the present claim of the N.A.C.C.P that the attorneys Roody and Moody — who secured death sentences are still in the case, but this is not true, the nine youth having repudiated this defense in writing.

The International Labor Defense's objective is to save the lives of the nine innocent boys. It recognizes that the best legal defense must be fortified by the most tremendous mass protest, if this objective is to be gained. According to the Southern attorney, Chamlee, the two victories thus far gained are the result of the tremendous pressure caused by the protest which poured in from all over the country. These protest were the result of the agitation made by the International Labor Defense. This organization realized that judicial proceeding are no guarantee of justice. Legal lynchings have been too tragically numerous for that.

The International Labor Defense has placed in this case all the forces at its command. Two investigators are trying to locate the white boys who fought on the train; to uncover the character of the chief witnesses against the boys; attorneys are working on the legal forms; protests are being made and the case being brought to the attention of the entire nation. The case is now in excellent hands, as proven not by promises, but by swift and able deeds [Chamlee, Reel 4, Box 4, ILD].

On April 11, 1931, two days after the jury in Scottsboro, Alabama, found the nine defendants guilty of raping the two white female hoboes, Secretary Walter White of the National Association for the Advancement of Colored People received a "Strictly Confidential" letter from a W.H. Hunt, an apparently influential "colored man" living in Birmingham, Alabama. Concerned about his own safety, W. H. Hunt wrote:

Birmingham, Alabama
April 11, 1931

Hon. Walter White, Secretary
Nat'l Asscn. For The Advancement
Of Colored People, #69 Fifth Avenue
New York city, N.Y.
(Strictly Confidential)
Dear Sir:—

No doubt you have read the newspapers and know of the case of the nine negroes, or rather eight, who was convicted at Scottsboro, Jackson County, Alabama, during the past week.

Eight were sentenced to die in the electric chair on July 10, 1931, and the other, because of his youth, will be tried in the Juvenile Court of that County.

These boys — reputed to be all under twenty one years of age — should have a new trial and change of place of such trial, and strong reasons presented to the Goverernor of this State, Hon. B. M. Miller, for clemency.

The writer, being a colored man, and living here in this city, can not act openly in this matter, but I am willing to aid in any way possible without publicity being given of that fact.

I have already talked with a few influential white people in this city, and they think, that something can be done for these boys.

If you will take up this case we think that some funds to aid can be secured among our group in this State.

Please advise at your earliest convenience. I am,

Yours very respectfully,

W.H. Hunt, 804 14th Court,

North Birmingham, Ala. [Reel 2, Group 1, Box D-68, #000629, NAACP]

On April 19, 1931, a written appeal for unity from a well respected NAACP Field Organizer and Director of Branches to the ILD was prefaced in the following manner:

William Pickens, Field Organizer of the National Association of Colored People, has published an appeal for support of the campaign to have the nine Negro boys framed-up and condemned to death at Scottsboro, Ala. The fight is being conductded by the International Labor Defense and the League of Struggle for Negro Rights. Mr. Picken's call for support of the United Front proposed by these organizations to save victims of the Alabama "court-house lynching" was made known in a letter received yesterday by the Daily Worker, a New York Communist newspaper which is taking a leading part in the fight.

NATIONAL ASSOCIATION FOR THE
ADVANCEMENT OF COLORED PEOPLE

69 Fifth Avenue, New York April 19, 1931
Kansas City, Mo.

Dear Daily Worker:

I am writing from Kansas City, where I have just seen a copy of the Daily Worker for April 18th and noted the fight which the workers are making, through the International labor Defense to prevent the judicial massacre of Negro youth in Alabama.

Enclosed is a small check for that cause. Please send it to the I.L.D. in an enclosed stamped envelope.

The promptness with which the white workers have moved toward defending these helpless and innocent Negro boys, sons of black workers, is significant and prophetic. The only ultimate salvation for black and white workers is in their united defense, one of the other. Other causes and movements may do a good work, but all other causes are good only as preliminaries to that consumption. The one objective for final security is the absolute and unqualified unity and cooperation of ALL WORKERS, of all the exploited masses, across all races and color lines and all other lines.

In the present case the Daily Worker and the workers have moved, so far, more speedily and effectively than all other agencies put together. If you do not prevent Alabama from committing these horrible murders, you will at least educate working people, white and black, to the danger of division and the need of union. In either event it will be a victory for the workers.

Enclosed is an article which I had written on the mere probabilities of the case when I received the first meager details through the lying daily press.

They gave few details, but that was the only way, out of my experience as a southern Negro, that I could make sanity out of the madness. I see by the reports of the investigations of the workers agents that I was not so far wrong, not wrong at all in the conclusion that these children are innocent and that they were framed.

This is one occasion for every Negro who has intelligence enough to read to send aid to you and the I.L.D.

Very sincerely yours William Pickens [Reel 4, Box 4, #000231, ILD].

One day later, on April 20, all nine defendants in the Scottsboro case agreed to allow the ILD to represent them in court, signing their names with an "X" that permitted Attorney George Chamlee to become Chief Counsel for their defense. The following statement became a critical move in the early days of the case that, in all likelihood, saved the defendants' lives.

We, the undersigned, being all the defendants in the Scottsboro case now pending in Jackson County, Alabama, hereby affirm and ratify the retainer by The INTERNATIONAL LABOR DEFENSE of GEORGE W. CHAMLEE, Attorney-at-law of Chattanooga, Tenn., as Chief Counsel in our defense, appeal, application for a new trial and any and all other necessary legal proceedings arising out of or incident to our defense.

We call upon all workers and others who are interested in preventing a gastly miscarriage of justice and affording us a fair opportunity to prove our innocence to cooperate with and assist the INTERNATIONAL LABOR DEFENSE and our Chief Counsel in every way possible.

Signed at Birmingham County Jail, April 20th 1931.

NAME	his Mark	NUMBER
Andy Wright	x	710 West 22nd St. Chatt. Tenn.
(Roy Wright)	x	710 West 22nd St/ Chatt. Tenn.
Ozie Powell	x	170 Gilmore St. Atlanta, Ga.
Willie Roberson	x	992 Michigan, Ave. Atlanta.
Haywood Patterson	x	910 W. 19th St. Chatt, Tenn.
Olen Montgomery	x	Rt 1 Box 1 Monroe Ga.
Clarence Norris	x	Molinena Ga.
Chas. Weems	x	Riverdale Ga.
Eugene Williams	x	Rear of 24 7th St. & Carr St. #3 Clarks Dept. Chatt. Tenn.

[Reel 4, Box 4, #000225, ILD]

In a manner reflecting utter dismay, attorney Raymond Alexander, president of the recently formed and predominately black National Bar Association, sent the following letter to a fellow bar association member and a vice president of the NAACP, William Andrews, inquiring about "any actions" contemplated in defense of the nine Scottsboro defendants:

The National Bar Association
Incorporated
1925
April 22, 1931

William Andrews, Esq.
65 — 5th Avenue
New York, N.Y.
Dear Mr. Andrews:

I read with a great deal of surprise and shock the article in the "New York Sun" on April 9 to the effect that eight Negoes were sentenced to die in the electric chair for an alleged attack on two hobo white girls.

Let me know if your office of the National Association for the Advancement of colored People has taken any action to determine the parents of these boys, their families or contact counsel in this case or any of the colored people of Chattanooga, Scottsboro or the environs, for the purpose of rendering assistance in any of these cases.

I should like to offer my assistance in any way possible to avoid such a wholesale slaughter of human flesh that is contemplated by these Alabaman bloodhounds. I should like to put the whole machinery of the National Bar Association to work against such a calamity taking place.

Very Truly yours,
Raymond Pace Alexander
President [Reel 2, Group 1, Box D-68, #0006680, NAACP].

Indicative of the confusion and uncertainties among the defendants about who should represent them within the Alabama judicial system, just after three days in accepting the ILD as their legal representatives, the defendants, while misnaming the ILD, issued a series of perplexed statements:

We, Roy Wright, Andy Wright, Ozie Powell, Charlie Weems, Clarence Norris, Eugene Williams, Olin Montgomery and Haywood Patterson, convicted of rape at Scottsboro, Ala. wish it understood that we desire our defense be left with the Interdenominational Ministers Alliance of Chattanooga, Tennessee, and that Messrs. Milo Moody and Stephen Roddy continue to act as out chief attorneys as they did at the trial in Scottsboro, Ala. Dr. H. C. Terrell, pastor of St. John M. E. Church is the only man we will advise with except Mr. Moody and Mr. Roddy.

We have not signed any paper or in any other way employed or authorized any attorney or person to act for us. Men claiming to be attorneys or interested in us have been to see us at the jail in Birmingham a Mr. Traub presented a paper for us to sign but we refused and he said he would sign for us. We did not touch the pen or tell him to sign our names. We told the men they would have to see Mr. Roddy.

None of us want to have anything to do with the Interdenominational Labor Defense its representatives and have not had. We did not send for the Interdenominational Labor Defense Organization, or its attorneys, or others who may be connected with it. They came to see us and we told them to see Mr. Roddy. We do not want our parents or other relatives to employ them or have anything to with them.

Witness our hands this 23rd day of April, 1931.

Olin Montgomery	Ozie Powell
Haywood Patterson	Charlie Weems
Andy Wright	Clarence Norris
Roy Wright	Eugene Williams
Willie Robinson	

Witness our hands and marks this he 23rd day of April 1931
H.C. Terrell, Pastor St. John A.M.E. Birmingham
R. J. Grolan [Reel 2, Group 1, Box D-68, #000693, NAACP].

While the defendants appeared to be indecisive and split as to their legal representation, a religious association in Chattanooga, Tennessee, that was in contact with the NAACP sent the following letter to Walter White:

OFFICE OF
PRESIDENT
1917 Citico Avenue
Chattanooga, Tenn.
LAYMEN'S ASSOCIATION
The Methodist Episcopal church
East Tennessee Conference
April 24th 1931

Mr. Walter White
New York City
My dear Mr. White:—

Thanks for your letter of the 20th and your wire of the 23rd. I thought at first that your telegram meant for us to send you amount necessary for transcript. It was late afternoon before we got its meaning, hence the delay. Now as to communicating with the boys, Mr. Roddy and two of our men were down there, Birmingham, yesterday and found that these "reds" had been down there and the boys say the "Reds" signed their names to some papers and claimed that the boys signed them. The boys however signed paper in the presence of Mr. Roddy, Mr. James, the Rev. L.P. Whitten, of Chattanooga, Rev. Terrell, and the Sheriff, and two deputies of Birmingham as a witnesses giving us and Mr. Roddy priority in the case. I may state that this committee reports that feeling in Alabama is very high the "Reds" and their activity will hurt the boys' case.

Now as to question number (1) How satisfied are we with Mr. Roddy? The committee with one or two exceptions is fairly well satisfied, or at least decided that they should keep him as he was first in the case. Some members of the alliance are not satisfied but the majority decided as above mentioned. (2) As to public opinion, as I see it, a majority of the white people and none one of the colored believe that the boys are really guilty yet this is the south and some politics are being played. (3) As to the amount of money that can be raised in this section, I might state that so far these last three weeks we have raised by public collections in churches about one hundred and sixty five dollars. Some of our larger churches have been lukewarm. Yet our prospects are good. We have assurances in the last three days that Birmingham, Gadsden, Anniston, and Huntsville will cooperate with us to the limit.

(4) I believe that we are safe in saying that the Interdenominatonal Ministers Alliance will cooperate with the N.A.A.C.P. to the fullest extent. I could not say any definite amount but they will "stick" till the case is won or lost in the supreme court of the United States, and then to the President. Very Truly Yours, (signed) Dr. P.A. Stephens Secretary of Committee [Reel 2, Group 1, Box D-68, #000707, NAACP].

April 1931
TO WHOM IT MAY CONCERN:

We, the closest relatives of *Ozie Powell* fully endorse every move of the International Labor Defense, and hereby express full confidence and agreement with the organization's handling of the case.

We repudiate most strongly the actions of the inter-denominational Ministers Alliance of Chattanooga, which by attempting to make our boy denounce the International Labor Defense, is helping send them to the electric chair. The hiring of Attorney Stephen Roddy by the Inter-denominational Ministers Alliance, who according to even the court records, refused at the start to even state he was there in Scottsboro to fight for the nine boys. And not making one move for weeks to get the court proceedings, the case, or publicize the boys' innocence, makes us state emphatically that the Inter-denominational Ministers alliance should have absolutely nothing to do with the case.

The move of the National Association for the Advancement of Colored People to get the mothers of the Chattanooga boys to get rid of the International Labor Defense, to sign statements without telling them what they contained, to play dirty lawyers' tricks while each day brings the boys nearer to the electric chair proves to us that the National Association for the Advancement of Colored People, too, have no real interest in helping our boy to get a new trial and a fighting chance to prove his innocence. One and all we State we will have nothing to do at all with these traitors, and will support unreservedly the policy and work of the International Labor Defense in defending our boy.

We realize that only mass protest of the working class, white and Negro, which is being rallied by the International Labor Defense, can save the boys from the electric chair.

We, therefore, wholeheartedly approve and support the International labor Defense and its chief counsel, George W. Chamlee, as the only parties that have any any legal jurisdiction in the defense of our boy.

[signed].....................................

Date..

[Reel 2, Group 1, Box D-68, #000823, NAACP]

From: the INTERNATIONAL LABOR DEFENSE
80 E. 11th St. Room 430
New York City

April 26, 1931
FOR IMMEDIATE RELEASE

9 CONDEMNED ALABAMA BOYS AND PARENTS DENOUNCE THEIR FORMER ATTORNEY

New York, Apr. 26;— The nine Negro boys condemned to death in Alabama on alleged rape charges issued a statement today, in which their parents joined them denouncing Stephen R. Roddy, local attorney and the two ministers who had reported thru the press that the defendants have dissociated themselves from the International Labor Defense.

"In an attempt to play the game of the white ruling class off the South, Roddy" the I.L.D. charges "who had originally 'defended' and betrayed the boys at Scottsboro, in company of a truant officer and two ministers and without the knowledge of the parents came to the Birmingham jail and with threats and promises tried to convince the boys that they would surely save their lives if they quit the I.L.D." The boys are all minors and two of them are only 14 years of age.

When the parents heard of this treachery they immediately visited the boys in jail and in conjunction with them issued the following statement: "We, Haywood Patterson, Andy Wright, Roy Wright and Eugene Williams, after a Conference with our parents, Claude Patterson, Ada Wright, and Mamie Williams desire to re-affirm our written contract with the International Labor Defense to engage George W. Chamlee as chief counsel in our defense, and we Ozie Powell, Olin Montgomery, Clarence Norris. Willie Robertson and Charlie Weems join with the above named defendants in ratifying our written statements to the International Labor Defense concerning the employment of counsel for us. A statement yesterday obtained from us by Steve Roddy and by W. M. James, L.P. Whitten and H. Terrell under circumstances we did not understand indicated that we are not satisfied with the International Labor Defense. This statement was obtained without the consent and advice of our parents and we had no way of knowing what to do. We completely repudiate that statement and brand those who obtained it as betrayers of our cause."

FOUR ATTORNEYS ENGAGED BY ILD FOR CASE

Four attorneys have been engaged by the ILD to fight the attempt to legally lynch the nine young Negro boys for the alleged rape of two white girls on a freight train. The attorneys are Geo. W. Chamlee of Chattanooga, Tenn/.,

Albert Taub of New York. The International Labor Defense is rallying tens of thousands of people behind the cause of theses nine Negro boys and mass meetings are being held thru out the entire United States.

In a statement issued by Geo. W. Maurer, assistant Secretary of the ILD it is pointed out that "we here appreciate the importance of this case and have from the very beginning been active in militant protest against this merciless butchery of the white ruling class. In the words of William Pickens, nationally known Negro leader, 'In the present case, the workers have moved, so far, more speedily and effectively than all agencies put together. This is one occasion for every negro who has intelligence enough to read to send to the International Labor Defense.' "We shall fight and fight vigilantly with Negro and white workers uniting against the program of the ruling class. The nine Negro boys will not burn" [Reel 2, Group 1, Box D-68, #000720, NAACP].

On April 28, 1931, in an unofficial NAACP report on Steve Roddy the following observations were compiled:

Report on Steve Roddy:

Steve Roddy is a drunkard recently released from an asylum where he was treated for mental disorders brought on by excessive drinking and "fast living."

He has not practice and no reputation in Chattanooga. His only clients are a few minor ones in police court. He never has a case big enough to be seen in the county court-house.

He was retained because he once won a small litigation for a relative of W. M. James, a crooked Negro politician of the town, who suggested him to the Interdenominational Ministers Alliance.

Upon his arrival at the first hearing in Scottsboro, he denied to the Judge that he had been hired to defend the boys, but claimed that the ministers had only sent him down to look thing[s] over.

During the course of the trial itself he offered no defense whatsoever. Newspapers report that he attempted to compromise with the prosecution by offering to plead guilty in return for life imprisonment for the boys. During the trial he also issued statements to the press that the boys were receiving a fair trial. From the transcript of the Haywood Patterson case, already in our hands, it is clearly shown that he refused to argue the case before the jury when offered the opportunity by the court, that he called not one witness for the defense except the boys themselves, that he overlooked all pertinent questions that might have been asked state witness, especially when they flagrantly contradicted each other, that he made no effort to call as witnesses any of the white boys thrown off the train, even though they were being held in the Scottsboro jail. It is reported that these boys refused to identify nine defendants as the ones with whom they had fought, and for that reason was never called as witnesses by the state.

The boys report that he constantly tried to get them to plead guilty although at the beginning of the trial, a newspaper reported him as saying he thought the boys were innocent.

Under Alabama law, appeal to the supreme court of the state must be made on the basis of court record, and new evidence cannot be used. New evidence can, however, be incorporated into the record as part of a motion for a new trial. The record at the trial contains, naturally, practically no defense evidence, nothing about the character of the two girls, about the position of the boys on the train, etc. However, although the law allows 30 days to file motion for new trial, Roddy made oral motions for seven of the boys directly after the trial with no preparation, thereby condemning them to the chair with no way under Ala. Law to bring into their cases the actual truth, or any defense testimony of any kind. His oral motions were of course denied. This point alone branded him murderer and lays basis for rumor that he got a share for the purse raised in Scottsboro to aid the prosecution. He excused himself to the local ministers by saying that the best tactic was to let them be in the courts and then appeal to the governor for leniency on account of their ages, etc.

Even on the appeal, he made no moves. When the ILD entered the cases, no effort had been made to so much as order the transcript of the cases. ILD lawyer, Taub, pointed this out to the ministers' Alliance and they at once told Roddy to order the transcript, promising immediate payment. A long distance call to the court stenographer by General Chamlee two days later revealed that the transcript had not been yet ordered, in spite of the fact that no legal steps could be taken without that, Chamlee immediately ordered transcript and ILD sent $85 in full payment.

Roddy had not prepared one single paper, has not obtained one single affidavit, has started no investigation of the case, has made not one motion except to attack the ILD.

The committee of the Ministers Alliance, in conference with the representatives of the ILD repeatedly recognized the vicious role Roddy has a traitor to the case. They agreed to get rid of Roddy as soon as possible. At a special meeting of the Ministers' Alliance last Thursday the majority expressed themselves as in favor of immediate dismissal of Roddy as a betrayer, and a motion of endorsement of the ILD was defeated without being put to a vote by technical objections raised by Bowen, President of the Alliance.

Roddy was retained without ever consulting the parents or the boys themselves. Not until after George W. Chamlee had been definitely retained by the ILD by the parents, and by the defendants, did he sneak out to Birmingham jail, buldose several of the boys into signing a retainer and a denouncement of the ILD. He went to the inhuman lengths of getting the sheriff to issue an order that no one could see the boys and tremendous pressure had to be exerted to get this order set aside for a few minutes to let the boys talk for the first time to their mot hers when the parents were taken to Birmingham last Friday at the expense of the ILD.

Attorney George Lively of Chattanooga and Chief of Police Perkins both good personal friends of Roddy, organized, together with one of the leaders of the Klan who has an office in the same building, the recent attempt to exclude from its office Friday at the expense of the ILD.

Roddy has, up to the middle of last week, been paid according to himself and to the ministers alliance $100. He told us and the ministers he had given half of this to Moody. He told us and the ministers he had given half of this to Moody, a Scottsboro lawyer appointed by the court, Moody tells Chamlee he received nothing [Reel 2, Group 1, Box D-68, #000722, NAACP].

Supporting the NAACP's sharp critique of Steve Roddy is the following internal letter by Walter White, the NAACP's National Secretary, written while he was in Birmingham, Alabama. White informs his associates Robert W. Bagnall (Director of Branches) and Herbert J. Seligmann (Director of Publicity) about a host of anxieties he perceives about any future relationships with the ILD, the Scottsboro defendants and their parents.

The Thomas Jefferson Hotel
Birmingham, Alabama

May 3rd 1931

Dear Bob and Herbert:

Of all the cases we've ever had this one is by far the most tangled and ugly of them all. This letter, a copy of which I am sending to Arthur [Ed. Note: NAACP Director, Arthur B. Springarn], is by way of an effort to get down on paper the story to date. As I write the outcome is gavely in dodubt. Whatever the ourcome it is one which is going, to give us a lot of trouble and we will have to be exceedingly astute to prevent on the one hand serious consequences in so far as the reputation of the Association is concerned and at the other end do what we can for these unfortunate boys.

The Communist have raised hell with their blustering, intemperate and almost insane threats. Pickens' letter is being broadcast and it has done us immense harm. Even some of our best friends interpret his letter as either proof that we are definitely linked up with the Communist or as an indication that we have fallen down on the job and a split in the Association has resulted. It will be a long time before we recover from that blow and I say this most advisedly

To begin at the beginning the reputation of the boys is exceedingly bad with one possible exception. When one sees the terrible poverty and ignorance from which they come, however, one can readily understand why they should be what they are. The reputation of the two white girls is infinitely worse. They are notorious prostitutes and one of them, according to reputable individuals in Chattanooga, was arrested in a disorderly house in flagrante delicto with a colored man a few months ago.

The parents of the boys, as may be expected, are frightfully ignorant and several of them have been taken in completely by the I.L.D. I talked with Mrs. Williams, mother of 14-year old Eugene Williams the morning I arrived in Chattanooga. She had begun to get suspicious of the Communist when Wakefield, Chattanooga representastive of the I.L.D., was barred from the jail in Birmingham when he paid the way of some of the parents and of Chamlee, Chattanooga lawyer hired by the Communists down here to see the boys. I pointed out to her that the odds against her son were terrific at best — that when Red prejudice was added to Black, she would practically insure her boy's execution by remaining tied up with the Communist. After some discussion she was convinced and signed in the presence of witnesses who were Dr. Stephens and Rev. Bowens, president of the Ministers Alliance,. A statement I drafted turning over full charge of the case to the N.A.A.C.P. and the Alliance.

The following morning, however, she walked three miles (having not even carfare) to Dr. Stephens' house to withdraw from this agreement. Her husband who is the stepfather of Eugene has abused her terribly for forsaking the Communists and had threatened dire things to her if she did not at once rejoin the I.L.D. crowd.

Between her visits I had had a long conference with Stephen R. Roddy, the lawyer the Ministers had employed and who had, with the aid of Milo Moody, Scottsboro lawyer assigned by the court to the defense, represented the boys at the original trials. Roddy is a man in his thirties, a heavy drinker, and impressed me as not being diligent or well trained. For example he is the one who should have been insisting upon the ministers that the transcript be ordered — on the contrary they had had, as a result of my telegrams and letters, to keep after him. Becoming suspicious of his excuses they had phoned the court clerk at Scottsboro and found that the transcript had not even been ordered. Roddy through Moody then ordered it when confronted with this fact.

On the other hand Roddy was the only lawyers who had the courage to go down there and defend the boys. Feeling against him was so bitter the National Guard, according to Roddy, had to escort him to and from court. The Communist are very bitter gainst him and are assailing him from every angle because he denounced them and refused to have anything whatever to do with them. Roddy says he is willing to step out of the case if we wish and even seems eager to do so. Should we go in, however, we will need him and Moody as attorneys of record though we must have outstanding counsel as chief of the defense.

The minister made a loose, verbal agreement with Roddy to pay him $250 or $300 to take the cases through the Alabama Supreme Court. On this they have paid him $130 of which he has paid Moody $50.

Let me jump here a bit to the interview I had with Chamlee, former State Attorney for Tennessee, who has been retained by the I.L.D. Chamlee is reputed locally to be a pretty good lawyer for the vicinity. I don't trust him, however, for he seems to me to be quite shifty. He professes undying love for the Negro (to me who he thought to be white) but his reputation as state prosecutor so far as Negroes are concerned is far from good. Last Sunday he denied vehemently in the press that he had been retained by the Communist, alleging the boys' parents were paying him which is absurd as they are pathetically poor. The day I reach Chattanooga, however, there appeared in the papers a letter he had written under pressure from the I.L.D. admitting that they had hired him. And yet when I talked with him the same afternoon this story appeared he told me the parents and the I.L.D. were paying him — and one of the parents in that group was Mrs. Williams who declared she had not hired Chamlee or talked with him even about the case.

Chamlee declares that Roddy made verbal motions for new trials for the eight convicted boys as soon as the verdicts were rendered and that those motions were promptly overruled except in the case of Haywood Patterson on whose motion the judge reserved decision until May 6th. Chamlee declared that under the Alabama statutes "about sixty days are allowed for filing of notices of appeal."

Roddy, on the other hand, declared that motions for a new trial were to be argued on May 6th in all the cases, that affidavits must be signed by jurors that they were influenced by the demonstrations in the court room, that unless the motions were won the boys were hopelessly lost, and that Moody would not proceed to securing the affidavits and arguing the motions unless we "put down five or six hundred dollars." *He also "thinks" ninety days are allowed for appeals.*

I told him it was out of the question to pay that much in one sum, that the money would have to be raised, that he would have to abide by his agreement with the ministers, and that we never paid all to any lawyer until the case was ended

Faced with this hopeless contradictory set of statemens by the two lawyers I sought advice of a third white lawyer (there are no good Negro ones in Chattanooga) who is a friend of Dr. Stephens but he was unfamiliar with the Alabama laws. I then tried to reach Chambliss, the colored lawyer in Birmingham over long distance, but could not reach him. I then wired the office for one hundred dollars to be divided between Roddy and Moody in order to keep some lawyer in the case. But before paying it Mrs. Williams came to repudiate her signed statement. At the moment the Communist have complete control of the case so I went back to Roddy, told him I was coming here, get Rev. Terrell who is close to the boys, see the boys at Kilby Prison near Montgomery tomorrow and if we get control of the case I will wire Dr. Stephens Monday money to be paid him and Moody.

So, here is where we are. As I see it it would be suicidal for us to be tied up in any way with that outfit of lunatics — so far as this case is concerned — the Communist. Our choice is to withdraw completely from the cases and make public fully our reasons for doing so — the Communist and their tactics, and the ignorance and stupidity of the boys' parents. Or, to get absolute control of the cases. This afternoon I am to see Chambliss and Brown, two local colored lawyers, to learn if it is necessary to have also the parents' consent as to choice of attorney since the boys have repudiated the I.L.D. (copy of agreement is enclosed) and since the boys are old enough under Alabama customs to be tried for a capital offense.

If this is so I shall go early tomorrow morning with Rev. Terrell, who I am to see also this afternoon, to Kilby Prison to get the signatures of the boys to an agreement which I shall draft giving us absolute control. This will kick the Communist and the parents who are stringing along with them completely out of the picture. This will bring down upon us infinite abuse from them and we must recognize that and prepare for that. On the other hand public interest is so deep we cannot afford not to be in the case, provided it is possible to get in without endangering the reputation of the Association. Our chief mistake lies in my now [Ed. Note: probably meant to be "not"] coming down here at the very beginning as I wanted to. All this mess would then have been obviated.

To guard the Chattanooga end I drafted and left there with Dr. Stephens a statement of points to be included in a <u>written</u> contract with Roddy and Moody, should we gain control. Negotiations have been begun here with a Mr. Beddows who is said to be a ferless, first rate criminal lawyer here. Dr. Terrell has seen him and Beddows seems willing to consider entering the case. He is said to be expensive but a good part of his fee can be raised locally.

Now is the time for Bob to get the Chattanooga and Birmingham branches reognized. Dr. Stephens and Rev. Ridley are keen and I urged them as well as others to call a meeting this week, pointing out that had there been a strong branch all this mixup would never have occurred. Bob, write strong letters to Stephens and Ridley (with whom you have had correspondence on this lately) following this up. Also write McPherson, Strawbridge, Anderson, and Rev. H. C. Terrell, Pastor [of] the St. John A.M.E. Church here (residence, 712 N. 15th Street) to the same purpose.

I am to see here also Mr. Elliott, editor of the <u>Post</u> to whom Ludwell Denny (with whom I talked in Washington on the way down) telephoned about myself and the case. Through him I hope to get a line on Beddows and on the state of public opinion on the case. Feeling here is tense because of a recent case of abnormal nature with which as a matter of course a Negro has been charged. At the moment public sentiment seems slightly to be veering away from the notion that a negro committed the crime after wholesale arrests of Negroes have not produced one on whom the crime can definitely be pinned.

As things now stand I expect to leave Birmingham for Atlanta (where the parents of some of the boys live) on Tuesday night or Wednesday morning. I hope to leave Atlanta not later than Thursday on the Crescent Limited which will put me in New York Friday morningqt 10:10, Daylight Savings. I will come immediately to the office. Will Herb save all of page one of the press releases for this story. When that is done I feel now that I shall need to tumble into bed and leave a call for not less than forty-eight hours later.

I find that the carbon has slipped on this small paper so that the copy isn't complete. Will Miss Randolph have one of the girls make a copy and send to Mr. Springarn. Telegrams to me here to Tuesday mid-night had best be sent to "W. White" care Dr. McPherson. Wednesday I can be wired at 129 Houston St. N.E. Atlanta.

Ever sincerely,

Walter

P.S.

As a sample of the Communist tactics, Sheriff Hawkins of the Birmingham jail stated to Dr. Stephens, Rev. Whitten, and Roddy that if he should give to the press telegrams which had come to him from the I.L.D. in New York "the jail wouldn't keep a mob out two hours." Similar telegrams have flooded, I am informed, the governor. Fearing the effect of any of the messages being made public all the boys except fourteen-year old Roy Wright in whose case there was a hung jury, have been moved for safe keeping to Kilby prison.

I am going to try and talk with Sheriff Hawkins and with the governor who is said to be quite fearless.

Forrest Bailey is sending one of their agents, Miss Hollace Ransdell, here to make an investigation. She is arriving, he informs me by wire, on Tuesday. She can be immensssely helpful and I shall give her a full story before leaving here.

Please send also by messenger a copy of this letter to Forrest Bailey, asking him to keep this in strictest confidence until I return. He of course will understand [Reel 2, Group 1, Box D-68, 000825, NAACP].

The following day, May 4, the following affidavit was drawn up, ostensibly by Walter White and Rev. H.C. Terrell, and signed by six of the defendants:

We the undersigned, having been convicted of rape at Scottsboro, Alabama, during the month of April, 1931 and sentenced to death do hereby of our free will request that the National Association for the Advancement of Colored People and, with it such bodies as it shall wish, have sole and exclusive handling of any and all efforts to be put forth in seeking new trials for us or appeals to any and all courts from said conviction.

The said Association shall have sole and exclusive right to select any and all attorneys to represent us and said Association's decision or decisions in this regard and also as to conducting of efforts to save us from death in the electric chair shall be final.

The said Association shall exclusively be designated to raise and disburse any and all funds which the public may generously see fit to contribute in our behalf. The Association shall give its official receipt for any and all such contributions which shall be raised only by agents of the Association who shall be designated in writing to solicit such funds. An exact accounting shall be kept by the Association in accordance with it unvarying custom in such cases of all moneys contributed or disbursed for our defense. Payments shall be made by said Association only by voucher through its National office located at 69 Fifth Avenue, New York, or through such office or branch or branches as may be designated in writing by said National Office.

The said Association acting in our behalf shall diligently resort to every legal and legitimate means towards securing for us new trials through appeals and otherwise, in order that there maybe secured to us as American citizens and human beings our rights to fair trials before a jury of our peers in lieu of the farcical hearings dominated by a vengeful mob which were given us at Scottsboro.

This written agreement shall render void any and all previous agreements made by us or those who speak for us, whether such agreements were written or verbal ones. We appeal to our parents to abide to the fullest extent by the compact we here make in order that our lives may not be made forfeit in the electric chair.

Signed this fourth day of May in the year 1931.

Willie (X) Roberson   Charley (X) Weems
Haywood ( ) Patterson   Andy ( )Wright
Ozie (X) Powell
Clarence (X) Norris
Witnesses:
H. C. Terrell
Walter White [Reel 2, Group 1, D-68, #000837, NAACP].

The next day, May 7, 1931, Walter White sent a final communiqué from the Thomas Jefferson Hotel in downtown Birmingham, Alabama, with the following observations:

> May 5 1931
> Dear Herb and Bob:
>   Things begin to look a bit better though we're far from being out of the woods. Yesterday I inveigled the Rev. Terrell (who was scared to death) to go with me to Kilby Prison at Montgomery. After hours of red tape unwinding we got into Death Row with the warden (whose name appropriately enough is Walls), two deputy wardens, and a turnkey hovering over my shoulder while I talked to the boys. More of that — it is a long and exciting story-when I get back. I got four boys to sign an agreement, two others want to write their parents first for advice, and the other two want to stick with the I.L.D.
>   One thing is certain — no I.L.D.representative will ever get into see them! Today I talked with Roderick Beddow, the best criminal lawyer in Birmingham and who, though only forty or so, is the Darrow of this part of the country. He is a fighter and everybody agrees that if he will take the case, he can do more than any other lawyer in the country. He is interested, declares the whole trial an outrage, and will take the case. I have ordered a transcript for him by wire and he is going this weekend to Kilby to talk with the boys.
>   I have just come from a long and highly satisfactory talk with the editor and managing editor of the <u>Post</u>, a Scripps Howard paper. The editor used to be on the <u>World</u> and called me a number of times, he tells me, about stories. They believed the boys guilty but now are openminded and are going to keep us tipped off on all developments. Hollace Ransdell, the Civil Liberties investigator, arrives this afternoon and I am suggesting to her that she set out tomorrow for Scottsboro and Huntsville (the two "raped" girls live there) to see what she can dig up there. Am off tonight for Atlanta where the parents of four of the boys live to see what I can do about getting them straightened out.
>   Will see you Friday morning about ten thirty.
>   Walter [Reel 2, Group 1, Box D-68, #000845, NAACP].

A few days later Walter White received a letter penned from Roy Wilkins, a young newspaper reporter for the *Kansas City Call* in Missouri. Years earlier, while a college student, Wilkins joined the NAACP. Upon graduation from college he utilized his position as a reporter to periodically inform Walter White about a number of civil rights issues occurring throughout the country. Wilkins eventually left his job as a reporter and in 1932 became a full-time member of the NAACP and Assistant Secretary of the Association. While in this position he advised Walter White on the need to make the Association more assertive if not relevant in the public's eye by developing a "crusading type of journalism" that could deflect negative inquiries about it legal strategies and tactics, particular those assertions coming from organizations such as the ILD. The following letters, which are indicative of Wilkins' observations in the early days of the Scottsboro case, essential underscored the ideological struggle and stylistic differences between the NAACP and the ILD. As such, they also highlight both organizations' intense, if not passionate, grappling for judicial control of the Scottsboro Boys defense.

The Kansas City Call
1715–17 East 18th Street
Phone Victor 3804 Kansas City, Missouri
May 7, 1931

Mr. Walter White, Secretary
N.A.A.C.P.,
69 Fifth Avenue,
New York, N.Y.
Dear Walter:

I have just seen the Tuesday issue of the Daily Worker and it indictment of the Association for its policy in the Scottsboro case.

Bearing in mind, of course, that the Communist are always ready to shout anything from the housetops to create a sensation, I cannot refrain from noting that their shouting in this case has caused no little embarrassment to the Association in this particular place.

It began, publicaly, on the occasion of Dean Pickens' speech at the Linwood forum here April 19. The front part of the hall was packed with liberals and extreme left wing members and during the question period there were some very direct questions asked Mr. Picckens about what his organization was doing for the boys in Alabama. He answered as diplomatically as possible by saying he had been on the road for some time, but he was sure his office was on the job.

The Communist have staged several demonstrations since that time and have held three mass meetings including their open air May Day celebration which drew about 400 persons, mostly negroes. At each one of these gatherings the Scottsboro case has received much attention and many copies of the Daily Worker containing the stories and pictures have been distributed.

A member of the local staff of the ILD has been to see me twice and has kept in touch with this paper by correspondence on the case. The national offices of the Communists and the ILD are sending out publicity and generally whooping it up.

The latest release from them, received late yesterday states a motion for a new trial was to be heard yesterday (May 6).

In the face of this activity, the official releases of the NAACP were silent until last week when I read with some amazement that the association was negotiating with a lawyer who had been previously reported both through the ILD and through southern newspapers as being eminently satisfied with the verdicts against his clients! With Chattnooga, Memphis, Birmingham and Scottsboro newspapers before me and with the Reds clamoring in their sheet, I thought the kindest thing I could do would be to junk the NAACP release on the story and not expose the situation to our readers.

Several weeks ago, rather than not carry any news at all about the case, I did rewrite some southern stuff and inserted without authority that the NAACP was looking into the case. Carl Murphy in his paper seems to have been similarly "up a tree."

I do not wish to appear unduly alarmed. Yesterday I saw Mr. Pickens on his way through from Omaha to Wichita and he assured me the matter was being taken care of. He seemed some put out because the Daily Worker had used his letter to the ILD as a sort of attack on the association. He said he had formerly been a member of the executive committee of the ILD and had frequently contributed to their various funds.

It does strike me from this vantage point, however, that the sooner the association can release a definite, clear-cut statement on this case the sooner it can secure united support from the newspapers, which are, after all, the only method the association has for reaching the masses of the people. As matters stand now, the situation is considerably mudddled and there is nothing for editors to get behind and push. I believe they would rather push the NAACP, but in the face of its silence and indefinite pronouncements, they hesitate between it and the ILD. You see, Walter, simply publishing news stories about what this one is doing and that one is doing will only confuse the public. To get the people into action, there must be a crusading type of journalism rather than the reporting type. But before the crusade there must be an objective. Name the objectives. Name the methods to be pursued and I believe you will have the press to a sheet behind the association.

Very sincerely yours,

Roy RW:FC [Reel 2, Group 1, Box D-68, #000890, NAACP].

On May 11th defendant Ozie Powell wrote the following letter to NAACP's National Secretary, Walter White:

> Kilby Prison
> Montgomery, Ala.
> May 11th 1931

Walter White
69–5th Avenue
New York, NY

Dear Sir:—

I had a letter from my mother telling me that she talked with you the day you were in Atlanta. I am sure glad you saw her and explained everything. She advised me that I did right in signing the paper for you requesting the International Labor Defense to keep hands off.

If you remember, Clarence Norris was occupying the cell with me and signed the paper for you at the time I did. He ask me to tell you that he preferred the help offered thru you from the Nat. Assn. for the Advancement of Colored People.

We both feel that your organization will do everything in our power to help us and will us and will do it in the right way.

I aint approve of the manner in which the Nat. Lab. Defense has handled things with their demanding telegram. They have only been agitating. It has given them lots of publicity which no doubt helped their personal gain. But does that help us? I cant see where it does.

The I.L.D. learned of your visit the day following visit and neither do I approve of method used by them of trying to poison our minds such as "you being our deadly enemy." As for the International Labor Defense I don't want them to have anything further to do with my case. Clarence Norris feels the same as I.

We will both put X by our name.

We learned that applications had been grant for a motion for new trial before the trial Judge. Hope your paper will have allowance them to represent us. Please let us hear from you?

I don't support the I.L.D. will send us fellows that [   ], any more money. With best wishes, I am sincerely yours,

Clarence Norris   Ozie Powell

[Reel 4, Group 1, Box D-70, #000003, NAACP].

By early May, criticism of Field Secretary Pickens' letter complimenting the ILD's thrust to defend the Scottsboro Boys not only raised indignation within the NAACP's leadership, but counterproductively raised questions among the public about the Association's overall policy on dissent within its own ranks! In this context, a trenchant letter from a former NAACP member to Walter White advised:

W. W. Wolfe
383 Mulberry Street
Newark, N.J.

May 11, 1931
Mr. Walter White,
69 — 5th Avenue
New York City
My Dear Sir:—

I think it would be a grave mistake to allow Drs. Pickens to leave the N.A.A.C.P., the Association has just suffered one irreparable loss in that of Mr. James Weldon Johnson's resignation, and now the lose of Mr. Pickens. I am afraid the loss would be so great, the Asociation would not overcome it very soon.

The Negro psychology is very peculiar. You may not have received many letters protesting the resignation of Mr. Johnson, but if you could stand around in disguise and hear all of the terrible things that are predicted that will happen to the Association since he has left, it would cause you to think more than once.

I don't know how it will be with Messrs. Johnson and Pickens out of the Association, but I do know with them in it, whenever a Mass Meeting was going to be held in behalf of the Association, those names served to be the best drawing cards — at least that was my experience when I was active in the N.A.A.C.P.

The public may become equally, if not more, attached to you, and we can always count on Doctor Dubois to draw the intelligentia — both Negroes and Caucasians.

If it is the policy of the N.A.A.C.P. to wait and see if justice is done to the accused — and I think that is right and proper — and Mr. Pickens knowing that — comparison of the organizations giving assistance to the accused could have been left out of his article, otherwise, I think it was allright.

I am a believer in free speech and would not be willing to live in paradise if I found it did not exist there.

That minister who hiked all the way from the South to New York City should have been placed in jail upon his arrival. His coming only meant one of two things — he was either looking for publicity or he was too ignorant to know that we knew what was going on down there as well as he did.

Yours very truly,

W. W. Wolfe

WWW/SV [Reel 2, Group 1, Box D-68, #000917, NAACP].

May 14th 1931

My Dear Mr. Montgomery:

I am writing you in further reference to the efforts which the National Association for the Advancement of Colored People is willing to put forth to secure a new trial for you, or to appeal your case to the Alabama State Supreme Court.

After visiting you at the prison on Monday, May 4th, I returned to Birmingham, and there, together with Rev. Terrell, Dr. Charles A.C. McPherson, who is Secretary of the Birmingham Branch, and others who are interested in your case, we called upon Mr. Roderick Beddow, who, as you perhaps know, is considered the ablest criminal lawyer in the State of Alabama. I told Mr. Beddow of my visit with you and the other boys, and of the facts as I learned them from the transcript of record from your trial at Scottsboro and as I had heard them from various sources.

Mr. Beddow agreed to appear as your counsel, provided you wished the National Association for the Advancement for the Advancement of Colored People to act in your behalf. We shall associate with him other attorneys if necessary and desirable, and with Mr. Beddow and such other attorneys as we may retain will be associated our National Legal Committee, composed of some of the most outstanding lawyers in the United States. You will note their names in the lower left hand corner of the sheet. Prof. Felix Frankfurter is of the Hartford University Law School, and is one of the greatest authorities on constitutional law in the United States. Mr. James Marshall is the son of the late Louis Marshall, and is, himself, one of the outstanding lawyers of New York City.

The Advancement Association is willing to put forth every legal and legitimate effort in your behalf that can possibly be put forth. No person can do any more, and if anyone tells you that he can do more, he is not telling the truth. It is most unfortunate for you that the International Labor Defense has, as Ozie Powell and Clarence Norris write me today, "only been agitating." We do not approve of the sending of threatening telegram simply to get in the newspapers.

Mr. Beddow will be down to Kilby Prison to see you within the next day or two if he has not already been there by the time you receive this letter. For your own sake, I strongly urge that you definitely indicate to him that you wish the Advancement Association to defend you. Unless you do state this clearly to him, and unless you very soon indicate that you wish the Advancement Associate to handle your case, it is possible that the plans for your defense may become so badly tangled that it may be almost impossible to defend you successfully.

Besides being able to get the best lawyers in the United States, the Advancement Association has also for twenty-two years been defending, under the Constitution and the laws of the United States and of the various states, the constitutional rights of the Negro as a citizen and as a human being. I enclose a leaflet which tells of some of these cases which we have won.

We are deeply sympathetic with you in your present difficulty. We will do all that we can for you, but as I said to you in Kilby Prison, we cannot and will not be associated with the International labor Defense or with any organization which uses tactics which hinder instead of help.

Let me hear from you by return mail. Ozie Powell and Clarence Norris today write me that they want the N.A.A.C.P. to defend them, as they both feel that our organization will do everything in its power to help them. They also asked the International Labor Defense to keep hands off. May I, as a friend, urge you to take similar action promptly, and to write your parents that you want the Advancement Association and no other to defend you.

> Ever sincerely,
> Secretary
> Walter White

Mr. Olen Montgomery
Kilby Prison
Montgomery.
Alabama [Reel 2, Group 1, Box D-68, #000985, NAACP].

By May 25, 1931, attorney George Chamlee was receiving letters from the Scottsboro defendants that expressed extreme frustration about the situation. While many of these letters were related to information about the trial process and their innocence, other letters underscored the horrible living conditions and racism that they received from prison officials. It is also apparent that as time wore on, the ability of these nine youths to withstand and resist the terrors of incarceration and a continual threat of jailhouse lynching rested primarily on their individual strength and innovativeness in overcoming unforeseen obstacles. In this regard their letters, whether they were dictated by or actually written by the defendants, provide the reader with a narrative steeped in the historical richness of the African American experience and a people's determination, albeit often encumbered by institutional and personal

Model train used by attorney Samuel Leibowitz during the second Scottsboro trial, in Decatur, Alabama, April 1933 (photograph by the author).

racism, to define their own existence. Not the least important in these developments is the June 10, 1931, affidavit prepared by Clarence Norris that decisively indicates the ongoing pressures the defendants were under.

AFFIDAVIT OF CLARENCE NORRIS

STATE OF ALABAMA,

Montgomery County,

Before me, Leo L. Cawthon, a notary public in and for said county and State, personally appeared Clarence Norris, made known to me as such, and having been duly sworn to speak the truth, the whole truth, and nothing but the truth, the said Clarence Norris deposes and says the follows:

My name is Clarence Norris, and I am at present confined in Kilby Prison, having been tried at Scottsboro, Jackson County, Alabama, on the 6th day of April, 1931, before Judge A. E. Hawkins, and having been found guilty of rape and sentenced to death by electrocution; and I state the truth and facts to be as follows;

I was put on trial for the offense of rape in Scottsboro on April 6th 1931, before the aforesaid Judge and a jury, and testified on that trial on my own behalf. I was represented in that court by Mr. Roddy and Mr. Milo Moody, an attorney of Scottsboro, who was appointed by the court to defend me. A short while before I was put on the witness stand I talked to my lawyers, who

Model gondola car used in the Decatur trial by Leibowitz to depict where the fight between the black and white hoboes occurred (photograph by the author).

were present in a room of the courthouse with the other Negro prisoners who were charged with the same offense, namely, Haywood Patterson, Ozie Powell, Willie Roberson, Andy Wright, Olen Montgomery, Eugene Williams, and Charlie Weems, and at that time was questioned by Mr. Moody and Mr. Roddy, and I told those lawyers at that time that I did not rape or have anything to do with either of the two white girls who were on the train, and that none of the other defendants who were charged with that offense did. On the 25th of March 1931, I had been on a freight train coming from Chattanooga, Tennessee, and was bound for Sheffield, Alabama, to visit my aunt who lives there, in order to get a job. I had a job in Atlanta, Georgia, working for the Capital Stone Company, and was let off. The only man I knew on the freight train when I boarded it at Chattanooga was Charlie Weems, colored. I didn't know until I got off the train at Paint Rock that Charlie Weems had boarded the same train at I did not see any other negro boys on the train, and did not see any white boys on the train. Neither did I see any white girls in overalls, or otherwise dressed, on the freight train, until I arrived at Paint Rock.

I rode on an oil car, with my feet hanging over the side. The oil car was back toward the cab-car. I am nineteen years old, and my mother, Ida Norris, lives at Molena, Georgia. My home was in Atlanta, and I had been living there about five years, and had never been in any trouble, except that I was arrested for late hours one time and served a term of ten days hard labor at Atlanta, Georgia.

I was arrested after arriving at Paint Rock by some officers, and I was taken across the country and put in jail at Scottsboro, on the night I was arrested about six o'clock. There were eight other Negro boys arrested. About an hour after we arrived in the Scottsboro jail, there were four men who came and took me away from where the other prisoners were to a cell in the jail and beat me there with sticks. I was slapped and kicked and told that if I did not tell that the other Negro boys who were arrested on the train had something to do with those white girls, that they would kill me; that they would shoot me down in the courthouse. I was afraid of them, and told them that I would do what they said. I was asked by one of these men if he Negro boys on the train did not throw the white men off, and I told them I didn't see that, and then they slapped and beat me; and then they asked me if I saw any of those Negro boys on the train have anything to do with those girls, and I told them no, and they went to beating on me again. They told me I had better get up in the courthouse and say that, and I told them yes, I would do it.

I was moved with the other prisoners from the Scottsboro jail to Gadsden jail the next day after we were put in the Scottsboro jail. We stayed in the Gadsden Jail two weeks, and about two days before the trial in Scottsboro several men came in the jail where the Negro prisoners were, and beat all nine of the colored boys that had been arrested and taken off the train. They tried to make us tell that we had had something to do with the white women on the train. All of the prisoners, even after they were beaten, said they did not have anything to do with the white girls. One of the men that beat us turned to me and said, "You told me down yonder at Scottsboro Jail that you would tell it," and then I told him that I would do what I told him and say in court that I was these other prisoners have something to do with the white girls on that train; and this man told me that if I didn't do it, he was going to shoot me down in the court.

When I testified in my trial at Scottsboro, I was afraid for my life, and did not there testify to the true facts. When I was on the stand testifying for myself, I stated that I was not engaged in a fight, but saw a fight in the gondola car. This was not true. I did not see any fight on the train, and did not see any fight in the gondola car; but made this statement that the Negro boys and white boys were fighting in that car in order to save my life, thinking that I would be shot down if I did not make this statement. I stated in my testimony that Haywood Patterson started the fight, and that he came across the flat car where I was, him and the rest of the colored boys, and that he, Haywood Patterson, said he was going over there to run the white boys off, and going to have something to do with the white girls. All of this statement was untrue; nothing of that kind happened in my presence. I did not see Haywood Patterson and other Negro men come across the flat car, or any other car, an say they were going to run the white boys off, and were going to have something to do with the white girls. I made this statement because I was fearful of losing my life in the courtroom while I was testifying.

I made the statement in my testimony that these Negro men knew the girls were on the train and that the white boys were with the white girls on the gondola car. This statement was not true as I did not see anything of the kind, I did not see any white girls at all, an any statement that I made to the contrary on the trial was untrue and was made because I was afraid of losing my life by those who had beaten me and threatened me beforehand. I did not see any white boys fall off or get off the train, and I did not ask two white boys what they were getting off the train for, and I did not get on the train to see if they were being put off. I did not get up on the box car, and did not see the Negroes putting the white boys off. All this statement was made up by me in the hope of saving myself from the threats which had been made.

I did not see any Negro boy have a knife around a white boy's neck, trying to push him off the train, and I did not see any other boy take hold of him and pull him back up in the car. I did not see any [flight] or trouble or difficulty on the train at all. When I testified that I saw Charlie Weems in the gondola, I was testifying to something that was untrue, as I made that up, I did not see Charlie Weems or any other Negro in the gondola. I do not know what a gondola car is. I did not see any white girls in overalls in any car on that train, and I did not see any Negro boys or men in any car on that train with white girls in overalls. When I answered in my testimony that I saw every one of the Negro boys have something to do with the white girls after they put the white boys off the Train, I was telling an untruth. I did nothing of the kind, but was testifying in order to save myself from what I thought was certain death if I did not swear this way. I was not sitting on the box car, and did not see any one of these Negro boys have anything to do with the white girls or rape them or do anything to them.

I did not see them together at any time on that train, but testified to this on my trial, because I was afraid that I would be shot down in the court room, as the men told me they would. I was never on a box car, but was on an oil tank car all the way from Chattanooga to Paint Rock. In my testimony, I stated that I saw Charlie Weems rape one of these girls, but that was not true. I saw nothing of the kind, but testified to this because I was afraid for my life under the treats which had been made and the punishment which had been inflicted on me. I testified truthfully on my trial that I didn't have a pearl-handle knife on me when I was arrested. If any of the officers found such a knife on the boys, it was not on me, as I did not have such a knife on the train or in the pockets when I was arrested. So far as I know, of my own knowledge, no one of the negro boys raped either of the white girls. I was not with them and did not see anything of the kind.

When I testified on my trial that a certain one of the negro prisoners in the court room had a knife around one of the white girls throat, pointing him out in the court room, I was telling something that is not true, under the influence of the threats and fear of bodily violence that had been inflicted on me twice before the trial. I did not see any negro man or boy have a knife around the throat of any white girl on that train. I did not see any white girls lying down when I got up on the box car, and did not see any Negro boy have a knife on the throat of either of them. My testimony on the trial to that effect was forced out of me by fear that I would be shot down in the court room. I did not see ny Negro boy or man on that trial force any white girl or woman to lie down while other Negro boys or men raped her, and my testimony to that effect is untrue and was forced out of me by fear and the threats that had been made to take my life in the court room if I did not testify to such facts.

I was on the ground, off the train, when I was arrested. I got off the oil tank car and was on the ground when arrested at Paint Rock. I was on the train, but not in the gondola. My testimony to the effect that I could see the faces of the women, but could not see their bodies or clothing, was untrue, and was made under fear and on account of the threats and bodily harm I have mentioned before. So far as I know, of my own knowledge, there was no fight between white men and Negroes on the train, and no raping of white girls by any negroes; and my statement I have made to the contrary on my trial was made under a sense of fear, because I was afraid they would shoot me down in the court room, as they told me. I told my lawyers that I did not see any of the Negro men have any-thing to do with the white girls, and that was the truth; but I was afraid to tell it that was in court. I never saw any Negro man or white man attack any white girls on that train, or do them any harm, and I did not see Charlie Weems ravish and white girls on that train, and did not see [   ] about her.

I am now in Kilby Prison and am not afraid of bodily harm at the hands of anybody; and the above statements I have made are true, and are made in the Prison, in the presence of Officer F. Partin, of Montgomery, Alabama, who is Deputy Warden of Kilby Prison. No inducements have been offered me to make this statement by anybody, and I have been cautioned to speak the whole truth.

(Signed) Clarence Norris

Sworn to and subscribed before me this 10th day of June, 1931

(Signed) Leo L. Cawthon)

Leo L. Cawthon

Notary Public, Montgomery County.

Alabama [Reel 3, Group 1, Box D-69, #000431, NAACP].

On June 22, the defendants received a stay of execution pending an appeal submitted by the ILD to the Alabama Supreme Court.

June 19, 1931

Blair County Jail

Dear Mother:

While in my cell, lonely and thinking of you. I am trying by some means to write you a few words. I would like for you to come down here Thursday. I feel like I can eat some of your cooking Mom. Beatrice may like she was going to send me a chicken but I haven't got one yet. I would like for you to bring or send me a chicken. If you please, send me some paper and stamps so I can write more often. Be sure to send me that chicken, if nothing else and don't forget that. Please don't write or tell me anything to make me feel good. You cant send Andy anything to eat, but you can me. Send or bring me a big bag of peanuts. If you send me a box you don't have to come because I have your picture and I can look at it, or the cake slice it up when you send it. Tell Sis I say hello. Write back. Let me know if you send it or come down. Either one. Put in box or let it come on to me. I have gone chicken crazy so I close for this time,

> Your devoted son
> Roy Wright
> waiting [Reel 5, Box 5, #000960 (folder c64), ILD].

> Montgomery, Alabama
> June 21, 1931

International Labor Defense
80 East 11th Street
New York City
Dear Friends,

Every single one of those boys in Kilby prison is with the ILD. We talked to them for more than an hour this afternoon and had a chance to explain to them what the ILD is doing. Every one said that now he knew the truth he was going to stick to the ILD and never sign anything for Walter White.

The boys had been worried to death by the warden not giving the boys our letters and by those NAACP people telling them all kinds of lies and showing them clippings from small town newspapers saying they were going to burn in the chair July 10. When we heard from them Walter White was coming here soon to try to get them to sign over the case to his organization we rushed right down here to clear any poison out of their brains that might make them think of doing a thing like that.

The boys told us they had never signed for Walter White and didn't expect to. Walter White is a liar if he says that we or any one of the boys wants him and his organization in this case.

Fraternally yours,
Janie Patterson
York Maddox
Ida Norris
Josephine Powell [Reel 4, Box 4, #000230, ILD].

Though Olen Montgomery was 17 years old when arrested in Paint Rock, Alabama, and nearly blind in one eye, he envisioned that once reaching Memphis, Tennessee, with enough luck and money earned from day labor work he could purchase a better set of glasses and embark upon a musical career. However, exactly two months after being arrested in Paint Rock, he was writing his attorney, George Chamlee, from Kilby Prison's death house in Montgomery, Alabama:

From Olen Montgomery   May 25–31
Kilby Prison
Montgomery, Ala.
My dear Frind Mr. George

Why sitting down warred nilly crazy i want you all to rite to me and tell me how is things going on a bout this case of us 9 boys bee cause i am in here for something i know I did not do my pore mother has no one to help hur to make a living but me she had a little girl Luft only 5 years old to take of and she has no job at all and i guct you all know how times is on the out side i hard i did all i cud for my pore mother to help hur live and my little sister i was on my way to Memphis on a oil tank by my self a lone and i was not warred with any one un till i got to Paint Rock alabama and they just made a frame up on us boys just cause they cud any way them grond jurys come out of the room and said us five boys punishment shall bee like time in the Kilby Prison and the judge sent them back in the room and they come back out the next time and said their punishment shall bee by death in the chair

Eugene Williams
Haywood Patterson
Charlie Weems
Clarence Norris
Ozie Powell
Andy Wright
Willie Roberson

We want you all to send us some money so we can bye us something what we can eat this food don't degree with me at all i supposed to be at home any way i did not do whay they gat me for i ant give no one any cause to mist treat me this way i know i ant and i hope you all is doin all you can for us boys please sur and we supposesd to have a nother trial be cause it was not a fair trial i ant crazy no way either lost my mine [Chamlee. Reel 5, Box 4, #0015 (folder c52) 1931, ILD].

One of the first letters written by 19-year-old Scottsboro defendant Clarence Norris appeared in the fall of 1931. Born on July 12, 1912, Norris was one of eleven siblings born on a sharecropping farm in Molina, Georgia. Attending school up to the second grade, he had to give up this privilege because his labor and that of his family was needed in order for them to survive the Depression. At the age of seven, he was fully employed in the cotton fields. By 1930, Norris left his sharecropping family and began looking for better employment by working on a number of mining and construction sites throughout Georgia. Receiving only 25 cents to 30 cents an hour, he took to the rails in March 1931, hoping to reach Memphis and eventually save enough money to attend a school and become literate. However, as fate would have it, the events of March 25 landed him in American and international judicial history books as a Scottsboro defendant. Because Norris was illiterate, all of his jail and prison letters were either dictated to a trusted inmate or written by a fellow Scottsboro defendant. His mother, Ida Norris, became a spokesperson for her son's welfare and an outspoken critic of the public conflict between the two defense teams.

Aug. 3rd 1931
Friday night
Kilby Prison

dear Mr. White How are you i am Well Say Mr. White this is Willie Robinson Righting tow say Mr. White i have wote you one tellers i want you have my case i wote and told you one i am looking for you tow all you can for i have know Mother and father to Want you tow take my case I don't want ILD tow have anything tow do With me so mr. White ples take my case and you Right tow my auntie 992 Michigan avenew Atlanta G Mrs L Mo Cox and tell her you are going to take My Case So if you are going to take my Case ples Right and let Me know So if you don't Right me i know our are not going tow my case ples Mr White take my Case i Want You tow have My case i have wote you a letter and told you tow Stop So Mr.White ples take My case I want you tow have my case i don't want the ILD tow have to my Case So goodby from Willie Robinson

Right Soon [Reel 4, Group 1, Box D-70, #00037, NAACP].

August 4th 1931

My dear Mr. Robinson

I have received your letter, and I want you to know that the N.A.A.C.P. is going to do everything within its power for you and the other boys there in Kilby Prison. We are working constantly on the cases, but as you must realize it will be at least two months before the motion for new trials will be heard by the Alabama Supreme Court.

Do not think for a moment that we are going to leave anything undone which we think will help to secure your freedom.

Ever Sincerely,

Secretary

P.S.— We have asked Dr. Stephens and other friends in Montgomery to visit the boys there from time to time and to take them such things as candy, cigarettes, etc. I am sure they will do this.

W.W.

Mr. Willie Robinson

Kilby Prison

Montgomery, Alabama [Reel 4, Group 1, Box-D70, #000049, NAACP].

A review of Walter White's August 5 and 6 daily memoranda of telephone calls, meetings, and seemingly continual political exigencies similar in many aspects to the Scottsboro case, undoubtedly required a major multitasking ability for the NAACP as well as its judicial competitor, the ILD. Noteworthy in this regard is White's August 5 memorandum where it is suggested that the NAACP must come to grips with its rejection as legal counsel by most of the Scottsboro defendants, and that a hostile atmosphere existed between these youths and the Association's defense attorneys. And as if this was not enough, the memorandum also notes that the opinions of respected NAACP field organizer William Pickens on the positive value of the ILD in the Scottsboro case were not received well by many in the Association's leadership. Finally, in a somewhat despondent manner he notes the "discouraged" attitude of "Negro leader" after an alleged interracial assault and murder of four whites that had the potential for additional racial explosion in Birmingham, Alabama:

MEMORANDUM RE: TELEPHONE CONVERSATION
With Mr. Beddow — August 5, 1931

Mr. Beddow called the Secretary over long distance, from Birmingham, Alabama, about 4:00 o'clock, P.M., August 5.

Mr. Beddow stated that he had visited the boys at Kilby Prison twice and that on both occasions the boys had been most insulting saying, "We do not want you. You are representing the capitalists and are just trying to get us electrocuted."

Only Ozie Powers, Clarence Norris and Charlie Weems still expressed the desire to have the N.A.A.C.P. and Mr. Beddow defend them. Oleen Montgomery, Heywood Patterson, Eugene Williams and Andy Wright absolutely refused to talk with Mr. Beddow; also Willie Robinson.

The Secretary promised Mr. Beddow he would talk the matter over with Mr. Arthur Spingarn and then call him on long distance Thursday morning, August 6.

<u>August 6</u>:

The Secretary talked with Mr. Spingarn (at Amenia, N.Y.) over long distance and discussed with him the advisability of the Secretary going to Birmingham and Montgomery. Mr. Spingdarn felt that this should be done; that final offer of the Association's help should be made to the eight boys, and that if any wish to remain with the I.L.D., the N.A.A.C.P. should publicly announce that fact and wash its hands of those cases, continuing of course to defend those who wish our aid.

Mr. Spingarn approved of the suggestion of the Secretary that we communicate with Major Moton at Capahosic, Virginia by long distance telephone, and ascertain if he would be willing to go with the Secretary to Montgomery to talk with the boys.

The Secretary talked with Dr. Du Bois who agreed with the position taken by Mr. Spingarn. Dr. Du Bois felt that the full facts should be made public when the boys make their decision.

At 11:15 today the Secretary tried to reach Mr. Pickens to talk with him but no one answered at his home.

At 11:00 the Secretary called Mr. Beddow but he had not yet reached his office. He left word for Mr. Beddow to telephone him.

In the afternoon Mr. Beddow telephoned that the situation in Alabama is tense on account of the recent assault by a negro, near Birmingham upon four white women, two of whom he killed, wounding the other two.

Mr. Beddow suggested that the Secretary come first to Birmingham nd then proceed to Montgomery.

Mr. Beddow reported that the man who committed the Birmingham crime had not yet been caught but that Birmingham is a veritable powder-keg ready to explode; that the Communist are industriously, and with some some success, spreading the report that the N.A.A.C.P. formented and caused the trouble at Camp Hill.

Mr. Beddow declined to express an opinion as to the advisability of asking Dr. Moton to go to Kilby Prison, saying that he was in no position to judge — that he was leaving the decision entirely to the National Office. At any rate, he feels the Secretary should come to Birmingham as soon as possible. Mr. Beddow will be out of Birmingham Saturday but says if the Secretary gets there Sunday or even Monday it will be time enough.

Mr. Bedow says the minds of the parents of the boys have been so poisoned against the Association's Secretary that he doubts that they can be changed; but he agrees that one final effort should be made to show them the probable consequences if they are defended by the Communist.

Mr. Beddow seemed very much discouraged, saying he had never in his life encountered such a nasty situation.

The Secretary told Mr. Beddow that he would wire him today as to whether he can go to Birmingham on Friday or Saturday.

5:30 P.M. — Telegram from Mr. Beddow saying, "Come immediately. Not necessary bring other party. If needed can communicate with him later."

The Secretary wired Mr. Beddow that on account of a Speaking Engagement in Philadelphia tonight he could not leave for Birmingham until Friday, and asked if Mr. Beddow would be in Birmingham Saturday [Reel 4, Group 1, Box D-70, #000055, NAACP].

> Montgomery, Ala.
> Kilby Prison.
> August 7, 1931

Mr. Walter White,
My dear Friend:—

Just a few lines to let you hear from me. This leaves me well and I truly hope when these few lines reach your kind hands they will find all well and doing fine.

Now, Mr. White listen here. It has been sometime since I have gotten a letter from you But I want you to know that I am depending on you to fight my case. The I.L.D. is trying to get us but I think that you can do us more good than they can. Mr. Beddow was down here to see us a few days ago and I wrote my mother and told her that I had more confidence in you all than I have in them.

I would like to hear from you sometime. I am looking for a answer soon.
From Clarence Norris
Kilby Prison
c/o Mrs. Porter [Reel 4, Group 1, Box D-70, #000080, NAACP]

August 9, 1931
Saturday Night
Montgomery, Ala.
Kilby Prison

    dear Mr. White How are you i am well and hope you are the same say Mr. White i get you letters tow day and gold tow know this you are going to take my case I Wish you Wood right and tell my auntie this you are going tow My case she Stay at 992 Michigan Ave. N. W. Mrs. Lomax i Wood think you if you Wood take my case i don't know what the other boys is going tow do But i What i am tow do i am going Stay With You So don't for get ples Mr white take my case and tell the I.L.D. tow Stop i see How it is now So I am going tow Right tow and tell my aunty and let her know about itI have get know mother and papa tow come and see a about me like other boys So i will Say good to all from Willie Robinson [Reel 4, Group 1, Box D-70, #000081, NAACP].

The following binding statement from the NAACP was sent to Mrs. Lila Cox in early August 1931. It in effect allowed the Association to represent Willie Robinson's legal interest in court.

    <u>Lila Cox,</u> living at <u>992 Michigan Avenue NW Atlanta, Georgia</u>, as the <u>aunt</u> of <u>Willie Robinson</u> and under sentence of death on a charge of rape alleged to have occurred on March 25th, 1931 in Jackson County, Alabama. Said <u>Willie Robinson</u> was born on <u>July 4, 1913</u> and thus is now <u>eighteen</u> years of age.

    I hearby turn over full charge of all efforts, legal and through appeal to public opinion, towards securing a new trial or in seeking appeal to higher court or courts to the National Association for the Advancement of Colored People through its national Office, located at 69 Fifth Avenue, New York City and through its <u>Atlanta, Georgia</u> Branch.

    I further agree that the organization above named shall have sole and exclusive right to select and retain attorney or attorneys, raise funds for defense through appeals to the public and to have full authority to act in any and all other manner towards providing the most effective and adequate defense for my <u>nephew Willie Robinson</u>

    I further agree to abide in every way by the decision of the bodies above named as to choice of attorney and as to the number of such attorneys. I further stipulate that only such attorneys shall represent my <u>nephew</u> as any be chosen by the above named body. I distinctly stipulate that should any additional attorney or attorneys than those chosen as above provided, enter the case, they do so without authority or consent from myself and the above named body shall not b held responsible for the whole or any part of fees or disbursements of such counsel.

    I further agree that all money or monies paid by my _____ or myself or any Other member of my family shall be paid through the Defense Fund established by The above named body. Further, all money or monies which may be sent for help in defending my <u>nephew</u> shall be turned over to this Defense Fund. My <u>nephew</u> will also follow this procedure.

It is understood by me that an official receipt shall be given to each person for money contributed for defense, said receipt to be official acknowledgement of such payment by the said National Association for the Advancement of Colored People; that said body shall be held responsible only for such monies paid it; that payment shall be made only by voucher; and a strict accounting kept of all payments received and disbursed and that the public shall be kept informed not only of the progress of the case but of receipts and disbursements.

> Signed, this <u>10th</u> day of <u>August 1931</u>
> in the city of <u>Atlanta, Georgia</u>
> <u>Lila Cox</u>

Witnesses:

_____

_____ [Reel 4, Group 1, Box D-70, #000095, NAACP].

However, in an adamant manner, Haywood Patterson's father, Claude, rejected any role for the NAACP in his son's legal defense.

> 910 W. 19th St.
> Chattanooga, Tenn.
> 1931 Aug. 13.

Mr. White.

I happen got your employ take care none them boys. That what to matter with the world today. People will teach them one thing and other people will teach them another. I learned you was in down there teachering the boys. I got George Chamble, me and all the mothers. We don't need you and none your crowd for nothing for all you all is no good. We learn you went down there, said we was miss lead. Like we was grown and we have five since, If you want to help anybody go to Camp Hill, help those boys. We ask you with all love and all kindness to stay out our bizeness for Havy is mine. When I here from you agin I hope you are going on about your bizeness for you cant do know good at all. If you want anybody to sing [sign] come to West 910 I will sing [sign] this. Claud Pattson talking to you. Stop and read this letter carefully.

From Claud Patterson [Reel 4, Group 1, Box D-70, #000115, NAACP].

Though Claude Patterson's harsh but short letter to Walter White expressed in no uncertain terms that NAACP involvement in his son's case was not welcomed, this sentiment is also indicative of an increased sense of psychological pressure upon the defendants as they sought both legal and emotional support. Herein, one may discern that Walter White's contact with the defendants is indeed tenuous but hopeful.

> Montgomery, Ala.
> Kilby Prison
> August 16, 1931

Mr. Walter White,

My dear Friend:—

Just a few lines to let you hear from me. This leaves me well at present and I truly hope when these few lines reach your kind hands they will find all well and doing fine.

Mr. White the other boys and I was talking about you today. I think all of them have made it up in their minds that you were write and Mr. White I am sorry that the boys acted like they did when Mr. Beddow was down here. Please don't think hard of him because I really don't think he knows any better. I am too glad for somebody to help me out of this trouble because I dont not know anything about what I am charged with so I am looking for you to do what you can for me.

All the boys send regards to Mr. White. I sure would be glad if you would send me some camel smokes. So I will close, from all

(signed)   Clarence Norris [Reel 4, Group 1, Box D-70, # 000117, NAACP].

August 17, 1931

Dear Mr. Robinson:

I have your letter of August 12 and am, as always, glad to hear from you. As I stated to you and to all the other boys when I was at the prison last Tuesday, the N.A.A.C.P. is now doing and will continue to do everything in its power in your behalf, which can be done in a legal and proper fashion. As I said to you when I was leaving, it is necessary for you to stand firm in your determination that the N.A.A.C.P. defend you.

Due to the fact that some of the boys were discourteous when he came to see you recently, Mr. Beddow was inclined to drop the case because some of the defendants were not standing firm. After I had talked with him, however, for a while and pointed out to him the necessity of remaining in the case, he agreed to do so. So you see a very great deal depends upon your doing everything you can to help us help you. You must not be changing your mind again, for that will mix up things so that it will be more difficult to help you.

I am writing to your aunt today and am sending you enclosed a copy of the letter I am writing her.

Ever sincerely.
Secretary

Mr. Willie Robinson
Kilby Prison
Montgomery, Alabama
WW/RR [Reel 4, Group 1, Box D-70, # 000132, NAACP].

Aug. 17 1931
Riverdale Ga

My dear friend I will rite you in the care of charlie weems who is in Prison and he rite to me for me to rite you for easier mantion of His case and want to no if you can help save Him, are clear Him. If so rite me let no one no he rite me down there to see Him I has letters from His now so I Will Give you His age He is 17 teen years old so I will close for this time your truly Paulene Leroy and all so Gussie c Leroy is Charlie Weems.

Antie

So rite soon

Please [Reel 4, Group 1, Box D-70, #000134, NAACP].

---

thursday night
Montgomery Ala.
Kilby prison
August 20 1931

My dear friend Mr White How are you i am well and hope When you get My letters i hope it Will fine you the same this is Willie Robinson Right tow you Say Mr White did you get home all Right this Make tow i have Wrote you i did know way was anny thing tow matter You and i did know Way you have get hirt Say Mr White the ILD Was tow See Me Sunday Say Mr White you know What i told thim i don't want thim tow have My case Say Mr White like told When You Was tow See us I want you tow have My Case So ples tow My case i hope you have Wrote tow My Aunte in Atlanta Ga 992 Michigan NW ave Mrs L M Cox So ples Wright her So i Will Say good night tow all from Willie Robinson Right Soon [Reel 4, Group 1, Box D-70, #000171, NAACP].

August 21st 1931

Dear Willie:

I have your letter of August 20th. By this time you have no doubt received my letter to you together with a copy of the letter which I wrote to your aunt, Mrs. Cox.

I am happy to say that the information given you that I have been hurt is not true.

I hope that you did make it sufficiently clear to the I.L.D. that you had definitely and for all time decided that you want the N.A.A.C.P. to defend you. As I have said to you before, we will do everything in our power for you and you need have no fear to the contrary.

You will hear from me again from time to time and we shall keep you informed of all that we are doing in your behalf.

Ever sincerely,
Secretary

Mr. Willie Robinson
Kilby Prison
Montgomery,
Alabama [Reel 4, Group 1, Box D-70, #000175, NAACP].

August 22nd 1931

Dear Clarence:

I have received your nice letter of August 16th and I am glad to learn that all the boys now feel that what I said to you last Tuesday when I was at the prison is right. After going back to Birmingham from Montgomery I talked again with Mr. Beddow and explained to him about the situation when he visited the prison. We also agreed that whatever the other boys decide we will defend you, Charlie Weems, Ozie Powell and Willie Robinson to the utmost.

You will remember that I told you both times when I visited the prison that we will do everything within our power to aid you and you can rely absolutely on this. I am sending a little story to the press on your letter this week and am including in it what you say about cigarettes. I am sure that you will receive many cigarettes as a result of this which I hope you will share with the other boys, both those who wish to be defended by the N.A.A.C.P. and the others as well. I am also asking Dr. Grey and Mr. Saffold of our Montgomery Branch to come to see you as frequently as possible and to bring you cigarettes and candy.

Ever sincerely,

Secretary.

Mr. Clarence Norris
Kilby Prison
Montgomery,
Alabama.
WW:CTF [Reel 4, Group 1, Box D-70, #000182, NAACP].

Wednesday night
Montgomery Ala.
Kilby prison
August 25 1931

My dear frend Mr White

How are you i am well and hope When You get my letters i hope it Will fine you the Same i Was glad tow hear from You i get Your letters Sunday and glad tow know you have Wrote tow My aunt in Atlanta Ga I am look for you all tow help me now you See i have Wrote tow i ILD and told them this i don't Want them tow have My case You see Mr White i Would Be glad if You all good people will keep me from the Chair and When my case come up i Want you com and See about it for Me and try tow keep us Wither it Say Mr White how is the Walden I Wist i cood See him tell com tow see Me i get some tolk for him. Say mr. White i am getting the Birming ham post You know the news paper i don't see What the Walden it have come out in the news paper way he is going tow take my case i want him tow my case Well i am look for you tow help Me now So i Will Say good night all

from Willie Robinson

Right Soon [Reel 4, Group 1, Box D-70, #000202, NAACP].

Wednesday night
Montgomery all
Kilby prison
Aug 26 1931

My dear frend Mr White How are You i am Well and hope When you get
My letters i Hope it well fine You the Same this is Willie Robinson Wrighting
tow You i did Want you tow think cause the other boy Wrote and told you
this he did /want You tow have the us othe 3 boy Still Want you tow have the
Case Say do you know When you come tow See me you know What i told
you i told this i Want you tow take My case and i Want you tow do this for
me Say i am glad you have Wrote tow My aunt i Wist you other boys know
like i did a about the ILD they want the ILD tow have they case and Say Mr
White When my case come up in am look for you tow help me now Say Mr
White i Wist You Would ples Send me Some Cigarettes ples Sir i hope you
Will do all you can for Me i have Wrote and told the ILD this i did Want
them tow have my case So good by from Willie Robinson

Right Soon [Reel 4, Group 1, Box D-70, #000203, NAACP].

In the midst of a series of letters that might suggest an improved struggle
against the ILD for the allegiance of the Scottsboro defendants, NAACP secretary Walter White received the following letters of rejection:

FORT, BEDDOW & RAY
ATTORNEYS AT LAW
206–210 Bankers Bond Building

William E. Fort   Birmington, Ala.
Roderick Beddow   August 26, 1931
Ben F. Ray
G. Ernest Jones
Counselor
Roderick M. Macleod
Willard McCall
Mr. Walter White,
Secretary of N.A.A.C.P.
69 Fifth Avenue,
New York City, N.Y.
Dear Sir:

Our relations in the past have been so pleasant that it is wth some hesitancy
and no little reluctance that I begin this letter. When we first met and discussed the Scottsboro cases, the probability of the guilt or innocence of the
eight defendants and the circumstances attending their conviction, I was actu-
ated by high motives when I said to you that I would recommend to my associates that we join you and your altruistic association in seeking, as far as
humanly possible, justice in behalf of the said defendants. As our conversation
progressed, I gathered from what you said that you were here for one reason,
and one reason alone, that being your interest in the great struggle for human
right.

I was persuaded to believe without equivocation, that this was a fact when you told me that an effort would be brought about by a misguided organization to promote race strife, and that the Scottsboro case had resolved itself into something more important than the lives of the convicted boys. I understand very well that cases of this kind provide the most fertile soil into which seeds of radicalism can be sowed. I know too, that the facts concerning your interest will not be truthfully related; the truth will not be told and that every resort and cunning known to just such organization will be brought into play to distort the truth.

I have always believed, as I have heretofore told you, that if everyone who claimed to be interested in the boys could bring themselves to believe that their interest, if left in our hands would be safe, we could get for them perhaps a new trial, or procure for them Executive clemency as a last resort. Of course we could before applying for Executive clemency, carry the cases to the United States Supreme Court, provided, however, a constitutional question was raised. The probability of proceeding in a dignified, orderly way seems to have faded into oblivion. The Governor has received many threatening letters coming of course, from perverted minds. Senseless and contemptible articles have been written in newspapers, dripping with Red propaganda, charging the trial judge with being an ignoramous; stating among other things that he is corrupt and illiterate,—some of them over the signature of a supposed attorney who claims to be one of the attorneys of record for the defendants, who as a matter of fact did appear at the time the hearing was [had] on the motion for a new trial.

In addition to all of this and to add to the burdensome task of trying to persuade the public that it must at all hazards and risks be fair, we had the Dadeville riot and other numerous difficulties which I do not deem it here necessary to recount. Frightful scenes of this kind were deliberately brought about through Communistic effort to injure your interest in the cases. The parties guilty of exciting the trouble even disseminated literature to the effect that your representatives called the meeting that culminated into the hideous orgies.

Now Walter, frankly, in justice to your organization and to ourselves, we cannot allow ourselves to be retained where there is so much strife, misrepresentation and internal misunderstandings. Long before we were approached in these cases the International Labor Defense had taken charge of the mothers, guardians or next of kin of the several defendants. They had them (the relatives) retain their counsel. Then to add to our already complicated situation, the boys cannot agree among themselves whom they desire as counsel. I am not, you understand, blaming the boys. Their position is analogous to that of a man drowning. They are panicky. They are stupefied, stunned and we may say without equivocation, placed in a predicament where they cannot wisely decide for themselves. I do no blame them. I do not even resent the insolence of one of the boys when I last visited him at Kilby. I charge his conduct to ignorance and misinformation.

You will remember when you and I agreed that I would urge the other members of my firm to join me in proffering your organization our help, we thoroughtly understood that the task was to be undertaken as and when the Communistic element was withdrawn. This we have been advised they will never do, not even if they were convinced that it would be for the best interest of the condemned individuals for they have found a medium through which they can spew their slime and false propaganda. As my associates and I told you in our last conversation held in our offices with Mr. Burton, yourself and others, the interest of all of the defendants are so intermingled and interwoven it can be likened unto a bolt of cloth. Positively there can be no separation of interest. To allow a separation would be to remove their cause from a foundation of rock to one of sand.

In making this decision and in behalf of ourselves I may say that Judge Fort loves humanity and would gladly sacrifice this all in its interest. Mr. Ray is possessed of the same proclivities and public opinion plays no part when he is called upon to make a sincere decision. As for myself, all I have to say is that space does not permit the privilege of extolling my own virtues. My record in behalf of the defenseless will speak for itself. However true all this may be and remembering the sacredness of an individual's constitutional right to a fair trial, we have concluded that we must decline to accept employment in the Scottsboro case.

I trust that you will understand our motive in making this decision. Our conclusions were reached after long conferences and much reflection. We have catalogued the insurmountable difficulties thrown in the road that leads from the trial court to the highest tribunal in the State; the charges of capitalistic interest, etc. We believe that even though we were allowed to proceed without interference, which of course is impossible, that if the worst should come, we would always be damned as having deliberately allowed the souls of our clients to be delivered into the hands of their enemies. I say this because it has been charged that capitalistic influences seek their execution and not the State of Alabama. Then too, we cannot be put in the position of fighting for the right to represent a client or clients. They have sufficient barriers to bridge from without. If this is true, certainly everything should be in harmonious accord where their interest is concerned.

We make our decision with the knowledge of the absolute confidence you reposed in us in tendering the cases. Believing as we do that we cannot get desired results with the taint of radicalism in the cases and knowing that their methods will produce irreparable injury to the cause of the several defendants, we cannot afford to continue for the reason that we would be identified as one of them. Then too, believing as we sincerely do, that the case has thus been injured, we would not be honest if we accepted your money, contingent upon an implied promise to do the thing we knew was impossible.

The near relatives of the defendants are scattered throughout the country. The following names and addresses are the only ones in our files. Whether they are correct or not we do not know.

Ozie Powers: (Josephine Powers, mother, 315 Washington S.9 Building 7, Chestnut Street, Philadelphia, Pa.)

Clarence Norris: (Ida Norris, mother, 4869 Russell Street, Detroit, Michigan)

<u>Charlie Weems:</u> (Gussie McElroy, mother, Route #6, Box 12, Riverdale, Georgia).

<u>Willie Roberson:</u> (L. M. Cox, aunt, 992 Michigan Ave., Atlanta, Georgia; another relative, Alberta Howard, 1010-A Washington St., San Francisco, Calif.)

I return herewith two checks drawn in favor of Fort, Beddow and Ray, one of said checks bearing date July 29, 1931, for the sum of two thousand dollars and the other bearing date of August 19, 1931, amount five hundred dollars. We are not returning you the five hundred dollars paid our firm June 4, 1931. The time consumed by members of our firm and associateds, namely, William E. Fort, Willard McCall and myself in making trips to Scottsboro, Chattanooga, Montgomery and New York and the expense incident thereto, approximate a larger sum than the remuneration received. Although there is an actual monetary loss to us, we gladly contribute the same, as we have no way of measuring the actual expense we have been put to in loss of time and money expended.

To have met you and known you has indeed been a pleasure. Your organization, I am sure, will make rapid strides in bringing about a better relationship between the races. You follow the proper procedure and your methods, as I understand them, are wholesome and beneficial to your people.

In closing I wish to say that our sincerest prayers sare that the Omnipotent Power will bring about ultimate right.

With every good wish, I am,

Yours sincerely,

(Signed) Roderick Beddow Encl.— 2

RB:sl [Reel 4, Group 1, Box D-70, #000205, NAACP].

Montgomery Ala. Kilby Prison   August 26, 1931

Dear Sir

Just a few line to let you hear from me i am well and hope when these few Line reach you they will found you the same listen Mr. Walter White save your time i has a letter from mother today and She told me to write you and tell you to keep hands off of me Becast She has some one to Fight for me and i will like for you to keep hands off Becast i am going to do just as my mother say She no The Best for me and that will also save you Time

So i will close

Yours truly

Ozie Powell

Answer Soon P.S. [Reel 4, Group 1, Box D-70, #000217, NAACP].

By the early fall of 1931, NAACP Assistant Secretary Roy Wilkins attempted to keep an open written dialogue with those defendants and their families, who continued to state that they would prefer the Association as their legal defender in court:

September 3, 1931

Mr. Willie Robinson
Kilby Prison
Montgomery, Alabama
My dear Mr. Robinson:

We have your letter of August 26th and are glad to know that you continue to believe that the N.A.A.C.P. is the right organization to fight your case. You may expect us to do everything possible for you.

Under separate cover we are mailing some cigarettes.

Sincerely yours
Assistant Secretary
RW/ID [Reel 4, Group 1, Box D-70, #000297, NAACP].

September 3, 1931

Mrs. Ida Norris
4869 Russell Street
Detroit, Michigan
My dear Mrs. Norris

This letter is to inform you that the National Association for the Advancement of Colored People is steadily at work on the case of your son, Clarence Norris.

Mr. Walter White, the Executive Secretary of the Association is now in the South conferring with attorneys and arranging the final details so that the bill of exceptions can be filed before the Alabama Supreme Court in the latter part of this month.

We have just received a letter from Willie Robinson stating that the boys are doing as well as could be expected. He asked for some cigarettes and we have mailed him today a carton of Camels in answer to his request.

Under separate cover I am mailing you two pamphlets of the Association, the last Annual Report which gives the history of the work for 1930, and the "First Line of Defense," which tells you about the cases which the Association has successfully handled during the last twenty-two years.

If there is any information you have which you think we ought to have, or if there are any questions you wish to ask we shall be pleased to hear from you.

Very Sincerely yours,
Assistant Secretary
RW/ID [Reel 4, Group 1, Box D-70, #000294, NAACP].

The following letter was also sent to Mrs. Josephine Powell and Mrs. Mamie Williams Cox.

NATIONAL ASSOCIATION FOR THE
ADVANCEMENT OF COLORED PEOPLE
69 Fifth Avenue, New York

Telephone: Algonquin 4-6545
Official Organs: *The Crisis*

Mrs. Andy Wright   September 4, 1931
c/o Mr. Butler R. Wilson
24 School Street
Boston, Massachusetts

My dear Mrs. Wright:

I am writing to you again on behalf of your son who is in Kilby Prison in Montgomery, Alabama, so that you may have clearly a picture of the situation as it now exists.

When Mr. Walter White, the Executive Secretary of the Association, was at the prison early in August, your son stated to him that he was remaining with the International Labor Defense solely because you wished him to, and he urged Mr. White to write to you again and explain the whole situation to you, and see if you would not change your mind. At that time your son said that he believed the N.A.A.C.P. was the proper organization to present his case to the Alabama Supreme Court.

The National Association for the Advancement of Colored People, which for twenty-two years has been defending colored people in the courts of the land both North and South, has gone to very great expense in this case because the Association believes that your boy has not been given a fair trial.

In all these twenty-two years, most of the people defended by the Association have been poor people in humble circumstances, share croppers, laborers, and ordinary workers who have been caught in situations where they could not help themselves. While it is true that there are some friendly, wealthy white people and some well-to-do Negroes and members and workers of this Association, it is also true that the bulk of its membership and the officers of its branches are made up of hard-working, dependable colored people in moderate and humble circumstances. They are interested in the case of your boy, and the hundreds of other persons this Association has defended, because they are kin to them, both as to skin color and to circumstances in life. You can be sure that an organization with a membership of this kind is interested only in the welfare of your son and others like him.

This case, already a very difficult one because of the nature of the crime charged against the boys, has been complicated considerably by the activities of the Communist working through the I.L.D. It is our opinion that the activities of the Communist in this case have endangered the lives of your boy and the rest for the reason that the Communists are interested in this trial partly to save the boys, but mostly to make propaganda for their political beliefs. The N.A.A.C.P. has no quarrel with the Communist as an organization. They have their beliefs and we have ours, but we do think they do your boy and the rest of them an injustice by using this case as an argument against the capitalist system, against the courts of the South and against the leading white people of Alabama, including the Governor.

This is the way the situation stands today. The appeal for a new trial for your boy must go to the Alabama Supreme Court. If it is denied there, an appeal for mercy must go to the Governor of Alabama. Against both the Alabama Supreme Court and the Governor, the Communist have made many threats, the Governor alone receiving more than 1700. How much sympathy do you think this court and the Governor can have for the case of your son when he is represented in court by the very people who have accused them of being unjust and heartless, by people who have actually threatened their lives?

In contrast to this method the N.A.A.C.P. has but one object in mind, and that is to save the life of your boy and those of the others. We realize that if this is to be done it must be done through the courts of Alabama and the regular processes of law set up for trials of this kind. We do not threaten anybody. We do not say the courts are unjust. We are assembling evidence of the innocence of the boys and putting it before the court, asking that justice be done. For twenty-two years we have followed this method and for twenty-two years it has brought results. Many men have been saved from prison and from death in cases which were just as bad as that in which your son is involved. So far we have been able to determine the International Labor Defense has never undertaken and won a case for a Negro defendant in a difficult crime such as the Scottsboro case. The ILD is further handicapped in that it knows practically nothing of race relationships in the South and of effective modes of procedure under those relationships.

I ask you to study this letter carefully and to think over the case once more, and if you still wish to continue with the International Labor Defense you may do so, but you must remember that your boy has put the final decision up to you and whatever result comes will rest with you. He is in trouble and in prison. He can't think, he can't make contacts and get information like you can, who are on the outside and free, and so he leaves this matter, which is the most important in his life to you. We shall be glad to hear from you when you have made your decision.

Sincerely yours,
Roy Wilkins
Assistant Secretary [Reel 4, Group 1, Box D-70, #000308, NAACP].

September 5, 1931

Mr.Ozie Powell
Kilby Prison
Montgomery, Alabama
My dear Mr. Powell:

Mr. Walter White has turned your letter of August 26th over to me for an answer. We understand that you wish the International Labor Defense to have charge of your case, inasmuch as your mother has decided that she thinks it is the best organization to do so. Mr. White is now on a trip in the South and may see you by the time this letter reaches you.

Yours very truly,
Assistant Secretary
RW/ID [Reel 4, Group 1, Box D-70, #000328, NAACP].

September 11, 1931

Dear Willie:

I have much pleasure in telling you that the N.A.A.C.P. has succeeded in retaining in the Scottsboro Cases the most famous and the greatest criminal lawyer in the United States if not the world — the great Clarence Darrow known throughout the world as the defender of the defenseless and as the man who always takes the part of the oppressed. Mr. Darrow's fame and great legal ability have won many battles which at first seemed hopeless.

A few years ago a mob attacked the home of a Negro doctor in Detroit. When a member of the mob was killed this Negro doctor, his young wife who was then the mother of a very young baby, the doctor's two brothers, one of whom was a dentist, and the other occupants of the house were arrested and charged with first degree murder. It was due to Mr. Darrow's great ability that all of the eleven defendants were acquitted.

When we first took up with Mr. Darrow the matter of defending you he felt that his time and strength would not permit him enter the case, but when we told him of the facts he consented to serve with the other counsel which included Messrs. Fort, Beddow and Ray of Birmingham. I am sure you will be happy to hear this

Ever sincerely,
Secretary

Mr. Willie Robinson
Kilby Prison Montgomery, Alabama [Reel 4, Group 1, Box D-70, #000372 NAACP].

Fri. night
Montgomery ala
Kilby prison
Sept. 11 1931

Mr dear frend How are you i am Well and hope When You get My letters i hope it Will fine You the Same i get the Box What You Send Me and Charlie Weems is with the NAACP the other boys is this the ILD and i am So glad this you all good people have get my case. Say Mr. Roy Wilkins i have a from Your friend tow day C Laue gmes So ples do all you can for Me So i am look for you all tow do all You can for Me ples Sir So if it have Ben for You all i Would Ben dead a long time a go So i Will Say good by from Your frind
Willie Robinson
Right Soon [Reel 4, Group 1, Box D-70, #000382, NAACP].

Sun night
Montgomery ala
Kilby prison
September 20 1931

My dear frind Mr. Roy
How are you I am Well and hope When you get My letters I hope it Will

fine you the Same I Was glad tow hear from you tow day and I Was think a
about you all When I get Your letters Say am so glad this you have Wrote and
talk with my auntie about it Say Mr. Roy the ILD people Was tow Me tow
day they Was from Chattanooga Tenn. and the man Was Mr. Lowell Wakefled
I he is With the ILD people I told he Sunday this I did Want he tow have my
case I have told he this I Want the NAACP tow have my case Say Mr. Roy I
am wrighting tow the man officers of the ILD it is 8 est a 11st New York NY
and I am telling them this I don't want them tow have my case and stop crying to get it. Mr. Ray I am So glad this Mr. Clarence darrow is going tow
help With My case I don't know he But I have heard So much talk of him Wel
Mr. Roy I am Worry yound yct I am oly eighteen now it worry me this my
First time in truble Mr Roy I get the Stamps what you Send Me [   ] you all
good people Send Me I have know one tow Send any But you all good people
So I think for what you have Send Me and please Mr. Roy keep my case I
have Wrote and told the ILD stope I don't Want them tow have My case How
is Mr. White So I Will Say good night tow
    all from
    Willie Robinson
    Right Soon [Recl 4, Group 1, Box D-70, #000476, NAACP].

Mr. Willie Robinson   October 3, 1931
Kilby Prison
Montgomery, Alabama
Dear Willie:
    The National Association for the Advancement of Colored People is glad to
inform you that last week it filed with the court at Scottsboro a bill of exceptions in your case, of nearly 800 pages. This bill of exceptions in your case, of
nearly 800 pages.
    This bill of exceptions will be placed before the Alabama Supreme Court,
and will be used by our attorneys in asking the Supreme Court to reverse the
decision in your first trial and grant you a new trial.
    The argument before the Supreme Court on this bill of exceptions will be
made during the third week in January, 1932. Clarence Darrow, the world
famous criminal lawyer, will make one of the arguments for you before the
Supreme Court.
    We thought you would be interested in knowing that the N.A.A.C.P. is
steadily at work trying to secure a new trial and freedom for you.
                           Sincerely yours,
                           Assistant Secretary
(Similar letter was sent to the other Scottsboro defendants) [Reel 5, Group 1,
Box D-70, #000570, NAACP].

Mr. Charlie Weems   October 29, 1931
Kilby Prison
Montgomery, Alabama

Dear Charlie:

Some weeks ago we wrote you informing you that Clarence Darrow, the great criminal lawyer, has agreed to help defend your case and will make one of the arguments before the Alabama Supreme Court next January.

We are very pleased to tell you at this time that Mr. Arthur Garfield Hays, one of the great lawyers of New York, who is recognized throughout the country, has agreed to associate himself with Mr. Darrow and help defend your case. Mr. Hays has won a great reputation for fighting the cases of down-trodden groups. He has always been willing to help colored people where the principle of freedom is involved. He and Mr. Darrow were the two lawyers who defended Dr. O.M. Sweet and his family in Detroit when Dr. Sweet's home was attacked by a mob.

We feel certain that with Mr. Darrow, Mr. Hays and the other lawyers who are working on your case you have now through the N.A.A.C.P. the greatest battery of legal talent in the country to defend you.

We wanted you to know this in order that you may realize that the N.A.A.C.P. is leaving no stone unturned to successfully fight your case.

Sincerely yours,
Assistant Secretary
RW/ID [Reel 5, Group 1, Box D-70, #000688, NAACP].

Kilby Prison
Montgomery, Ala.
Nov. 10 1931

Mr. Walter White
Dear Sir

I rec'd your letter Sometime ago. Was indeed glad to hear from you. My delay in writing was due that I cannot write myself and I were waiting on the other boys to answer you letter but I don't think any of them did. so another disinterested party wrote for me. As I before said when you were down here. I wanted your to do what you could for me, of course the International Labor Defense is still sending each one of us boys money. I don't know where my mother is in favor of your Association or not. I dont think she is. Mr. Beddow were here twice talking [   ] but since I've heard that he wont take the case unless the (I.L.D.) lay off And Mr. Chamlee says he is going through with the case. I believe ou are best Please. If you don't handle it for us I want to have your letter read to all of them because they will understand better. answer soon.

Sincerely Clarence Norris
P.S. Who have our case?

Write each one & explain to them because some of them can read & write & some cannot [Reel 4, Group 1, Box D-70, #000750, NAACP].

Mr. Clarence Norris   November 13, 1931
Kilby Prison

Montgomery, Alabama

My dear Clarence:

Mr. Walter White has turned over to me your letter written November 10th in which you tell of the I.L.D. You also say that some of the boys do not understand the situation clearly. This is the way your case stands at present.

The appeal to the Alabama Supreme Court has been filed and is now waiting to be certified by the judge at Scottsboro, Alabama. He had by law from September 22nd until November 22nd to read and sign this bill of exceptions. After that, it will go to the Supreme Court of Alabama for a hearing during the third week of January, 1932. At that hearing one of the arguments will be made by Clarence Darrow, the great criminal lawyer of Chicago, whom we have engaged to help fight your case. Mr. Darrow will be assisted by Arthur Garfield Hays of New York City, another famous lawyer.

Those are the facts to date and we hope the boys will not be made uneasy by anything that is told them to the contrary. We have written to your mother and to the mothers or relatives of all the other boys, advising them from time to time of each step that we have taken for your defense.

If there is anything you do not understand further about this case, or that the other boys do not understand, please write to us again asking questions and we will do our best to make it all clear to you.

Sincerely yours,

Assistant Secretary

RW/ID [Reel 4, Group 1, Box D-70, #000757, NAACP].

Though Scottsboro defendant Haywood Patterson was continually labeled by Alabamian prosecutors and generally local and State media as the prime defendant in the Scottsboro case and as a leader among the other eight defendants, his aggressive resistance to Alabama's vicious exploitative prison system made him a prime target for brutal retaliation by racist wardens, guards and white inmates. However, contrary to public perception, Patterson's interaction was extremely problematic with his co-defendants and on several occasions hostility and violent conflict emerged. Yet, he is the only Scottsboro defendant to successfully escape from Kilby Prison's death house and its accompanying prison farm system, in 1948.

In the 1950 novel *Scottsboro Boy*, Haywood Patterson, with the assistance of writer Earl Conrad, documented Patterson's personal struggle to become literate while imprisoned, and most significantly his escape from Kilby prison's farm system (Conrad, 1950). Interestingly enough, the horrific dynamics surrounding Patterson's imprisonment and his innate will to dominate his immediate environment led to a series of clashes between himself and fellow Scottsboro defendants as they sought various means to survive the Alabama prison system. In this respect, Haywood Patterson personified what most southern whites feared and hated about blacks, and what many blacks feared about the south: racial supremacy.

It is also apparent that Haywood Patterson's assertive personality was most likely shaped by his outspoken parents. Throughout Haywood's years of incarceration both his parents, Claude and Janie Patterson, left their mark on the historical narrative of the Scottsboro case. Claude Patterson's August 13 letter to Walter White, reproduced above, minced no words in dismissing the NAACP's usefulness to his son's case and rejecting its involvement.

> Condemned Dept.
> Kilby Prison
> Montgomery, Ala
> Dec. 10 1931

Mr. J. Louis Engdahl
Dear Sir:

While sitting all alone in prison i thought I'll express you a few lines to let you here from us boys. We all are well and hoping to be free soon and also hoping you all will remain in fighting for us boys.

Mr. Engdahl i am ask you a question and i would like for you to answer it in your write, and here it's are. Have you all got Mr. Darrow to fighting for us boys. The reason why i ask you that becost i heard that Mr. Clance Darrow was going to fighting for us boys, and i would like to know if possible becost i am innocent, as innocent as the tiny mite of life just beginning to stir beneath my heart. Honest, Mr. Engdahl, i haven't did anything to be imprisonment like this. And all of the boys send their best regards to you all and best wishes. So i would appreciate an interview at your earliest convenience.

Very truly yours,
Haywood Patterson [Reel 5, Box 5, #0213 (folder c54), ILD].

> Montgomery
> Kilby
> 948 Violet Ave. S.E.
> Atlanta, Ga.
> Dec. 14 — 1931

Mr. White,

Kind sir I visited the home of Charlie Weems aunt that lives at Riverdale Ga. Route 1 — and I learned that they had heard from you all. I have wonder why I haven't learned anything else I am quite anxious to learn some Charlie is one of the Scottsboro boys.

Respectfully Mrs Lula B. Jackson [Reel 4, Group 1, Box D-70, #000896, NAACP].

Dec 20 1931

Dear Mr. Roy How are you i am Sick n get Your letter tow day and Was glad hear from you I get a from aunt tow day She Want you all tow have My case I am glad you all Get my case I do Want the ILD tow have it Mr Roy When you get time Wright tow My aunt in Atanta Ga Mrs Lulu B Jackson 948 Violet Ave S E Wright tow My aunt 992 Michigan ave Mrs L M Cox Atlanta Ga So if you all get My case Keep it I am Looking for You all tow help me from Right Soon

Willie Robinson [Reel 5, Group 1, Box D-71, #000027, NAACP].

Mr. Ozie Powell   December 23, 1931
Kilby Prison
Montgomery, Alabama

Dear Ozie:

Under separate cover the N.A.A.C.P. is sending each of you small gift for Christmas and our hearty greetings of the season. You may be interested to know that Mr. Clarence Darrow, Mr. Arthur Garfield Hays, Mr. Walter White, and the law firm in Birmingham, Alabama are having a conference in Birmingham on Sunday, December 27th, to make the final plans for the argument of your case before the Alabama Supreme Court on Januarys 18th. These men will meet in Birmingham and go over every detail of your case to see that you have the best possible defense.

It may be possible for these famous lawyers to visit you on Monday, December 28th. We are not absolutely sure about this but we are trying to arrange it so that you can personally talk to the famous men who are to argue your case. We know they will be glad to see you and we hope that if they do come you will receive them with the courtesy which they deserve because of their great interest in you and their hard work on your case.

Sincerely yours,
Assistant Secretary

RW/ID [Reel 5, Group 1, Box D-71, #000046, NAACP].

Mrs. Lula B. Jackson   December 23, 1931
948 Violet Avenue, S.E.
Atlanta, Georgia

My Dear Mrs. Jackson:

We were very glad to have your letter inquiring about Charlie Weems and the other boys in the Scottsboro case.

The N.A.A.C.P. is doing everything in its power at very great expense to see that these boys get another trial at very expense to see that these boys get another trial and win their freedom. We have gone about the legal investigation, the drawing up of the appeal and the hiring of lawyers with the greatest caution, because we wanted to be sure that there would be no slips in the case. We have been criticized by the Communist and their supporters because we did not use the same methods used by the I.L.D. However, we have gone on in our own way wishing to be safe and sure rather than rash and sorry.

When the Alabama Supreme Court hears this case in the third week of January, 1932, Mr. Clarence Darrow, the world famous criminal lawyer of Chicago; Mr. Arthur Garfield Hays, an equally famous lawyer of New York; and a leading law firm in the state of Alabama will argue the appeals before the court. Recently, the bills of exception prepared by the N.A.A.C.P. lawyers, covering almost 800 pages, were approved by the judge at Scottsboro and sent up to the Supreme Court. The size of this document will give you some idea of the great care and detail the N.A.A.C.P. has used in getting together every scrap of evidence which can help the boys in the higher court. The judge did not approve the bills of exceptions filed by George Chamlee, I.L.D lawyer, on the ground that they were not properly drawn up.

This will give you an idea of what the N.A.A.C.P. has done up to date. We believe that we have left no stone unturned in the defense of the boys and we are placing all the power of our organization and its branches, scattered from coast to coast, behind the case.

Sincerely yours,
Assistant Secretary

RW/ID [Reel 1, Group 1, Box D-71, #000034, NAACP].

However, a momentous decision was made by the defendants that forced the NAACP to consider the viability of a co-defense relationship with the ILD.

Kilby Prison
Montgomery, Ala.
[date unknown, however after December 27th]

Dear Mr. Geo. Maurer:

I will write you a few lines to let you hear from me. I am well and I hope when this reaches you, that it will find you the same. I wrote you a letter and would like to know if you got it.

I would like for you to stop Mr. Walter White from butting in my case for I don't want him to have my case for he is gots a run talls people that he had taken my case but I dont want him. I want you all to take my case, the I.L.D., for you all had my case first and I want you all to keep my case for me please.

I would like for you to send me some cigarettes, please for I haven't anything to smoke. I would appreciate if you would send them and I would like for you to write my sister Dorothy Weems for me please in Charlotte, N.C.

413 Est Bland for I wrote her a fine letter and I cant get a letter and I would appreciate if you would, so I will close for this time from.

Charlie Weems [Reel 5, Group 1, Box D-70, #000689, ILD].

PRESS SERVICE OF THE NATIONAL ASSOCIATION
For The
ADVANCEMENT OF COLORED PEOPLE

Moorfield Storey   69 Fifth Avenue, New York City   James Weldon Johnson
President   Telephone Stuyvesant 6548   Secretary
Sent to the:—
Colorado &
California Papers   Negro Aid States Position
     In Scottsboro Cases

New York, Dec. 30.— Commenting on the withdrawal of its counsel, Clarence Darrow and Arthur Garfield Hays, from the case of 8 Negro boys sentenced to death in Scottsboro, Alabama, the National Association for the Advancement of Colored People today issued the following statement:

Air Mail   December 30, 1931

The National Association for the Advancement of Colored People advised by its attorney, Clarence Darrow and Arthur Garfield Hays and notes from the press that the 8 Negro boys sentenced to death in Scottsboro, Alabama, have chosen to be defended by Lawyers appointed by the International Labor Defense, and that the I.L.D. declines co-operation with attorneys not controlled by the Communists. Messrs. Darrow and Hays offered to issue joint statement wih the other attorneys in the cases couched as follows:

> "We represent the defendants. We represent no organization. The lives of 8 boys are at stake. It is unimportant who enlisted our interest. We will engage in no controversy between groups. We have agreed to work together to try to save these boys and our responsibility is to them and to them only.

This proposal was rejected by the attorneys for the International Labor Defense. The Communists have stated that they will not have Messrs. Darrow and Hays in the case unless under Communist auspices. This statement directly contradicts the Communists' claim that they have no interest greater than saving the boys.

The N.A.A.C.P. had retained a corps of lawyers which included the best criminal lawyers in Alabama and the leading criminal lawyer of the United States. It is our fear that the connection of the Communist with this case in the prevailing attitude towards Communists in Alabama will hurt the case of the boys, but we are not without hope in view of th excellent effect on public sentiment in Alabama of the work done by the N.A.A.C.P. and the elaborate bills of exception presented to the court by N.A.A.C.P. attorneys,

The N.A.A.C.P. had and has no interest in the case other than to extend help to the boys. the boys have vacillated in their choice of counsel. When they were last seen in Kilby Prison by Walter White, Secretary of the N.A.A.C.P. , 4 of them asked to be defended by the N.A.A.C.P., while the other four expressed their personal desire, subject to the consent of their parents or guardians, that the N.A.A.C.P. obtain counsel to defnd them. Relying on these statements of the boys the N.A.A.C.P. obtained the counsel enumerated above. The N.A.A.C.P. still hopes that the lives of these innocent boys may be saved.

Walter White, Secretary [Reel 5, Group 1, Box D-71, #000098, NAACP].

Kilby Prison
Montgomery, Ala
Dec. 30, 1931

Dear Mr. Walter White:

I received you letters a few days ago and I would wrote you before but I was looking for you all to come down here and I am sorry that Mr. Clarence Darrow and them did not take the case for I want Mr. Clarence Darrow to take it and tell them I say do not forget me please for I haves signed for you all first and I want you all have my case and no one but you all and I signed the pact but I did not no and dear sir, Mr. Walter White, I received your cigarettes and I was glad to get them and please sir write and tell me about this as soon as you get this letter.

From Charlie Weems
To Mr. Walter White
Write soon [Reel 5, Group 1, Box D-71, #000096, NAACP].

The following statement was published in *Daily Worker*, on December 31, 1931:

We, the undersigned Heywood Patterson, Eugene Williams, Andy Wright, Charlie Weems, Clarence Norris, Ozie Powell, Olen Montgomery, and Willie Robertson, heretofore in April 1931, made a written contract retaining George W. Chamlee, of Chattanooga, and Joseph D. Brodsky and their associates, as our attorneys to make motions for a new trial, and to appeal our cases from the Circuit Court at Scottsboro Alabama to the Supreme Court at Montgomery, Alabama, and in May 1931, we made an other agreement ratifying the first contract.

Now, in December 1931, we hereby renew our contract with them and authorize them to appear for us in the Supreme Court of the State of Alabama, as we did in our other agreement, and to make the best effort possible, to get our cases reversed and to get us a new trial.

We authorized our parents and next of kin to employ Mr. Chamlee and his associates and we hereby ratify all their actions and agreements in reference thereto. We desire that all notices, and all communications relative to this case, intended for the appellants, or their counsel, be given to Mr. Chamlee, as our attorney. We desire a private conference with him.

Eugene Williams   Charlie Weems
Andy Wright   Haywood Patterson
Ozie Powell (his x mark) Willie Robinson
Clarence Norris (his x mark) Olen Montgomery

[Reel 5, Group 1, Box D-71, #000112, NAACP].

2

LETTERS FROM 1932
Counselors for the Wise

January: The NAACP withdraws from the Scottsboro case.
January 10: Ruby Bates' letter to friend Earl Streetman repudiates rape charge.
March 24: The Alabama Supreme Court, voting 6–1, upholds the convictions of seven of the defendants, while granting Eugene Williams a new trial because he was a juvenile at the time of his conviction.
May 27: The United States Supreme Court agrees to hear the Scottsboro case.

WESTERN
UNION
Received at 657 West 145 St New York   1932 JAN 3 AM 10 17
NH44 225 NL 22 EXTRA 1/140 VIA SD=CHATTANOOGA TENN Jan 2
CARE WALTER WHITE AND ROY WILKINS. NAACP=
409 EDGECOMBE AVE=

NEWSPAPERS ARE CARRYING STORIES THAT CLARENCE DARROW AND
ARTHUR GARFIELD HAYS REPRESENTING THE NATIONAL ASSOCIATION
FOR THE ADVANCEMENT OF COLORED PEOPLE HAVE REFUSED TO
HELP THE SCOTTSBORO BOYS STOP WE THEREFORE WISH YOU WOULD
WIRE THESE GENTLEMEN AND ALSO MAKE PUBLIC ACKNOWLEDGE-
MENT OF THE FACT THAT NEITHER ONE OF YOU NOR YOUR ORGANI-
ZATION IS NOW OR HAS EVER BEEN IN ANY SENSE OR IN ANY WAY
CONNECTED WITH THE CASES OF THE SCOTTSBORO BOYS AND THAT
THESE CASES ARE NOW AND HAVE BEEN EVER SINCE THE SCOTTSBORO
TRIAL IN THE HANDS OF OUR ATTORNEYS HEADED BY GENERAL
GEORGE W CHAMLEE OF CHATTANOOGA CHIEF COUNCIL AND SUP-
PORTED BY THE INTERNATIONAL LABOR DEFENSE JOINTLY WITH US
STOP WE REQUEST THAT YOU PUBLISH IMMEDIATELY A LIST OF THE
NAME OF ALL PERSONS WHO HAVE CONTRIBUTED MONEY COLLECTED
BY YOU WITHOUT AUTHORITY ALLEGEDLY FOR THE DEFENSE OF
THE SCOTTSBORO BOYS AND THAT YOU RETURN THE SAME AT ONCE

TO THE DONORS WHOSE GOOD INTENTIONS AND CONFIDENCE HAVE
BEEN ABUSED BY YOU STOP WE REQUEST FURTHER YOU TELL THEM
THAT YOU ARE NOT NOW AND HAVE NEVER BEEN LEGALLY CON-
NECTED WITH THE SCOTTSBORO CASES AND THAT YOURE NOW
ABSOLUTELY AND COMPLETELY DIVORCED FROM ALL CONNECTIONS
WITH THE CASES=

CLAUDE AND JANIE PATTERSON   MAMIE WILLIAMS   ADA WRIGHT
IDA NORRIS   VIOLA MONTGOMERY   JOSEPH POWELL
LULU JACKSON   GUSSIE MCLEROY   BEATRICE MADDOX
AND   JULIAN PATTERSON [Reel 5, Group 1, Box D-71, #000181, NAACP]

Januarys 4, 1931(2)

Willie Robinson
Charley Weems

Mr. Wilkins has referred to me your letter of December 28 in which you
make the statement that you do not want the I.L.D. to have your case but
wish the N.A.A.C.P. to defend you.

Upon your statements to Mr. Pickens and to me when we visited Kilby
Prison, and upon various letters written to us by you and by certain others of
the boys, the N.A.A.C.P. at great expense and trouble secured as [lawyers] for
you the two greatest criminal lawyers in the United States if in the world,
Clarence Darrow and Arthur Garfield Hays. In addition to these famous
lawyers, we engaged the best law firm in Alabama to aid in your defense. Our
lawyers prepared in your behalf bills of exception to the Alabama State
Supreme Court totaling 790 pages for which the stenographic and photostatic
service alone cost us $600, which sum we paid. Six trips have been made from
New York to Alabama in your behalf, and all preparations had been made for
the most effective defense possible.

But when Mr. Darrow came to Alabama from Chicago and Mr. Arthur
Garfield Hays and I came from New York the telegram signed by you and by
the other seven boys in Kilby Prison stated to Messrs. Darrow and Hays that
you wanted the I.L.D. to defend you and that you did not want Mr. Darrow
and Mr. Hays unless they would leave the N.A.A.C.P. and work under the
I.L.D. Mr. Darrow and Hays refused to do this, doing so of their own accord,
for they knew that with the methods used by the I.L.D. it would be most
difficult if not impossible to put up the best defense for you. They have therefore, withdrawn from the case.

Neither the N.A.A.C.P. nor anybody else can force upon you counsel which
you do not want. I have before me copy of *The Daily Worker* of December 31
in which your name is signed with the other seven boys to a statement reading: [insert]

You have chosen your counsel and that settles the matter so far as the
N.A.A.C.P. is concerned.

May I say in closing that you and the other boys have vacillated, changing
your minds so frequently that it impossible for any organization or individual
to know what you do want. May I say to you, however, that we have no bitterness against you; we understand how perplexed you and your parents have

been. It is unfortunate that you have not been able more fully to understand all the factors involved in your case.

We wish for you every success under the auspices you have chosen about the case.

Sincerely yours,

P.S. We are enclosing copy of press release answering the telegram from your relatives which gives the official decision of our Board of Directors. [Reel 5, Group 1, Box D-71, #000182, NAACP]

January 6, 1932

Dear Charley:

Mr. Wilkins has referred to me your letter of December 28 in which you make the Statement that you do not want the I.L.D. to have your case but wish the N.A.A.C.P. to defend you.

Upon your statements to Mr. Pickens and to me when we visited Kilby Prison, and upon various letters written to us by you and by certain others of the boys, the N.A.A.C.P. at great expense and trouble secured as counsel for you the two greatest criminal lawyers in the United States if not in the world, Clarence Darrow and Arthur Garfield Hays. In addition to these famous lawyers, we engaged the best law firm in Alabama to aid in your defense. Our lawyers prepared in your behalf bills of exception to the Alabama State Supreme Court totaling 790 pages for which the stenographic and photostatic service alone cost us $600, which sum we paid. Six trips have been made from New York to Alabama in your behalf, and all preparations had been made for the most effective defense possible.

But when Mr. Darrow came to Alabama from Chicago and Mr. Arthur Garfield Hays and I came from New York the telegram signed by you and by the other seven boys in Kilby Prison stated to Messrs. Darrow and Hays that you wanted the I.L.D. to defend you and that you did not want Mr. Darrow and Mr. Hays unless they would leave the N.A.A.C.P. and work under the I.L.D. Mr. Darrow and Mr. Hays refused to do this, doing so of their own accord, for they know that with the methods used by the I.L.D. it would be most difficult if not impossible to put up the best defense for you. They have, therefore, withdrawn from the case.

Neither the N.A.A.C.P. nor anyone else can force upon you counsel which you do not want. I have before me copy of *The Daily Worker* of December 31 in which yours name is signed with the other seven boys to a statement reading:

"We, the undersigned Heywood Patterson, Eugene Williams, Andy Wright, Charlie Weems, Clarence Norris, Ozie Powell, Olen Montgomery, and Willie Robertson heretofore in April 1931, made a written contract retaining George W. Chamlee of Chattanooga, and Joseph D. Brodsky and their associates, as our attorneys to make motions for a new trial, and to appeal our cases from the Circuit Court in Scottsboro, Alabama to the Supreme Court at Montgomery, Alabama, and in May 1931,we made an other agreement ratifying the first contract.

Now, in December 1931, we hereby renew our contract with them and authorize them to appear for us in the Supreme Court of the State of Alabama, as we did in our other agreement, and to make the best effort possible, to get our cases reversed and to get us a new trial.

We authorized our parents and next of kin to employ Mr. Chamlee and his associates and we hereby ratify all their actions and agreements in reference thereto.

We desire that all notices, and all communications relative to this case, intended for the appellants, or their counsel, be given to Mr. Chamlee, as our attorney.

We desire a private conference with him."

You have chosen your counsel and that settles the matter so far as the N.A.A.C.P. is concerned.

May I say in closing that you and the other boys have vacillated, changing your minds so frequently that it is impossible for any organization or individual to know just what you do want. May I say to you, however, that we have no bitterness against you; we understand how perplexed you and your parents have been. It is unfortunate that you have not been able more fully to understand all the factors involved in your case.

We wish for you every success under the auspices you have chosen.

Sincerely yours,

Secretary

P.S. We are enclosing copy of press release answering the telegram from your relatives which gives the official decision of our Board of Directors about the case.

Mr. Charley Weems
Kilby Prison
Montgomery, Alabama
WW/RR [Reel 5, Group 1, Box D-71, #000229, NAACP]

Sunday night
Montgomery
Kilby, ala
Jan 10 1932

My dear frend Mr. Roy i get your letters tow day and was glad tow from you Mr. Roy When Mr White Was here tow see Us Boys I told him that i Want him tow have my case and if you all don't take the case i Will all Way Say that i Want you all tow have it i know Who i Want tow have My Case and i am So Sorry that you think i don't know Who Want Well Mr Roy i look like you cood take Us 4 boys Case and let the other Boy go With the ILD and any way My annt You all tow have it and i do tow Well Mr Roy i Will Say I am Sorry that you all did take Us 4 Boys ples take it the I LD ink Wright i see it now Well Mr Roy i Will all Way Say that i Want You all

So

Right Soon

from Willie Robinson [Reel 5, Group 1, Box D-71, #000279, NAACP]

Januarys 13, 1932

Mr. Willie Robinson
Kilby Prison
Montgomery, Alabama
My dear Willie:

I have your letter written Sunday night, Januarys 10th , 1932, in which you say that you wish the N.A.A.C.P. to have your case and that you have always wanted the N.A.A.C.P. to have your case. You say, also, that you think we could take four of the boys and let the other boys go with the I.L.D. You also state that you now see that the I.L.D. is not right.

Now, Willie, you must realize that we took your word last summer when you said you wanted us to have your case and we spent thousands of dollars and much time and energy for you and the other three boys who said they wanted to go with us. Then, at the last moment, on December 27th, the great lawyers, Clarence Darrow and Arthur G. Hays, whom we employed for you, received a telegram with the names of all of you eight boys signed to it, telling them not to come in the case unless they come with the I.L.D. You see, there was nothing for us to do but quit when such a telegram was received by our lawyers.

Did you sign that telegram? Have you ever seen that telegram to Mr. Darrow and Mr. Hays? Did the other three boys who said they wanted the N.A.A.C.P. sign that telegram?

Please answer and tell me if you signed the telegram to Mr. Darrow and Mr. Hays.

Very sincerely yours,
Assistant Secretary

RW/ID
[Reel 5, Box D-71, Group #000307, NAACP]

Jan 17 1932
Sun night
Montgomery
Kilby ala

My der Mr. Roy how are You i am all OK tow night i Was glad tow hear from You and do all Way is Mr Roy i am not going tow tell you a Story i having Seen know telegram of Signed one of mr. Darrow and Us 4 Boys Want you all tow take the Case But i hope you all take it But if you all don't take it and you know i will have to have Some one tow help poor me Come on in tow my Case i Want You all and all so Wish that i cood get You all and the ILD face tow face So i can tell who i want tow have My case now you know my time ink long now and Would you please Sir Wright and tell me if Mr. darrow and Mr. hays going tow take My Case or not you See Mr Roy i Want Be knowing who get it so i wont B worry who fighting for me But lik it is now it Worry me tow and then tow you all Wright me and Say that you all are going tow take it i all way know who i Want have it So Wright and let me

What you all are going tow do please Sir at one and all so if I did Want you all tow have it Would keep on worry you all tow take it i Would gusst Stope Wrighting tow you all you See i Must Want you tow have it i keep on Worry you all tow take it You see the other Boys who Want the ILD they don't worry like i do they must Be please With them and When you Wright and tell me what you are going tow do them i Will Be please then i am going tow keep on Worry tell you Say Yes from
Willie Robinson
i am looking for an answer
    this Week [Reel 5, Group 1, Box D-71, #000378, NAACP].

In early January 1932, when the Scottsboro defendants were trying to resolve exactly who they wanted to represent them court, one of their complainants, Ruby Bates, unwittingly repudiated her earlier testimony of being raped by the defendants. A letter that was found quite by accident on the person of a drunk driver who was stopped by the police in Huntsville, Alabama, raised subsequent questions as to the veracity of Bates's letter and her later claim that she was at the time "so drunk that I did not know what I was doing." This letter became the first major incident to suggest that the prosecution's case was under severe stress. Addressed to her boyfriend, Earl Streetman, the letter stated:

> Jan 5, 1932
> Huntsville, Ala
> 215 Connelly Alley

dearest Earl
    I want too Make a statement too you Mary Sanders is a goddam lie about those negroes jassing me those police man made me tell a lie that is my statement because i want too clear myself that is all too it if you want too Believe ok. if not that is ok. you will be sorry some day if you had too stay In Jail with eight negroes you would tell a lie too those Negroes did not touch me or those white boys. i hope you will believe me the law don't or i love you better than Mary does or any body else in the world that is why i am telling you of this thing i was drunk at the time and did not know what i was doing i know it was wrong too let them negroes die on account of me i hope you will Believe my statement Because it is the gods truth i hope you Will believe me i was jased But those White Boys jased me i Wish those negroes are not Burnt on account of me it is those white Boys fault that is my statement and that is all I know i hope you tell the law hope you will answer soon
    P.S. this is one time that i might tell a lie But is the truth so god help me
> Ruby Bates
> [Reel 4, Box 4, # 0360 (folder c36) ILD]

In an explosive social and judicial atmosphere, both the NAACP and ILD received written inquires about the Scottsboro case from a wide political spectrum of American and foreign intellectuals, college students and lay persons. The following letters are indictive of broad-ranging public interest in the case: From France leftist philosopher Magdeleine Paz wrote Walter White of the NAACP asking for clarity and specific details about the case so that she could assist in promoting international support for the nine defendants. In this respect, the following translated "letter of inquiry" by Paz, dated June 25, 1932, and its July 15 response — apparently by NAACP Assistant Secretary Roy Wilkens — underscored the existing difficulties confronted by contentious defense teams and the confusion this may have wrought upon the defendants.

Charleston, S.C. Mar. 26th 1932
To the NAACP.
   It is regretable To learn of the fate of 7 negroes Doom to die for a crime that they are inocent of for the sake of white supremacy in alabama.
   being negroes and the children of slaves which alabama played such an important part in barbarites which will ever remain a blot on america civilization the decision of alabama supream court it is a decision That has always condem negroes. For the sake of a government for negroes and with negroes, for 7 negroes to goe to their doom for such a crime As rape on two [   ] distiluted hobo white girls it will only serve the 12 millions blacks of this country as the greatis piece of injustice which holds every negro in this country with no rights that white men is to respect
   the negro needs more than a n.a.a.c.p. to demand this justice he need a government he needs what Japan has which is Power which demand justice for the Japanese not until then will — it need not be such organization to Advance his cause. how is it that black race isi the only race in This country needs such an organization as the n.a.a. c.p. to advance the cause of justice for them? it is A shame on the part of the negro Leadership of this country to let Those boys be lynch in the electric Chair of Alabama. their case should be taken direct to the president and not bleeding the negro public for funds To save those boys lives. lynching must be stamp out in this country an I am one negro willing to die to make thiscountry the Land of the free and the home of the Brave for negroes.
J. B. Howard
9 Fludd St. [Reel 5, Group 1, Box D-71, #000770, NAACP]

MEHARRY MEDICAL COLLEGE
Nashville, Tennessee
April 3, 1932

Mr. Walter White
69 Fifth Avenue
New York, N.Y.
Dear Sir:
   The case of the eight negro boys at Scottsboro, Ala. continually rested heav-

ily on my mind. Recently I thought of a movement to have every negro college student body to sign a petition to the governor of Alabama to take the necessary stetps to insure justice to these unfortunate individuals.

I present this matter to you since I read recently that you say the N.A.A.C.P. is still willing to work on the case. I believe that if your organization will prewent a petition to the student bodies of all of our colleges there will be a gratifying response. I believe also that such action on the part of the college youth will have a good and effective influence upon the governor of Alabama, or other proper authorities, in this case. I believe that such a petition should express our unalterable disapproval of the methods of the Communist in the case, since it seems that these people have aggravated the already prejudiced feelings.

Would it be of advantage to try to enlist in such a movement the Commission on Interracial Relations and a few of the more liberal southern white student bodies, such as Duke, North Carolina and Tulane?

I am a senior medical student at Meharry.

Yours sincerely,

Frederick Rhodes [Reel 5, Group 1, Box D-71, #000688, NAACP]

June 25th 1932

My Dear Walter White,

It has been a long time since I have had any new from you.

I am writing you today on the subject of the affair of the young Negroes at Scottsboro.

As soon as we heard of the matter we became nantually as busy as we could be on it. Since the month of March I have snet out articles in "Monde."

I have learned that the Communist (Secours Rouge) (ILD) have taken over the campaign of defense. While having hardly any illusions on the efficacy of the Communist, and general, we have responded, Maurice Paz and I to the appeal that was made to us to join in their efforts; but at the meeting of the Committee, the first thing that we asked was the broadening of the campaign. Our point of view was that only great manifestations in which individuals repesenting all phases of social life would participate could carry much weight. We argued that political divisions must be put aside and an appeal must be made principally to the sentiments of humanity & justice, and not to adhere to the handful of converts who are influenced by the Communist. We must try to touch public opinion in its entirety, so to speak.

This conception was not admitted. It was reported to us that the communist had quite decided not to make an appeal to the Socialist Party (which numbers about 140,000) nor to the C. S. I. (which numbers about 800,000) because the leaders were renegades and traitors; they were willing to take a unique stand with the infinitly restrained Communist public & only to hold conferences with communist orators.

With the same views in mind we decided to make the effort that the Communist refused to make. Two months ago we founded a committee for rhe liberation of Tom Mooney (I am taking a very active part in this matter); (I wrote to all of the Committee (which included Henri Barusse, Romain Rolland, George Duhamel, Rene Maran, Bertrand Russell, Karin Michaelis, Langeain, etc, etc.; about one hundred individuals with scientific degrees and liberal art degrees from Universities) to ask them to join in the campaign in favor of Tom Mooney, an action in favor of the Scottsboro Negroes. Their acceptance was received and the Committee for the Liberation of Tom Mooney also became a Committee of Defense for the Scottsboro Negroes; we organized a meeting at the Salle Wagram, which was held day before yesterday.

By the enclosed clippings you will see what took place at the time. We made a quite diversified appeal (two various persons) and naturally made an appeal to the Communist & the I.L.D. The Communist began by stating their refusal to attend, but said that a member of the I.L.D. would speak at the meeting. We registered their reply and announced the name of the delegate from the I.L.D. at the same time as the names of other orators. There appeared the next day in "Humanite" a violent diatribe saying that we usurped the name of the delegate of the I.L.D., and inviting workers to denounce our actions which was a "manaeuvre," etc., etc. Their articles were thus written in the "Humanite" before holding our meeting in order to boycott our actions. They engaged workers to come to the meeting to contradict us.

This did not prevent our meeting from assembling and from being a great success. There were 4,000 enthusiast present, vibrant with indignation; there were also Communist rumblings which happily did not trouble the conference. At the last moment, since we had at first refused the presence of Eda Wright, she was brought in through the Commnist; her presence and her speech produced a great feeling. Engdahl (ILD) took the opportunity to say, among other things that if the Negroes were executed the fault would be with the Socialist, and he also attacked the NAACP — I refused to translate this part of his speech.

My dear Walter White, the purpose of my letter is as follows: 1st, take an active part in the campaign for Scottsboro, in those divisions sustained by the ILD and the difficulties which this organizations is going to meet in an action where unity must be the first principle. Second, I am asking you to send in a hurry all articles/documents which you possess on this matter and its results. We would like to continue our efforts to reproduce articles in the Socialist press and the "left wing?" press and to hold meetings. We must have precise & abundant Documents. We would also like to be well informed on the part taken by the ILD since the beginning of the affair. We have a circular dated January 5th, but that is all the information we have.

Now, you know that the ILD spread the rumor that the NAACP has interfered with the defense of the boys and that it had wished to make them plead guilty; that the boys revolted that the NAACP had given them a lawyer only a fool brought out of an (insane) asylum. Who has since returned to the asylum.

We would like to answer these statements with precise assertions based on extra statement (documentes). I am asking you to send me all that you have with the shortest possible delay, in order to end the campaign of discredit againset the NAACP and to revive the action of defense.

Excuse the hurried letter & accept from Maurice Paz & myself all of our
sentiments of great sympathy & our faithful remembrance.

In a general fashion, this affairs has revived a line interest in the race question. I am asked for articles and conferences. Send me also general documents
on the recent situation (latest developments).

Enclosed are some articles from "Populaire," organ of the Socialist party.
(Signed) M------------------Paz [Reel 5, Group 1, Box D-71, #000897,
NAACP]

7/11/32
Kilby Prison
Montgomery, Alabama

Miss Dillon
Dear Friend

Your most kind and welcom letter has been received, and also highly appreciated.

Your letter found me well and getting along just about as well as I could
expect. And I do hope when these few lines are yours they will find you as
well and injoying the best of life.

Now Miss Dillion I was so glade to know that my letter was injoyed, not
only that but we all appreciated hearing from Mrs. Wright and the great work
she is doing for us, and also to know that she is being treated nice and kind.

And one great thing we all were so please to hear and that was that our
friends are goint to stick with us.

We realize that all of the workers are working hard for us and are sacrificing
them selves for us, and to send us little things which we realy do thank them
for.

Now Miss Dillon I know that it is very exciting in New York, and every
body is kept busy, but how be ever I hope to meet you all there some day.

I suppose you are busy most of you time,

So I will ask you to accept these few remarks.

I am yours,
Charlie Weems [Reel 5, ILD, 00691, ILD]

July 15th 1932

Mme. Magdeleine Paz
8 Rue Cesar Franck
Paris XV
France

My dear Madam Paz:

Your letter of June 25th to Mr. Walter White, our Secretary, arrived when
he was away on vacation and I have been delayed in answering you this long
because of my inadequate knowledge of French.

I am enclosing herewith certain documents having to do with the questions you raise in your letter. there is a pamphlet by Mr. White which is a reprint of an article published in Harper's magazine last December. It sketches the case in detail and points out its significance. Then there is a statement by Mr. Clarence Darrow, the eminent lawyer, explaining the circumstances of his withdrawal from the case last December.

We found early in the controversy between our organization and the communists and the I.L.D. that it did little good to issue denials and counter-denials in reponsse to statements made by the Communist. They have little regard for truth and accuracy and one of their spokesmen told us that the habit of telling the truth was a bourgeoisie virtue. They are not concerned with the means to an end, but only with the end. Thus the N.A.A.C.P. has been the victim of a vicious and persistence campaign of vilification from the outset. Even in January when our Board of Directors officially withdrew from the case and left it in the hands of the Communist the attacks did not cease and have not yet stopped. We could not please them by remaning in the case and we have not pleased them by getting out and leaving them in charge. I suspect that you will find it a difficult matter to deny every charge they make.

I am enclosing also copies of news stories which went out in our press release from time to time last year in which we deal with certain phases of the controversy. I hope these documents will serve the purpose you desire and if there is any further specific information ou wish if you will write again I am sure Mr. White will be glad to send you promptly any information. He has much of it at his fingertips since he was actively and personally in charge of our organization's negotiations. He will be back at his desk on August 8th.

Very sincerely yours,
Assistant Secretary [Reel 5, Group 1, Box D-71, #000917, NAACP]

Kilby Prison
Montgomery, Alabama
July 27, 1932

Dear Mr. Engdahl,

Just a few lines so as to let you hear from me this leaves me well and getting Along alright as the time being and I do hope when these few lines are yours they Will find you well and enjoying a pleasant life. I were so very glad to hear of the Good news that our Europe friends are willing to help to us in this hard struggle in their doing so we feels as we can soon gain our freedom again as we should have it because it is so hard to be cut off from the things are due us more so when are being punished for something we did not do.

Mr. Engdahl please have some of the Europe friends to write me. I be very proud to hear from them if it be possible without putting to much responsibility on them, all of the Boys are well and are still cheerful they also sends their heartiest regards. So I will come to a conclusion by asking you to please accept my best regards and extend my best wishes.

I remain yours truly
Andy Wright [Reel 5, Box 5, #000810 (folder c62), ILD]

* * *

On November 7, 1932, the United States Supreme Court in *Powell v. Alabama* 287 U.S. 454 ordered new trials for the Scottsboro defendants on the basis that in the defendants' first trial they were "denied effective" counsel. The court explained that missing factors in their defense, primarily protections derived from both the 6th and 14th Amendments of the United States Constitution, were:

a) They were not given a fair, impartial and deliberate trial.

b) They were denied the right of counsel, with the accustomed incidents of consultation and opportunity for trial, and

c) They were tried before juries from which qualified members of their own race were systematically excluded [http://en.wikipedia.org/wiki/Powell_v._Alabama].

The Supreme Court also made the following observations: the trial took place in a social atmosphere of a "hostile and excited public" and the defense counsel, Mr. Moody and Mr. Roddy, demonstrated "little experience" with the consequence being "little defense." The Court concluded: "In light of the fact outlined in the forepart of this opinion, we think the failure of the trial court to give them reasonable time and opportunity to secure counsel was a clear denial of due process [14th Amendment]."

Overjoyed over this decision, Olen Montgomery sent the executive director of the ILD, William L. Patterson, the following letter:

Kilby Prison
Montgomery, Alabama
Nov. 9. 1932

Atten: William L. Patterson,
Dear Friend,

Since the supreme court has granted we boys a new trial I thank it is my rite to express my thanks an appreciation to the whole party for thair care of me and the wonderful and faithful struggle for my rites. I am so happy over it until I don't hardle know exactly how to thank them for thair kindness love of us poor ones. But I do appreciate it to the very highest respect. I know that my dear mother is joyses over it as many hard thangs she have hade throwen in her face about my trouble. Oh! well they aint the only ones are happy over it. I my self feels like I have been born again. for worrying and heartbroken I have had thanking of my poor innocence life.

and mr. Patterson since you all are going to have us transfered I will ask you to have some one to send me a pair of cheap slippers dark tan and size seven English toed. now mr. Patterson, I don't want you to thank I am choicey because I cant be for the circumstances I am under, But really my feat is small and leen and boney, an a Broad toed shoe don't fit my feat what so ever. and color I just like dark tan because my mother always liked tan for me. and of course I would ask my mother for shoes. But she are disable to buy them and you all are the only one I can ask for support. and I will gladly accept them and appreciate them to the highest because I am in need for them and it is getting real cool here and concrete never stays warm in the winter part of year

    I remain yours as ever,

    Olen Montgomery

    P.S. answer at your earliest conveniences

    Bye" Bye, [Reel 5, Box 4, #00020 (folder c52), ILD]

On November 7, 1932, Andy Wright received the good news through a postal telegraph exclaiming:

STUGGLES OF THE NEGRO AND WHITE WORKERS HAVE BROUGHT YOU A NEW TRIAL UNITED STATES SUPREME COURT REVERSED THE DECISION SENTENCING YOU TO THE ELEC-TRIC CHAIR WE WILL CARRY ON THE FIGHT UNTIL YOU ARE FREE DO NOT LOOSE YOUR COURAGE COMPLETE VICTORY IS AHEAD

                    INTERNATIONAL LABOR DEFENSE

                          NATIONAL SECRETARY

[Reel 5, Box 5, #000812 (folder c62), ILD]

                    Kilby Prison

                    Montgomery, Ala.

                    Nov. 6 1932

Mr. Patterson,

Dear Sir:

    It affords me the greatest of pleasure at this present time to let you know that I received your kind and welcome letter today and was more than glad to hear from you and to hear the good news of mother.

    Being well and able to carry on the fight. It also made me feel good to learn that You all's going to carry on the struggle until we are in the arms of our dear mother,s we certainly do appreciate any afford you all's make towards we poor innocent and unfortune boys. and we are very thankful to have you all's as our dear friends. Needless to say how proud we is of you all's I also wish the day will soon come when I have the greatest of pleasure in meeting you all so as to express my sincere gratitude for you all kind deeds a towards me while I were in confinement of Prison for some thing I did not do. I also notice enclosed of your letter you had a eight dollar's money order which was one dollar for each of the boys we also accepted and preciated to the verriest of highest now I beg to say that I was glad indeed to re,cd. it because I were in debt for $1.45 and was without smokes stamps also stationery and haven't been able to write to my dear mother for eight weeks. fact I am still in debt for 95 [cents] we will also be very proud indeed to be able to received a little more money so as to help us get out of debt. now I wish to say these few lines leaves us one an all well and getting on as well as we could expect owing to our present condition now I must come to a conclusion by saying I am anxiously waiting for an promptly reply.

Comradly yours,

Andy Wright [Reel 5, Box 5, #000809 (folder c62), ILD]

B'ham, Ala.

Nov. 6 1932

My dearest workers I receive your letter and was glad to here from you all and all so the money and I will be glad when I can be abll to see you all and when you here from mother tell I say hurry up I want to see her bad and all so your all so I will clos my letter but not be hard amis you.

Roy Wright [Reel 5, Box 5, #000963 (folder c64), ILD]

Kilby Prison

Montgomery, Ala.

Nov. 7, 1932

Mr. James L. Patterson,

Dear Friend:

We boys received your letter which was mailed to Andy Wright and was also glad to no that Andy's mother is O.K. and we all was to glad to receive the money because we was really in need for it and I really apprcciate it to the very highest respect. and I am well and getting along just fine. and to morrow is the day for our decision and I do hope we will get the results of our appeal. and I sure will be glad to get some more money quick as possible because Im in debt of 90 [cents] for of this already.

So I remain yours,

As ever,

Ozie Powell [Reel 5, Box 5, #000588 (folder c58), ILD]

A series of letters by Olen Montgomery and his mother, Viola, underscore a desire that in the pursuit of justice, victory will somehow prevail. Interestingly, indicative of the growing interest and network of supporters for the Scottsboro Boys, Montgomery notes that he sent out some six hundred post cards to supporters within about a week's time.

Atlanta, Ga.

Nov. 7, '32

My Dear Comrade Pattison

Just a few line to let you no that I reseved the telegraph to night was to glad to here that the boys got a new trial corse it was no more than I expected. I had seen it all ready in the Atlanta World the Negro paper here I am more than glad to night and as you say the fight must develop that rite and I am willing to continue the fight. I have ben selling the Post Card all day to mailed to the Supreme Court. *I have mail over 6 hundred from here since last thursday* [Note: Ed. italics]. Well I wont rite much more you rite me a letter. I rite you last week and sent you some of Olen drawing. did you get it. Tell me all the news. I am all ways glad to here from you I had a nice letter from Olen the other day he ask me to send him a box but I did not have a bit of money to fix it with. I don't have nothing much since you all don't send me any more more money. Well I wont rite any more to night I am tired. I work pretty hard to day.

You rite me now, from comrade Montgomery

Atlanta, Ga. [Reel 5, Box 5, #000988 (folder c65), ILD]

Atlanta, Ga.
Nov. 7, '32

My Dear Comrade Pattison,

Just a lines to let you no that [your] letter was reseved a few days a go. it found me and the rest of the Comrade OK. As for as I no hope when this reach you it will fine you all the same. I also reseved the money order it come in good because it was very much needed at the time. I can all ways fine a place for it. I need some rite now for house rent.

I have moved a cross town with comrade Carrie Jackson and the rent man come out to day and put up a rent card so that mean money or move so if you can I will be to glad if you can send me $10.00 so I can rent me a good house for the winter and so I will have a place for the comrade when they come to Atlanta. I had a very nice letter from Olen to day I am sending it over so you Can see what all he wont and I ant got money to buy it with.

Well I wont rite any more I got to be going to a meeting at once.

From comrade Montgomery

of Atlanta, Ga. [Reel 5, Box 5, #000980 (folder c65), ILD]

Montgomery, ala.
Nov. 9 1932

Mr. William L. Patterson

Dear sir mr. Patterson just a few lines to let you hear from me I am well and and getting along alright all with me the conception of been free. But I do hope to be real soon. Now I hope when these few lines have been delivered to you it will find you and the whole party doing just fine. Well mr. Patterson I know you have heard of the boys great success and to say I am [   ] happy sure as silk because that will help me out a lots and know that you al are still busie in getting me and Ray out on bail and to I really will be glad when the day comes when Ray and I can go out in the street where I can excise my worried bones. for I sure ain't getting any in here. now mr. Patterson I know that you all ar going to get us all a way from this prison as quick as possible and I sure wish you would get some of the members to get me a pair of cheap slippers I am not choise about them what so ever although if they sould happen to be gotten I wish they would be kindly of and english toed pair of slippers size seven and color Black. I have seen in the newspapers a few times of some slippers that's call a friendly five now that's a cheap slipper and looks to be a good slipper altho I have never owned a pair of them But if only the members get me a pair of them I will gladly accept them and will appreciate it.

Oh! my and so as I am coming to a conclusion I will ask that you give my best regards to the whole party.

I remain yours as Ever.

Eugene Williams [Reel 5, Box 5, #000788, ILD]

Montgomery, Ala.

Nov. 16, 1932

My Dear Mother, [Ed. note: Mrs. Viola Montgomery]

I received your letter Sunday and more than ever glad to hear from you it found me well and getting along just fine. And I hope when these few lines are yours they will find you all OK. You say the next thang to do is get us out of there. I sure will be glad when that time come and you say your wish I was there to eat dinner with you. I wish I was there to eat dinner and supper also breakfast in the morning.

Oh! well tell Mary Alice I say hello and be a good little girl for me. and I don't know when you are comeing to see me but I don't want you to slip up on me and so you take this little list and keep it so you wont for get to brang what I ask <u>for this is it.</u>

A franch harp note E. this is the name, M. Hohner, and south meat, and some fried pies instead of baked potatoes, and some fish, and some good biscuits and some cheeses if its necessary. That's all I taste them now. And what did James do with the pictures I drawed. He said he would snap them and send me one. Are did they take are not.

Oh! well I must close for this time from your son,

Olen

Bye" Bye

and you write to Mrs. Mamie William Eugene's mother and see what's wrong with her. Eugene is worried almost to death about her he cant hear from her, and you tell me in your letter.   (over)

This is the address

Mrs. Mamie Williams

2202 Read Ave.

Chattanooga, Tenn. [Reel 5, Box 5, #000982 (folder c65), ILD]

Kilby Prison
Montgomery, Ala.
December 7, 1932

My Dear mother:

I received you letter and was glad to hear from you it found me well and getting along just fine and I do hope when these few lines are yours they will fine you and all OK. now mather Mr. Chamlee was here Sunday to see us and mather since the people of the I.L.D. are going to give you all a little money to buy us our Christmas I am sending you a list of what I want you to bring me when you came. and if they don't do that I do hope that you will be able to get much of this as you can. Because last Christmas I didn't have nothing wurth a dime and I do hope to enjoy this one the best way possiable. and don't forget to brang that Belt and brang little sister with you to so I will close now this is what I want you to brang me

1 coconut
2 nice cakes chocolate and coconut. I pond of mix nuts
a dozen of apples
a dozen of oranges
a dozen of bananas. And candy. 3 blocks of grape
    chewing gum. 2 pairs of socks. And some cheese.
    and some fried rabbit
    and sausage. and some fried potato pies. and
    some sauce meat. and some rex-all tooth paste
    and some stamps envelopes
    and tablet.

[Letter from Ozie Powell was not signed] [Reel 5, Box 5, folder c58, #000599, ILD]

Kilby Prison
Montgomery, Ala.
Dec. 19, 1932
William L. Patterson

Dearest Sir,

I was move then happy as received your most kind and welcome letter which had enclosed money order for the amount of $200 which we one and all surely did appreciate your kindness sure very much. Not only that but everything which your dear friends have done for us and are being done. We do appreciate it and we would be sure happy if you all only could make arrangement as soon as possible and get us removed from this place so that we can receive exercise which we need very badly and that is exercise.

Now I only wish I was more educated so that I could express my sincere appreciation to the people in New York for all that they have did for we boys while here in prison. And we are well please in the way you all taking of things for us. No matter what they says about the I.L.D. I have all ways wish for the I.L.D. to take care of me and all ways will. So I will close for now hoping an early answer. hoping you are well and getting on all right. Sincerely yours,

Haywood Patterson [Reel 5, Box 5, #000209 (folder c54), ILD]

3

LETTERS FROM 1933
Clash of Concerns

March 6: Judge A. E. Hawkins grants the Defense a change of venue to Decatur, Alabama, for a new trial.
March 13: William L. Patterson, Executive Director of the ILD, retains attorney Samuel Leibowitz as the lead attorney for the defense.

By 1933, mothers of the Scottsboro defendants, as personified by Viola Montgomery, were exhibiting an adept ability to describe their physical and emotional anguish in words that resonated far beyond the printed pages of newspapers and journals. As they found increased access to the public through media savvy political organizations they also became sophisticated in their attempts to reach the hearts and minds of thousands of curious and outright sympathic readers and listeners. For example, in the early spring of 1933, Viola Montgomery expressed as a mother both her anguish and increased social awareness in an open letter addressing the concerns of millions of mothers in Georgia, the nation and around the globe. Describing how they shared their children's suffering under what appeared to be egregious and unsympathetic political systems, she appealed:

February 1933
Viola Montgomery
<u>A Working Mother at Georgia</u>
   I have been reading a wonderful storie of a poor working woman and it appealed to me varry much. I am a woman and I no a lots about just what work mean for I have work every since I was twelve years old and no I am forty one and I can't see any good at all. I did me only runt my health when I worked I work so hard and regular until it upsit all my nerves and now I ant able to work if I could get it to do. It has ben years now since I worked any worth why and I am just as fat as I was when I worked so hard course I gess I wood have ben working some place if I had not laid of for a few days to vissied the nine Scottsboro boys.

See one of them are mine and because I wanted to go and see my sun the lady wood not have me when I got back. It seem to be a crime here in Georgia to fight for your child life when you no it is framed up for a crime it did not do. I gess by now everyone have hurd about the letter that Ruby Bate rote her friend telling hime that she lied on the poor children but that all rite no one can every pay me enuff to tell a lie like that on nothing.

I tell the world that I am a working woman and a unhappy one because I all ways worked and I could not have nothing that I wanted nice to eat or wear. I have oftime wondered how was it the one do work of some kind had nothing much I no one thing I work most on a farm and in the fell we owed it so say the boss man so that where mine went to. I worked all the year round just for what I eat and wore and that was fat back and surp and bread and to cotton dress and one pair of shoes. I never new what it was to rest until Sunday because when it rain I had to clean up new grounds, cut bries, they was always something to do on a farm for a woman I no, and if you go to some of the landlord for Sunday cloth he wood tell you not take up to much if you do you wont clear nothing in the fall and I desided I wood not take up no more than I could help, thinking I wood clear more, and when fall come it wood be the same thing, so I say to myself in 1930 that I will not farm anymore for anyone. The last landlord I work for I ask him for a 98 [Ed. note: 98 cent] hat and he told me to see if I could make out until Fall because it might come a hail storm and destroy our crop and I wood not clear enuff to to pay him up and that was in N.C., that is a farming country.

They ar a good many Georgia workers out there and they work hard and mad a plenty cotton and earn but a little. They got the first year that I and my family was there we made over one thousand dollars and I seen 75 of the dollars and I begain to wake up and left there. But listen worker, just as soon as you get tird of starving wegs and begain to take about it you must die or go to jail, because it make the ruling class mad with us. But just don't let that stop us from fighting for our rite for I never will forget how hard I wash and iron when I live in Chattanooga. I was to be confined and I work so hard until when the baby was born it was dead. I was told that I was to week to bring it to the world alive and I am satefide there have ben a plenty of them kind of case among the working women of Georgia.

Rote by one of the Scottsboro mothers.

Viola Montgomery [Reel 5, Box 5, #000990 (folder c65), ILD]

Viola Montgomery's letter appealed not only to the "working women of Georgia" but to an expanding array of women and men of varying class, ethnic and racial backgrounds throughout the country and abroad. One example can be drawn from the efforts of shipping family heiress, social activist and writer, Nancy Clara Cunard. Campaigning in the early 1930s to free the Scottsboro defendants, Cunard brought together a number of writers and artist in France and England to sign a petition appealing for the defendants' release.

In the pamphlet *Writers and Intellecutuals in England: Scottsboro Appeal*, Nancy Cunard explained:

"HELP US SAVE OUR BOYS"

"Help Us Save Our Boys." Group photograph of Scottsboro Boys mothers. Top row, from left: Mrs. Ada Wright, Mrs. Janie Patterson, Mrs. Ida Norris. Bottom row: Mrs. Josephine Powell, Mrs. Viola Montgomery, Mrs. Mamie Williams (courtesy the Daily Worker/Daily World Photographs Collection, Tamiment Library, New York University).

This Appeal was launched by me, Nancy Cunard, in France, in the beginning of 1933, and was sent to the writers and artists and other intellectuals that I knew. It was done all along without any built-up plan, such as consultation of literary "Who's Who," but in an informal and personal manner, without the aid of printed lists or of any organizations.

In London, in March, April, 1933, I was much helped by George Burke, an unemployed or itinerant pedlar-newspaper-seller, who became so interested in the case that he volunteered to get signatures in pubs, etc. and sell the Scottsboro postcard.

Cde Llewellyn, of Cardiff, also organized the collection of signatures and Donations.

Bob Scanron, ex-boxing champion of Colour, and Norah Andrews, English wife of Gordon Andrews, then secretary to Paul Robeson, also had lists, and Mrs. Kirk, and the "Busmen's Punch," London.

Protests were later sent American authorities, and Funds to William Patterson, Sec. of Scottsboro Defense, ILD, New York.

Scottsboro Appeal

You have no doubt read and heard of the *Scottsboro* case in Alabama, U.S.A., the most outstanding and appalling example of race hatred and white prejudice against Negroes. This culminated after a farcical trial, in the death sentence for 8 out of the 9 Negro working lads, all under 21, framed up on a false charge of raping two white prostitutes: the ninth being under age received a life sentence. At the trial a lynching mob surrounded the court house. The supposed victims of the attack, the two white girls, denied even having seen the coloured boys. But after being put through the usual American 3rd degree methods they were terrorized into saying they had been raped.

This happened in March 1931. The 9 lads have been in jail since then, facing the electric chair — and facing it in the literal sense too. For several times during the different stages and successive appeals in the case (all rejected by Southern courts) the chair has been wheeled in front of their cells and left there as each new date set for execution approached.

BUT THE AROUSED INTEREST AND MILLION-FOLD PROTESTATIONS

throughout the entire world — from workers and intellectuals, and all classes and creeds of men — the funds raised towards the exceedingly heavy cost of the defense, and the militancy and skill of the defending lawyers have resulted in the case being brought for appeal before the United States Supreme Court, in Washington, the highest court in America.

[Ed. note: (Some)] other writers and intellectuals who signed this Appeal in the spring of 1933 in England and whose names are found on the collective lists (herewith) that were carried about by me or by helpers, are as follows:

Alastair Crowley — Scientific Essayist: "This case is typical of the hysterical sadism of the American people — the result of Puritanism and the climate."

Lionel Roberts — Artist

Richard Wayman — Film Artiste.

Samuel Beckett — Writer

Shane Leslie — Author, M.A. of Cambridge: "I think Christ was very fortunate not to have been tried before a Southern judge."

B. Malinowski — University of London/Professor of Anthropology: "The Scottsboro trial has been one of the most notorious miscarriages of justice. It means that lynching has now penetrated the courts of justice."

Andre Gide — homme de lettras.

Ezra Pound & Dorothy Pound — author: "I not only protest, but if this sort of judicial sanction of murder and frame-up continues I shd. be disposed to advocate direct action. We have had enough criminals in high office

already. A state even a state sanely founded can not indefinitely continue if it condones and sanctions legal murder of innocent men."
Sinclair Lewis — writer.

John Banting — Painter: "International Civilization is at stake. Anyone with a sense of justice must help these victims of dangerously insane race-hatred."

Nancy Cunard — Publisher, Printer, Writer: "There is no use in pleading when (mis)justice is so completely controlled and directed by race-hatred. The old lynching and legal-lynching habits, and oppression of Negroes in U.S.A., and the brutal exploitation of native people elsewhere have got to cease.

Knowledge of such cases of vicious Frame-ups that take place uninterrupt-edly in America — more particularly against Negroes, and more particularly in the Southern States, where they are kept in utmost economic misery and peonage is no longer confined within the geographical boundaries of these States, or of America. The entire world is aware of them and is protesting to the maximum against their continuation.

The Scottsboro case has "lit such a candle as will never be put out."

In the name of justice and equality (concepts which emphatically do exist also in a very large proportion of the American people).

Free the 9 innocent Scottsboro boys unconditionally:

Free them at the coming re-trial" [HRHRC: Nancy Cunard Collection, 28.6].

Birmingham, Ala.
Mar. 16, 1933

Dear Mr. Patterson,

I received to money order OK and was very glad to receive it. I am also glad to know that you all will give me some consideration about the 20th of this month. I am also glad to know you all have succeeded in having an trial in another place and at this trial I hope to prove my self not guilty of the crime charged against me. any wasy I am keeping faith and courage. Hoping to hear from you at once. Yours respectfully,
Roy Wright, County Jail
Bham. Ala. [Reel 5, Box 5, #000964 (folder c64), ILD]

Roy Wright   March 20 1933
Birmingham
Alabama
Dear Roy,

I was very very glad to hear from you this morning and glad to know that the money came in handy.

We also are pleased that the trial is going to take place in another town. We are preparing it in the best possible manner. You must keep your hope and courage up for we are going to fight with you and for you until you are free.

We have the best criminal lawyer in New York, who is going to try your case. Thousands of friends are supporting you. Do not be afraid.

Very truly yours
NATIONAL SECRETARY
William L. Patterson

Wlp-ea [Reel 5, Box 5, #000967, ILD)

> **April 6: Ruby Bates appears in court for the defense and denies that she or Victoria Price were raped. She explains how after spending a night with their boyfriends it was likely semen would be found in their vaginas.**
> **April 9: Haywood Patterson is found guilty and sentenced to death by electrocution.**

NIGHT LETTER   April 17, 1933
HEYWOOD PATTERSON
BIRMINGHAM COUNTY JAIL
BIRMINGHAM ALABAMA
    EMERGENCY SCOTTSBORO CONFERENCE ASSEMBLED NEW YORK
APRIL SIXTEENTH REPRESENTING SIXTY FIVE ORGANIZATIONS SENDS
MILITANT GREETINGS TO YOU AND EIGHT OTHER BOYS PLEDGE
UNCEASING STRUGGLE TILL YOUR FINAL UNCONDITIONAL RELEASE
BEN DAVIS JR. CHAIRMAN

[Reel 5, Box 5, #000214, ILD]

However, almost two weeks later a "violent" disturbance in the Jefferson (Birmingham) County Jail involving the Scottsboro defendants was reported in *The Birmingham News*. The disturbance was allegedly instigated by the International Labor Defense. The newspaper, in an apparent support of the prosecution, addressed the incident in the following manner:

The Jail Riot Staged by the Scottsboro Negroes

The riot staged in the Jefferson County jail by the nine Negro defendants in the Scottsboro case must be put down as just another unfortunate consequence of the senseless and vicious agitation of the case by the International Labor Defense and other radical groups or individuals.

There can be no doubt that the prisoners were aroused to their mutinous attitude by the Communist propaganda that has been bearing in upon them, and not by any grievance over the treatment they have received in jail. It is not surprising that the propaganda which has reached them should have had this effect. The fact that the Negroes, after their violent outburst and some hours of sulking, have abandoned that attitude and promised to behave themselves, indicates that their own better judgement has now prevailed over the incitements to which they have been subjected. Let us hope this better judgement will continue to rule their conduct. It is obviously better for them to behave themselves, and it is better for everyone and everything else concerned. It ought not to be difficult to persuade them of this. However they may feel about the case itself, they surely have no cause for complaint at the treatment they have received in jail.

If we realize that their spell of misbehavior was a more or less [a] natural result of the propaganda which has surrounded the case, we may dismiss it as a matter of no serious concern. It is unpleasant for Alabama to have this sort of thing happen. But there has been much in connection with the case that has been unpleasant to Alabamians. Our people on the whole have tried to bear it all with patience, which under the circumstances is the sensible attitude for us to take, and certainly we can be patient with respect to this latest consequence of the reckless and unscrupulous agitation on the part of radicals who have sought to make of the case a cause célèbre in the interest mainly of themselves, and not the defendants [*The Birmingham News*, April 29, 1933].

A few weeks later, in May 1933, a respected African American Communist leader, Benjamin Davis, who would eventually become chairman of the International Labor Defense, visited the Scottsboro defendants. His observations of the defendants' lifestyle is also enlightening:

REPORT ON INTERVIEW WITH SCOTTSBORO BOYS IN BIRMINGHAM
May 13, 1933

Presented letter of introduction and identification to Warden, Jefferson County Jail, Saturday Morning. He and two other officials conferred over it about 5 minutes, and within 15 minutes I was speaking with 6 of the boys. (The letter of introduction and identification was from Joseph Brodsky, chief ILD attorney). Neither the warden nor the jailer asked me any questions with reference to my identity. There was no effort whatever to prevent me from seeing the boys. I expected some difficulty in being allowed communication with the boys, inasmuch as no Negro attorney had ever before appeared in the case or demanded recognition as such. (Undoubtedly, the ease with which I was admitted to conference with the boys was due to the fear of exposure on the part of the jail officials, if Negro attorney was refused recognition in the Alabama courts.)

FACTS OF FIGHT BETWEEN BOYS

Thursday, May 11th, Haywood Patterson on the one hand and Roy and Andy Wright on the other, became embroiled in serious mutual "kidding." Before the boys were arrested in 1931, they were interested in the same girls in Chattanooga. There was a sort of friendly rivalry between them. This rivalry has followed them through the whole three years of their imprisonment. On this occasion the kidding became extremely personal, and before either of the boys knew what had happened, Roy Wright, the younger of the two Wright boys, seized a knife and stabbed Patterson. The wound while not serious, required the immediate services of a physician who closed it with two stitches. The wound is on the left side, on an approximate line with the lowest rib. Patterson is not seriously affected, the only serious consequences being the fright and pain. There is a conflict between Patterson and the Wright boys as to where the knife came from. Patterson stated that the knife was slipped to one of the Wright boys by their friends at the jail; while the Wright boys say that the knife was taken from Patterson at the time of the incident.

As a result of the incident the Wright boys and Charlie Weems have been moved to a separate cell from the other 6 boys. Weems was not compelled to go, but chose of his own volition to be with the Wright boys. I talked over the incident with the Weems and the Wright boys, also.

Patterson and the Wright boys both regretted sincerely that their tempers "got the bests of them," and wish to be placed in the same cell together again. They stated that it is very likely that incidents of that sort will occur, inasmuch as they have no literature to read and no diversions to occupy their time and minds. They say that they are frequently nervous and irritable from the terrific strain from the "frame-up" ordeal.

I impressed upon the boys the necessity of their refraining from any such internal dissension as it weakens their case, and exposes them to additional "frame-up" by the authorities. I told them that this was but a scheme to separate them and thus weaken their united front of militancy and courage. I instructed them to demand to [be] placed in the same cell again, and I took this question up with the warden who stated this would be done when they were certain there would be no more fights. My own impression is that the knife was slipped into the possession of the boys, in order to frame them on another charge.

GENERAL TREATMENT OF BOYS

The boys stated they were getting on fine, and wished me to so inform their relatives and friends. Since the Patterson second trial, they have been given more attention by the bosses, who fear mass power and pressure. They attribute this "better treatment" to their general militancy in resenting the maltreatment of the guards. They rebelled at the cursing and swearing of one Dement, one of the jail officials, and there has been no such abuse since.

When I entered the cell to talk with the boys the jailer refused to allow me a private consultation with them, but this privilege was demanded, and upon demand was forthwith accorded me.

CONDITION OF BOYS

All boys in excellent spirits, and show an extraordinary realization of the tremendous significance of their cases in the struggle of the Negro People in the United States for National Liberation. They reiterate an unabated confidence in the ILD and its policies with reference to their cases. They evinced a powerful courage and determination to fight their "framers" until the rights of the oppressed Negroes were won.

I studied their faces carefully. They are beautiful. Their chins are up, their eyes bright with confidence, defiance, vigor. Without doubt this has been instilled into them by the world sympathy aroused by the ILD. They are militant and unafraid.

NEEDS OF BOYS

Olen Montgomery is fast losing his eyesight. He cannot see a match stem in his own hand. When he was first arrested his glasses were broken and he has had none since. It is virtually impossible for him to read. The jail authorities have done nothing for his eyes. I suggest that this question be taken up with the Birmingham ILD at once, and that funds be rushed to the jail for Montgomery's glasses. Protest should be sent at once to the jail denouncing the blinding of the Montgomery boy. This matter was taken up with the warden who stated that this would be "looked into."

The boys complained about the food and I took this up with the warden, who immediately pointed me to the kitchen to show that the food was first-rate. While the food is not first-rate, it appears that it is not as bad as is found in the Georgia hell-hole-jails.

A number of the guards complain about the special attention given to the boys, claiming they are spoiled. The warden is apparently afraid to deny the needed attention, afraid of the publicity policy of the ILD. For instance, when Roy Wright gave me a belt he made for a relative, the warden stood about a half hour until he had finished it and didn't attempt to rush Roy at all.

Incidentally, Roy who is 15, is a very cocky lad, giving no quarters to any of the prison officials. He is very clever, showing considerable ingenuity with his hands. Patterson is very militant especially along the lines of the ILD. Exceedingly aggressive and brave.

The boys should be sent the Daily Worker and other literature. They had absolutely no money and funds should be sent to them regularly. This is imperative.

They need shoes, shirts, overalls, toothpaste, soap and other such necessities [Reel 5, Box 4, #0220, ILD].

June 22: Judge Horton sets aside Haywood Patterson's conviction and scheduled electrocution date of June 16 and grants him a new trial.

July 31st, 1933
80 E. 11th St.
c/o I.L.D,
New York City

Dear Richard,

I received your letter Friday and was very glad to hear from you and to hear that you was having very good meetings. I spoke in new London the night you left that day we had a very good meeting.

I have been at camp almost two weeks. I am at Unity and I try to read but some how are other I cant get interested in reading but I read the daily worker every day. I have two more weeks to stay in camp then if I am strong enough I will start speaking again.

Yes I read about Haywood getting a new trial and I realize that we have got to put up a harder and stronger fight for their freedon as you say we must not let these nine innocent boys die.

I know there is plenty here in the east for me to do but if you all contending the tour to the coast I hope that I will join you for I miss you and Mrs.

Patterson when I go to a meeting and since I came to camp and I am thinking of you all and wondering how the meetings are and wishing that I was a long.

If I don't get to join you all I am going to help carry the help an here for the freedom of the boys not only the Scottsboro boys but for all other class war Prisoners. I hope you are reading the Mirror if you cant get it while you are traveling when you return I will let you read the story by the time you return the whole story will be out I already have two issues of it.

When I spoke in new London I make a better speech than I had been making. I spoke more about the movement they all seamed to like my speach better I talked for about an hour and fifteen minutes.

give my love and best regards to Lester and Mrs. Patterson.

I hope our struggle for the boys will be successful. I close with love and best regards to you and best wishes for the meetings. Comradely greetings Ruby Bates [Reel 4, Box 4 (folder c36), #000360, ILD]

Molina, Ga.
August 19, 1933
Dear Comrade Nancy Cunard,

Just a few lines to let you hear from me and let you know how much i thank you for the money you sent i thank you so much you just dont know how much i thank you for the money. Dear comrade ann glad you has been suscefull in raising money for the Boys. Dear comrade of course: how never seen you personal but hope i will see you some Day. of course it has been some time since i has travel but I havint forgot Yet. My little girls sent love to you all.

Dear Comrade i am just still praying for freedom for the Boys trusting that they will soon be free some day. Well the last letter i got from my boy he said they was all getting along all wright i get a letter from him every week well I guess This is all for This Time.

your Ida Norris [HRHRC, Nancy Cunard, 17.5, Ida Norris]

October 20: Upon the insistence of the State prosecutor, Attorney General Thomas Knight Jr. a new trial judge is appointed, William Washington Callahan.

Reputed Ku Klux Klansmen Judge William Washington Callahan's entrance into the Scottsboro trial on November 27, 1933, was both portentous and racist. Quickly, attorney Samuel Leibowitz realized that Callahan's judicial strategy was to rule in favor of the prosecution's case, while attempting to lower the political profile of the case and "take the case off the front pages of American newspapers" (Linder, 2009). Significant in this regard was Callahan's apparent understanding of the saliency of the media, both nationally and internationally speaking. As such, Judge's Callahan's decree that photographers would be banned from the courtroom grounds, and that "there ain't going to be no more picture snappin' round here"—and even more problematic, his imposing a three-day limit would on each trial, and having each trial run late into the evening if necessary—was not surprising. Whether or not he developed this strategy by himself, clearly Callahan and his conservative view of the law in practice was meant to cripple the growing political interest in the case. Accordingly his banning of typewriters from the courtroom was simply a further extension of a kind of mindset steeped in judicial arrogance and dispensation (Linder, 2009, p. 571).

Judge Callahan's awareness of the potential impact of media such as radio and newspapers, even in the early years of the 20th century, was credible in that he was clearly concerned that it would strengthen the Scottsboro defendants' image locally, nationally and internationally. For Callahan, concerns related to potential white mobs or vigilante violence were problematic but controllable. He apparently preferred to personally select a group of "men with sound judgement" as opposed to having National Guardsmen present, as they "irritate people," as he explained in the following letter to Alabama Governor Bibb Miller. This is an interesting point pursued by Callahan, particularly when it appears that it was the presence of the National Guard that probably saved the nine defendants' lives in Scottsboro in March 1931.

When the Scottsboro trial resumed in November 1933, Judge Callahan's linear logic during the first days of the trials unfolded as he established a series of prohibitions within his courtroom. For instance, he was unrelenting in his overruling of defense attorneys' objections, while consistently sustaining the prosecution's objections. His involvement in the prosecution's case was such that at times it became difficult to separate one from another. Enjoying his power, he even chided defense attorney Samuel Leibowitz with comments such as, "Judge Horton can't help you now." Callahan would in fact walk a very fine line among his racially oriented courtroom constituents as he assured them that he was no Judge Horton. However, as a strict southern legal constructionist, his concerns about maintaining a specific racial order were so pronounced that it can only be queried, was he not also aware that his judicial behavior was establishing a high potential for judicial appeals by the defense team right up to the United States Supreme Court? Though assuredly many of Callahan's contemporaries must have asked the same question, the fact is that the Alabama of 1931, like the rest of the country, was only 35 years away from the 1896 *Plessy v. Ferguson* decision and its racial doctrine of "separate but equal," and 68 years from the end of the Civil War. The lynching of "Negroes" was less a crime than a sport throughout most the South and many other parts of the country.

James E. Horton,
Judge

W. W.Callahan
Judge

State of Alabama
CIRCUIT COURT
J. H. Green, Clerk
Decautur, Alabama
November 14, 1933

Governor B.M. Miller,
Montgomery, Alabama.
Dear Governor:

It has fallen to my lot to try the Scottsboro negroes. I am opposed to trying any case with soldiers in the courtroom unless it is absolutely necessary, and I am very much inclined to the opinion that when the conditions are such as to require soldiers, they are such that a defendant could not get a fair trial.

I do not believe now and have never believed that soldiers were necessary in the trial of these Scottsboro negroes at Decatur. Of course you could find, I presume, numbers of people who would probably make statements that they [throught] the negroes ought to be convicted, or that they ought to be hung, and probably some would say that they ought to be mobbed, but I can't believe that the sober minded people of this county have such feeling as that; in fact I have never heard but very little expression of feeling against the negroes. There has been some feeling expressed against the lawyers in the case.

I believe that the militia not only advertises the case and thereby brings an extraordinary number of people to court, but that it also irritates the situation. I think it would be decidedly better to try the case just as any ordinary case is tried, except that I feel that there should be a number of bailiffs and deputies. I have somewhat looked into the law, and it appears that I have power to appoint only four bailiffs. I do not think that is enough. What it appears to me that I need, is about a dozen men of sound judgement and stamina, and who have had experience in handling of crowds and in dealing with the criminal minded. The jail at this place is so insecure that in ordinary cases it requires a guard all the time to prevent escapes from the jail, and of course on this occasion some extra precaution must be taken about guarding the jail.

When the Attorney General was here I went over this matter with him and he said that he would see to it that I had all the necessary men that I needed, but I did not then see just what authority he had, and I have heard nothing from him since. I do not know the extent of your authority, but it would appear that you would have authority to send a sufficient number here to have an orderly trial. I presume that I would have the inherent power to appoint sufficient number of men to protect the prisoners and to insure an orderly trial, but under my appointment the question comes up: How would these parties be paid?

We are confronted with another complication and that is this: The trials were drawn out at great length here before and considerable bills were incurred at the boarding houses and hotels. Those bills have never been paid, and the Sheriff informs me that the hotels and boarding houses are declining to feed and house the jury.

I am laying these matters before you to see what suggestions you feel justified in making.

The prisoners are to be arraigned in Decatur on the 20th, and the trials are set for the 27th of this month.

Yours very truly,

W. W. Callahan

WW/NH [Morgan County, ADAH Archives].

4

LETTERS FROM 1934
Scottsboro Mothers

By 1934, the Scottsboro trial had evolved far beyond the borders of Alabama or the United States. The trial had in fact become an international judicial *cause célèbre* that pitted the ideological forces of racism and colonialism against those of civil rights and economic parity. Suddenly the trial and its appeals and retrials were becoming a social, political, and constitutional drama that attracted national criticism and international responses that questioned America's claims of being a democracy, since it rationalized the sanctioning of judicial inequality, racial apartheid and mob or judicial murder. In this sense, the Scottsboro case and its accompanying issues of civil and human rights enforcement were becoming a testing ground for the American judicial system's conception and interpretation of social equality and justice under the law. As such, the notion that the pursuit of justice was always and irrevocably linked with heightened considerations of impartiality under the law, regardless of one's social status, learned abilities or comprehension of the law, was now being seriously challenged.

Some foreign observers of the trials viewed the Scottsboro Boys primarily from an internationalist perspective that inquired whether Europeans could continue to philoposhically maintain political and economic hegemony over non–European populations throughout the world without wholesale destruction of their own "raison d'être." In this cauldron of political, economic and racial thought, the subjugation of these nine young "Negroes" was quickly being transformed into a symbol of political and judicial resistance for millions of disenfranchised people around the globe.

From 1932 to 1934 a number of events impacted the course of the Scottsboro trial. Of major importance was the defendants' retaining criminal trial attorney Samuel Leibowitz as head of the defense team. Secondly, Ruby Bates's recanting of her earlier testimony, denying being raped, set in motion a number of accusations between herself and Victoria Price. Similarly, the scheduling of a new trial in 1933 for Haywood Patterson and Clarence Norris and their subsequent guilty verdicts set the stage for an appeal process that allowed Judge James E. Horton to order a new trial due to the suspect nature of the prosecution's evidence.

Though these unfolding events further ensured that the Scottsboro case would be both politically and judicially significant for the foreseeable future, for the defendants, the daily battle for survival was full of psychotic fury, violent madness and all of the uncertainty of war. On this human level, daily battles to stay alive in Birmingham's county jail and Kilby Prison's Death House were matched by the ongoing struggle to maintain sanity.

In a letter to Frieda Brown of the Prisoners Relief Department of the ILD, Roy Wright expressed his frustration and anger about incarceration. Mistaking Brown's gender, he writes:

> B'Ham, Ala.
> Jan 4, 1934
>
> Mr. Freedie Brown
> Dear Sir:
>
> Your letter came a few day past, indeed was I surprised to get it.
>
> Now Mr. Brown, the thing that Eugene and I want to know is it that we are unable to get any information from you all, here of late.
>
> And we have written to Patterson time and again and also Spector for information.
>
> But none however have we received, so now we are writing you for some information and see if this will stop us from hearing from you. Now, Mr. Brown the thing we want to know, just what you are going to do for us, anything or nothing?
>
> From what we can see there is nothing being done for us, because for me myself have been 33 months and have not been tried as yet, and Eugene have been granted a new trial nearly two years ago, and he has not had a trial either. So we want to know now are you all going to let Alabama try us or are you all going to continue to keep us held in confinement or not. Now, Mr. Brown, you ask us to write you and let you know how we spent the holiday season.
>
> They were spent somewhat in despare as usal, because you know there was nothing done for us by you to make us anyways comfortable and as for greetings we have not received any or letters either.
>
> Oh! yes, Mr. Brown you said that our stories could be used in your press. We do not think Mr. Brown that our stories would be agreeable with you all, and to with the public because we would be letting the public just how we are fairing and just what we think about you all, for we feel toward you all that you all are just as crooked as the rest of them are including our attorneys, because I have myself have paid very close attention to the spaces that Patterson have left in his writings and I too have paid very close attention to Mr Chamlee's talking and also his writings so that is why we believe that all of

you are crooked and if things dont change from where they are now I am myself let the public know just how crooked you all are.

Because Mr. Chamlee himself said that Eugene and I cases was nothing much and he could easily get us out and we want know why he does not get us out.

Now dont you all think that we would be a great help to you all speaking to the public than we would being held in here.

Now do not think that you all are for the right thing, and so you all have about got what you want out of us and now don't care anything about us, so that is why I am going to let the public know just what you darn crooks are up to.

I am
Yours truly,
Roy Wright
    and
Eugene Williams [Reel 5, Box 5, #000960 (folder c64), ILD]

Bgham, Ala.
County Jail
Jan 7, 1934

Dear Sir:

Just a few lines to let you hear from me and how I am fairing in this place. those who are interested in our Welfare in this place I Beg that you Will please send some one down here just as soon as possible these people here are just half feeding We Boys I ask them for something more to Eat and they put me in the dog house, please send some one down real soon, as you know how these people treat we poor Boys, here in this miserable place do please send some one real soon, so I'll close,
Yours Comradely
Charlie Weems [Reel 5, Box 5, #000693, ILD]

Jan 14, 1934
Atty B J. Davis
250 Auburn Ave. N.E.
Atlanta, GA.

My Dear Attorney,

No Doubt you will perhaps feel a little surprised on receiving these lines. Yet I do hope four surprise will be of an agreeable kind. I just wish to let you know that I feel certainly confident that you all are putting Forth every conceivable effort in our behalf which is a righteous cause and again I am praying — trusting in you all and god allmight for the outcome.

Now Lawyer please, Clarence Norris and myself are in Dire need of a little money here for smokes and other things. And we wish that you see that we get some as soon as possible. You must understand circumstances underconditions here are very very Differents in the way Birmingham we could make

Friends and have them to bring us such as we need. but here we cant see anyone and we are badly in need please dont Desert me in case if I isn't asking to much of you please send a little money or see that we shell have some in the earliest possible future I remain yours very truly Haywood Patterson

Clarence Norris [Reel 5, Box 5, #000224 (folder c54), ILD]

Haywood Patterson
Clarence Norris
Kilby Prison
Montgomery Ala.
1–15–34

Mr. William L. Patterson

Dear Mr. Patterson

We Clarence & myself have just received enclosed a money order for a Dollar But some how did not receive a letter with it. however just now I hardly realize just how to express my appreciations to you and the many friends for the untold Happiness you offord we poor Boys while pent uphere from the pleasures and freedom which life holds. however we are praying and trusting in you all and the good Lord for freedom and salvation.

now Mr. Patterson I wish to ask you to favor Clarence and myself by sending a little money all along as its will mean much toward our happiness and god will Bless you one and all. and then we can keep in newspapers magazines stamps writing paper and others little things such as something good to eats now Mr. Patterson you must understand this place are a very very different place from Birmingham when we were there we could make friends and have them to Bring us such as we need But here at this place we cant get even a cigarette unless [unless] we have the money now again I wish ot express my supreme appreciations for the many kind little Deeds that you and your members have done for me.

now Mr. Patterson we only ask a Special interest in seen that we get a little money more often in the future again thanking in advance for prompt favorable response.

I am yours very truly

Haywood Patterson

Clarence Norris [Reel 5, Box 5, #000227 (folder 54), ILD]

Continuing with her letter writing campaign despite her own tenuous living condition, Viola Montgomery's ethnographic styled letters to her son are instructive about a mother's resiliency to support her imprisoned and endangered son. In effect, her letter to her son's accuser, and to her friends associated with the ILD functioned to support various strategies to forestall her son's execution:

January 18, 1934

Dear Ruby:

Just a few lines to let you know that I have been to see Olen and the rest of the boys. I found them all well as you would expect. They all looked mighty well to me and still got the faith that they will be free some day. I hope you will keep well and able to fight for the freedom of the boys. They seem to understand that the only thing will free them is mass pressure. Well, I won't write much more. I am a little upset. I got to move some place I will write you when I get moved. I guess you think I sure move a lot but I ain't able to pay rent and it all ways easier for me to move than to pay rent. I ain't got nothing but my trunk and a few quilts. I had a bed and a few chairs but the boss got them back but that's all right too. Well I must close.

You write anytime. From your friend, Viola Montgomery.

[Reel 5, Box 5, # 000991 (folder c65), ILD]

Atlanta, Ga.

Birmingham, Ala.
County Jail
Jan. 25th 1934

Mrs. Essie Brown,

Dear madam, it affords me the greatest of pleasure in addressing you these few remarks in regard of your most kind and lovely letter of which I recd to day. It found me getting along very fine in health. But a little worried in mind this day. But I really do hope that these few remarks will find you an all OK in every respect. now (Mrs) Essie my dear friend I certainly did enjoy reading your letter. and absolutely proud to know that the many friend are still with me an are going to continue the fight until I am free. and (Mrs) Essie my dear, I sure do appreciate the many kind things of which people are doping for me. And I hope that I will Be able to meet them all some day how happy I will be to meet them and tell them what it means to me to be free again. (Mrs) Essie, you ask me was I allowed to receive candy. Why certainly (Mrs) Brown. But I would much rather for you to send me something else. I am in need for a little money so I can buy cigarettes and stamps, and pay for my news papers and read about how things are going on — on the out side that's the only consolation I gets reading news papers and its hard for me to keep them up. I am taken too the Birmingham news, and the Birmingham Post. I am behind on them and I am suffering for smokes and stamps. the people sure did treat me cruel Christmas. They didn't send me any thing for Christmas, and (Mrs) Brown, I will appreciate very much if you will send me a little money soon as possible. I am looking to hear from you real soon. Please give me Best regard to all. So I will close.

Faithfully Yours,

Olen Montgomery [Reel 5, Box 5, #000033 (folder c65), ILD]

Feb. 24, '34

Dear Friend and Fellow Worker;

I have been reading of the great work that has been carried on in Moscow among the working class and the good work that they are doing for the political prisoners in America. I have a son in Birmingham jail waiting with pretty good patience for the working class all over the world to get together and demand the boss caste to let them go. He understands well that is the only way that they ever will be free is we workers will have to face them up to it, because they won't find much sympathy among the boss class here for the Negro. It's the same way with the Negro boss. He don't give a dime for a poor Negro and I don't give one for him. I had a letter from Comrade Frieda Brown. She asks me to join the ILD here in my section. She don't know that I am a CP member and I would not be anything else because if the C. P. had not push the ILD the nine Scottsboro boys would have been dead two years ago. So I am with the Party as long as I live. I don't care who likes it or who don't like it. I do, and I think every fair minded person would like it as well as I do. I like it because it believes in every man or woman to have a right to a decent living.

Not only that, I like the whole program and the one I like best is to get rid of this so called government and the big boss. He keeps up pressed to death. I tell the world I want to be somebody but I can't under this government. This so called government has put a many good women in the garbagecan, and put the lid on it, but I tell the world I will fight like hell to stay out and I want the rest of my comrade to do the same.

Well, I guess that's all for the time being.

Long live our ILD and CP movement. And best regards to all my fellow workers both white and Black.

From Mrs. Viola Montgomery of 588 Reed St., Atlanta, Ga. [Reel 5, Box 5, #000993 (folder c65), ILD]

Early Spring, 1934

Dear Friends and Fellow Worker of This World

I am just setting here all alone, thinking over these times, and just wonder if I will be able to stand them much longer. Course, I will tell the truth. I am getting along very well at the present for something to eat, but I ant got a decen place to sleep. I was sleeping on a friend of mine Bed and they wanted it so that left me on the floor rite at the mean time I need it worse it looks mity unfair to me to have to live here in this great Big world a mong a plenty of Everything and have to worrie and wish for it. I tell you what so this thing cant last much longer because if Every worker feels like I do it would not be hard for them to orginize for Better conditions because I sure is tird of the way I have to live. I am not a Bit well and have to live in a close place. No where to get a good Bath that enuff to kill any one and I mean it if you ant a good one you cant stand it be corse the Boss class mean to Press hell out of the worker.

Xmas came and gone and I did not get a thing for the ILD. Sent me $10.00 this week. I owe the Daily Worker a little money. I will Pay that and go to see my Son Olen next week with that money. I sure was glad to get it, so I could go to see Olen as he has look for me so long and when I return Back I will rite another storie tell how I find him, so that all for the time ben. From Viola Montgomery [Reel 5, Box 5, #001007 (folder c65), ILD].

Atlanta, Ga
Feb. 13, 34

Dear Friend and Fellow Worker I want to gave thanks to the working class Bouth White and Blacks that be long to our great world wide movement the ILD for the good work that you all has done for the Freedom of My son and others that I has Ben reading a bout for more than to years. I cant say any more than that be cause I did not no anything a bout the ILD until my son Olen was Framed up But I am glady say to day I am verry well aqcuinnted with it and glad I iam maby I will be a little help to the movement. I never has Ben able to tell any one just how I do feel towards the movement and I never will. But I will say this, I am with the ILD as long as I live be cause I made a promas to one of the Cormody that I wood Fight for my sun life sid by side and I ment that the Carmod was Dave Daron. He was the first one that come to my home in Monroe, Ga.

He told me say if you all mothers will stick to the ILD we can save your sun and they has did that be cause I talk with my sun Olen three week a go and if the ILD had not fought so hard they wood have ben dead. Soon will be three year now and to think some Old Mrs. Hucks from B-ham have the nerve to used the jail and ask the Boys to let the NACCP help them she say we cant do nothing for you unless you all say so. I will tell the World I am not Willen for them to speak a bout my sun unless they join hand with the ILD. Now if they degre with us as we first ask them to do it OK with me for them to work with us if not to hell with the naacp be cause any Body now days don't feel that the world shourd be together and degree on the same don't need to be in the world.

Well I wont talk any; more a bout the naacp I will get on our great gourment. A man told me yestaday that the gouerment was given us a liven and that we auto be thank full. But if the worker see it like I do the gouerment ant given us nothing. It all ready ours we has worker all our day under this so call gouerment and we that work so hard got nothing for it so how can a man are woman feel like they are getting any thing now what little we get the way we have to get it don't do much good. Tell the world I don't care for thear little old relief ticket. I hear are plenty of work to do if thay wood let us do it. No they try to fool us make us think that thear doing something for us, But they ant fooling me and if they find out ya ant no fool they wont give you nothing. Now I ask for more relief last week and this week they did not send me any thing at all. I ant got no cold are wood and snow on the ground. So worker in my cecloson don't let this so call gourment fool ya. Rote by a scottboro Mother, Mrs. Viola Montgomery of 588 Reed St., Atlanta Ga.

P.S. if this gouerment was any good it wood not stand for so many lynchen and so much other dirtie work to go on. [Reel 5, Box 5, #001016 (folder c65), ILD. Transcribed as written in original letter.]

B'Ham, Ala.
County Jail
Mar. 1, 1934

Dear Friends:

It affords me the greatest of pleasure in addressing you all these few remarks so as to let you all know how I am getting along.

I am getting very fine in Health. Dear Friends, I was informed today by a member of the I.L.D. telling me how glad you all would be to hear from me and I am awful proud to have the pleasure to write you all and tell you all how Proud I am to have many friends on the outside. I am so glad that you all are going to continue the fight to free me, and I only wish I could explain to you all in words as I desire but under the circumstances I can not. I will say I do appreciate the many kind deeds are being done towards me and my companions.

That kindness will never be forgotten by these nine boys. Oh well, I must close.

Faithfully yours,
Olen Montgomery [Reel 5, Box 4, #000027 (folder c52), ILD]

Haywood Patterson
Kilby Prison
Montgomery Ala.
March 5, 1934

Mr. John Wexley
My Dear Wexley

Sir,

This certainly is a great moment for me To take the pleasure in trying To Write a greater friend as you are of course. I hardly realize just how to express my sincere appreciation to you and the congregation for the great trouble which you and all of you are putting forth in my Behalf and I am sure grateful To hear of the play, Oh I trust that it will be of great success — and it only Gives me great joy To realize that I have the Heartfelt sympathy of you all. I hope you know Mr. Liebowitz I love him more than life its self. He is such a mighty great man I think such a lot of him in case I should live 19 years from today I will remember him. Now Mr. Wexley you will excuse my expression which it are a little Different from yours. Now I wish the play will Bring forth good results. Please extend my sincere appreciation all of the workers
Yours truly
Haywood Patterson [Reel 5, Box 5. #000212 (folder c55) ILD]

In April 1934, ILD attorney Benjamin Davis made a second visit to Birmingham's Jefferson County Jail to investigate the living conditions of the defendants. His report though sheathed with ILD political bias, reveals the levels of inhuman treatment being doled out to the Scottsboro Boys:

> The last time I visited the Scottsboro boys in Jefferson county Jail, I carried them a carton of cigarettes, matches and stamps. Following the usual custom, I expected the packages to be examined and returned to me for distribution as I interviewed them. But this time Deputy Warden Rogers, refused to permit me to deliver them. He took the packages and marked on them for "The Scottsboro Niggers." This was done plainly and conspicuously so that I might be intimidated into understanding the treatment accorded to all "niggers" whether they were lawyers or prisoners.
>
> Then Warden Rogers, as he led me to the cells for interview stated, "he didn't know what had gotten into them Scottsboro niggers. They're the worse bunch of niggers he ever saw. Always raising hell when they get the best treatment possible."
>
> But the seven Scottsboro boys in Jefferson County jail tell a different story about the "best treatment possible." Andy Wright was confined in solitary for more than 3 weeks because he refused to go "outside in the snow and sleet to catch a death cold. This was at the request of Warden Dan Rogers. Then Montgomery was placed in solitary because he kicked against the starvation portion put on his food plate. Warden Rogers considered this "the best treatment possible."
>
> Warden Rogers asked one of the boys "who is that nigger lawyer who came in here, a son of a bitch. I wish I could catch him sitting in the court house here. I'd hang him." He also told the boys, that "as long as that nigger lawyer keeps coming down here swelling your heads you're going to stay in solitary. You'd better keep him away."
>
> Once Warden Rogers brandished his pistol on one of the boys threatening to kill him. As the boy pleaded for his life, Rogers belched, "I ought to kill you now, they're going to kill you anyway, just like they're going to burn Patterson and Norris."
>
> The boys all are mortally afraid that Warden Rogers will someday shoot them down in cold blood. At every opportunity be curses them browbeats them and attempts to provoke them into defending themselves in order that he might murder them for "resisting an officer of the law." He plants stool pigeons in their cells. These stool pigeons provoke fights which result in the boys being thrown into solitary while the stool pigeons are never punished. Then he boasts to the boys "that I'll always believe my stool pigeons in preference to you niggers."
>
> A stool pigeon framed one of the boys a month ago by claiming he had stolen 50c from him. This boy has been in solitary now for more than five weeks without change of clothes or a bath. This same torturer Rogers also claims that the boy has a razor in his possession, and threatens to keep him in solitary until the razor is delivered up. The truth is that this boy has never had

a razor in his possession and obviously has no way of obtaining one even to secure his release from solitary.

Warden Rogers has repeatedly informed the boys that as long as people come to see them they will stay in solitary. Recently when Myra Page, well known writer, visited them, Warden Rogers called her a white whore and yelled "as long as white whores come down here to see you, we're not going to let you out."

In spite of all the concentrated terror and brutality unleashed upon them recently, the boys understand clearly that it is not accidental or spontaneous. As they said to me, "We know they're trying to divide us, but they can't. They're trying to force us to take the NAACP, but we don't want it. Warden Rogers is trying to find an excuse to kill us in jail, but we know and we're going to stick together and watch him."

These 7 innocent boys in Jefferson County jail still have confidence in the ILD and the fighting unity of the Negro and white workers who alone can save them. They are daily realizing that the sadistic tortures of Warden Rogers are a part of same bloody system which framed them 3 years ago, and they look hopefully to the same ILD, the same world protest to save them from the new intensified campaign of terror against them [Reel 4, Box 4, #0240, ILD].

While Scottsboro defendant Haywood Patterson waited for a new trial due to Judge Horton's dismissal of evidence in his case, and Clarence Norris's execution date of February 2, 1934, was suspended on appeal, the mothers of the defendants began a massive appeal by sending letters directly to President Franklin D. Roosevelt. Supporting this effort, the ILD organized a May 13 "Mother's Day March" in front of the White House. Regarding this, the following letter was sent to President Roosevelt:

May 2nd 1934

President Franklin D. Roosevelt
Washington, D.C.

Dear Sir:

On May 13, 1934, on the day when the American people will celebrate Mother's Day, we are asking the President of the United States to receive five American Mothers, Mrs. Jane Patterson, Mrs. Josephine Powell, Mrs. Mamie Williams, Mrs. Ida Norris, Mrs. Viola Montgomery. They are the mothers of five of the Nine innocent Scottsboro boys, who three years ago were condemned to die, and whose lives were saved by thousands of Americans, Negro and white, who Have protested their innocence and supported their defense. (Their innocence has been proven in the courts, and admitted by Judge James E. Horton, in his opinion of June 20, 1933.)

These mothers have suffered great unhappiness. In their suffering they symbolize thousands of mothers today, whose young sons and daughters, unemployed, despondent, demoralized, during the long period of the crisis, have left their homes in search of work, in the hope of recovering lost manhood and lost womanhood. These mothers have long known this deprivation. For three long years they have known the torture of the threat of death to their innocent children. These are mothers to whom the Government owes the safeguards for the realization of their right to "the pursuit of happiness."

This appointment with the President on Mother's Day is made at the request of the five Scottsboro mothers named above. We ask that acknowledgment be made to them in care of this organization.

Yours truly,
INTERNATONAL LABOR DEFENSE
National Secretary

Wlp:hs [Reel 4, Box 4, #0463 (folder c38), ILD]

May 2, 1934

(copy)
Haywood Patterson
Kilby Prison
Montgomery, Ala.

Dear Son:

Everywhere I've been along, all people know a bout Scottsboro boys. So don't you change your mind to the N.A.A.C.P. You stay with the I.L.D. because it is fighting hard for your freedom.

I may be down to see you in a few days.

Mr. Brodsky is coming to see you. I sent him the letter you wanted him to read. All the people send you love. People at home are well. I am in the I,L.D. office in New York and all send love.

Your Mothcr

P.S.— Don't forget that I am depending on you and Clarence to keep your faith in the I.L.D. just like I am doing.

Your Mother
(signed) Janie Patterson

[Reel 5, Box 4, #000091 (folder c53), ILD]

Haywood Patterson
Condemned Department
Kilby Prison
Montgomery Alabama

May 4 1934

My Dear, Darling mother

This certainly a great pleasure for me here trying to write you these lines in regards of how I am. Well darling, at this time I am getting along as best as I can under the circumstances. Now mother, precious dear, I received yesterday a letter from Sebill. She was well so far as I am concerned. I have not heard from Louise this week therefore, I can't give an account of how they are getting on.

Mother Dear I hope that you will get to see all my Dear good friends those of whom has Been sure faithful to me, although I never heard from my friends on a certain account but yet, they should know that does not discourage me as I know they carry the great struggle on and there will be no end to that until I am freed.

Yes there are at least two or 3 friends whom are not a member of the I.L.D. that I hear from. Tell Wm. Patterson and also my many good friends that I am being held incommunicado. If there is any one who wish to give me help by sending me such; as cigarettes, magazines, money and stamps I will get it all right and will appreciate their kindness as if I were before where I could write them. Just to-day I received one dollar from 80 E. 11th St., but received no letter with it that is the way it has been ever since I am here.

I realize that you all know all about it and that is why it does not worry me or discourage me therefore, it is necessary for you all not to feel discouraged anyway I am innocent of this mess and I will die with that word regardless to what may come or happen. I am innocent and I will always say I am innocent so you all need not worry as I dont worry.

Wish you are well, and enjoying a lot. I hope you can read this as I have not with anything to write with.

Close for this time.

Your loving sun;

Haywood Patterson

P.S. I sincerely hope that it want be much longer before someone comes down to see me as I wish for a few things to be known [Reel 5, Box 5, #000218 (folder c54), ILD].

In the late spring of 1934, Olen Montgomery, imprisoned a little over three years, was beginning to exhibit an impatience that comes from relentless brutality and incarceration. And while this development was probable and observed in some of the other defendants, more frustrating for the defendants was knowing that their supporters' efforts to obtain wider support, even from President Franklin Roosevelt, went unabated but unproductive. The following demanding letter by Olen Montgomery to his mother, Viola, is a case in point:

> Birmingham, Ala.
> County Jail
> May 3rd 1934

My dear mother

I read your letter today and was more than glad to hear from you. It found me feeling very well in health and I hope that these few lines will find you O.K. in every respect. Listen my dear mother, it's one thing I want you to do for me and that's to be careful. And listen mother, that's all right about the things I ask for. I want some money and I can get what I need. The I.L.D. don't send me enough to buy 3 packages of cigarettes hardly. And I got my shoes in pawned and my hat and I want them out before the fellow get tried and go off and I want my shoes and hat. I had to pawn them so I could smoke. I didn't have no money and I had to smoke and have other things I

needed. I want you to send me three dollars so I can get my shoes and hat, and get me some smokes. I know you can send me three dollars in a few days. Just ask some of the friends to help you send me the money and I know they will help you. I want three dollars and I want it before the 12th of May. I don't want that fellow to take my things with him. I get my shoes in pawn for $1.25 and my hat in pawn for 50c. If you would use your head for something else excuse raising for the I.L.D. you could have something and would be able to send me something worth while. You just ask the friends to help you send me some money and I know they will help. Just explain my condition to them and tell them I need shirts and pants, cigarettes, socks and stamps, stationary. Tell them I wear size 30 x 32 pants and I know they will be more than glad to help you. It ain't no harm for you to ask friends to help me. Oh! well mother you take care of yourself and be sure to do what I told you to do for me and send me the three dollars soon so I can get my things out of pawn before that fellow leave for Kilby Prison. So I will close from your son
Olen Montgomery [Reel 5, Box 4, #0028 (folder c52), ILD]

A day later, Olen wrote his mother a second letter in which his demands were more explicit:

> Birmingham, Ala.
> County Jail
> May 4, 1934

My dear mother
   I read your other letter today. And listen you ask me how was my health. My health is bad. And listen you ask me about a meeting or something down here. Listen I don't care anything about it. Other words I didn't see it and I didn't want to see it. Such as that ain't no good. It only making it hard on me here in jail and I know it. That thing they had here May Day, what good did it do. Not any at all. I'm still locked up in the cell. Instead of the I.L.D. trying to make it better for me here in jail they are making it harder for me by trying to demand the people to do things. Listen, send me some money. Send me three dollars like I told you in my first letter. I need it, and send it soon. So I will close from your son
Olen [Reel 5, Box 4, #0030 (folder c52), ILD]

Approximately a week after the five mothers of the Scottsboro defendants and the ILD sent a request to speak to President Roosevelt they received the following telegram [Reel 4, Box 4, #0481 (folder c38), ILD]:

NAI29 35 GOVT

   THE WHITE HOUSE WASHINGTON DC 347P MAY 11 1934

WILLIAM L PATTERSON
NATL SECRETARY INTERNATIONAL LABOR DEFENSE 80 EAST 11 ST

   THE CASE TO WHICH YOU REFER IN YOUR LETTER OF MAY SECOND AND YOUR TELEGRAM OF MAY SEVENTH IS ONE OVER WHICH THE STATE OF ALABAMA HAS JURISDICTION I MUST THEREFORE

RESPECTFULLY DECLINE YOUR REQUEST
MARVIN H MCINTYRE SECRETARY TO THE PRESIDENT.

405P

Upon receipt of the rejection telegram, the "Scottsboro Mothers" drafted the following letter to President Roosevelt. It was later modified and forwarded to the President.

May 12, 1934

Franklin Delano Roosevelt
President of the United States of America

Mr. President:

Today has been designated as Mother's Day. In thousands of cities in this country mothers whose sons and daughters have been forced from home by the tremendous burdens of the crisis, anxiously desire some word from them. Thousands of boys who have been herded into the Civilian Conservative Corps anxiously seek today some ( ) from their sons. For these Mothers we have the greatest of sympathy.

For three years our sons have been taken from us. This loss cannot be attributed to an accident. Our boys are held from our embrace by the ruthless hands of a still more ruthless government. The State of Alabama has them imprisoned and is torturing them. Its duly elected Judge James Horton, in the city of Decatur in his opinion, touching upon the right of a new trial, declared them to be innocent. Yet Alabama's authorities, its landlords and its industrialist persist in their imprisonment and torture.

What can be the reasons for this other than an attempt to terrorize the Negro people. Our sons were tried without the benefit of people of their own race and nationality acting as judges of the facts. In the prison in which they are housed, Negroes who seek to visit them are intimidated and brutality humiliated.

Mr. President, we ask you to intercede in behalf of our sons. We ask you as chief executive of this country, as one who is supposed to take an interest in the welfare of the people of this county and in the administration of just and impartial law, to add your voice in open protest to the continued murderous persecution of our children. Your word Mr. President, would have tremendous weight throughout the land. Already hundreds of thousands of people in America and in Europe have raised their voices in protest against this brutal thing. Men in high circles here and abroad have openly declared their belief in the innocence of our boys. Ruby Bates, young southern girl who in fear of her life was forced to unjustly condemn our sons, has heroically come forward with a statement of the full and complete facts in the case. Is this not accumulated evidence of their innocence? Will you not, as President of the United States add your voice to theirs.

We shall anxiously and tearfully watch the press, expectantly awaiting your public reply.

Very truly

Scottsboro Mothers [Reel 4, Box 4, #0467 (folder c38), ILD]

June 12: The Alabama Supreme Court unanimously denies the defense a new trial. Attorney Leibowitz argues that qualified blacks were systematically kept off the jury rolls, and the names that were currently in the rolls were forged after the fact.

Though these attempts to gain President Franklin Roosevelt public support were frustrated, the hopelessness of imprisonment began to push the incarcerated Scottsboro defendants to make demands upon their supporters. As these demands increased in both material and psychological ways, many supporters were themselves pained in their attempt to fulfill basic requests from the defendants. The following few letters between ILD National Secretary William Patterson and defendants Roy Wright, Haywood Patterson and Olen Montgomery are indicative of a litany of supportive challenges that defense teams and family members faced when communicating with these incarcerated men.

June 15th 1934

Roy Wright
Jefferson County Jail
Birmingham, Ala.

Dear Roy:
    We are please to tell you that we were able to get you what you wanted. Under cover we are sending you a pair of gray tweed pants. Please write us and let us know how they fit. We hope you will like it and that it is the correct size because we are unable to make exchange. It was a little hard to get, but we are very happy to send it to you, and the pleasure you will get in receiving them is worth the little effort we have made here.
    Last week we wrote you that Frieda Brown of the Prisoners Relief Dept. was ill and she was therefore unable to write to you. We know you will be sorry to hear that she is still ill and has not come back to the office yet.
    We are enclosing $2.00 with which you can buy a few necessities.
    Our heartiest greetings,
William L. Patterson
NATIONAL SECRETARY [Reel 5, Box 5, #000967 (folder c64), ILD]

June 15, 1934

Haywood Patterson
Kilby Prison
Montgomery, Ala.

Dear Haywood;
    We are pleased to tell you that we were able to get you the fountain pen you asked for. We are sending it to you under separate cover. Please write to us and let us know how you like it. It has given us great pleasure to be able to send it to you.
    Last week we wrote you that Frieda Brown of the Prisoners' Relief Depart-

ment was ill, and she was therefore unable to write to you. We know you will be sorry to hear that she is still ill and has not come back to the office yet.

We are enclosing $2.00 with which you can buy a few necessities. Keep up your good spirit.

Our heartiest greetings,
INTERNATIONAL LABOR DEFENSE

Wm. L. Patterson, National Secy. [Reel 5, Box 5, #000231 (folder c54), ILD]

June 15th 1934

Olen Montgomery
Jefferson County, Jail
Birmingham, Ala.

Dear Olen;

We are pleased to tell you that we were able to get you some of the things you wanted. Under separate cover we are sending you a pair of pants. Please write to us and let us know how they fit. We hope you will like it and that it is the correct size, because we are unable to make an exchange.

We are sorry that we could not get the white lumber jacket. We believe what you want is a white sweat-shirt. If this is so, let us know and we will make every effort to get it for you.

It was a little hard to get some of the things for the boys, but we are happy to send them to you, and the pleasure you will get in receiving them is worth the little effort we have made here.

Last week we wrote you that Frieda Brown of the Prisoners' Relief Dept. was ill and she was therefore unable to write to you. We know you will be sorry to hear that she is still ill an has not come back to the office yet.

We are enclosing $2.00 with which you can buy a few necessities.

Our heartiest greetings
WM. L. Patterson
NATIONAL SECRETARY

[Reel 5, Box 4, #0031 (folder c51), ILD]

After sending Olen a letter of support and addressing his basic needs, William Patterson sent the following letter to President Roosevelt that clearly and succinctly placed the political and moral adjudication of the Scottsboro case in the lap of the nation's Chief Executive. Underscoring the "surly manner" and rejection by the White House staff to accept the delegation of Scottsboro Mothers on May 13, the following statement, though replete with International Labor Defense rhetoric, highlights the judicial duplicity and racism within the American judicial system.

STATEMENT TO PRESIDENT ROOSEVELT
ON THE SCOTTSBORO CASE

Mr. President;

On Mother's Day the Scottsboro Mothers' Delegation was shamefully turned away from the White House gate by naval attaches, detectives and police, though several communications had been forwarded to you requesting that you hear their petition against the continued imprisonment and torture of the nine innocent Negro boys who are the victims of the monstrous Scottsboro lynch frame-up.

When the delegation returned the following day, the White House gate was again similarly barred and manned, and the delegation was informed in a surly manner that you had issued orders to allow no other members of the delegation to pass beyond the gate except the Mothers and their spokesman. A fierce denial met the request for the admission of Miss Ruby Bates, one of the two white young women involved in this case, whose conscience compelled her to repudiate the false charge of rape at the second trial in Decatur, and who came with the Mother's Delegation to ask that you intervene to secure the release of these boys whom she knows to be innocent.

The four mothers and accompanying spokesman were kept in the lobby, where Secretary MacIntyre appeared, only to inform them of your refusal to hear their petition on the grounds that "the Scottsboro case is the business of the State of Alabama and not the business of the President." After listening for a brief period and reading the statement which these poor, outraged, suffering mothers brought to present to you, Mr. MacIntyre left, purporting to interview you. Upon returning, your Secretary requested that a copy of Judge Horton's decision and other material be forwarded to you.

A copy of the decision of Judge Horton is herewith enclosed together with the printed brief of the appeal now pending before the Alabama Supreme Court and a copy of the communication forwarded by President Wilson to Governor Stephens of California, intervening in the case of Tom Mooney to stop the hanging of this labor leader, the innocent victim of a similar vicious ruling-class frame-up.

Judge Horton's decision was handed down on June 22, 1933, in the Morgan Circuit Court of Alabama, granting the motion for a new trial in the case of Haywood Patterson who was convicted and sentenced to death at his second trial held in Decatur. This trial followed upon the decision of the United States Supreme Court which ordered a new trial and reversed the death sentences passed upon seven of these boys by the Scottsboro court and upheld by the Alabama Supreme Court. This decision of Judge Horton reviewed at length the entire evidence submitted both at Scottsboro and at Decatur. (A digest of the most important findings of this decision is appended hereto.) This decision adjudged the case for the State of Alabama in the following significant words:

> "This is the State's evidence. It corroborates Victoria Price slightly, if at all, and her evidence is so contrary to the evidence of the doctors who examined her that it has been impossible for the Court to reconcile their evidence with hers.
> "The testimony of the prosecutrix in this case is not only uncorroborated but it also bears on its face indications of improbability and is contradicted by other evidence, and in addition thereto the evidence greatly preponderates in favor of

the defendant. It therefore becomes the duty of the Court under the law to grant the motion made in this case."

Please mark, Mr. President, that this decision was handed down by a white Alabama judge in the face of deliberately organized and actually menacing lynch terror. This decision must, therefore, convince all but the conscious and venomous upholders of barbarous lynch oppression that these nine Negro boys are absolutely innocent of the foul charges brought against them, and that they are the victims of a ghastly lynch conspiracy which contravenes every principle of justice and every democratic right which is supposed to be guaranteed by the Constitution of the United States.

The history of this case, extending now over three years, is the stark record of a ruthless ruling-class conspiracy to carry through the hideous, wholesale lynch massacre of nine innocent, unemployed Negro boys. Thrust into starvation by the capitalist crisis, these boys set out to look for jobs (two of them being ill, to seek medical attention), only to find themselves in the clutches of official lynch torturers, faced with the electric chair and the constant menace of savage mob lynching.

The significant circumstances and events of this outrageous frame-up are too many to enumerate in this statement, but a few must be mentioned. The legal lynch orgy at Scottsboro when eight of these boys were railroaded to the electric chair in 72 hours, to the sadistic gloating of a deliberately organized lynch mob of 8,000 which surrounded and jammed into the court-room. The terrorizing of witnesses and defense attorneys at the Decatur trial; organized lynch mobs actually started from Scottsboro and Huntsville and were turned back only when Judge Horton declared from the bench that the mobs would be met with bullets.

Highly important is the brazen denial of the right of Negroes to serve on the jury, though numerous Negroes took the witness-stand in the terrorist atmosphere of the Decatur court and proved their qualifications. The violent appeals to chauvinist prejudice and race hatred by the prosecuting officials and Attorney-General Knight. "Free that 'nigger' and every white man will tremble for his daughter tonight. We have built an Anglo-Saxon civilization and we mean to maintain it." The burning of the house of the witness Lewis, a Negro worker, in Chattanooga, following upon the Decatur trial; the threats of Ku Klux Klansmen against him and his subsequent death from "mysterious" poisoning.

Still further demonstrative of the true nature and ruling class origin of this lynch frame-up are the following unmistakable maneuvers. The introduction of Judge Callahan, a reputed Ku Klux Klansman, into the case, after Judge Horton rendered his decision reversing Haywood Patterson's conviction, because of the too rank nature of the frame-up and the pressure of international mass protest. The subsequent railroading of Haywood Patterson and Clarence Norris under his openly biased direction at the second Decatur trial.

Flagrant and indicative is the forging of the names of Negroes to the Jackson County jury roll and the despicable maneuvers of Judge Callahan, acting in collusion with Attorney-General Knight, in connection with the delaying of the trial transcript, granting extensions of time and reversing these a few days before the time for appeal would expire in order to deprive these boys even of the right of appeal.

In addition, there is the refusal during these more than three years to give a trial before a juvenile court to Roy Wright, who was 14 years old at the time of the Scottsboro trial when a mistrial was declared in his case. The similar refusal in the case of Eugene Williams who was 13 years old when framed-up, despite the decision of the Alabama Supreme court ordering such a trial. The denial of the right of bail to all these boys and their torture and several at further frame-ups in the jail.

All these events and deeds prove conclusively that the Scottsboro case is no ordinary "criminal" case, no accidental "miscarriage of justice." Nor is this an isolated case. Witness, the murderous terror in Birmingham around the frame-up of the tubercular Negro war veteran, Willie Peterson; the fascist attacks and wholesale slaughter and imprisonment of starving Negro share-croppers at Camp Hill and at Tallapoosa; the lynchings of Harden and Pippen following upon the forcible driving out of their defense attorneys by Judge Foster, and the lynching of the paralytic, Dennis Cross, framed on the usual charge of "rape," at Tuscaloosa; the lynching of James Royal at Decatur after the second trial of Haywood Patterson; the wholesale legal lynching of five Negroes on February 9th of this year—all in the state of Alabama. On that same day, three Negroes were legally lynched in Texas and another in Arkansas. These are typical instances of the outrageous lynch-frame ups, ferocious sheriff's man-hunts and murderous police attacks perpetrated against innocent Negroes, which are rampant all over the South and are increasing rapidly throughout the entire country.

Savage mob lynchings and burnings of Negroes rise at a rapid rate. In 1932 the reported ghastly toll of lynchings reached 37; last year 47, of which 42 are Negroes; this year already nine. The facts of the recent lynching of two Negro farm-workers in Bolivar county, Mississippi, clearly show the oppressive slave origin and fascist character of these frightful lynch orgies. For the "crime" of asking for decent food, these Negro toilers were charged with "insulting" the landlord's wife, arrested and turned over to the lynch mob by the sheriff. Moreover, a characteristic feature of these lynchings is the increasingly open and direct participation of officers of the law and the brazen incitement of lynching to lynching by the highest state and government official such as Governor Rolph.

The Scottsboro case is thus a flagrant instance of the whole system of national and social oppression of the Negro people in the United States. Under this system, thirteen million Negroes are crushed into slavery and starvation, victims of discrimination, segregation, disfranchisement, persecution, chain-gang torture and murderous legal and extra-legal lynch terror. This is in open contravention of every democratic right which the United States Constitution statedly guarantees.

This oppression is most violent on the Black Belt of the South where the Negro nation, a majority of the population, is barbarously enslaved and suppressed. A small but powerful ruling-class of white landlords and capitalists, ruthlessly maintains this frightful system of oppression, slavery and exploitation in order to wring super-profits out of the toll and misery of the down-trodden Negro masses. And these white ruling class slave-masters utilize the machinery of government, courts, fascist lynch bands (Ku Klux Klan, White Legion, etc.) and every means at their command forcibly to suppress the Negro people and to keep them isolated and divided from the white workers and poor farmers who are also oppressed, exploited and terrorized.

Aggravated by the capitalist crisis and still further intensified by the ruinous cotton plow-under program and differential labor codes of the N.R.A., this oppression has reached unprecedented and unbearable heights. The enslaved Negro toilers on the land and the oppressed Negro masses in the cities are now menaced with wholesale extermination by starvation and murderous terror, which rapidly engulfs the white workers and poor farmers as well. Unbridled bloody terror is let loose by the capitalist landlord ruling class against any and every attempt of the starving Negro and white toilers to struggle against hunger and death and to unite for the improvement of their miserable slave conditions and for their defense.

This violent oppression and terror against the Negro people and white toilers is of the same infamous pattern as the bloody suppression of the working class and the persecution of the Jews and other minority groups in Hitler's fascist Germany. The monstrous Nazi frame-up at Leipzig was in essence parallel with the vicious Scottsboro lynch frame-up. The Nazi terror, culminating in the present drive to butcher Ernst Thaelmann, the heroic leader of the German working class, differs only in degree from the fascist attacks now rapidly developing here in the U.S.A.

In Atlanta, Georgia, Angelo Herndon is being brutally tortured in the Fulton Tower jail. Charged with "insurrection" under an old barbarous slave law, this 19 year old Negro working class leader has been sentenced to 18 to 20 years on the chain-gang for the "crime" of leading a demonstration of starving Negro and white workers to demand relief. The recent decision of the supreme court of Georgia upholding this savage sentence, which means death by terrible torture, has been the signal for a reign of terror against the Negro and white workers and their organizations — arrests and brutal police attacks, the illegal raiding of the workers homes and the office of the International Labor Defense, the rushing to trial of the Atlanta Six, four white and two Negro workers, charged with "insurrection" and faced with the death penalty, for attempting to hold a meeting of Negro and white workers in 1930.

In Polk County, Florida, James Franklin, the Negro organizer of the citrus pickers' union was framed-up on a charge of "attempting to assault" the white landlord's daughter, arrested and held by the sheriff while this slave-driving, landlord murderer shot him to death. Shortly after, Frank Norman, the white organizer of the International Labor Defense, was kidnapped and killed by a landlord's fascist band.

In Alabama, six Negro miners have been murdered in cold blood, and one white miner shot, scores brutally beaten and arrested by company thugs, police and national guardsmen. This is the bloody fascist terror let loose by the coal and steel barons and their governmental agents to break the strike of thousands of coal and ore minors, 75% of whom are Negroes, against the starvation, differential wages and unbearable slave conditions imposed upon them under the N.R.A. The brutal breaking up of the May Day demonstration of Negro and white workers in Birmingham has been followed by wholesale attacks, arrests, illegal raids upon workers' homes and the raiding and smashing of the offices of the International Labor Defense by police, Ku Klux Klan and White Legion fascist bands.

The murder of three striking Negro longshoremen in Galveston and New Orleans and of a white longshoreman in San Pedro, California; the shooting of two striking workers and a woman and child on the picket line in Buffalo; the murder of two workers and the wounding of hundreds in the lethal onslaught of national guardsmen upon the Auto-Lite strikers in Toledo — the blood of the Negro longshoreman just murdered in Mobile, Alabama is still fresh — these are frightful instances of the rising, bloody fascist suppression of the Negro and white toilers throughout the entire country under the N.R.A. Will you now permit that to this bloody scroll there shall be added the legal lynch massacre of the nine innocent, Scottsboro boys?

It is because these nine, innocent, unemployed Negro boys, who are the victims of the Scottsboro lynch frame-up, symbolize the oppression of the entire Negro people and the exploitation and suppression of all the toiling masses, white as well as black, that this case has assumed national and international proportions of tremendous magnitude and immense social and political significance, calling forth the indignant protest and stern struggle of millions of toilers, middle-class people and outstanding intellectuals all over the world.

The power and duty of the President as chief executive to intervene in such a case, where every constitutional democratic right is violated by state officials, is clear and is established by precedent. The Constitution prescribed for the President the oath, "to preserve, protest and defend the Constitution of the United States." Article Six of the amendments declares: "In all criminal prosecutions, the accused shall have the right to a speedy and public trial by an impartial jury." (Our Emphasis)

The Fourteenth Amendment, written into the Constitution after the Civil War, dealing directly with the rights of Negroes, specifically states: No state shall make or enforce any law which shall abridge the privileges or immunities of citizens of the United States; nor shall any state deprive any person of live (life), liberty or property without due process of law; nor deny to any person within its jurisdiction the equal protection of the laws." The Fifteenth Amendment plainly states: "The right of citizens of the United States to vote shall not be denied or abridged by the United States, or by any state on account of race, color, or previous condition of servitude."

The intervention of President Wilson in the Mooney case is a clear precedent. President Wilson empowered Secretary of Labor, Wm. B. Wilson to appoint J.B. Densmore, Director-General of the U.S. Employment Service, to conduct a thorough investigation into the Mooney frame-up. The report of this investigation, conducted through the installment of a Dictaphone in the office of district attorney Pickert of the state of California is Document No. 157 of the first session of the House of Representatives of the 66th Congress. President Wilson further appointed a Federal Mediation Commission which reported on the Mooney case on January 16, 1918. On January 22, 1918, President Wilson addressed a communication to Governor Stephens of California, urging him "to postpone the execution of the sentence of Mooney."

The reasons for the intervention of President Wilson in the Mooney case are clearly set forth in these documents. The Densmore report stated: "The Netherlands Federation of Labor, the British Trades Union Congress, the General Federation of Labor of Milan, and other similar organizations all over the world had taken official cognizance of the methods used in securing the conviction of Billings and Mooney, and had entered their solemn protests against what they considered a gigantic frame-up on the part of unscrupulous capitalistic interests to discredit the whole cause of union labor. The liberal sentiment of Russia was aroused..."

The Report of the Mediation Commission declared: "However strange or however unexpected it may be, the just disposition of the Mooney case thus effects influence far beyond the confines of California.... But the feeling of disquietude aroused by the lowliest and even the unworthy against false accusations. War is fought with moral as well material resources."

In his communication to Governor Stephens, President Wilson stated the grounds for his action "in these troubled times," and "because the case has assumed international importance." The communication of the U.S. Ambassador to Russia reporting the gigantic protest demonstration of Russian workers before the United States embassy, also shows that it was the realization that the mighty struggle of the working class against the frame-up of Tom Mooney was crippling the prosecution of the imperialist war which compelled President Wilson to stop the hanging of Tom Mooney.

You, Mr. President, have declared a national emergency under which you found the power to intervene in all states to close and re-organize the banks, thus protecting the swollen fortunes of the bankers. You have secured the power to organize a special federal forces to operate in all states to protect the rich and their children against kidnapping.

You have inaugurated the N.R.A. and have found the power to enforce this program in all states, to limit the production of cotton, etc. and to enforce discriminatory differential labor codes in the southern states. But you declare through your secretary to the anguished mothers who came with bleeding hearts to petition for the release of their innocent, tortured boys: "The Scottsboro case is the business of the state of Alabama and not the business of the President."

Can the millions of oppressed Negro people and suppressed white toilers believe that you can do nothing to stop the frightful wholesale legal lynch massacre of the nine innocent Scottsboro boys? Can they hold the impossible idea that you are impotent to enforce the democratic rights plainly written in the U.S. Constitution? Can they imagine in the face of your sweeping powers and action under the N.R.A., etc. that you are powerless to do anything to stop the rapidly increasing production of lynchings, legal lynch massacres, and murderous fascist attacks with which the rich ruling-class exploiters and their governmental agents ruthlessly attempt to crush the Negro and white toilers into starvation and slavery under this very N.R.A.?

In the name of hundreds of thousands of members of our organizations and affiliated bodies, and in the name of millions of toilers and other people in the United States and throughout the world, who support the struggle for the freedom of the nine, innocent Scottsboro boys, we protest vehemently against this statement of yours to the Scottsboro mother. This statement gives direct aid and support to the Alabama ruling-class lynch terrorists in their attempt to burn the Scottsboro boys and also to the fascist suppressors of the Negro people and the entire working-class throughout the whole country, and, indeed, throughout the world.

We protest further against your refusal to receive and to hear the Scottsboro mothers and their entire delegation and against the humiliating and hostile treatment accorded them. We protest also against your similar action toward the delegation of 5,000 Negro and white workers and other people who marched to Washington on May 8 last year with a petition signed by hundreds of thousands, demanding the freedom of the Scottsboro boys and the adoption of the Bill of Civil Rights for Negroes, presented by them for the enforcement of the thirteenth, fourteenth and fifteenth amendments to the Constitution.

Your actions in these and other instances compel us to recall the following statement among the catalog of oppressive acts set forth in the Declaration of Independence as the occasion and the necessity for the revolution of 1776. "In every stage of theses Oppressions, We have Petitioned for Redress in most humble terms. Our repeated Petitions have been answered only by repeated injury."

We demand that you act as chief executive of the United States government to secure the immediate, unconstitutional and safe release of the nine, innocent Scottsboro boys. We demand that you act to enforce all the democratic rights of the Negro people and the working class enumerated in the Constitution. We demand full equal rights, economic, political and social, for Negroes, and the right of self-determination for the Negro people in the Black Belt of the South. We further demand the release of Angelo Herendon, Tom Mooney and all victims of class oppression. We demand that you take steps to stop the lynching and oppression of the Negro people, the murder pf striking workers, and the increasing brutal attacks upon the masses of impoverished and unemployed workers and poor farmers and their organizations.

INTERNATIONAL LABOR DEFENSE
National Secretary
Spokesman of the Scottsboro Mothers
June 21, 1934 Delegation [Reel 4, Box 4, #0495-0504 (folder c38), ILD]

Clarence Norris
Kilby Prison
Montgomery, Ala
8-18-34

To the members of the
American Federation of
Musicians Local 802

Dear Friends it give the greatest of pleasure to try an show my appreciation toward you all for making it possible for me to have an guitar. I was imform throu mine lawyer Mr Brodsky that your all are fighting for local autonomy. I trust that you all will have the greatest success in your struggle. For the last three years a great fight have been going on for my freedom But I have lost my faith in the ones that are putting in every effort of their time to bring about my freedom. I am sure that this worthy cause which you all are struggling to accomplish will end and be a great benefit to all. The Guitar will help me a great deal during these trying days.

So again I thank you all. And many appreciation.

Whishing the A.F.M. No, 802

Much success in the future to come.

Sincerely yours

Clarence Norris [Reel 5, Box 4, #0078 (folder c53), ILD].

Kilby Prison
Montgomery, Alabama
September 14, 1934

Kilby Prison
Montgomery Ala
8–20–34

Mr. Joseph R. Brodsky
Dear Sir,

Your kind and encouraging letter received It found me in fairly good health. But not doing so well under the conditions.

Things are not going so well with us. We have made several requests asking for some one to come down. I would like to see you or some one else on some very interesting business. We are trusting that some one will be down in the near future as early as possible

I saw in the paper where a request was made for a special session. It would please me, greatly if they would call one.

If by any chancing in your work you should see any friends whom have some old True Detective magazines that they have finish reading for them to remember me, and send them down. Detectives are my favorite magazines, But any books or magazines that have good reading will be appreciated. They will help a great deal to pass away the time while waiting on actions.

Attorney Fraenkle sent me some but they were not the exact kind I prefer reading although they were highly appreciated. Will you please excuse me for not writing myself. I don't feel good, not the very best therefore I am getting some one else to write you.

Well, let us hope that the future will bring some favorable. Warmest regards to all.

Confidentially yours,

Haywood Patterson [Reel 5, Box 5, #000232 (folder c54), ILD]

Birmingham, Ala.
Sep 15 1934

My Dearest Mina

Why how are you felling to night Fine I really hope. I am not felling so Well my Self I am unhappy my self but I really hope When this letter come to be your that it will fine you well and in joy the very best of life yes my Dear I received you letter now why I havening rote to you do you no what I told you about correstpond now with me Well I Still felling the same Way about what I told that why I Rote to you See Darling it make me fell very very bad When I Write people and they don't Seems like they don't wish to correstpond with me and you no how I fell about you not writing Back to me now My Dear you Say on your last letter to me that Some times you listen Darling Why not do this if you don't have times in the day times. Now I am not asking you to do to much I hope not But now if you don't have time in the office when you go home at night do you have times to Write me then oh By the Way about my sister I received a letter From her to night she say She will Write you When She have so Dont Worry about that Darling I will Will See to her Writing to you But I am Still thinks that you don't care to correstpond with me that the Way I am telling about it.
Write Soon that if you Correstpond With me
Yours only
Willie Robinson [Reel 5, Box 5, #000653 (folder c59), ILD]

Molina, Ga.
September 18, 1934

International Labor Defense:
  Dear Sir:
  Received the ($10.00) ten dollars.
Thanking you very much.
Inez Norris,
Molina, Ga. [Reel 6, Box 5, #000002 (folder c66), ILD]

Bham, Ala.
Sept. 22nd 1934

Dear Mina

I recd' your letter today and was very glad to hear from you. It found me feeling just fine in health and I hope that these few lines will find O.K. listen mina I answered your last letter and I cant see why you didn't get it I'm awful sorry of it. and I am glad to hear such report about mother. and listen send me mr. Peter Caldwell address her in B'ham. and listen Roy Wright is getting along OK. I'm sorry he wont write you he dont like to write. any way he is OK. Oh well give me best regard to all.
Yours faithfully
Olen Montgomery [Reel 5, Box 4, #0032 (folder c52), ILD]

Editor's Note: Roy Wright was 12 years old when arrested at Paint Rock. He was the younger brother of Andy Wright. When Judge Alfred E. Hawkins sentenced all of the defendants to die in the electric chair on July 10, 1931, Roy Wright was given life imprisonment due to his age. In 1937, Roy Wright and three other defendants were released with all charges against them dropped. In 1938 Roy Wright and three other defendants appeared in Harlem at New York's Apollo Theatre as a "Special Added Attraction." In 1959, Wright stabbed his wife to death and then committed suicide after discovering that she was involved in another relationship.

Bham. Ala.
Sept. 22, 1934

Dear Mina:

Today you kind and welcome letter was received and also the two dollars which I was very glad to receive. and you ask me what was the matter with my eyes. ah know it aint the matter of dark it is something wrong with them. and for one thing they is weak. and they gives me trouble all times and at times I can't read or write at all for them gives me so much trouble. ah Mina I show do enjoy reading your letters only wish that they was longer one.

and if my eyes get any better I am going to try to Write a long letter so that you all can read it to all the Comrade workers for I do want them to know how much I really appreciate them for all they hard fighting that they has did for my freedom and do hope that they will continue until I am a free man which I do believe that they will. oh well I will come to a close hoping to here from you soon.

yours truly

Charlie Weems [Reel 5, Box 5, #000705 (folder c60), ILD]

Birmingham, Ala.
Sep 22, 1934

the very very Dearest and my heart Why I rite you loving letter a few days ago and I was Very Very glad to hear From you now my Dearest your letter Found me not felling so Well I have ben sick several or 3 Days now? But in the means times My Deareste I how you are felling Why don't you tell me on your letters some times how you are Felling So I will no how to address my letters to you and tell you how I be feeling. Why not you do me same Ways Darling 2 now if I and you are going to correstpond Why not let I and you correstpond right my Dearest now. What I means Darling that is tell Me how you are Felling and all So tell me how you are getting along now Darling I no I am not asking you to do t much now is I? But any way Darling I really do hope When this letter come to be yours that it will fine you well and injoying a happy life asI am long to be doing myself Very Soon. Oh Gee Darling you don't know how much I injoy myself correstpond With you 2.

now my Dearest it See now that I cant getting along without yours letters 2. Now P. S. tell me What Will I do without yours letters. Oh by the way my Dearest I am glad you seem to no how I felt when I writing to you and you didn't write back now Darling what other way could I tell but to tell Best 2 But I and you want are forget about that Darling

now Dearest you Say that you Wish you could do some way to make me be happy. I all so Wish So myself for I am Not happy Darling, oh. Gee Dearest Why not tell me something to make me happy I no you can if you care to Darling tell me Something about New York City I have heard So much talk of New York City that why I am long to see New York City I have been to 5 Big City I have stay in Chicago illinois 833 So Jackson Blvd Chicago Ill. And all so to 524 E. mason St. Milwaukee Wis 992 Michigan Av and Los angeles Cal. 689 indiana Ave. Kansas City Mo. 978 Broadway Atlanta GA But still Darling that not like New York City Do Please Write me along sweet letter and tell me something to make me happy Darling. I will Write more next time Darling tell me something about New York City

Your only

Willie Robinson

Write soon Darling [Reel 5, Box 5, #000654 (folder c59), ILD]

Bham. Ala.
Sept. 28, 1934

Dear Mina:

I received your kind and welcome letter today and also the two dollars which I highly appreciate, and in the mean time your letter found me well in health but still having trouble with my eyes and I do hope that I can get something done to them for they burn all the time just like I have got pepar in them and I think that a pear of glasses would help my eyes a lots and I do hope that I will soon get some. and oh gee you ask me what do I do to pass a way my time. oh well I have to read such as a love story books and letters from anyone but of course I don't receive very many letters,

which you can realize that letters give me the greatest of consolation to read them, and you ask me did I ever receive letters from any of the [Branches] of the I.L.D. know I haven't got a letter any of them. but I do wish that I could hear from them. and oh gee you wrote such a nice and lovely long letter to me and gee I enjoyed reading it. And you stated that you want to keep in contact with me, oh well I should say that we both want to keep in contact with each other and other words you will always keep in contact with me that is if you will continued on writing me I am always willing to write you.

So I will close by saying you have best [   ] hoping to hear from you real soon.

yours truly

Charlie Weems [Reel 5, Box 5, #000708 (folder c60), ILD]

Sep. 29 1934

My Dearest Darling

Why tow night I rice your letter and Was very very glad to rece a letter From a Dearest Friend as you are. I am Felling much better now then I was the last times I Writing to you Oh Dearest. I also rece the light you send to me and oh Darling You know Without I tell you that I thank you for it. Now Dearest I really Don't know how to thank you Now darling how are you feeling you really do tell me how you feeling but dearest any ways I really do Hope When you do rece my letter that it will Fine you Well and injoying a Very Happy Sweet life, as I am wish and Hope to Be Doing Very Soon My Self. Oh say Dearest have you rece a letter from my sister she say she have writing to you but no hearing from you She have gone west now to my aunt now My aunt name is Mrs. A.L. Howard, 1017a Washington St. San Francisco, Cal. Oh Darling when you have time write her I know she will be Very Very glad to rece some letters From you. Oh Dearest I all so have one in Atlanta, ga Mrs. L. M. Cox 992 Michigan Ave. N.S. I know they will be very very glad tow correstpond With you. Oh Gee Darling, you know what it seems like to me that I Ben hear life times. Oh By the way dearest I really Be glad when I get out want you Darling oh PS Say yes For me. Now tell me how can I see a happy life in here. it unhappy to me Dearest but any way Darling I am in good hope and also in good spirits. When 1935 come wish to be in New York City My Self. Oh Dearest Want you do Please say yes for me and really means it when you say yes.

PS Don't say anything just to make me feel happy. Oh Gee Dearest I know you Woulding tell me any thing juss tow make me feel very happy. Oh Darling, the next thing I Wish for you to answer What I Be asking you I would so much like for you to answer them right. Do you read my letter or just look at, at them? Why I say so Dearest I ask you something on my letter last week and you diding answer anything I ask you right. Do please From now on read my letter good and answer some of them right. Do that much for me darling, and also I Wish for you to answer my letter write away and Dearest this [Please] just about have taking my help I Stay sicking all the times and I am really suffering unnecessarily in jail Say darling in your next letter to me do Please Send me a book of 3 cent Stamps they are very head For me to get in here I hope some day that I can do some niced thing For you. Oh Gee Mina I think I Will like New York Very Very much they all tell me that are nice City tow Stay in. Oh I guess this Will Be all For this times Oh PS Dearest give my Best Wishes to all that I no. I am hoping to hear From you Very Very Soon

Sincerely yours,
Willie Robinson [Reel, Box 5, #000664 (folder c59), ILD]

Kilby Prison
Montgomery Ala.
10–15–34

Mr. Osmond K. Fraenkle:
Dear Sir:

Your most highly and appreciated letter received. Indeed happy to know that you are taking the case right ahead. It is true that I wrote Mr. Leibowitz telling him that I wanted him for my Attorney. But I only ment under conditions that he cooperate with the I.L.D. He is a fine and able Lawyer and I would like very much for him to be continued connected with my case in the behalf of the I.L.D. If not he is out for as I am concern.

My mind will never lead me to drop this organization. They have did to greater work in this fight to see that I get justice for a crime I am absolutely innocent off. My mother was down to see me Saturday & Monday also Benjamin Davis. They straighted out things and give us advice what to do in the future.

I do ardently hope that every wise stept that be taken will be a stept toward my freedom. I am not loosing my faith and courage but I do hope that this struggle will come to an close in the very near future. I want you and all others who are interested in my case in my behalf to turn a death ear to all gossip conserving Leibowitz and me.

Wishing all much success in the near future.
Very Truly yours
Clarence Norris [Reel 5, Box 4, #000080 (folder c53), ILD]

Birmingham Ala.

Nov. 8 1934

Dearest anna

Why How are You Felling to night? Fine I really do hope I am not Felling So we to night. I am Felling Very Very Blue to night. But any Way anna Dear, I really do Hope When this letter come to be your that it will fine you well an injoying a happy Sweet life as I am hoping tow Be doing Very Soon Be doing Very Soon My self.

Oh anna Dear I rece you letter to night and anna Dear I cont tell you how happy I Was to hear From you. Now listen anna Will you tell Mina that I also rece her letter to and Was Very-Very glad to hear From her. and all so tell Mina I am Very glad to hear her Say that She are Felling Fine. And tell her I say that I Hope She will Stay that way. Now anna Dear PS tell Mina that I Say I Dont think She are doing me right. Now What I mean She Want answer my questions, and tell her When answers my questions right then I Will answer he letter. Gee Why I Ben asking Mina 3 questions For over Seven Weeks She Wont answers them? Why goe ilt not but to thing.

For Mina to Say that yes are know. See anna I Don't like to Write to people When they Wont answer my questions. I just you are the Same Way. Say may I ask you some questions to. Do you go to Dancing are you interested them? Why I ask you I am interested Dancing Show, and parties and Swim and Playing the Piano and Playing the guitar, and Playing tennis. Now anna Dear, I am interested and all these thing I Was ask you. Now I Don't know Way you are interested in What I like. But the thing I Want to no, can you tell me what Dance out? If you dont No, aks Mina. She love to dance. And if no she no the latest Dance out. Now do PS tell me what I ask you. Now anna Dear. I told you that I Would be Glad to exchange Snapshots With you. Now you no snapahots mean more than one thing. I like so much to have a snapshots are you and Mina. But I no that Will be impossible For me to get it. I am not saying that you all Want

Send it, but you no what I mean Don't you anna Dear? You no what it all about Down heur. Now Snapshots mean Pictures But it For more then it For more then one thing, and tell mina She ask me what sort are a questions I what to ask her. Oh well tell her, it not any thing to make her angry with me. And When She tell me What I have ask her and infarmed me to ask her some more questions then I will tell her What Sort are questions I Want her to know. I am not going to Write to Mina until She answer my questions right.

Your only

Willie Robinson [Reel 5, Box 5, #000672 (folder c59), ILD]

November 13, 1934

Willie Robinson
Jefferson County Jail
Birmingham, Ala.

Dear Willie:

I was sure glad to receive your letter of November 8, but sorry to hear that you are feeling blue. I know that you are having a very hard time in jail, suffering for a crime which you did not commit. I wish I could tell you that my life is an easy one, as I am sure you would like to hear, but that is not the case either. On the outside for us people who are working to improve the conditions of the workers, is not a song and dance, but still it is a lot to feel that one is free, and not behind the bars.

I do wish, I could tell you something that would gladden your heart. But I don't know what would. You say Mina didn't answer the questions that you asked her. Well maybe she couldn't, for she is a fine girl and thinks very highly of you.

I will try to answer some of the things you ask me. No — I don't go to dances. I used to go to dances years ago but now I don't. I do go to shows. I see lots of moving pictures. It is very good to sit down and look at things on the screen and imagine things. Of course the things one sees in the movies are not true to life, but they amuse one and keep our minds off some of our very serious troubles.

I don't go to many parties either because I am too busy, but I go to some now and then. I don't play the guitar , but I used to play the piano, but I don't now.

I used to play tennis, but I don't do that now either. I am too busy now to engage in sports. I also swim, but now it is too cold.

I hope that this will tell you a little bit about the things I do, and what I am interested. If you want to know more about myself, you ask me and I will answer you.

I am sending you a snap-shot, but I find that I haven't got one by myself— I seldom take pictures. The one I am sending you is with two other girls and a baby. I've got my arm around the child and I am the first one on the right. I hold a book in my left hand. I have a mark on the side where I am.

Keep up your fine courage,

Your [   ]

Anna Damon

Acting National Secretary [Reel 5, Box 5, #000678 (folder c59), ILD]

5

LETTERS FROM 1935
Black Jurors Wanted

Mrs. Ida Norris (Clarence Norris's mother), often erroneously referred to as "Inez" Norris, is reputed to have strongly influenced her son to select the International Labor Defense as his legal representative. Undoubtedly, by 1934 at least three other mothers were sufficiently satisfied with the ILD's legal strategy to make this choice for themselves. Soon they were making speechs at ILD sponsored rallies around the country in support of the Scottsboro defendants. Accordingly, their first hand experience as African American mothers provided audiences with a poignant perspective on racial conflict and its direct threat to their child's life. For that reason, letters exchanged primarily between mothers and their incarcerated son, or to supportive persons were in essence an assemblage of human emotions that personified lives constrained by a society that attempted to imprison them as captives within their own skin. Needless to say, their deeply felt pain coupled with stubborn pride speaks volumes about the human will to do more than simply survive.

January 23 1935
Mr. William H. Davis,
N.Y. Amsterdam News
New York City

Dear Sir:

I am the mother of Clarence Norris and I am hurt to see what you said about my Boy and the case in your paper last Saturday. Don't you think we mothers and our poor boys have enough to bear without your making it worse for us? Why don't you tell the truth?

You know that the I.L.D. got the Supreme Court to give Clarence and Haywood another hearing, but you try to make out that Mr. Leibowitz get it and he will carry on the fight for my boy before the U.S. Supreme Court. You print a letter to make people believe that Clarence wants Mr. Leibowitz and the American Scottsboro Committee to take his case from the I.L.D.

I can say that Clarence wants for I am his mother and I talked with [him] in the Jail a few weeks ago and I have letters from him. Clarence wants Mr.

Fraenkel, Mr.Pollak, Mr. Brodsky and the I.L.D.to go on with his defense. My boy wants Mr. Leibowitz and the American Scottsboro Committee to stop fighting the I.L.D. and join with them and all our true friends to fight together to get justice and freedom for him and for all the other boys.

I can say that is what Haywood wants and the other boys and all of us mothers now that we all see through the whole thing. We are poor and we never had a chance to get much learning, but we have sense enough to know that it is the fight of the I.L.D. lawyers and united mass protest behind them that saved us up to now. We know this is our only hope.

Now I want you to print this in your paper so the people will know the truth. My son and Haywood would have been burnt on December 7, if Mr. Fraenkel and the I.L.D. hadn't got the stay from the Alabama Supreme court. Mr. Fraenkel and Mr. Pollack filed the papers for the I.L.D. with the U.S. Supreme Court. They really won the new chance for the boys and are carrying on the defense with all right. I ask you from the depths of my suffering heart, please tell the people the truth, so they will know how they can really help to save my boy and the other innocent boys. I ask you and the other leaders of the American Scottsboro Committee, please don't hurt the boys' defense now. Their lives are hanging on a thread, and only a strong, united defense can save them now.

So I ask you all to unite behind the boys' real defense. I want you to turn over the money you all have collected to the I.L.D. so the boys' defense can have the mone(t) it needs now. I ask you and all who really want to help to join the I.L.D. and the Scottsboro-Hernden Action Committee [see editor's note]. Please, everybody, unite now, and help free our poor, innocent boys. Sincerely yours,
Mrs. Ida Norris [Reel 3, Box 3, #000909, 1935, ILD]

Editor's note: In 1934, the Angelo Herndon case turned into a major political trial that pitted workers suffering economic and physical starvation against the economic interest of the State of Georgia. Angelo Herndon was a political labor organizer who became involved in organizing black and white workers to demand economic relief from the City of Atlanta and the State of Georgia. Because of Herndon's strong organizing appeal, he was charged with "attempting to incite to insurrection." In a trial in which he would be sentenced to 18 to 20 years, but would only serve a few months due to the international appeal of the case, Herndon stated to the jury, "You may send me to my death, as far as I know. I expect you to do that any way, so that's beside the point. But no one can deny these facts. The present system under which we are living today is on the verge of collapse. It has developed to its highest point and now it is beginning to shake. For instance, you can take a balloon and blow so much air in it, and when you blow too much it bursts; so with the system we are living under — of course, I don't know if that is insurrection or not!"

April 1: In *Norris* v. *Alabama* the United States Supreme Court finds the exclusion of blacks from jury rolls deprived blacks defendants of the equal rights protection under both the 6th and 14th Amendments. The case is remanded to the lower court. However, Patterson's case is not argued before the Supreme Court due to technicalities in filing dates. It was suggested that his case should be reviewed by the lower courts due to the *Norris v. Alabama* decision.

Birmingham, Ala.
April 6th 1935

To the Students of the Southern District Training School

Dear Comrades:

It affords me the greatest of pleasure to address you these few remarks so as to let you hear from me in regards of your welcome letter of which we just received that found us one and all well and truly hope when these remarks are yours they will find you and all well in every respect.

Now I must say that we are proud indeed that the other two boys got a new trial. Congratulations to all of you for the hard and faithful fight you all are putting to prove our innocence and that we deserve our freedom.

Yours sincerely,
Andy Wright.

Comrades of the Labor Defender and Daily Worker

This is a copy of the letter sent to the Southern District Training School in answer to a wire of congratulations sent to the Scottsboro boys by the school on the recent victory.

The letter sent by the school pledged support to the fight for the freedom of the Scottsboro boys.

Comradely,
Ann Miller [Reel 5, Box 5, #000814 (folder c62), ILD]

July 15th 1935
Mrs. Ida Norris
Molena, Ga.

Dear Mother Norris,

Somehow letter in which you inform us that you returned to Molena is not at hand and I was under the impression that you were at Atlanta. I expected to see you there, However, when I arrived in Atlanta I found that you were not there. This is too bad, because I had your teeth with me and I had planned to make arrangements in Atlanta for a dentist to see that the teeth were properly fitted for you. Now I really don't know what to do.

It is impossible for you to come to New York at this time but if you can arrange to go to Atlanta and stay there a while with Mrs. Powell, or perhaps someone else we would see that the teeth are sent down and we will also send you the cost for getting them fitted.

In so far as getting any dentist is concerned. Try to see Ben Ronin, his address is 313 Wellborn Street, Atlanta, Ga. and he will see someone who will be able to find a dentist for you.

I am enclosing herewith $10.00 from the Prisoners Relief Department. Please write me as soon as possible what arrangements you are able to make Very best wishes from everyone,

ANNA DAMON, Acting National Secretary
International labor Defense
AD:EB
Enc. [Reel 6, Box 5, #000003 (folder c66), ILD]

1928 Cedar St.
Chattanooga
Nov. 18, 1935

Dear Rose,

I received your telegram you send to me yesterday Nov. 17, 1935. Very glad to hear from you, also glad to received the $10 you send to me. Yes I have been keeping up with Mooney and Herndon. I am praying for them to come out of that mass. I received a letter from Anna today and she gave me understanding about the scottsboro boys, now I am please and feeling fine about the case. I am praying and hoping we will win this victory which I believe we are going to get. I will be looking for the dress for Louise Christmas if nothing happen to us. All send love to you. Anna wrote me a very nice letter and it was a very sweet one. Hoping to hear frm you again. I thank you a lot for the $10 for Claude isn't working now.
Sincerely
Jannie Patterson [Reel 6, Box 5, #000096 (folder c67), ILD]

1928 Cedar St.
Chattanooga
Nov. 25 1935

Dear Comrade Anna,

I received your letter today very to hear from you. Yes I understand every thing about the case and the joint organizations that are helping in the case. I am glad that Haywood is in excellent health and in good mental spirit. I am glad that you all are working, I read in the paper when the boys trails are going to be. Yes I will be glad to go sown to see Haywood any thing. Haywood wrote me after Claude come home from down to see him, how he enjoyed seeing him. Give all my love there in the office, also the other Comrades.
Sincerely
Jannie Patterson [Reel 6, Box 5, #000099 (folder c67), ILD]

December: Due to the prevailing sentiments in Alabama, both Attorney Leibowitz and the ILD are considered by many to be liabilities to the defendants and the defense is reorganized. The Scottsboro Defense Committee is formed with Allan Knight Chalmers as Chairman. Clarence Watts is named local co-counsel.

1928 Cedar St.
Chattanooga
Dec. 24, 1935
Dear Rose,

We received the box last night very glad to received it sure do thank you for the dresses you send to me, I am crazy about the skirt you send to me, it is my fit. I like guess any way it is very pretty. I thank you for every thing you send to me. Every thing you send fit me, I sure do thank for the dresses you send. We hope you a merry Christmas. We recieved a letter from Haywood yesterday. I was very glad to hear from him. We all thank you for the box. Yes and the rain coat I thank you for it.
Sincerely
Louise Patterson [Reel 6, Box 5, #000102 (folder c67), ILD]

6

LETTERS FROM 1936
Psychology of Oppression

Though the previous five years of incarceration for the Scottsboro defendants were underscored by psychological threats, physical beatings, restrictions to dungeon-like cells, little or no exercise, improper food, the "hole" and their close proximity to the prison's electric chair (which allowed them to hear the screams, crying and pleas of condemned men being executed), there is also evidence of individual and collective resistance on their part. One senses that while the defendants were continually abused behind the walls of Birmingham's City Jail and Montgomery's Kilby Prison, their individual and different personalities became steeled to the unforeseen challenges that they faced.

This is apparent in the tone of letters from Norris, Patterson, Weems and Andy Wright that follow, as they lay bare their frustrations, innocence and visions of being freed one day, while contending with the prospect of being sentenced to life in prison or to death. Not surprisingly, their actions and defiance propelled the guards and prison administrators to take great pains in trying to rationalize the "uniqueness" of these incarcerated black defendants.

Alabama's judicial system and their prison officials found their answers in a social analysis construct premised on racism and an extreme trepidation about Northerners, Communists and Jews as a threat to southern American traditions and culture.

> **January 23: Haywood Patterson is found guilty and sentenced to 75 years in prison. The decision suggests that there was disagreement among the jury as to Patterson's guilt.**

Atlanta Ga.
Jan. 1–2/36
   Dear anna just a line er to as I am riten for mr Narris to let you no that I got my Box OK thank for it But all the thing was to small for me mas [Christmas] I was looking for a coat that I could wear. Now why the ice is on,

the gown brown one is Big Enuff for me But it to light for now But I like it
fine well that all for this time I will rite you a gain soon
  From Viola [Reel 5, Box 5, #001018 (folder c65), ILD]

January 15, 1936
Mrs. Viola Montgomery
61 Rawson Street, South East,
Atlanta, Ga.

Dear Mrs. Montgomery:
  I was very pleased to receive your letter of January 1st and to learn that you
have received the package O.K. I am really very sorry that the coat did not fit
you. We tried our very best to pick out the most suitable coat for you. There
is no large coat available now, and so we cannot send ou one. I am glad at
least that the brown one fits, and if you wear nice warm clothing underneath,
I think you will be able to keep yourself warm.
  Enclosed heresidth you will find $10 for the month.
  By this time you have received a letter signed by all the organizattions in
the Scottsboro Defense Committee. The committee is doing all that it can,
and you can be sure that everything that is being done, is in the best interest
of the boys. We, of course, are very active on this committee, and everybody
is working very hard. The trial will start on Monday, and as we understand,
Haywood Patttterson is to be brought up first.
  Let us hear from you soon, and keep us informed on how things are with
you.
Very best greetings,
ROSE BARON [Reel 5, Box 5, #001019 (folder c65), ILD]

> **January 24: While being transported back from court to the Birm-
> ingham Jail, Ozie Powell gets into a verbal disagreement and then
> a physical altercation with Deputy Sheriff Edgar Blalock that ends
> with Blalock's throat being cut by Powell. Sheriff Jay Sandlin stops
> the car and shoots Powell in the head. Both Powell and Blalock
> survive the altercation and receive medical attention in a Birm-
> ingham hospital.**

February 3, 1936
Atlanta, Georgia

*Mrs. Josephine Powell's account of her visit with Ozie Powell (in a Birmingham
Hospital)*

I went to Birmingham with James Thomas in his car. With us were Ozie's sister, Charlie Ray; his brother, James; his sisters "baby," Ruby Ray; and his girl
friend Emma Loy Rucker.
  "They wouldn't let anybody go to the hospital but me and the Sheriff didn't
want me to go but he let me go after I made him know I was Ozie's mother. I
showed him a furniture receipt (to identify myself).

"Two deputy sheriffs took me to the hospital in their car. One of the deputies said there were two things he wanted me to do. One was not to 'break down' and the other was that he wanted me to question Ozie concerning where he got those knives from. [Note: there seem to be three knives now.]

"When we got to the door of the room, a nurse (Negro) said 'Is that your son in there' — I shook my head — just then a deputy stepped up and told me not to talk with any of the nurses.

"The sheriff (probably deputy) went in and asked Ozie how he was feeling — Ozie said 'very well' — in a feeble voice.

"Then he let me go in."

"He was lying there like asleep — most likely doped up sclf.

"The deputy said, "here's your mother."

"Ozie jumped up and then fell back and started crying.

"I said, 'Hey boy,' he said, 'Hey Momma'

"'How you feeling' 'Very well'

"'Anything hurt you' 'Not now'

"'How long were you unconscious,' he said, 'I haven't never been unconscious,' he said, 'I haven't never been unconscious, only when I was asleep.'

"Then I sort of started away and looks around and the room was most full of deputies.

"Then I asked him, 'Why did this, thing just now come up when they been transporting you from jail to jail and from town to town.'

"He said, 'Well Momma, I don't feel that there's no need for me to express any further cause. I done give up.'

"I asked him what he give up for and he said, 'cause I feel like everybody in Alabama is down on me and is mad with me.'

"What they mad with you for"

"Because I done what I did"

"I asked him what had he did"

He said, "Well — I wont talk any more about it."

"I said, 'you have told everybody else, why don't you tell your Mother?'

He said, "Momma, aint but one thing I want to tell you right now. Don't let Sam Leibowitz have anything else to do with my case."

He said "Will you write to that effect."

"I told him I will.

One of the sheriffs broke in and said,

"It's not left up to your mother, you're supposed to have any lawyer you want."

"One of the sheriffs bent over the bed and said, 'Now Ozie, tell your mother the truth. Who gave you this knife?'

"First Ozie said, 'I don't know now.'

"The Sheriff said, 'Here's your mother, now — wont you tell her the truth about the knives?'

"Ozie said, 'I think it was a boy named Ernest that gave me the knife.'"

"While I was talking to Ozie there were about 20 deputies in the room and all out in the hall. They all had guns and black-jacks and I didn't know what they was going to do to me. I was scared hey was going to shoot me down.

"Then we left and went back to the courthouse where James was. The sheriff and James started talking and I walked off.

"The sheriff called me back & said 'Nothing to hurt you Auntie, this is just a news man' (another man, a reporter joined the sheriff).

"The sheriff and the news man were standing there. The news man asked me some questions about who I was and where from and then he asked, 'your boy wants another lawyer, don't he?'

"Yes, he asked for one." I said.

He asked was I going to get him a lawyer. I said, "I'm going to try to, when I see further."

Parenthesis mine [JSG].

Joseph S. Geldeis [Reel 15, Note 70, Part 6, #0843, NAACP]

Atlanta, Georgia
February 3, 1936

Mr. Morris Shapiro
320 Broadway
New York City
Dear Morris,

I just had a long talk with Mrs. Josephine Powell. I am enclosing, herewith her statement as nearly as I could get it down and partially organized.

She seems to realize now, that the officers were using her as a tool (partially against her will, partially without her knowledge) in their effort to break the solid defense. She kept saying, as we discussed the matter "I looked around and the room was full of sheriffs" or "I just give up. I haven't got the strength to fight" or "I was scared. I didn't know what they was going to do to me," which indicates that she pressed her questions on Ozie unwillingly and under duress.

She is now anxious to continue with the Scottsboro Defense Committee and Liebowitz & Watts. But she is an exceptionally weak, emotional and vacillating person.

She was anxious to go back to see Ozie again this week, possibly Wednesday or Thursday. I urge her not to do this but to wait and come to Birmingham on February 12 which she agreed to do. In the meanwhile I think it <u>very important</u> for Ben Davis to come to Atlanta and see Mrs. Powell. She has complete confidence in him and I think he can restore her hope and will to fight. If so, she can have a good influence in rallying Ozie when she does see him. I think the next visit should be in the presence of Watts, who can, in some measure, protect her and Ozie from the pressure of the armed guards.

Everything points to the fact that enormous and brutal pressure has been exerted on that poor boy and that under this constant bombardment he has lost courage.

I'm going to get to the Negro nurses in the hospital in Birmingham while there. They will have a story to tell or I'm no judge.

Please show this to Anna — and make proper financial arrangements for Mrs. Powell to get to B'ham on the 12th if you so decide.

Sincerely,
Joseph S. Geldeis [Reel 15, No. 71, #0840, Part 6, NAACP]

1928 Cedar St.
Chattanooga
7/17/36
Dear Rose,

I recieved your letter today very glad too hear from you, I also thank you for the $10. Which you send too me for this month. I am glad that your received a letter from Andy Wright. But I dont wont you all too put Haywood with those other boys because, when ever Haywood are with those other boys it is always something going on wrong, for my sake dont put Haywood with those owher boys, I don't wont him with the other boys and Haywood wouldnt like too be with them, for everything happens they say Haywood does it and I dont wont no trouble about haywood being with them other boys, now answer and let me know about Haywood not being with those other boys dont put him with those other boys. Yes we have being have hot weather but now it is very cool an clouday we had rain three days straight, it isnt raining now but it is cool. Thanks for the money and dont move Haywood with those other boys. I owe you all three dollars for books but I been in such a tight until I senpt the money for my Husband get sick I couldnt work but if I live and nothing havent too me I will make it good. When we get straighten out good in our bills I will send you all those three dollars. I don't wont you all too think I am trying to beat you all out of it, for I try too be straight and square with the world.
Sincerely,
Jannie Patterson [Reel 6, Box 5, #000105 (folder c67), ILD]

B'ham, Ala.
Jefferson County Jail
July 18th 1936
Listen Anna,*

this is a matter of business no fun. Now listen you realize how long I have been cut off from pleasure don't you? And you realize it hard on me don't you? especially me a young man. And you or any one else should have sympathy and feeling for me. now listen please dont get offended over what I am fixing to say in your Present. I cant help it Anna. I am almost crazy in this place. This is what I want to say it's a new warden on here at night. and he will let me to a woman for all night for $5.00 which it is worth it. I know its worth $5.00 of mine because if I don't get to a woman it will soon run Poor me crazy. I really have stood it long as I can. I just got to get to one. I have been in jail over five years. And it's a shame. Now Anna Please send me $5.00 and take yours out of my eight. Now Please send it rite away. I am looking for it Friday. And I will appreciate that to the very highest. Now since I have explain the situation to you. I am sure you will feel my sympathy, wont you? sure you will! I am looking for it Friday with out a fail. Please give my regard to all.

Yours very truly.

Olen Montgomery

Please answer soon

Anna Damon was Acting National Secretary for the ILD in 1936.

[Reel 5, Box 4, #0042, ILD]

July 21, 1936

Mrs. Janie Patterson

1928 Cedar St.

Chattanooga, Tenn.

Dear Mrs. Patterson:

We received your letter of July 17 and was glad to hear that you and your family are well.

You don't have to fear about Haywood being together with the other boys. If he does not want to, nobody will compel him to do so. We are trying hard to do everything that is good for the boys. We want to get them out of the solitary confinement cells and we thought they were anxious to be together. But is Haywood does not want to be with them, we will not have them together. Don't worry.

Best regards from all our comrades here.

Fraternally,

ROSE BARON

Secretary [Reel 6, Box 5, #000109 (folder c67), ILD]

Haywood Patterson

County Jail

Birmingham, Ala.

August 22, 1936

My Dear Anna Damon I have just received you letter which was dated August the 10th 1936 and am taking the pleasure writing you once again. I am ashamed for this long silence But the truth is that I have felt so unhappy and Horribly Disappointed and resentful over the outcome of my last trial and the way the case are now Being conducted. Altho I am most certainly that you have felt in my silence too. Now I wrote you a letter some time ago telling you in particularly about How you your self Had taken to done But you shunned me for a while. I though nothing of it though and I need not to Have worried for my long silence and delay on I realize that it came about larglly on account of your conduct. Now I want spare myself the trouble to comment an I fell that you are not the one to blame. I cant believe you have done such things that have been told to me and I think I am going to like you more better now But you must behave of your self and not to bother me too much by telling people untrue things.

Now I Have received some clippings which friend sent to me which a reporter pressed. You see I do try to give every man an fair deal as He give me therefore I do not wish to hurt his pride an He have tried to hurt me. He was a negro reporter him self and a woman companion came Down to see we boys and they Distrubed me the minute I saw them Because I was in bed taking a rest from what He tells me in five minutes why I was forced to the conclusions that every word He spoken was spoken against me. And from the clipping I have the reporter talked too much and most everything He said was absolutely false. I did show him a letter from Mr. Leibowitz and why I did it because He Had said something which I didnt like. now I am going to expect to Hear from your during next week also please send me some postage Stamps for they are not Handy to get Here. Please write and let me know something about my case.

Hopefully yours Haywood Patterson [Reel 5, Box 5, #000236 (folder c54), ILD]

1928 Cedar St.
Chatta. Tenn.
Sept. 11, 1936

Dear Rose:

We wrote you all some time ago about Haywood trial and you all wasn't interested emough about it to answer it. I wont to go down to see Haywood and I am asking you to scnt me my railroad fair too go down to see him. If I was working more than two or three days a week I wouldnt ask you for my fair down to see Haywood. Will you please send me my fair down to see haywood. You all are acting mighty funny about the trial, I ask about Haywood trial.

Sincerely
Claude Patterson [Reel 6, Box 5, #000113 (folder c67), ILD]

September 14, 1936
Mr. Claude Patterson
1928 Cedar Street,
Chattanooga, Tenn.

Dear Mr. Patterson:

The appeal in Haywood's case has been filed with the Supreme Court of Alabama by Mr. Frankel and Mr. Watts, and it will come up in January, at Montgomery. There is no way in which we can make it come up sooner.

We agree with you that you should go down to see Haywood, and we have recommended to the Scottsboro Defense Committee, which controls all the finances in the case, that they send you the fare to go to Montgomery to see him.

Very sincerely
ANNA DAMON [Reel 6, Box 5, #000111 (folder c67), ILD]

B'ham, Ala.
Sept. 20th 1936

   Anna what is the matter with you? I need pair of shoes real bad and I have written and ask you just as nice as I could to send me a pair I am not going to take the money that you sends me and Buy any thing else to wear because its all I can do to keep up in smokes and other little things that I need and you know it. I cant eat the most of this food here and some time I buys something that I can eat. you all think you are smart. Rose Baron wrote and told my mother that she had a letter from me last week and I was getting along fine. I aint wrote that woman in three months and she know it. I am not getting along fine I am not doing any good at all. You all got sense enough to know I am tired of being in jail. And you could have done got me out too I do believe. the longer I stay in jail is the richer you get. and better you feel But yet we are staying trying to keep faith. And you all wont do a dam thing to encourage us you wont do a thing we ask. you know I am not able to Buy no shoes and clothes. But yet you will sit up there like something dumb want even answer my letters. look like you would let me know something so I could make other arrangement and get me some shoes. whats the matter with you any how woman you aint never did me this way before! let me know what you going to do so I can make other arrangement
Yours truly
Olen M. [Reel 5, Box 4, #0046 (folder c52), ILD]

Haywood Patterson
County Jail
B'Ham. Ala
September 21, 1936

   My miss Damon I have gotten your and the contents. and Have finally decided to write you although I have written you. and I just do not understand why you never mention anything about these letters I am most certainly. You Have gotten these letters Because they are being mailed out to you. anyway, I Have delayed in Writing you for a long time, and I ceased for some reasons or other. now I understand that the workers Have greatly Increased I know it is so of a truth the innumberable substance of friends whom Have pledge to give support all too well I know. and what more you say that are for always ask about me and the boys and desires to know how I am getting along. well it is Hard to describe my feeling and therefore it is rather Hard to tell just How I am getting on Because I haven't felt Happy even a day since I left my Home. there is no Happiness nor pleasure to be seen Here and never will be for the days Have seemed very very long and tediously which makes it seems very dark for one. and make one feel very sorry for him self. and the wearisome nights is all made up with nightmares and restless moments why I am full of tossing to and fro into the better of each Day before I can be able to get much sleep.

So you see it is very hard indeed. none the less I try to take whatever hardness there is with a smile. And determinedly, I have kept on looking and trusting that something favorable will soon turn outright in my favor. of course I am overconfident that all good things will soon comes unto me. But I hope sincerely it will be in the shortest possible time, because shut a way from the outside world for so awfully long — the longest for no just cause, is a life of unbearable misery to one to come to think of it. I tell you that it is very Hurtfully and most dreadful and Discouraging to one. of course I am going on trying to make the very Best of it and also try to make myself know and see the Bright side and be wholly at ease and keep quiet. now I can Have nothing whatever to say right now except I am wishing you well and everything. I notice you do not enclose me postage Stamps anymore. Kindest regards and Best wishes to you. and in your spare time write me.

Commardely Haywood Patterson [Reel 5, Box 5, #000239 (folder c54), ILD]

September 30, 1936
Olen Montgomery
Jefferson County Jail
Birmingham, Ala.

Dear Olen;

We are enclosing $8.00 for the month. I hope you are well. I expect an answer about the shoes real soon.
Very best greetings,
Anna Damon
Acting National Secretary
AD:rm [Reel 5, Box 4, #000051, ILD]

Bham, Ala.

Oct. 2 1936
Dear Anna!

I received your letter and was indeed glad to hear from you. these few lines leaves me not feeling so well but I truly hope when thee few lines reaches you they will find you enjoying the best of health. I recollect explaining you why I don't write you is because you shows such little interest in my letters, you always as usually Ignores my letters matters what I write about so I figure from that you wasnt interested in nothing I say because I have tried every way I possibly no how to interest you in my letters but it seems that I am a failure so I decide to give up trying but it actually hurted me to the depths of my heart and I would appreciate knowing just why your so rude to me? now I know you're wondering why I asked you such question. Well I could explain the whole situation just how it stand though you may not be interested so

therefore I decline to do so at the present. many — many Thanks for the money. appreciates it to the highest. give my best regards to all.
I Remain
Yours Most Sincerely
Andy Wright [Reel 5, Box 5, #000818 (folder c62), ILD]

Cleveland Ohio
Oct 2, 1936

Dear Mrs Baron your letter was received and read found me well so far. I needs Dresses, bloomers, Siks and also sweater. also if you have any underwear for men please send me 2 suits and a nice suit of cloth for my husband, also sox.

I have received a letter also from Clarence and he said it was getting cold down there he ask me to send him 5 dollars, but at present I did not have it to send I will also be very glad if you all could send my check a little early every month. I had a letter from Ines and the children and they were all getting along alright. Give all the Comrades my best regards hoping to here from you Again soon.
From ida Norris
7021 Kinsman Rd.
Cleveland Ohio
P.S. also my husband needs an overcoat and I am in need of bed covering bad so if you have any blankets send me some.
[Reel 6, Box 5, #000006 (folder c53), ILD]

October 7, 1936
Eugene Williams
Jefferson County Jail
Birmingham, Alabama

Dear Eugene:

How are you? You know I have no way of telling how you are because you don't write. You also know that I am very anxious to hear from you.

I hope that you are in good spirits. I realize Eugene, that these are times when it is very hard to keep your chin up, but at these times, you must remember that your tens of thousands of friends are working, day and night to free you and all the boys. They are working to make new friends for you, and all the world over there are people who go about their daily work with the thought: The Scottsboro Boys Must Be Freed! I am sure the thought of this will make you feel you are not alone.

I am enclosing $8.00 for the month. I hope that you will write soon.
My very best greetings to you,
Anna Damon
Acting National Secretary [Reel 5, Box 5, #000796, 1936, ILD]

October 7, 1936
Roy Wright
Birmingham, Ala.

Dear Roy:

How are you? You know I have no way of telling how you are because you don't write. You also know that I am very anxious to hear from you.

I hope you are in good spirits. I realize, Ray, that there are times when it is very hard to keep your chin up, but at these times, you must remember that your tens of thousands of friends are working, day and night to free you and all the boys. They are working to make new friends for you, and all the world over there are people who go about their daily work with the thought The Scottsboro Boys must be Freed! I am very sure the thought of this will make you feel you are not alone.

I am enclosing $8.00 for the month. I hope that you will write soon.

My very best greetings to you,

ANNA DAMON
Acting National Secretary [Reel 5, Box 5, #000970 (folder c64), ILD]

B'ham, Ala.
Oct. 12 — 1936

Dear Anna,

I recd my shoes and I like them But they are not friendly Fives how much did you pay for them?

Anna when is my trial coming up? I want to know please see can you find out and tell me.

yours very truly

Olen Montgomery [Reel 5, Box 4, #000058 (folder c52), ILD].

October 14, 1936
Haywood Patterson
Jefferson County Jail
Birmingham, Ala

Dear Haywood:

I was so glad to receive your letter of September 21 and to find that you are not going to let yourself become sad and depressed. Your attitude is a very intelligent one and will do a great deal to preserve your health and resistance.

I shall look forward to your letters and hope you will write again very soon. I am enclosing $8.00 for the month and some postage stamps.

My best greetings to you

Anna Damon
Acting National Secretary [Reel 5, Box 5, #000243 (folder c54), ILD]

2709 E. 51st St.
Cleveland Ohio

Mrs. Anna Damon
80 East 11th St.
New York City

Dear Mrs. Damon: [Ed. note: Letter written early October, 1936]

I want Herein to To express my Heart Felt Gratitude to you and The I.L.D. For your letters of Consideration to me From you on the 26 inst. And I Can not Explain How Happy it made me and it Certainly filled my heart with much joy and hope and my Heart full of gratitude and Hope. And to Cinderely Thank the I.L.D. and the Peohle at large for their support in such a noble Cause in Defense of our people. To all (Concerned) they have given me much hope in My Plight and Bereavement for my Boy and all the others Boys that have Suffered in the Scottsboro Case. And again thank you kindly
Cincerly yours
Ida Norris
2709 E. 51st.
Cleveland Ohio
PS I will Thank you For other Names of The Boys that's Freed, By Return mail.
[Reel 6, Box 5, #000008 (folder c53), ILD]

October 15, 1936
Mrs. Ida Norris
Cleveland, O.

Dear Mrs. Norris,

We received your letter and were very glad to hear from you. We will try to send you the things you ask for as soon as possible. We are expecting some clothing in quite soon, and will make up your bundle immediately it gets in. We are sure that we will be able to send you most of the things you ask for, but as you know, it is very hard to get men's clothes. Right now we have no men's clothing in the office at all. However, if we do get some in, we will gladly send you some. Meanwhile please ssend us your husband's size suit, shoes, and so on.

I am very glad that your family is well and that you are getting along rather nicely. Enclosed you will find $10.00 for the month. Let us hear from you soon.

Fraternally,
ROSE BARON
Secretary [Reel 6, Box 5, #000009 (folder c66), ILD]

October 18, 1936
Olen Montgomery,

Jefferson County Jail,
Birmingham, Ala.

Dear Olen:

I am glad to hear that you like the shoes. They were brought at a Friendly five shoe store, but they were a special shoe and I suppose that is why there was no name engraved anywhere on them. I hope that they are comfortable. The cost was $4.08.

According to information received here the trials are scheduled for November 2, but I don't know which of the boys are going to be tried first. As soon as there is anymore information you may be sure that I will let you know at once.

I hope you are feeling well and are in good spirits.

Very best greetings

Anna Damon

Acting National Secretary [Reel 5, Box 4, #000057 (folder c52), ILD]

Haywood Patterson
County Jail
Birmingham. Ala.
October 19- 1936

Dear Miss Damon, I was So thankful on receiving you very short note and the contents of course I am always very grateful on getin your most needful letters and thank you fro your great Kindness and courtesy to me. How very nice of you and How very glad am I to see that you yet like and enjoying having my letters a great deal and I assure you that Hereafter I shell press forth my uttermost and try an I might an make my letters more amusingly an interestedly like, an I might an make my letters more amusingly an interestedly like an I use to do when once I were being Held incarcerated at Kilby Prison the Horrible place you know! And you seemed to Have liked my letters there too of course I can hardly ever say anything which will be of great encouragement to anyone especially to the unaccountable friends whom Have did Marvelous wonderful-Splendid work in my befalf and whom Have been wonderful-splendid work in my behalf and whom Have been wonderfully kind and generous and considerate of me and the Boys and I am most certain in my own mind that the workers are forever doing something great for we boys even if we dont know about it

But myself are always confident that the workers are continually a pledging their support and giving of their best assistance purposely for the freedom of the nine innocent Scottsboro boys and I supposes you no doubt know that yet I am Having the selfsame perfect faith in the workers and admire them tremendously as I usual do, and again I suppose you know that I havent lost my good courage and Hope for liberty. We Havent done it yet and I doubt if we ever do.

I think of you workers daily with the kindest thought and pray for the great success especially the success to Earl Browder and James W. Ford. I wish they shell Be greatly successful for the successful of these men will better for me and others poor and needy ones. I imagine by now you Have gotten a letter from my baby Sister Louise telling you about the merciless unjust which were done like unto Her with-out the least cause. You see I have a letter from Her and she says that she have written you, see it too terribly bad and I feel my sorry for my Sister at least more sorry than I have felt for myself, and it I absolutely too miserable that she Had to make a trip way from Chattanooga very happy on her way, But were made sad and horribly disappointed I dont know why such extreme misfortune Had to happened But It happened and she wasnt allowed to see me. I was wistful expecting Her, but I were badly grieved and disappointed please Anna for my sake always make better arrangement when ever anyone of my family should come to visit me. please Have Lawyer Powell or some other good Christain white person to Bring them out to see me so that they can be respected for they are Human being as I am sure my Sister have wrote you about the indecent comments which was expressed before Her. She tells me that she Have never been hurted by a person Before in Her life not until she came in alabama to try to get to see me. It is bad and Hereafter I want you to please arrange so or for Lawyer Powell or some other good Christian white person of Birmingham Here to Bring them out when they should come to see me again.

Now I can Have nothing more to say except am hoping you will be able to read this letter. My best regards and wishes to everyone especially for you.

Comradely

Haywood Patterson [Reel 5, Box 5, #000245 (folder c54), ILD]

October 21 1936

Ozie Powell,
Jefferson County Jail,
Birmingham, Ala.

Dear Ozie:

How are you feeling? I am beginning to get worried about you since you don't write.

I am enclosing $8.00 for the month. Will you write soon?

Very best greetings.

Anna Damon

Acting National Secretary [Reel 5, Box 5, #000600 (folder c60), ILD]

October 28, 1936
Ozie Powell,
Jefferson County Jail,
Birmingham, Ala.

Dear Ozie:

We have just had news that your trial is to be postponed for at least a month because the Judge is very sick. Just when it will take place we do not know as yet, but we will write you as soon as we get further information.

Meanwhile I am sure you are going to be as brave and in as good spirits as you have been up until now.

I hope that this letter will find you in good health.

Very best greetings.

Anna Damon

Acting National Secretary [Reel 5, Box 5, #00091 (folder c58), ILD]

October 28, 1936

Olen Montgomery,

Jefferson County Jail,

Birmingham, Alabama

Dear Olen:

We have just had the news that your trial is to be postponed for at least a month, because the Judge is very sick. Just when it will take place, we do not know as yet, but we will write to you as soon as we get further information.

Meanwhile I am sure you are going to be as brave and in as good spirits as you have been until now.

I am enclosing $4.00 for the month, since your shoes cost $4.00. I hope that this letter finds you in good health.

Very best greetings.

Anna Damon

Acting National Secretary [Reel 5, Box 4, #000059 (folder c52), ILD]

* * *

After five years of incarceration, convictions, death sentences, beatings by guards, solitary confinement, physical and psychological torture and more, passionate resistance can and in the case of the Scottsboro defendants was often turned destructively inward. Abnormalities outside the walls of a stockade or prison become norms within and with fierce consequences for the weak. Friends and associates become competitors, prisoners long for life on the outside, guards view their occupation as tormenting confinement, and within this violent milieu all compete for control and dominance.

The Scottsboro Boys, now five years in confinement, were no longer "boys," in age or experience. Power conflicts and notions of territoriality within the confines of prison cells presented opportunities for violence, something that became omnipresent and ubiquitous.

Haywood Patterson

Jefferson County Jail

Birmingham, Ala

October 28–1936

Dear Miss. Damon, I suppose you will perhaps feel a little surprised on receiving these few words, but its most important that I should write you at this time. first I want to tell you about my being informed of your present being there in Seattle Washington a few by-gone days and How very wonderful of you to Have made a nice comment an you did. and you also made mention of me and the Boys in your comment. I do so appreciate all the splendid wonderful work you Have done in my behalf. I can never forget it. wish that I had more schooling so that I could show you how greatful I am.

now anna I want to tell you about How things in going on and How some of the Boys are doing or rather If in only Roy Wright and Charlie Weems, an of course to tell the truth. I have try in every way there Is open to me to get along with Roy Wright especially when I am in his present but that Have seemingly an impossible thing to do and for some reason or other they Have put him in confinement near me in my company and I regret it terribly because He is a most Disagreeable boy. Honestly Roy Wright is an unreasonable foolish sort of Boy. I never knew he wan such a fellow. Why He is In human and very unkind you see Roy Have abuse me terribly on many occasions, and are yet abusing me for no reason or cause that I can figure out simply Because I never bother him and Have less to say to him at any time or any where. I always Have none or less to say to him and I fail to see why must He abuse me and He is a piecebraker among the boys and myself. you see He always set their Hearts against me by saying things concerning me. I am going to show you Here How miserable and unjustly He Have did unto me. Of course I do not feel against him and do not wish to harm him unless He tryest to Harm me. you see I can not afford to allow him to ingure me anymore like an you can recall or remember once about 3 years ago him and his Brother andy Wright over power me and cut and beat me terrible you see the Doctor Had to use six stitches on the cut and every since then He Have Had a extreme dislike and a perfect pick on me you see.

Just last month He taken seven dollars a way from which you all Had sent me an a monthly allowance saying that He Hate to see me with anything. Well I let him go with it Because I dont wish to fight so I didn't resist. and about Charlie, He Have also taken money from me which you all sent on 2 occasions say that I had been unfair, Says that Leibowitz and him associates John Terry Had told them that I had been unfair and so on.

Now you need not to suggest even a words to them concerining this because they are angry at you all and I mean they stays Half angry always they Do say things about you and so to Do me a favor just Write to their people and Have them and advice them to keep a way from me Because I do not wish to be fighting anyone. Also I hope you will see that Mr. Powell come to see me you know I dont ever want to be In Roy Wright present He thinks himself something when He isnt nothing. He thinks Himself better than anybody and He will mistreat others, and I dont care to Be around him. I told you that When you were down to visit us on both occasions.

I must come to a close by begging you to please find time to answer this letter and send me a few postage stamps.

I am very hopefully yours,
Haywood Patterson [Reel 5, Box 5, #000215 (folder c54), ILD]

October 28, 1936

Andy Wright,
Jefferson County Jail
Birmingham, Alabama

Dear Andy:

I have your letter of October 2 at hand. I am so sorry that you feel that I have ignored your letters. You know I am so anxious to get them and really sorry when I don't hear from you. I am always so busy that it is possible that I overlooked something very important in your letter. I hope you will forgive me and write real often now.

I have just had news that your trial is to be postponed for at least a month, because the Judge is very sick. Just when it will take place, we don't know as yet, but we will write to you as soon as a we get further information.

I am enclosing $8.00 for the month. Hoping that this letter finds you well, and in good spirits. I remain,

> Very sincerely,
> ANNA DAMON Acting National Secretary

[Reel 5, Box 5, #000816 (folder c62), ILD]

October 28, 1936

Charlie Weems,
Jefferson County Jail
Birmingham, Ala.

Dear Charlie:

We have just had news that your trial is to be postponed for at least a month because the judge is very sick. Just when it will take place, we do not know as yet, but we will write to you as soon as we get further information.

Meanwhile I am sure you are going to be as brave and in as good spirits as you have been up until now.

I hope that this letter will find you in good health.

Very best greetings,
Anna Damon
Acting National Secretary [Reel 5, Box 5, #000717, ILD]

Haywood Patterson
Jefferson County Jail
Birmingham Alabama
October 30–1936

Dear Miss Damon I cant begin to Describe my feeling of How glad I was on getin your joyful words to-day. I can say that your letter certainly did brought some comfort and joy and gladness to me and thank you a great deal for giving me some information concerning the coming tirals of the other Boys. and thank you some more for giving me a little definite information especially concerning when my case will develop again a second time. that's awfully kind of you to tell me. you see I have to depend solely upon the local newspapers to obtain any Information concerning the case affairs in particularly. I say again it was wonderfully kind of you. an of course you have for always been heavenly good and considerate. Constant you have and I going to expect you send me some good candy for christamas time like an you always have done. You know last christamas you set me good candy but myself alone didnt eat it all. you see I was having a most beautiful girl friend at that time so I shared with her. I gave her half and myself half and after we had complete eating all the good candy we both wished for more anyway, you must know I will have a birthday on the 12th day of December. I wonder Do people gets presents on their birthdays? Why I suggest this is because I Have see almost six birthdays and no presents. you know miss Damon I thought of you daily after Having a letter from some of my Dearest friends of Seattle Washington whom impart to me of your present being there in Seattle douring that time so I-Decided that I should write you an it was important that I should tell you the things which Have been stated in that letter which I had mailed out to-day, just before. Receiving yours I mailed it out in morning and in the afternoon time I received yours.

I Hope you are going to understand all things you see I was so excited I Hardly knew what I was doing in according to writing concern. but fortunately I Hope you will by some meaning comprehend the fact of what I Have suggested, therefore I shell not spare myself the trouble to repeat it, you see try to know that I Have no desire to be fighting or to do evil. you see sometimes I have Wrote you mean things but try to know that it wasn't Intentional. You see I was mostly forced to the conclusion by Being told continual that so long an you write and talk nicely to them why they will forever do wrong and so on. You it is a great Honor for a man to clare from strife But it is the most Hardest thing to do because every silly fool will be medding. and an I forth said in my letter which you should have by now. I cant afford to allow anyone to cause Harm to me of I can help and keep from being Hurt, I couldn't very well do that you know! I will be glad when my care comin up. of Course I do expect them to do justice and judgment in it. I must come to a close by asking you to please try and send me some postage right soon so that I will be in a position to answer some letters kindest regards. Hopefully yours, Haywood Patterson. [Reel 5, Box 5, # 000259 (folder c54), ILD]

November 4, 1936

Eugene Williams,
Birmingham, Alabama

Dear Eugene:

I have just recently had a letter from your mother and you will be glad to know that she is well.

I am enclosing $8.00 for the month.

It is very hard for me to write to you Eugene, because you never answer my letters.

I am sure it is not hard for you to sit down and write a few words telling me how you are. You know I am anxious to hear from you and I cannot understand your silence.

I hope his letter finds you well.

Best greetings

Anna Damon

Acting National Secretary [Reel 5, Box 5, #000798, ILD]

November 4, 1936

Haywood Patterson,

Birmingham, Ala.

Dear Haywood:

I have your letter of October 30 and am so happy to hear that you are feeling well. I have made a note of your birthday on my calendar.

I certainly understand that you have no wish to fight, and I think we should both forget those old letters of yours when you were not in such good spirits.

Your mother and father were certainly happy when we told them about your letters. I am sure they enjoyed hearing about them as much as I enjoyed reading them.

I will remember how much you liked the candy I sent you last Christmas and try to do as good a job next month when Christmas comes around again.

Enclosed is the postage you asked for.

Very best greetings.

ANNA DAMON

Acting National Secretary [Reel 5, Box 5, #000258 (folder c54), ILD]

[Probably written, November 5th 1936]

Haywood Patterson

Jefferson County Jail

Birmingham, Ala.

Dear Haywood:

We have just had the news that the trial of the other boys is to be postponed for at least a month because the Judge is very sick. This of course does not affect your appeal to the State Supreme Court, which comes up in January.

I hope that this letter finds you in good health. May I expect to have one of your letters real soon?

Very best greetings.

ANNA DAMON

Acting National Secretary [Reel 5, Box 5, #000257 (folder c54), ILD]

Haywood Patterson
Jefferson County Jail
Birmingham Alabama
November 6–1936

Dear Miss. Damon your very nice letter cam to me to-day, and I have wondered miserably on what I should suggest in regarding to your letter. an you
may see that I am not in the mood for doing any particularly thing to-day,
especially when I am having a awfully terrible bad cold which makin it very
difficult for one can hardly knew what to say. Anyway I sure am always glad to
Hear from you and to act promptly in giving you a early reply without a
Delay. Now I Have noticed from reading your letter it Have seemed that you
Received only one letter from me on the appointed date which was the 30th
of October, when you should of Have gotten 2 letters from me on that date.
because of the fact in that I mailed you one letter Oct. 30 and another one on
the 31. probably you have gotten both of them. I most sure you have obtained
them. But you half forgotten to make mention of them is that right? anyway I
received enclosed the postage stamps which was so kind to send me. I thank
you a great deal for them. it was Kind of you to do so Because I Had ran out
completely and Had no particular way of getting any. and I sure am thankful
for these which present me with you see.

You suggested that you had made a note of my birthday on your calendar.
Why It was Heavenly sweet of you to do so. and I now believe you are going
to surprise me. when it finally getting around to the appointed day. in concerning the old dirty letter which I written you while in a bad mood and
upset in mind. of course that Have been a Degree of forgetfulness with me
apparently I Have forgotten about all of it. and by reason why I refreshed your
recollection is because I didnt want you to believe that it was Intentionally. for
it wasn't Intentional. I did it against my better judgment. I promise to take
perfect good care to see that wont happen anymore. For I felt so terribly sorry
after Having done an I did for all of a suddin I came to realize that you had
worked so Hard and cared so tenderly for we Boys. I myself was so miserably
sorry and grieved over it all and wanted to Write and impart to you of How
terribly sorry I was, because I know you are a good natured little girl an of
course generous to a fault. Yes, I sure did enjoy the nice candy you sent last
Christmas. and it Have seemed that I can never forget the great kindness of
you, and every little kind thought of shell always be Remembered.

I think of you daily and all the kind things you done too, and what more I
thank You for writing to my Home an you Have done so to inquire of my
family welfares and Health. You know all my family are absolutely good people except me and my 2 Brothers and we wasnt say bad boys, but we would
get in Bad company and go places and seening and doing things. You see I
have a good Christain Hearted mother. Honestly She have Been a faithful
church worker most of Her whole entire life. You to known that I have a good
wonderful splendid mother and I just loves Her all the times. once I was a
Chirstain and church goer, But you know How that is. I quitted it and my
father He is a loving and kind daddy I like Him so much that it is painful. He
Have always tried to bring me upright. I can never forget the Beatin He gave

me. sometimes for not attending school. of course I have again reformed some goodness that Have been lying latent with in me Have came already to the front, and I Have made a sacred vow to god that if only I am freed again. Of course I am never free. I say the word free even if I were out I yet wouldnt be free. You understand, I shell never gone a way and leave my mother so she would never again feel sorry on account of me. of course I am absolute inno-cent of any wrong-Doing. they just usurp we boys and I fail to see How they ever could convict me just on Half-Caster So-say. I suppose I be convicted in men minds. well this is all for the time being and I thank you again for the most need postage stamps. be well and extend my Heartiest Regards to everybody, and in the meantime you accept my kindest Regards and all good Wishes.

I a sincere comrade Hopefully

Haywood Patterson [Reel 5, Box 5, #000274 (folder c54), ILD]

By late fall of 1936, Olen Montgomery's plans for a musical career resurface in a series of letters sent to ILD National Secretary Anna Damon. Though Olen's letters are increasingly written in a direct if not demanding manner, it also appears that Anna Damon is very much aware of the impact of incarceration on the ability of all of the defendants to resolve their simplest needs and deal with their daily circumstances.

B'ham, Ala.

Nov. 1 1936

Dear Anna

Just a few lines to let you hear form me this leave me worried. listen Anna I Want me a six string guitar and I want it rite now please. listen take all of my $8.00 and get me a six string guitar of course I will need a few smokes but I will do with out. because I want me a six string guitar and must have one. I want to make some recards I could make at least one recard here in jail. you all want do nothing to help me. I wrote you and Begged you like a dog to send me one and you wouldn't ever answer my letter. But that's alright. Just take my next $8.00 and get me one. don't get such large one if you can help it. You can get some small six string guitars and send it rite away please I need it. If I live I am going to Be the Blues king. I want to surprise every Body some day. Anna please don't wait a munit send it rite on to me so I can Be practuceing on these too songs that I have made up oh well it wont seem like I am ever going to get a trial. well maybe my chance will come some day. I am going to loose my mind thinking about a guitar oh well I will look for it by Friday.

Yours very truly

Olen Montgomery

P.S. Anna get a Black guitar if you can and I want the strings to be good if you don't mind it I will appreciate if you send me a extra set. Just put them inside the guitar, and please send a letter along with the guitar so I will know about it. [Reel 5, Box 5, #0035, ILD].

November 10, 1936
Olen Montgomery
Jefferson County Jail
Birmingham, Alabama

Dear Olen:

I have your letter of November 1st.

Olen, you know that I try to make things as comfortable and as pleasant as possible for you. You asked for an 8 string guitar last time and you remember that we tried so hard to get it for you, but couldn't because these guitars are so expensive.

I will try to get you the kind you want now. I am very sorry that I couldn't answer you about this sooner, but I was so busy, that I had to put it off until now.

I wrote you a few weeks ago that your trial and the trials of the other boys was postponed for a least another few weeks or so, because Judge Callahan is ill. I will let you know as soon as I get my further information about it.

Now I want you to be patient, and I will try to get your guitar for you a soon as possible.

I hope this letter finds you well and in much better spirits.

Very best greetings,

Anna Damon

Acting National Secretary [Reel 5, Box 5, #0034, ILD]

Nov 12th 1936

Listen woman I aint ask you for no 8 string guitar I told you plain as I could speak to take my $8.00 and get me a 6 string guitar. and I cant see why you aint done sent it to me. woman you will run a person crazy. I begged you like a dog once before to send me one. and you wouldn't even answer my letter. do you call that making thing comfortable for me? that worry me. and hurt me to my heart for you to do me like that you wouldn't send the guitar. or either answer. now I am willing to pay my $8.00 and go with out smokes and you still wont sent it. Anna please dont worry me like that I cant stand it. if you were in my condition I would do every thing I could for you to make you happy. or any one else. Please don't worry me like that. I am already weak cant stand much. stays worried. and so please send the guitar rite [now] I throught I would have it By now. I want to Be learning how to play it and so send the thing on if you going to please. send it By air I want it now

Yours truly,

Olen Montgomery [Reel 5, Box 5, #0063, ILD]

Bham, Ala.
Nov. 21, 1936

Anna Damon
Hello Miss Damon

I received the money glad was I to get it meanwhile I am well in health. now anna I am asking you to make me a present of a six string guitar right away and don't say that you are not able to send it and I don't mean for you to take it out of my allowance either now I am looking for it before this months gone now I am looking for an answer Soon now don't Disregard this letter and don't wait until next month to answer it, and to if you wish to you can first send the money right away and I can Send out at one because I wants a guitar bad and now I am looking to received it Soon. Charlie Weems [Reel 5, Box 5, #000721, ILD]

Charlie Weems,   November 26th 1936
Jefferson County Jail
Birmingham, Ala.

Dear Charlie:

I have your recent letter and am glad that you are well.

About the guitar — we cannot afford to send you more money than we already are doing. If you would like to spend your $8.00 allowance on one, as Olen Montgomery did, please let me know.

Very best greetings,
Anna Damon
AD:RB
BSSAU
12646
A F L [Reel 5, Box 5, #000724, ILD]

November 24, 1936
Olen Montgomery
Jefferson County Jail
Birmingham, Ala.

Dear Olen

I sent you the guitar last week and I hope you like it. As you probably noticed from the price tag, the cost was a little over $8.00. Therefore, as per our agreement, I will not send you your monthly allowance until next month.

I hope this letter finds you well.

Very best greetings.
Anna Damon
AD:
BS&AU
12646
A F L [Reel 5, Box 5, #00064, ILD]

County Jail
Birmingham, Ala.
11–25–36

Miss Anna Damon.

Dear Madam

I am writing asking a favor. Something which I do not understand. That is about some stamps I have. I am asking you to exchange them for me and to know how much they value I would like to know very much and Send me the money for them. they were sent to me from some friends of England. thier names are Mrs. Edith Odonnell, and Husband. I am enclosing a letter with this for you to mail to them for me please. they live, 6 Oxford road, Southsea Hants, England, and please do this at once. You can send the money for these coupons next week when you send me the money for the month. I'll close wishing you a Happy Thanksgiving.
Sincerely yours
Clarence Norris
County Jail
Birmingham, Ala. [Reel 5, Box 5, #000085 (folder c53), ILD]

December: Lieutenant Governor of Alabama Thomas Knight meets with Attorney Leibowitz in New York City to negotiate a possible compromise.

December 2, 1936

Clarence Norris
Birmingham, Ala.

Dear Clarence:

I have your letter of November 23 on hand and am very glad that you are well. I sent the letter to England as you requested. I am sure it makes you feel good to know that you have friends all over the world that are interested in you and are working to set you free

I am sending you back the English postage. It is worth very little, and I suggest that you exchange them for American postage at the Prison Post Office

Enclosed is $8.00 for the month. I hope you will write again soon.
Very best greetings
Anna Damon [Reel 5, Box 5, #000086 (folder c53), ILD]

Opposite: A group photograph of the Scottsboro Boys and NAACP visitors. From left to right, Ozie Powell, Olen Montgomery, Willie Roberson, NAACP National Office Staff attorney Juanita E. Jackson, Charlie Weems, Clarence Norris, Haywood Patterson, Andy Wright, attorney Laura Kellum of the Birmingham NAACP Youth Council, and Dr. E. W. Taggart, President of the Birmingham NAACP. Roy Wright refused to appear in the photograph and argued that "all they do is talk, talk, talk." *The Crisis Magazine,* January 1937 (courtesy the National Association for the Advancement of Colored People).

December 9 1936

Charlie Weems
Jefferson County Jail
Birmingham, Ala.

Dear Charlie:

Enclosed please find $8.00 and an addressed envelope so that we can hear from you.

Hoping you and the boys are well. Rose Baron will send you your Christmas present so with good wishes and let us hear from you soon.

Fraternally yours,
Anna Damon
Acting National Secretary [Reel 5, Box 5, #000724, ILD]

In one of the last letters written in 1936, Patterson conveys some of the growing observations about the judicial process among the defendants.

Haywood Patterson
County Jail
Birmingham Ala
Dec. 11–1936

Dear Miss Damon I Have just received your letter and the contents. So thank you kindly. Now it Have seemed sort of an if you are not going to make me a present of anything for tomorrow is my birthday. and nobody to send me a present except one little Beautiful girl of Birmingham here and She have been a close friend of mine for nearly 4 years now. I shell send the letter which I received from Her to day so you an see, I am sending it in a Separate envelope.

You must know that I wish to be of some assistance to you all. I want to be Helpful to you, and utilize the organization, but it Have so seemed that you prime Leaders do not wish to be useful to me in some certain things. and I am forced to Acknowledge to the fact that I really loosing confidence In some of you. I regret to say this But it is best to be truthfully. I saw in Labor Defender magazine one of the Horrible looking pictures that you all could find to place in it and says that it was me. and the reading above it says send Him greetings. I dont like it. And I beg of you all to not to place another one like it In the paper or magazine please. of course I understand your reason for not sending me a birthday present, you feel that if you Should send a present all of the boys would want one if they knew about it, and the boys some of them is funny that way.

When Mr. Morris Shapior were down to interview we boys, some of the Boys made some complaint about you all send Montgomery extra things. Now Mr. Shapior can tell you that I gave him the best veneration that could be afford, and he promise me that when He had gotten back in the city that He will see about Montgomery getting extra things. I myself told him In this way, that I dont care if you all send Montgomery whole New York down Here for him to have, why I really mean that because it Doesn't concerns me. and I am not jealous like some people, and I asked Mr. Shapior to stop you all from use slanders against me Because it is Hurtful to my very Soul. and as far as or anyone of the boys can Have all that anyone should send them, and I will not think anything of it.

But only I fail to see why is that you all, Mr. Brodsky too do not listen to my Request since douring the time I have been in solitary confinement which is am being all alone most of the time. except on day out of each week and that is when Roy myself and Charlie and another fellow prisoner Have a little time to spend with together and what I am about to suggest is that I have Thought of myself a great Deal and haven't an yet figured out how I am being unjustly framed, and what can be holding me in prison.

Of course some says for an answer is that C.P. and N.Y. Jews is the bigger reason for my being kept constantly incarcerated. And relate that if I should keep a way from Them, you will more than liken to be released immediately. Why I dont know about that you see. I like the jew race of people and always have. and all my life nearly was spent among them daily. and I understand them all to well. Why they Have never caused me to grief or to suffer any misfortune, honestly some of them seems to like me so much an to try to teach me How to speak some things in their language which is not lawful. an of course I can say a few words an I recall. and you can see that I can never feel against jew or even anyone. I like them they are really the best sort of people and I gets a great kick out Hearing some of them talk.

Well now I have wander off of what I were Intend to say and Here. I believe Is the really interesting part of this amazing case; which I Have stood accused of all these long times the degree of my innocence you have read the facts just an they transpired in newspapers So see if in your opinion the jury awarded the just proper verdict In my former tiral. I myself have Recapitulated all the witnesses catumnys. Whom stand ready always to be present to declare the Different stories against me, why they always recantations them selves each time, and they still do me wrongfully. But I need not to comment on these matters, because by now my innocence Have appealed to everybody.

And I am in beholden to the many Friends and members whom are not familiar with me yet. They bemoan, and I am always Having the feelings that I really know everybody personal whom have an interest in me, and pledged Their Heartfelt support and are giving their very best assistance towards obtaining my complete release. I assure you anna that it certainly is a just cause to carry on continually purposely to gain me my freedom. I feel that every one knows that this is a [ ] affairs and a most dreadful situation which I am facing without a moving cause. Now anna I want you to write an acknowledge receipt of my letters please, and do send me postage between the months. Kindest regards and best wishes I am yours sincere.
Friend: Haywood Patterson [Reel 5, Box 5, #000274 (folder c54), ILD

Cleveland Ohio
Dec. 18, 1936

Dear Anna

I received the box and was surly glad to get it only one dress was all that I could wear. you did not send any thing for my husband. please see can you fine me a nice fur coat and a sweater if you do please send it to me real soon. I had a letter from the Children and they were all well. I hope you can send me my Check real soon as I want to send my children something for Christmas. please try to make it more as I need it very bad I had a letter from Clarence he and all the other boys are well. I am hoping and trusting they will all be free in this next trial.

   When you answer this please send me mother Patterson's And Mongermory Address for I want to write to them. give all the Comraddes my best regards and I am looking to here from you again soon.
Close from Ida Norris
3715 Cedar Ave.
Cleveland Ohio [Reel 6, Box 5, #000011 (folder c66), ILD]

Decber 21 1936
   Dear Mrs rose baron i reseave the check saday and was werry glad to reseave it because i came in good time because i neaded it werry bad try to make it parsable to send me my check the firs of every mat be shae to try to get me a cote and swetter and send it soo as you can because i real them for myself send me a large sise cote and swrter hope you a merrny Christmas and a happy nue year please dont forget to send my mail to
8751 Cedar ave rear Ohio
Myour truly Com
Ret ida Norris
Close wit much love [Reel 6, Box 5, #000013 (folder c66), ILD]

7

LETTERS FROM 1937
Four Down, Five to Go

In the new year, changing political and economic considerations seemingly impacted the judicial decisions made by both the prosection and the defense teams. And while these elements within the judicial process were significant, the struggle to maintain a semblance of sanity was paramount for this little band of brothers, and appeals for assistance through letters became their primary tool for survival.

Yet major events far beyond their ability to envisage in January 1937 began to unfold beginning in May, when the defendants' chief antagonist, prosecuting attorney Lieutenant Governor Thomas Knight Jr., died. However, this apparently had little influence on the Alabama Supreme Court, which on July 14 upheld Patterson's earlier conviction and sentencing of 75 years, nor did it seemingly affect Clarence Norris's third trial, which ended two days later on July 16 with a death sentence. Correspondingly, the trials for the rest of the defendants began and ended within a four-day period but with varying results.

Andy Wright's two-day trial, July 20–21, ended with a conviction and sentencing of 99 years. In a similar manner, Charley Weems' two-day trial, July 22–23, ended in a 75-year sentence. However, after Ozie Powell agreed to plead guilty to assaulting Sheriff Blalock, his July 23–24 trial ended with the rape charge being dropped and his receiving 20 years for stabbing the sheriff.

Seemingly demonstrating the weakness of their case, the prosecution agreed to drop all charges against the last four defendants, Eugene Williams, Olen Montgomery, Roy Wright and Willie Roberson. Needless to say, this in itself raised major issues as to the validity of the prosecution's original case, in that it implies the prosecution's witnesses and the foundations of the original trial were unreliable and baseless. However, the political and social realities that made it so deadly were as present as ever.

* * *

Jauary 11 1937

Dear Mrs. damon

   just a few lines to let you hear from me I ejanyed the cristmas and all so the Nue Year i hope you are well and gette a long all right. i am wrighting to you to give you my nue odress I sent it to you but I thurt you might have forgotten it. try to send me a little Mare money because my kids in the soth yet and they hafter handbook and other things and I hafter send them half what I gets and it dont leave much dont for get the Cart and dswetter and find me a copple shirts for my boy he is in [   ] yet i had a letter from the kids themy was all well and get along all right

   I close wit my bees regards to you

   Yours trully

ida Norris

3715 Cedar ave rear

Cleveland Ohio

tell me a bout the boys trile whe will it come up tell me I your next letter send me Mr patson odres and all so Mrs Montgomery. [Reel 6, Box 5, #000015 (folder c66), ILD]

Haywood Patterson
County Jail
Birmingham Ala.
Jan. 11–1937

   My dear Miss Damon yours was gladly received some few days ago in which I founded enclosed the regular monthly allowance and for which I thank you, now that I Have read this letter with interest. However I noticed the signature. And it Have seemed that you did not really written this letter because it wasnt your signature or so it seems to me. and I dont like that. you are my little Pal, and I desire Having you to write me always. So stop putting some one else up to do it or else up to do it or else I am going to cease my communication get that? because I dont like Having you shunning me. anna you know the doctor came to Enterview we boys yesterday and He gave examination. of course He Did not disclose anything to me and if there anything wrong. I dont know about it. of course I have thought and worried so much that my is feverish and sick. an I am weary and my very soul is being crucified, I am just bearing [tho] But I can not go on bearing much longer.

   You see it is terrible. Maybe a curse is upon me or something is the reason why I should go on suffering in such way. I say again that it is horrible to think that jail houses is killing me. I never once thought that I would Have to die a way in jail, and this longest stay incarcerated is becoming to be a slow death for me. and the rest of the boys likewise slowly dying too. anna I an lonely There is no one to be my comforter. I Have to amuse myself constantly alone poor boy am I? but above all else I think I am entirely sane of course you people in the East may not consider it like an I imagine. I suppose when you Have completed this letter and carefully consider all things. you are very likely to see things differently too. naturally the feet is by continual Brooding over this misfortune and troublesome situation. Have actually got a lots to do with one mental an especially when I Hear of How I am being slandered. its made me actually foolish. I will admit that the Hospitality of the north and all that sort of thing. You know I am not very well acquainted with it. of course I am sane in my own way. but being tortured continual by such an being scandalized. Keeps me in Rather some what bitter moods. You know that when especially my position is impossible to do anything at all about it. and those photos being publish of me Have really became outragous and indecent rembeance which they have resulted. and I beg of you all to close publishing them. I disapprove such Horrible looking things. and it is Hurtful and dispirited to me. for always there remained at the Root of my Heart the precious Hope that some day I would win out. That sometimes there would come the chance But How Long? Write me soon and send me some postage stamps please.

I Remain Hopefully

Haywood Patterson [Reel 5, Box 5, #000287 (folder c54), ILD]

January 15, 1937

Dear Haywood:

I just got your last letter and I cannot begin to tell you how deeply it moved me. In one way it made me very happy to realize that you feel that I am such a real friend to you that you can pour out your heart to me the way you did. You are a very brave and fine young man, Haywood. You have stood up under your terrible burden in a way that very few older people would have been able to do.

But really, Haywood, you must not brood so much about your mind. Anyone who just reads your letters can see that you have a splendid mind. Of course, you are not happy and could not be. None of us who know you and all the other boys, who think of you and want to help you can be happy while you are still in prison. All admire you for the splendid spirit you have shown thorough all these years.

As for slandering you — you must give up that idea. Haywood, I agree with you about the picture, but honestly, it is the only one we had of you and we would be only glad to use another one if we had it. Perhaps you can have a picture taken of yourself. We will try to have it printed all over so that the people will see you as you look today. There are thousands of people who would like to see it.

You know, Haywood, nothing would make any of us happier than to have you free. And none of us will rest until you are free. But it takes time, too much time, I agree with you, but you must realize we are doing everything that can be done to get you all out.

After I finished reading your letter, there were tears in my eyes and I felt that if there was anything in the world that I could do at that moment to make you a little less and [and] a little more cheerful I would have done it.

But our letter ended the right way when you signed it, hopefully yours. You must not give up hope. Haywood, and I promise you that I will try to write you more often from now on.

I am sending you postage stamps. Everyone here in the office joins me in sending greetings to you.

Fraternally,

Anna Damon

Acting National Secretary [Reel 5, Box 5, #000292 (folder c55), ILD]

Haywood Patterson
County Jail
Birmingham Ala
January 18 1937

My Dear Miss Damon, I was surprisingly pleased at having received such prompt favorable Response from my last letter to you. I am supremely pleased to say that I have read your nice letter through several times, with a great deal of pleasure. And however I have considered all words Honorable. Because to me your letters are always thrillingly comforting and they helps my feeling a great deal somehow above all else. And right now I am utterly unable to tell you how sincerely I feel for you Anna. But yet you seem to doubt my confidence I have in you But I suppose you have good reason for doubting and that comes about largely on account of my Conduct sometimes. I say things that I ought not to say But allow me to reassure you that I have certainly taken you into my confidence in so personal matter. And have liked and trusted you. And you know that.

Regardless to my pretends to be angry sometimes at why I hardly ever be angry at all you see? Of course Anna I feel always that you are a real friend whom I can confide in. I read in your eyes last time. I saw you. I saw there in them good things. And just where you were a good harmless little girl and wishes to be Friendly to everyone and you are my personal confidentar. And you may well remember when you were down to interview me last time. I assure you then I had lots of confidence in you. Why here is the Selfsame words. I told you when you were down. [is] you know I have confidence in you. You remember now my telling you dont you? Or I supposed you have half forgotten by this time Havent you? And douring your last visit I wanted then to confide something in you which I felt was quite important concerning some events which happened to me there incarcerated at Montgomery Alabama, and also some things concerning Leibowitz and his associates, and also I wanted to explain something about we boys, but couldn't have done it when you were down on account of our position an I thought you were going to ask to see privately which they would have shared a Special room for that purpose.

Anna I try not to brood much not worry about anything at all, but I feel Depressed and sometimes prison life seems unbearable [or something]. Please Anna I have not got anyways of having pictures made of myself right now but if you promise to cease using the ones you all Have got will try my uttermost to get some done when the weather get more pleasent here. You see I have been planning to get me self a Kodak, but I havent had the money to spare for such. You see I can get a pretty good Kodak for $5.75 and no soon then I have the money to spare I shell get myself one. And then you can rest assure of getting a picture every time. I have some made I promise. You know anna I can not understand why the committee Have ceased sending we boys our regularly monthly allowance. Why I am in dire need of those $2.00 right now. No fooling about it. I need my $2.00 So badly. I can Hardly knew what to think. You know that. So please find out what up. And try to know the reason why they haven't sent it. Anna you said after your having finished reading my last letter there were tears to come in to your eyes. Why I don't like for anyone to talk that way. For it will make me feel more sader. I want everybody to be Happy even the if I am unhappy. You see, of course I do appreciate your inner feeling so much more than I can now repeat and not only just that but I appreciate all the things you have done for me. And don't think I don't and there is not another one who are any dear to me than you are. Why you are one of the dearest friend I have and I sure am grateful for all what you are doing and Have done for me. No fooling I do so appreciate all of everything. And anna I am sending you here with this letter five small sheets of paper which I have removed from my little book, you see I would like you to autograph a sheet and then you have gotten them completed please return to me. So that my place the sheets Back in the proper place with in my little book will gladly appreciate your goodness to do that for me. Well I can have nothing more to say at this time except to say good bye until I hear again from you. And please don't ever think I am tired of you.

I don't get enough of you.

Warmest regards & all good wishes to every Body and especially to you I remain again very Hopefully Yours Haywood Patterson [Reel 5, Box 5, #000293 (folder c55), ILD]

January 26, 1937
Mrs. Ida Norris
3715 Cedar Avenue
Cleveland, Ohio

Dear Friend:

I have received your letter of January 22 and will try to answer all of your questions.

All the boys are still in the same place. I am enclosing an addressed envelope to Clarence, which is the address to which we always write him, and at which he receives all our letters. You can write to Mrs. Viola Montgomery at 405 Harris St. Monroe Post Office, Monroe, Ga., and to Mrs. Janie Patterson at 1928 Cedar St., Chattanooga, Tenn., Ruby Bates can be reached through our office — International Labor Defense, 80 East 11th St., N.Y.C.

About the trial of the boys, we do not know ourselves when it will come up. As soon as we geet this information we will let you know.

With very best greetings.

Fraternally,
ROSE BARON [Reel 6, Box 5, #000017 (folder c66), ILD]

February 2, 1937

Haywood Patterson
Jefferson County Jail
Birmingham, Alabama

Dear Haywood:

I certainly was pleased to get your very [   ] letter of January 18. That's the sort of letter I always look forward to, a letter that shows that are full of hope and confidence. I delayed somewhat in answering you, because I wanted to get the sheets from your autograph book signed in time to send them back in my next letter. I hope you like them.

We have been very busy here these last days getting ready for Angela Herndon's appeal to the Supreme Court which is coming on Friday. But no matter how busy we are on all the other hundreds of cases we have to attend today, we never forget about you for one minute.

Keep up the good spirits you show in your last letter and write to me soon. With warmest regards,
Sincerely,
Anna Damon
Acting National Secretary [Reel 5, Box 5, #000297 (folder c55), ILD]

February 3, 1937

Haywood Patterson
Jefferson County Jail
Birmingham, Ala.

Dear Haywood:

I feel a little jealous of all the letters you have been writing to Anna Damon without sending any to me. You know how anxious I am to hear from you all the time.

I am sending our regular monthly allowance of eight dollars with this letter and I hope to hear from you very soon.
Warmest greetings,
Rose Baron [Reel 5, Box 5, #000299 (folder c55), ILD]

Haywood Patterson
County Jail
Birmingham Ala
2-5-1937

My Dear Miss Baron I thank you for your generous kindness and courtesy an I have just received your most welcome letter containing the regularly monthly allowance. Now may I reassure that I don't want you to ever be conscious of a thought or never imagine that I am forgetting you even for a moment because am not. And in fact, why I while a way most of time sitting around thinking mostly of anna nd you all those whom are very Dear to me. An of course you can see that I would you to share in my contentment too. An frequently an an you would like. For I know fact that you too have worked so hard and cared so tenderly for me and the boys. And I am almost Sorry and ashamed for my acting in the past and neglecting you. All well I guess whats done is done. And no amount of Regret can change it. But hereafter I promise you solemnly to buck up and live right up to you all But some times you all made me tired. My dear friend an of course though I was afraid of the fact that I wasn't cheering you much by writing that way liked I did, but once in a while I too need to let off some Steam. And you and anna happen to be first on Deck to receive it, you see life wasn't or hasn't been easy for me lately and I suffer in need of lots of things.

You see its is true there will always be a dark cloud hanging lowly over Alabama for its injustices and hardship to we poor victims. Say you know I have Been carefully noticing the local papers for some Development in my case an once I was told that my case was supposed come off within last month but so far it didn't and I am rather bothered over so much delays. Yes I like writing Anna and I think she are a wonderful-spendid woman and what more I have like anna for a many things for her fineness and loveliness. And I like Her for her courage and strength. And my one satisfaction is that I think she are a courageous fighter. Now Rose I wish to thank you for self writing in autographing the sheet for me, its swell of you. I must close for now with warmest Regards to you, and all good wishes to the fellow workers.
I remain your good Friend
Haywood Patterson
P.S. don't ever imagine that I am forgetting you Because I can never do that, you Are one of my Dearest Friend too. And you may rest assure that am often times thinking of you & all and wishing fo the day to soon come so that I can be out there with you.
Yours Haywood [Reel 5, Box 5, #000300 (folder c55), ILD]

Haywood Patterson
County Jail
Birmingham Ala
2–7–1937

My Dear Friend Anna your nice letter was gladly received Some few days ago and am quite sorry for not having gave you a prompt reply. But the truth is that I wanted to write Rose and so on until I finally postponed yours for a while. I Have received the sheets in which you and the rest Have autographed and I can not attempt to tell you how greatly they have pleased me. I like them and especially the way you autographed yours. I was delighted to have the self hand writing an my one satisfaction is to keep my dear ones in rememberance.

You know! Anna, I would like very much to know why there haven't been any news in my case. Once you say In January, but January have gone by and I haven't obtained any news yet. You know that the Lawyers in this case does not necessarily give we boys any direct information concerning the case — affairs in particularly at no time — nice lawyers isn't they? Why I haven't had any words from either Mr. Leibowitz or Mr. Brodsky in nearly a full year and you can see now that I have to depend solely upon you all to o btain any definite information if an interesting fact develope in the case. I suppose you are going to say you don't anything about this. But it just happen to be true. Occasionally we never get any information from the good lawyers and just an it have occurred to me so far I have been unable to comprehend the meaning for their acting. Of course I am no ways disturbed about it. And I know you can not help because they haven't wrote any of us. And I dont expect you to maintain their acting or reasons for not, you are a dear good little girl. And I have shown special interest in you and that is all because you seems to be very popular, but really Havent concentrate any affection on you. I like you of course, and you know it does not take one long to tell when to like a person. And I like you better than anyone in the World, and always I do wish you health and happiness. And so long as you wish to be so nice to me, I will let you be a little nicer. Now can you conceive of anything nicer? I think of you constantly my heart beats in wild rapture for your sincere Friendship.

Now Anna, I wish to request a favor and it is for the benefit of all of we boys you see I hate doing it because you have been too nice already, but I don't seem to get around it, you see. I have been trying the hardest to get me a Kodak out the regular monthly allowance, but so far it have seemed impossible because what with the monthly allowance no sooner than I have it, I give it right out without returns and that's all because I owe it all out before it gets here. Now if you can and will I would like you to present me with $5.75 so to get me a Kodak. I shell enclose you a picture of the Kodak which I like and can get it if I had the money. And you can please return the picture Back. Now don't get the idea that I am begging of wanting to over do the thing, because I have no wish to take advantage of you all kindness, But the truth is because I am helpless and no ways of getting any thing except to ask and you know that. Well I can have nothing what ever more to say for now except to say that I shell be anxiously awaiting on your prompt favorable reply My deepest regards
I remain your good friend,
Haywood Patterson [Reel 5, Box 5, #000302 (folder c55), 1937, ILD]

County Jail
February 16th 1937

Dear Mother,

I received your letter a few days ago and it found me doing very well, and truly I hope when these few lines Reach your hands will find you well and Enjoying the Best of life. listen mother I need a little money. This food they feeds Don't agree with my Stomach. you know I suffer with the stomach ache. if you Send me a little money I can send out and get me something to Eat that will agree with my somach. Ofcourse the food is all right But it just Don't suit my appitipe. So mother I will be looking for it Soon. Send me much as $2.00 are $3.00 any way — I am awfully glad to know the children are still going to School and tell all of them I say hello and Be good. I hope to meet you all

Again Soon, so I will close.

from your son,

Clarence Norris

County Jail

B'ham, Ala.

Ans. Soon. [Reel 5, Box 4, #000088 (folder c53), ILD]

> Haywood Patterson
> County Jail
> Birmingham Ala
> March 7 —1937

Dear Anna, I will now acknowledge receipt upon my receiving your short note and the regularly monthly allowance. I shell be some what different from you, and to show you that I have courage enough to give answers to your letters promptly. Why I fail to understand why ou did not give some sort of an answer about the or my getting a camera. Why you are the wore little friend I ever know of. And of course I don't worth $5.75. I don't worth it, and you Did the right thing for not giving it. But I would be mighty pleased If you would kindly return the picture of the camera which I sent. So please dont take that a way from me, for maybe soon I will save up enough money to get it with. I thought you were so good a friend. Of course I don't feel anyways towards you for anything. But I do not feel that it is justified that I should contain myself any longer with the feeling that you are so good a friend to me. I have been sick with High blood pressure, and having a terrible cold but I am so much better now. I wrote Mother and told Her that almost I believed that I had the T.B. or something and I am sorry I done that because she becamed alarmed & upset about me. But I just have High Blood pressure that's all, and am well again.

Haywood Patterson,

Please will you answer about the camera? [Reel 5, Box 5, #000306 (folder c55), ILD]

B'ham, Ala.

March 22nd 1937

Dear Anna

I rec'd your little short letter. nothing said about trial. you always wants to know how I am getting along. you ought know just how I feel with out asking. if you stay in jail six years how would you feel you wouldnt even want no one to ask you that. in other words you people up there will help run a person insane the way you all act. i writes you and ask you to do things and you want even answer. But yet you always wants to know how some body is feeling and getting along. how can I feel up lifted?

I told you three weeks ago to have three or four pictures made from the one you have of mine and send them to me and you aint even mention it. But let it go now. listen I wants a Mandolene take $3.00 out of my money and get it get the second have one you was telling me about last year. send it rite away I am praying for it. it dont take you no three or four weeks to do nothing I want it that's all the pleasure I have now if you is going to send it rite away if you aint let me know. so I can write Mr. Brodsky he told us to let him know if any thing go wrong.

Olen Montgomery [Reel 5, Box 4, #000066 (folder c52), ILD]

Cleveland O.
Mar. 10 1937

Prisoners
Relief Fund.
Mr. Rose Baron:

I am witing this to leet you know that I am in thee best of health, and hope you are enjoying the same

I am forwarding my new address to you for future mail — 2212 E. 37 St. Please send me the amount I ask you for in my last letter the next check you send me. The reason I ask you send me the amount I did. Is because I want to Buy some clothing to send my children for-Easter.

Closen with the Best Regard
Always
Mrs. Ida Norris
2212 E. 37 St. [Reel 6, Box 5, #000019 (folder c66), ILD]

2212 — E 37 St
Cleveland Ohio
March 23, 1937

Prisoners Relief Fund
Rose Baron Secretary
Dear Madam:

I received the chick allright. It was not lost, but it went to the wrong address. Please don't address any more mail to Kinsman Road.

Miss Baron I am in a needy condition and I am asking you to please give me five dollars ($5.00) extra on the next check. My children are needing clothes and I want to send them some.

Please send me B. D. Amos' address. He lives in Chicago. Also send me the address of the I.L.D. office in Detroit and the name of the secretary.

Notify me when the trial is coming up.
Sincerely yours
Ida Norris [Reel 6, Box 5, #000023 (folder c66), ILD]

March 25, 1937
Olen Montgomery
County Jail
Birmingham, Ala.

Dear Olen:

We have been trying very hard to get a second-hand mandolin for you but have been unable to get one good enough to play on. None of those we saw were any good at all, and since a new one costs entirely too much money, we simply could not buy it for you.

We are very sorry to disappoint you, but as much as we would like to get you this Mandolin, our finances do not permit it

Very Sincerely,

Anna Damon [Reel 5, Box 4, #0070 (folder c52), ILD].

March 26th 1937
Miss Anna Damon & Rose,

Dear Miss Damon as I am to say that I look forward to get money twice in next month date, 2 and 30 and I would like to know can I get them both at one time? if so please send it on the early date. and if you and all will not be worried by me any more.

now anna I say that I need the money so I can get straight for trial. now dont throw this letter aside as you have did all the rests and then tells me that you haven't heard from me. I am looking for an answer. Charlie Weems. [Reel 5, Box 5, #000728 (folder c60), ILD]

March 31, 1937

Haywood Patterson
Jefferson County Jail
Birmingham, Ala.

Dear Haywood:

I just got your very beautiful and touching letter about your father. I can understand just exactly how you feel. I met your father for only a short time, but it was long enough to see what a really fine man he was. But one thing you must remember, Haywood, and I am sure that he would want it too — he would not want you to grieve too much. He would want you to think of all the nice times you had together.

So far we have not yet had a letter from your mother, only a wire thanking us for the money we sent her for the funeral expenses. But we know that she is surrounded by kind friends who are doing everything to make it easier for her.

I know that you will be as brave as you have always been.

P.S. I am enclosing your monthly money order.

With warmest regards,

Anna Damon [Reel 5. Box 5, #000309 (folder c55), 1937, ILD]

Montgomery Ala.
April 16–1937

Dear Rose:

I know I have neglected writin you for some time. An I will assure you it wont Happen again for I am about out of the insane mood I have been in since last fall. An to you want answers.

Yes I have been receiving the money and appreciate it very much. Rose I hope you All a lovely may day. An I do hope some kind of preparation will soon be made for our day.

Do you have any idea when an application for a parole or pardon will be sent into governor Dixon. It is time for some one during some thing for I am about to loose my mind.

Give my best regards to all an you accept my heartiest regards.
I remain
Andy Wright [Reel 5, Box 5, #000832 (folder c62), ILD]

* * *

The following nine letters reflect a range of responses by some of the remaining five defendants to the July 24 decision by the State prosecution to drop rape charges against Olen Montgomery, Willie Roberson, Eugene Williams, and Roy Wright. One letter however, from an irate white citizen bemoaning the fall of "Southern chivalary," uses colorful language in its damning of the defendants, their attorney and the "North."

July 24th 1937
Dear Rose,

It has Been sometime Since I have Written You. I am awful Sorry I waited so long to write. I was in good hopes of Bein out where I could talk with Each and Every one of my friends face to face. But although I was unsuccessful in my trial. But By chances I may overcome. Listen Rose I am in need for [   ] five dollars to buy me some things I

Roy Wright with his mother, Ada, July 31, 1937, after his release from prison (courtesy the *Daily Worker*/Daily World Photography Collection, Tamiment Library, New York University).

really need. and I would appreciate it if you send me Much as five dollars any way to buy me the things I need. listen Rose I hate to ask any one for no more than I can help. But I hate to weary you or any one else. But I am just really in need. and are at a place where I cant get anything unless Some one give it to me. So I hope you don't do like the rest Dispoint me in what I ask for. So I hope to hear from you very soon.

So I will close.

Yours Sincerely

Clarence Norris

County Jail

B'ham Ala. [Reel 5, Box 4, #000092, ILD]

Birmingham Ala.
County Jail
July 24th 1937

Dear Readers:

I am quite sure you all have read the outcome of my trial and seen how I was given miscarriaged of justice — but of course I feels that its my duty to write you all the facts of my case of which you probably overlooked or it was not published in the paper how I was framed, cheated and robbed out of my freedom.

(No. 1) first beginning March the 25, 26, 27 1931. I Wasn't charged of Criminal assault on neither girl nor identified and was carried through the first second and third degree and on the basis I Would gain my freedom by turning state evidence against the other eight boys and just because I didn't know nothing neither would I lie on the other boys the charge of rape!

I was framed and place on me the 28 day of march 1931 and was tried convicted and given the death Sentence and in November 1932 the Supreme Court of the Unite State Reverse the Sentence and a retrial order. the 19th day of July 1937 I was tried and Sentence to 99 years imprisonment. Now I Wish to call your attention is how the judge charged the juries. he charge them in a perjury way out of his one hour and 25 minutes Somnation he only mention acquiall three time and each time contradict it by saying if you juries finds a doubt Which gase to me reconsider it never did he mention a single defense witness in his hour and 25 mins. summation to the jurys. How can I receive justice in the state of Alabama especially of Morgan County when perjury is use against me and my attorneys to? and I beg you dear friends readers and all stick together work and struggle together and see that justice be brought to light. let us all pull and Struggle together and see that justice be done it not the matters i hates to go to Prison but I am innocence and the slander is being thrown on our race of people and family is my reason of Wanting to fight harder than ever.

Now in you all spare time I wish you well drop me afew lines frequently as possible.

Andy Wright

Jefferson County Jail
Birmingham Ala. [Reel 5, Box 5, #000833 (folder c62), ILD]

---

948 Violet Ave. SE
Atlanta, GA.
July 25th 1937
Miss Anna Damon

My Dear Friend Just a few lines to let you and All know just hear happy. I
am Oh, my little Nephew went free, Willie Roberson.

Please tell me where did Mr. Leibowitz take him I haven't heard yet, I
am so happy Oh, I am so glad I know you are happy with me. I wont able
to be present at the trial I read the news paper every day I knew our attorney
was doing his best he is wondfull. Oh I thank the ILD and all the hole New
York, I tried my best to organize my people down here in the Black Belt
but I was Put in we all got out we only stayed locked up [   ] two weeks
and a few days they had me charged with Incite Insurrection. Now as the
freedom is officially decreed by high court I guss I can get my group back
again. Angelo Herndon myself have walked side by side when he was in
the south. I must go to work and help save the other Boys. Please write
at once the news I will write you more next time hoping to hear from you
soon.
I am yours truly
Lulu B Jackson [Reel 6, Box 5, #000277 (folder c69), ILD]

July 27, 1937
Samuel Leibowitz
Negro Leibowitz
New York City, N.Y.
Dear Sambo:

Well you and some other trash free your "niggars." If you had been a
white man I would have been really surprised but since you are a little
dark too, naturally you would fight for a close race. Then too you made
money.

If the trial had been held in the North I wouldn't have been surprised but
to think that Alabama let a bunch of renegades come down here and fight for
a gang of blacks two white ladies methinks the South has lost a State. It really
should be called Leibotwitzville.

Well half breed take your niggars back North and keep them. The Ladies of
the South can mourn the fact that they have lost Alabama when it comes to
Southern chivalary.

This letter is from a white girl and a D__ Yankee besides. [Reel 4, Box 4,
#0931, ILD]

July 27, 1937
Mr. Clarence Norris
Jefferson County Jail
Birmingham, Alabama

Dear Clarence:

I was very glad to receive your letter. I am enclosing $5.00 as per your request, and hope you will be able to get the things you want for the money.

I am sure, Clarence, that there will be a time in the near future when you will be able to speak to every one of your friends face to face. I hope you realize that the I.L.D., the Scottsboro Committee and all your other friends will not give up the fight until you and the other four boys are free. I don't have to tell you how happy we are to have Montgomery, Williams, Roberson and Wright free. We are no celebrating this partial victory and hope to celebrate in the near future the full victory when you and the other boys will be free.

Write to me when you have a chance, and let me know how you are.

Fraternally,
Rose Baron [Reel 5, Box 4, #000093 (folder c53), ILD]

County Jail
Aug. 3, 1937

Dear Rose,

Yours was received a few days ago. and I indeed was glad to hear from you. and I Received the money and it come in a needed time. rose I wondered what do you call Soon a month are two are a year are said cant understand what some people call soon. Rose I only call a few days Soon. But I wont you to give me some kind of ideas about soon. Because I am anxious to know. Rose Because I am tired of bein in Jail suffering for something that I know nothing about. and a crime that I didn't not to commit, and never thought of commiting such crime Because I have not Right to commit Such crime. Rose I am hoping to Be out of jail Before xmas. Do you have any ideas about how long do I haft to Be in jail? if so tell me where I can Be satified. So I guess this is all for this time. I will write more in my next letter. I have a lot of letters to ans now so that why I am making yours short. So I am looking for a long encouraging letter from you Soon telling me about some things that I would like mighty well to hear about. So this is all for this time.

From yours Sincerely,
Clarence Norris [Reel 5, Box 4, #0095, ILD]

County Jail
Aug. 3, 1937

Dear Mr. Morris,

Charlie Weems and Clarence Norris in jail cell, 1937 (© Associated Press).

Yours was received this morning and I certainly enjoyed hearing from you. Your letter found me well and I hope when these few lines Reaches you they will find you the Same. Mr. Morris I wish one would help me out of the miserable place Now. Because I am tired of such place. Mr. Morris I appreciate having friends all over the world but it seems to me like all my friends are working mighty Slow. Mr. Morris I have Been in Jail for over six in a half years and I am tired of hearing the Same thing about what my friends are doing I have Been hearing about what peoples are doing trying too Do for the whole time that I have Been in Jail. And it don't seems like they have did anything for me. Because I am still in jail. and also in the same shape that I was in six years ago. Now I wonder how long do I have to stay in jail now Mr. Morris. Do you have any ideas about how long do I haft too stay in jail now. if so tell me where I haft to Be all the time studying and wondering about it. Mr. Morris I am in need for some money and I would appreciate it if you would send me much as $3.00 out side of the money order that I gets every month Because I am in for some things that I Realy need. I have a whole lots of letters to ans and also needs Cigarettes and stamps and stationeary to ans thems with and I cant Buy all of that out of the little Money that I gets Every month. Because I needs some more things awful bad. and I would appreciate it if you would send me the amount of money that I ask for. So this

is all for this time hoping to hear from you Soon. Telling me about some
things I ask you about my case. So this is all for this time from yours Sincerely.
Clarence Norris [Reel 17, Part 6, #000383, NAACP].

County Jail
Aug. 3 1937

Dear Anna, I receive your letter a few days ago it found me well and I hope
when These few lines Reach you they will find you well and enjoying the Best
of life. Anna I am wondering how long do I haft to Be in jail. could you give
me some kind of idea about it? Because I am sick of this place anna what you
was telling me in your letter I don't want too hear nothing about all of the
friends that I have on the out side. Because I have Been hearing that Same-
thing for over six and a half years. and I am tired of hearing that now what
peoples are Been doing it don't seems like it have did any good Because I am
in jail and also in the Same shape that I was in over six years ago. anna what I
wont to know now how long do I haft to stay in this miserable place. I wish
you would give me some kind of ideas about what I am asking you. I am not
interested in the dimertation that peoples are giving on the out side. What I
am interested is now that is getting out of jail. and then another thing that I
cant understand and that is why that Mr. Leiawitz had to repeal my case and
Didn't repeal the other Boys. if he had of taken a repeal in the other Boys case
it seems like they would have been here in Birmingham instead of Bein in the
State penitentiary. that is why I feel so funny about my case. anna I don't
guess I haft too Be in jail another xmas. Do I? if I Do I wish you all would
tell me. and then probly I could Be patience. anna I am asking you for $2.00
out side of the money that you send every month. Because I am in need for a
fews things and I also haft to Buy cigarettes and stamps and statinary. Because
I have a lots of letters on hand now. and havent got any stamps and statinary
to ans thems with. and I would appreciate it anna if you would send the
$2.00. that I ask You for next week when you send my money far the month.
So I guess I will close for this time. hoping to hear from you Soon.
From yours Sincerely
Clarence Norris [Reel 5, Box 4, #000097 (folder c53), ILD]

1037 Cutter St.
Cinciinnati, Ohio
August 18, 1937

Dear Miss Rose:
    Your letter of August 17, 1937 was recieved today and also the 25 dollars
check, but my mother is here now in the Geneeral Hospital, but we have to
pay them for giving her treatments because she isn't a citizen of this city She
will have to be here a year before she could get any treatments in the hospital
here free. So I am going to take this money and pay her doctor bill here she

have to pay $2.00 a day and I will have to sent the hospital doctor in Montgomery Ala. $10 for the time she was there. The doctor here in Cincinnati said she was paralyzed in her whole left side and a busted blood vessel in her head on the left side, her mouth was drawn around some but not it is coming back to its place.

the doctor said she was doing fine we was out to see her to day and she said she was feeling find and they was very good to her, but she wont to come home. The doctor said if she get over this stroke she may not walk no more but her case was a dangaus one I will be writing you often about her, she have her good mind she said haywood was doing find and he still have the face that you all are going to get them free just like the other boys he have all of the face just like us. Mother attend a I.L.D. meeting here in Cincinnati last Monday night August 9, 1937 and said it was a very nice meeting I am hoping the way I spend this money is O.K. it all is going for my mother.
Thank you.
Louise Patterson
Thank you for noticifing the members of Alabama about my mother's illness but she is here now. [Reel 6, Box 5, #000122 (folder c67), ILD]

Andy Wright   August 19, 1937
Kilby Prison
Montgomery, Ala.

Dear Andy:

On August 4 I wrote you a letter and sent the regular monthly prisoners relief allowance of $8 to you. As I have not heard from you, I am writing to ask how you are and how you are getting along. I should be very glad if you would write as soon as possible and let me know if you received the money.

I am sure you will be glad to know that the Scottsboro Defense Committee is going forward with your case and that a motion has been filed for a rehearing and will be heard on August 27. This, as you know, is the first step for the appeal and this being taken for all of the other boys except Ozie Powell, whose case is now on a different basis.

I assure you that we are working as hard as ever for your freedom and for the freedom of the other boys and hope to win it in the near future.

Fraternally,
ANNA DAMON

[Reel 5, Box 5, #000838 (folder c62), ILD]

Cleveland Ohio
8/21/37.
Dear Friend

Just a few lines to let you no I am well and doing find. Also send money and also glad to get it I got a letter from Children they all was Well I try to get up her with me. I had a letter from Clarence he geting along allright to be in jail. In your next letter write and tell me is Clarence is still in Birmingham jail or not I wount to no so I can Write to him. Please send me Mrs. Patterson address I wount to Write to her. In your Packer will you get me a larg fur Coal for my sells, also some shirt and [   ] Blanker, just anything you like to pack for Bed things. Clarence say he was worry list bed for me not to Worry he thank he be free a gain I allso going to write to Mr. Roosevelle [Ed. Note: President Roosevelt] for help 5 boys when I get a hear I will send you letter. Be sure not to get Mrs. Patterson address. realing I ask you for coat I not able to get one.

I closs my letter
But not my heart
From Ida Norris
Add, 2709 E 51 St. [Reel 6, Box 5, #000031 (folder c66), 1937, ILD]

August 12, 1937
Clarence Norris
Jefferson County jail,
Montgomery, Ala.

Dear Clarence,

I am enclosing our regular $8.00 for you. I have seen the other boys, who are here, several times and I hope that the time will not be to far away when we will see you too. As you know, motions for retrial have been filed in all the cases. These motions and the appeals are necessary to prevent the sentences form being carried out. There is no other way to do it.

The reason that you were separated from the other boys is that under the law, if you were moved to Kilby you would have been put in the death cell, which none of us want.

The Scottsboro Defense Committee is pushing as hard as it can to secure your freedom but the slow process of the courts is what is holding things up.

Hoping to hear from you soon.

Fraternally,
Anna Baron [Reel 5, Box 4, #000096 (folder c53), 1937, ILD]

Atmore, Ala
Sept. — 9 — 37

Dear Miss Anna Damon:

I am writing you in regards of my being transferred from Kilby Prison. I am now confined at a place, name Atmore, Ala. And now I have no protection at all for my life, and too I have no way of protecting my self. I am ill as no doubt you know. Here I can not get the proper medical aid that I need. I was transferred Tuesday on a moments notice, and had to go to work at once on my leg. I can hardly walk I am too ill to even be walking. But I must try to carry on until you and some of the rest of my supporters in this case can do some thing. I truly hope that they wont jail me now, for surely need that help in getting transferred away from down here in these woods. Now this letter was mail by one of my pals who went free. I could never have sent it out otherwise so when you write, you will know that all my mail is open before I receive it. There is so much more I could say, but it will wait until some of you all come to see me. No doubt the Pittsburgh Courier will be interest in what I have to say. It will be a plenty.

Now I wish for you to inform every one concern in my case of this incident. And write me at once letting me know that you received this letter O.K.

Now there has been several threats place on my life since I have been here. Most of the Free white and several of the officers are bitterly against me. You really don't know how bad I need some of you to come down here at once. This is a matter of life and death. I have been told that they are planning now to have one of the inmates to take my life. So to delay I this matter may mean my death. I am not writing this just to be writing, this is really serious.

In case you receive this send me a wire at once, letting me know what you all are going to do for me. I was sent [   ] for the people to get rid of me. Now by getting me a lawyer I can be moved a once.
Haywood Patterson

Answer at once. Please Dear Anna I am having a pal to write this for me and please believe me and know that is the whole truth from earth to heaven. Your friend Haywood Patterson.
Love to all the Friends. [Reel 5, Box 5, #000310 (folder c55), ILD]

1037 Cutter St.
Cincinnati, Ohio
September 16, 1937

Dear Rose:

Your letter was recieved today, also the check which you to my mother, we sure does appreciated the money very much, which it is a lots to help to my mother and she is yet sick. But the doctors have dismissed her from the hospital, and she is at home, but she will have to stay in the bed for three months. We had a hard time trying to get her check cash because the know her at the posted office and they wouldnt let us have it but we got it cashed at another posted office. Im senting mothers check sent it in my name until mother is able to go for herself. I am glad Haywood now have an appeal in Washington.
Sincerely,
Louise Patterson [Reel 6, Box 5, #000127 (folder c67), ILD]

September 17, 1937

Dear Friend:

Attached, for your confidential information is a copy of a letter smuggled out of Atmore State Prison Farm (Chain-Gang) by Haywood Patterson.

Under separate cover, we are sending you a memorandum and other material on the present situation, which must have you immediate attention. The danger to Haywood Patterson's life, as you can see in the attached letter, is serious.

This letter should be used by you to inform our members and friends of the desperate situation, to start action on this matter without delay.

UNDER NO CIRCUMSTANCES MAY THIS LETTER BE PUBLISHED! NOR ANY PUBLIC MENTION BE MADE OF ITS EXISTENCE. This is important as a protection for Patterson.

We trust you will take immediate action in this situation.

Fraternally,

Anna Damon [Richard B. Moore Papers, Box 6, folder 2, Schomburg Research Center]

September 17, 1937

Haywood Patterson
Atmore State Prison Farm
Atmore, Ala.

Dear Haywood:

We only just learned of your transfer to Atmore from your family and other friends. Rest assured that we will do everything that we possibly can to help you and to see that you are properly taken care of.

I hope that you[r] leg will heal, and that by now you are getting the hospital treatment which you need, instead of having to work in the condition you are in. Please write to me as often as you possibly can and let me know if there is anything that you need or that you would like to have.

Every day we get letters asking after your health. You may be sure that not one single one of your thousands of friends has forgotten you and they are on the job to get you free. Your appeal is now in the United States Supreme Court but there will be no word from them until October. Keep your chin up Haywood, just the way you always have, and remember that we're out here doing everything in our power for you.

I am enclosing some stamps and envelopes. Very best regards,

Fraternally,

Anna Damon [Reel 5, Box 5, #000316 (folder c55), ILD]

Birmingham, Ala.
Sept. 23, 1937

Dear rose I receive your letter and also the clippers a few days ago it found me well and I do hope when this letter reaches you it will Find you all o.k. listen rose I am in Solitary which I have already told you all I read and you all haven't made no kind of effect to get me out of Solitary. rose you all don't know how Bad I am suffering in this miserable place. I am treated bad From any other prison here. You all know as long as I have Been Bound in jail and

you all know how Bad I need Exercise and rose I wish that you all would make some kind of peparation to get me move From solitary. Because I need Some Exercise. you take the whole time that I have Been in jail I have spent the most of the time in Solitary and you all know at that rate I will Soon Be dead. Because half of the time I am so stiff until I cant hardly Walk for my limbs paining and hurting me. and then to this Food that they Feed here. it is not healthy For any one without Exercise. When I Eat it, it keeps me in pains all the time. I cant rest day are night in peace. and you all know how miserable I am as many places here that these peoples can let me get exercise they wont do it. listen I wish you all will hurry up and do something For me Because I am in miseral. rose I am writing this letter to you and Anna and all of the rest for you all to do something for me. and please let the rest read it. So this is all
From yours Sincerely,
Clarence Norris
County Jail
B.ham Ala. [Reel 17, Part 6, #000504, NAACP]

Haywood Patterson
Jefferson County Jail
Birmingham, Ala.
September 26 1937

My Dear Rose this is to inform you that I received your much welcome and highly appreciated letter just a day or so before my being transferred from Atmore Ala. Well I can sleep a bit more peacefully now. What a relief it is to have gotten transferred a-way from that place, the lonely desolate stretch of land and woods where Atmore is situated. Anything might happen at such a place and then again I had received several threats on my life and they would not give me any Medical attention there and worked me quite hard every Day when I couldnt hardly get around on my leg. You see they sent me right out of the Hospital one day and the next day I was put to work. I was very weak an I had lost a great deal of strength while there in the Hospital. I spent a month & two weeks in Hospital. After all I tryed to explain my condition to the Wardens there at Atmore but they told me that they didn't have any sympathy for me and so on. Then again in weight I had losted 16½ lbs, but the Wardens at Atmore told me that I would have to gain that back by working.

You know I can not bring myself to believe that my friends would ever let me go into Prism and suffer in the way you all Have done. And I can not tell you in words How my heart have pained over the way you all have done things. I never once thought Rose. That you all would consent to my going in Prism for such an untold crime. You know circumstantial evidence sometimes hangs a man — for something He did not do or knows anything of. Why you all nearly killed my mother with such change of attitude. Caused her to have a stroke when she came down to visit me while I was confined in Hospital at Kilby Prism. You see my Mother and I have always considered you all most capable & trustworthy. Well I want talk anymore on this subject. You know no sooner than I arrived here they placed me in solitary confinement. I wish you all would write the warden and ask him to allow me a little privilege to get exercise largely on account of my condition. Now I have written anna a letter and in it I asked for a little money so s that I could be able to get my self a few clothing. So will you please see to it that I should have a little money for clothing in the near future. I could go on talking to you Rose, an there is so much I wish to talk over with you but I will just save it for another time so good Bye and my whole Heart love to you yours feeling very discouraged and downcasted.

Haywood Patterson

Answer soon Please [Reel 5, Box 5, #000317 (folder c55), ILD]

Sept. 29, 1937.

Richard B. Moore
International Labor Defense,
200 West 135 Street
Room 204
New York City.

Dear Friend:

In my conversation with Mr. Shapiro, a few days ago, in respect to the tour in the defense of the five Scottsboro boys still in prison, I understand from him that the Scottsboro Defense Committee was willing to offer only cigarette money and money to buy newspapers

While I am whole-heartedly willing to do what is right by the boys, still the Committee will understand I am sure, that I have personal responsibilities. I would like to be in a position to help my mother and my little sister in the south, and like any other young man, I need a little money for myself. I would be willing at your earliest convenience to go on the tour provided that the Committee would see to it that I get adequate food and clothing and shelter, and pay me sixteen dollars per week. I could go for a period of two months, and if the tour is successful, maybe longer. In the end I would I would like to pursue my education.

I have a liking for music and am anxious to educate myself in that line. I would therefore appreciate it if the Committee would assist me in this respect.

Thanking the Committee for its most valuable assistance in the past,
I am
   Very sincerely yours,
      Olen Montgomery [Richard B. Moore Papers, Box 6, Folder 2, 1937]

Haywood Patterson
Jeff. County Jail
Birmingham Ala
October 12, 1937

My Dear Anna, I am writing you once again, although I have written you but an yet I haven't Heard anything at all from you and I begins to wonder why? In that letter I suggested a favor and my reason for asking you for an extra $5.00 is because I want only to get me a few articles of cheap clothing. An most of my clothing was destroyed and that is because I wasn't allowed to carry them into Prism with me. Now in your letter you asked me if there was anything I would like or need let you know, so I did. And I fail to understand why you Havent written me in & regarding my letter well maybe you will when you get this one. I do Honestly hope so anyway, Dear Anna an I understand from some friends that the boys hav deserted the I.L.D. and Insure themselves with some sort of Show. I am quite sorry for that if they have done such a thing. Of course I didn't so much an expect that those Boys would be of any aid or assistance to me or the remaining Boys, but I did so thought that they should go out with a determined mind to do all there was in their power to strengthen the I.L.D. the ones whom fought for them and saved their lives and saved them from Prison because you all knew that they was all innocent Boys.

I have nothing against either one of the boys nothing more than that they are most disagreeable at all times, but still I hope that the I.L.D. and Mr. Leibowitz do not hold anything in their hearts against these boys for they are rather young and stands in state ignorance of a great many things and can easy be deceived but after all they knew right from wrong. After we are all freed I think they would want to come back to you all, most likely they will. Why I myself can never forget the wonderful deeds and splendid cooperating that the I.L.D. Have shown me through all these years of misery and hardship and therefore my gratitude goes out to you all for the wonderful service you are daily rendering.

You know I haven't heard from the Committee for a good longtime now and I certainly miss the aid and assistance of the Committee and I wonder why such kindness should be taken a way from me especially when I am so appreciative. Now I am Honestly hoping for an answer from you please let it be soon

Yours Sincerely Haywood [Reel 5, Box 5, #000323 (folder c55), ILD]

Montgomery, Ala.
Kilby Prison
October 3rd 1937

Rose Baron:

A few lines in regards to let you hear from me I am not well at all thought I trust that these few lines find you well and getting along fine. Now I want to know from you all if our case are being appealed Why is it that we are down here slaveing as if we were dogs and a bit worse and the conditions at us Boys do not require the job that they have us working on and we don't have no special boss. But just anything that have a white face is sour boss including convicts and all. One says do on thing another say do another and because we cant do both at once they want to beat us up the reports so as I learned the

Deputy warden is trying to bribe the kitchen surgon to poison us and the return answer was if we be here and Haywood go free are get a new trial they will at which they will pay a convict to do it and if you all try to do anything about it they will get the convict to take it on him on self and plead guilty to it with their aid at helping him under cover. Now listen what I am telling you all now don't ignore it because things are very serious now.

We couldn't explain things to the gentlemen down here because we were in the presence of the Chief Warden and we know what would been the result if we did so. We are absolutely afraid to eat here and you all know just about how long we can hold up at this rate.

And again the Supder. at the cotton mill O. D. Edwards himself stated in our presence that he will beat our brains out when and if the Supreme Court act in Haywood favor and we are quite sure he have got the white convicts to pick at us in order for us to speak about it so they can mob us. They say that they are going to learn us how to rape white women in this part of the world. So we ask you all to regard this letter and statement.

Your truly,

Charlie Weem

Andy Wright

Ozie Powell [Richard B. Moore Papers, International Labor Defense & National Negro Congress, Box 6, folder 1, 1937]

Oct. 19th 1937

Haywood Patterson

Jefferson County Jail

Birmingham, Ala.

Dear Haywood:

I just got your very nice letter in which you complain about not hearing from me for a long time. I wrote to you several times recently and I am sure that by the time you get this letter you will have received the others.

What you say about the boys interested me very much. I was glad to have your opinion about them. You may be sure that none of us is in any way angry with them. We understand their problems and are trying to do our best to help them solve these problems. Two of them dropped into the office yesterday and send you their regards. There is no news yet about your appeal to the Supreme Court but there should be very soon, since the judges have had the papers for a number of weeks now. I hope that my next letter to you will be able to contain some very good news. I am sending you the $5 you ask for and hope that it will help you get everything t hat you need.

With very best wishes and regards. I am your friend.

Sincerely,

Anna Damon [Reel 5, Box 5, #000322 (folder c55), ILD]

Birmingham Ala
Oct. 25: 1937

Dear Mr. Brodsky I am writing you a few lines just to let you know how I am Bein treated here. Mr. Brodsky I am Getting are ill treatment here. I am not Bein treated Right. I think that I should Be treated as the rest of the prison here I am placed in Solitery in the Back Side of the jail that I should Be on. I have Been placed on the Back side of this jail Every since July When I was tried. I am on the side of the jail where they keeps all white prison where I cant Get No kind of out let are No Exercise are either see no visitors and I think I should see peoples who are interested in Me in trying to do what they can for me. Listen I had a Friend of Mine From ohio and these Dirty Sheriffs wouldn't let her in to See me. after spending Money for her rail road fare for over 200 miles. and after that these old Sheriffs here cursed and doged and abuse here around. and drove her away from the jail. they did that just Because I was a Negro Man and she were a Negro woman. they don't do these white prisons like that the colored only have one visiting day. and every day is visiting day with the white. And nare day is visiting day with me. I am Bein treated worser than any prison here, listen I am going to enclose the telegram that I rec.d after She was Driven away From the jail. to show you how dirty these No Good peoples is. listen I will Be dam glad when I am out of this No Good State. and I also wish that you all will hurry up and Do something for me. if I don't soon Be out of this place Something will happen badly with me Because I am Getting tired of Bein treated worser than a dog. listen I wish you would send me a little money where I can Get Me a Few things that I really need you promise me some time ago that you Would send me the amount of money to helps Get the things that I need. But haven't heard From you since. So I Guess this is all For this time. hoping to hear From you soon.
From yours Sincerely
Clarence Norris
County Jail
B.ham Ala. [Reel 17, Part 6, #000548, NAACP]

Birmingham, Ala.
Oct 27 1937

Dear Mr. Morris I recd your letter and also the $5.00 a Few days ago and you letter did Not Find Me Getting along so Well. Mr. Morris I don't think that I am Bein treated right By the Committee and Mr. Leibowitz are either the I.L.D. and I don't think you are mr. Leibowitz are the committee and the I.L.D. is not are Bit interested in Me Enough to try to regain My freedom. Mr Morris I am innocent of and don't Feel like I will every will Be able to over come this Frame up. Mr Morris I Believe that I am Being Framed to the chair are either prison for the resto of my life. By the Committee and Mr Leibowitz and the I.L.D. Mr Morris I have had plenty Faith in the Committee and Mr Leibowitz and also the I.L.D. in regaining My Freedom But now I don't have no Faith are either Coinfidence in None of you all who so call them selves My Friend. Mr Morris I feels just like you all have help the State Frame Me out the best of my life just to Get those four Boys Free who are Free now of course I am Glad to see those Four Boys go Free. Because they Got just what they Due. And I know I should have the same thing Because I am innocence. Mr. Morris I have Been asking some of you all to send Some of the Lawyers down. I wont to see Mr. Leibowitz But I haven't seen any one since I was tried in that Kingaroo Court in July. Mr. Morris its something is going on Crooky. That Why I cant see anyone are either can Get any kind of Detail about my case. Mr. Morris I have known the time that I could see some of you all at most any time But now I cant see any one. Mr Morris you know as long as I have Been in Jail and have Been pending on What Mr. Leibowitz and I.L.D. and the Committee and What they all was telling me and Nothing they hasse said have Been put to no action and that is Enough to make any one Feel Down hearted and Discourage and lose Faith and Coinfidence. Of course Mr. Morris I know that none of you all don't care about My Feeling I have Betoweard you all. Of course I cant help how none of you all Feel about what I am saying I am just only telling you about the way I Feel I have lost Faith in you all and it cant be helped. Because I always will Believe that I am Framed until I Be convience. Of course if I have been Framed By you all and the state I haven't Been treated just. So I hope God will Bless you and I am hoping all of you all a Good Success in Everything yo may do are doing. So this is all. From Clarence Norris [Reel 17, Page 6, #000555, 1937, NAACP]

Birmingham, Ala.
Nov 25 1937

Mr Morris Dear Sir I am Droping you a few lines to let you hear from me. I am well in health. And I hope when this letter reaches you it will find you o.k. Mr Morris when you read this letter I know you will know just about how I feel in mind. Listen Mr Morris I wont to know why that I cant get no kind of understanding from none of you all about my case. I think that Mr Leibowitz is a terribly lawyer he is the one that I look for to give me Some kind of understanding about What going on in my case. of course My idia about it I Don't think it is nothing going on in my case to Benefit me anything and I think Every since I have Been in jail it is nothing has Been Done By none of you all to Benefit me anything Everything have Been Done it was for a [ ] show and for the Benefit of Some one Else. Listen Mr Morris I wish that you all would Send Mr Leibowitz Down here to see me where I can talk with him myself. And I wont be satisfied until I see him. Listen Mr Morris ou all just don't know how Bat it is to be confined in jail and cant get no one to tell me anything about what going on in my case. Listen Mr Morris if my case go to go through the high court I Don't think it Should lay in Ala. Supreme Court a year are so before bein argue and acted on if it haft to I know you all don't wont to see me free as Bad as you all pretend if you all dont soon tell me something about what going on in my case if it is where I can have my repeal withdrawn I will do so. Because I have been suffering long enough for something that I didn't do. And as quick as I can get this long suffering over with it wont Be none to Soon. I am tired of laying around in prison suffering and

Bein use by all of these organizations. Now Mr Morris if I don't Soon know some thing concerning my case I will write to the Alabama Supreme Court and ask thems to withdraw my repeal and just take what come. And the administration that peoples have Been making over me will be all over with so this is all.

From yours Sincerely

Clarence Norris [Reel 17, Part 6, #000648, 1937, NAACP]

The mother of Scottsboro defendant Haywood Patterson died in Cincinnati, Ohio, on December 24, 1937. [See Appendix C.]

8

LETTERS FROM 1938
Jail Rot

Governor Graves's commuting of Clarence Norris's death sentence to life imprisonment did little to improve the lives of the remaining Scottsboro defendants. Continual hostile interaction with prison guards, particularly within the Kilby Prison cotton mill complex, could turn deadly. Norris would lose part of a finger in a machine accident, and like Weems, was also attacked by guards and other prisoners, and Haywood Patterson received word that Ozie Powell was beaten unmercifully at Atmore Prison. Though these violent incidents were indeed tragic unto themselves, they are reminders of the intense differentials in power among the Scottsboro defendants, as some complained about their plight and the possibility of being disregarded or valued less than others.

January 19, 1938

Andy Wright
Kilby Prison
Montgomery, Ala.

Dear Andy:

In sending your monthly allowance I am taking this opportunity of writing you a few words.

I am worried about the fact that you have not written to us for such a long time.

You know how anxious we are to receive letters from you. We just had a letter from your mother and Lucille and we were glad to hear that they are all well, and that they enjoyed their Christmas presents we sent them.

I am sure that Roy has been writing to you about his interesting trip, especially in California and of the good work that has been done for you and the other boys.

Fraternally,

ROSE BARON [Reel 5, Box 5, #000840 (folder c62), 1938, ILD]

New York City
March 22, 1938

I am very sorry for the statement which was made to the papers. I wish to apologize to the Scottsboro Defense Committee after reading that the appeals had been filed for the boys by their lawyer, Mr. Fraenkel. I am interested in the other boys and I felt that they had been sacrificed, but I see better and as long as I can see that something is being done for their defense I am willing to do what I can.

I had written a statement shortly after I came to New York and left it in Rev. Harten's office and more words were added to it and it was released without my knowing. Some things I didn't say and couldn't have said them with a seven grade learning. I couldn't and wouldn't say that the tour which we made with Mr. Richard B. Moore was a racket. I know that the tour did help the defense of the boys still in prison and that the money that was raised wasn't handled by us or Mr. Moore but Was sent into the Committee and the Committee sent Mr. Moore our expenses.

I hope that all my friends will continue to do what they can to help those boys get their freedom and I also will continue to help as long as the fight is carried on.

Olen Montgomery [Reel 5, Box 4, #0071 (folder 52), ILD]

* * *

The following correspondences were written by Alabama state officials and pertain to a violent encounter between defendant Charlie Weems and Kilby State Prison officials. Though these reports reflect an ongoing tension between the inmates who are forced to work for commercial interest and the guards who must ensure that this occurred, they also allude to a level of institutional violence predicated upon racist proclivities.

STATE OF ALABAMA
BOARD OF ADMINISTRATION
Montgomery

March 22, 1938

Statement of C.O. Edwards, overseer of Kilby Cotton Mills, with reference to encounter John Barton, guard in the mill, had with Charlie Weems, a colored prisoner, which occurred at 6:30 on the morning of March 22nd 1938

After Charlie Weems was cut by John Barton I stopped him at the door of the mill and took a stick away from him and made him throw the knife down.

C.O. Edwards

Witness:
Bishop Jones [Reel 18, Group 1, Box H-4, #000270, NAACP]

STATE OF ALABAMA
BOARD OF ADMINISTRATION
Montgomery

Statement of John Barton with reference to encounter with Charlie Weems, colored prisoners, which occurred in weave room of Kilby Cotton Mills on morning of March 22nd, 1938, at 6:30.

I spoke to Charlie Weems about not keeping up his work properly. He replied by stating that if I didn't like the way he was doing to take him to the Warden. He then wheeled around towards me and had a knife and a stick in his hands. He intended to attack me and I defended myself by striking him with a small knife I use in my work and around the looms.

John Barton

Witness:
C.O. Edwards [Reel, 18, Group 1, Box 4-H, #000271, NAACP].

STATE OF ALABAMA
CONVICT DEPARTMENT
Preliminary Report of Accident

_____Kilby_____ Prison, _____Montgomery_____ Ala., March 22, 1938

Name_____Charlie Weems_____ Serial No. 37521_____

County_____Morgan_____ Date of conviction_____July 24, 1937_____

Color__Colored__ Present age_____26_____ Class_____A_____

Contractor__Convict Department__ Date of accident__March 22, 1938__

Description of injury   One cut left side of face starting at cheek bone to chin,

Approximately four inches long. Cut thru to mouth. One cut down center of chest

Approx. five and half inches long. Muscles cut and torn but no serious damage by this cut.

How did accident happen? State cause, whose fault, what injured peron was doing, and could accident have been prevented:

_____
_____(See below)_____

Statement of injured person? I was scrubbing floor in the weeve shop. This morning when I walked in, the floor walker, Capt. John, stopped me when I came in the door. He told me to throw my apron away. I went over and started scrubbing. He came back where I was and told me to get up. He told me to quit an hour ahead told me to come to the office where Capt. Edwards was. I started to walk off then turned and looked back at him. Then he cut me with his knife. I grabbed a stick to keep him from cutting me any more. I backed off to the out side door. Capt. Edwards came out then and I gave him the stick. He told me to come to the hospital. I came by myself.

How long experienced in work in which he was injured_____

Probable length of disability_____

NAMES OF WITNESSES

_____   _____

_____   _____

_____   _____

(Signed)_____F.A. Boswell_____ Attending Physican.

_____

_____

WARDEN'S STATEMENT OF HIS PERSONAL
INVESTIGATION OF ACCIDENT

Go into detail____See letter attached_____

_____

_____

Signed: F.A. Boswell, Jr.____ Warden

[Reel 18, Group 1, Box 4-H, #000272, NAACP]

Understanding the additional political turmoil this "incident" could provoke, Kilby Prison Warden F.A. Boswell Jr. sent the following letter up the administrative chain to the State Board Administrator, Hamp Draper:

KILBY

Hon. Hamp Draper, Associate Member,
State Board of Administrator.
Montgomery, Alabama.

Dear Sir:—

I regret to report to you trouble that happened in the mill about 6:40 this AM. Charlie Weems, #37521, CM, Morgan County, had given cconsiderable trouble about his work in the mill. I am informed by Mr. Edwards that it had become necessary to change jobs with him several times. This morning he changed jobs and put this negro to cleaning floors, and instructed Mr. John Barton, Floor Walker, to put him to work. Mr. Barton tells me that he told the negro what to do and when he came around several minutes later he had not hit a lick of work. He had some words with the negro and he attacked the floor walker with a stick and knife. Mr. Barton to protect himself used his pocket knife inflicting two pretty good gashes in Charlie Weems, one in his face about four inches long on left side cutting to the hollow of his mouth — the other about seven inch gash down the center of his chest. It is my opinion that Mr. Barton acted to protect himself. Just a short while back this negro had a fit in the mill and threw his broom away. He has been more or less stubborn and rebellious since his confinement at Kilby. I regret this affair very much.

Yours very truly,

(Signed) F.A. Boswell, Jr.

Warden, Kilby Prison
[Reel 18, Group 1, Box 4-H, #000273, NAACP]

Assuredly "incidents" such as what occurred to Charlie Weems happened on a regular basis throughout the Alabama prison system and invariably received little attention beyond the prison itself. However once it was known that a Scottsboro defendant was involved, the political stakes were altered. Not surprisingly, State Board Administrator Hamp Draper found it politically expedient to inform Governor Bibb Graves of the "incident" involving a Scottsboro defendant:

State of Alabama
Board of Administration
Montgomery

March 22, 1938
Hon. Bibb Graves
Governor of Alabama,
Montgomery, Alabama,

Dear Governor:

I am herewith submitting for your consideration a report on some trouble that occurred in the cotton mill today between Charlie Weems, one of the Scottsboro negroes, and foreman John Barton, along with report of Mr. F. A. Boswell, Jr., covering same.

Ordinarily I would not trouble you with matters of this kind but on account of the notoriety of these cases, and knowing too that we can not keep such matters secret, I want you to be fully advised of the facts in the case.

These men were sent to us the same as all other prisoners and it is our duty to work them along with other prisoners under the same conditions as the other prisoners. This man was cleaning machinery, and has been doing this for quite a while, and is now on the third different class of work since being confined at Kilby. These negroes have never been satisfied, and we have changed this negro from time to time hoping to keep down trouble, but he has been very troublesome for the last two months and will not do anything that he is told to do unless some one is standing over him all of the time.

Mr. Barton has been a foreman in the mill for a long while and this is the first time he has had any trouble with any of the prisoners. I talked with Mr. Barton, [who had] to take some steps to keep this negro off of him.

Yours truly,
(Signed) Hamp Draper
Associate Member [Reel 18, Group 1, Box 4-H, #000274, NAACP]

State of Alabama
Executive Department
Montgomery

March 23, 1938
Mr. C. B. Rogers, Presdient,
State Board of Administration
CAPITAL

Dear Mr. Rogers;

Enclosed find copy of the official report of the Solicitor, upon the unfortunate occurrence at Kilby Prison on yesterday, in which prisoner Weems was
injured by official Barton.

This report is self explanatory and I am writing to request that in view
thereof, that you re-instate Mr. Barton in the position he formerly occupied.

Sincerely,
Bibb Graves,
Governor [Reel 18, Group 1, Box 4-H, #000275, NAACP]

Montgomery, Alabama
March 24, 1938

Hon. Bibb Graves, Governor,
Capital
Montgomery, Alabama.

Dear Governor:

Pursuant to your request to me this morning that I conduct an investigation and report to you upon the difficulty which occurred at Kilby Prison yesterday morning between Mr. John Barton, one of the officials at Kilby and the
negro Weems, a prisoner confined there, I beg to report to you that I went out
to Kilby today and made a thorough investigation, examining all witnesses
that were necessary to get a clear idea of the trouble, and what brought it
about.

I was afforded every courtesy and facility by those in charge at Kilby
Prison.

My conclusion, based on the investigation which I conducted, is that I
think the official, Mr. John Barton, should be immediately restored to his
position, that he was justifiable in any assault which he made on the prisoner
Weems, which assault was superinduced and brought on by said prisoner,
with no fault whatever on the part of Mr. Barton.

I investigated Mr. Barton's record, which is most excellent; he has always
conducted himself in an exemplary manner, and is really a fine official.

I find that this negro is unruly, disobedient and recalcitrant, and has been
that way since he has been in prison. He is hard to discipline, and I think the
officials there have been most lenient and considerate of him heretofore. The
fact is I think most of the Scottsboro negroes have had too much attention
shown them.

I don't think there is anything necessary to add to this report except that
my verdict is that Barton is absolutely justifiable in what he did.

With kindest regards, I am very truly yours
(Signed) Wm. T. Seihale

I am inclosing two copies of this report, as the press requested that I give it to them, and I deliver them all to your own disposition.

W.T.S. [Reel 18, Group 1, Box 4-H, #000276, NAACP]

* * *

Montgomery Ala.
Kilby Prison
June 12, 1938

Miss Rose Baron,

My Dear Rose! I received your kind and welcome letter today and was indeed glad to hear from you these few lines. [   ] me very well in health but am absolutely troubled in mind. I wants to know at once is you all going to appeal my case to the Unite State Supreme Court. Please answer this letter right back and send it by air mail because I want to know why mr. Frankel didnt come out to see us.

I tries to stays cheerful but my courage is failing me every day and you dont make a lot me attempt to help me informed of the effort you all are going to make in my Behalf. All I know is that I am in prison. You could at least write to me once every week but you wont even do that. Please explain me the reason why others beside you is busy you should get too busy to write to me. It cause I have explained enough to you to know how uplift it makes me to read a letter from you.

Andy Wright [Reel 5, Box 5, #000842 (folder c62), 1938, ILD]

5016 Holyoke Ave.
Cleveland Ohio
June 23, 1938

My Dear Friend,

These few lines [   ] me and family well. I have received not a word about the trial or the decision I was promise to be notified when the decision was handed down but received no word hve not received the daily worker [ed. note: *Daily Worker* newspaper] for a longtime. I have wrote Ben [most likely, Ben Davis] again and again but have received no paper yet. I want to know what being done and I want you to keep me posted on what being done for my boy. Please see that I get my paper right away. I'll be also glad when you can send me the amount of $10 as $6 don't go so far. Answer soon.

from truly your friend

Ida Norris [Reel 6, Box 5, #000033 (folder c66), 1938, ILD]

July 2, 1938
Haywood Patterson
County Jail
Birmingham, Ala

My Dear friend Anna. Your most welcome letter it arrived just nicely in time. And I was most delighted at having you feeling the way you do. It mighty decent of you to want me writing again. Your courage touched me deeply. You has been a brave spirit through it all. I have wanted to thank you for acting as you did by to writing me while I were angry. But it no harm Done to make sure you haven't done anything to distress yourself about. You see nothing can ever be wrong between us Anna. Know that we are all brother and sisters under the skin. I trust what I am saying Here would lay a warm light on your heart.

You see everything I have said in my former letter was perfectly true. It is just that I have got a dislike of being misled about anything. But you know I guess I have been a bit rusty for a long time, but tonight I feel oiled-up again Having only the will to live through and I think its wonderful the way you all are now working things out and I am not voicing my discouragement at the Hopeless task in fact I have tremendous confidence and absolute faith in the attitude that you all are now pressing forth and I think you all are wise in being fare-handed about the whole thing the matter. I believe can be satisfactorily arranged.

I would be so glad if you all would get me out of his as speedily as possible because the Heat here is intense, and as for air there seemed not to be any and it does weigh me down. I don't deserve this. I haven't chosen this life but I have Had to take what it gave me all the embarrassments its rather I had to be put into this kind of life. Now I wish to ask another favor of you all and I trust that I am not making another vain attempt that would bring me Nothing. May I remonstrate with you though getting quite plain But I beg you to pardon me for you have done something once for me and I has a tremendous capacity for gratitude.

See Anna, the committee Mr. Morris Shapior, has sent me $3.00 in which to get me a pr. of shoes with. So will you all be kind enough to present me as with $5.00 so that I can be able to get me a couple of suits of under clothing and a couple of pr. socks and a dress shirt. Now I can managed to do that with five Dollars. So please listen to me at this time and I want bother you again just this one time see and no more. Well I writing like mad Anna. So must complete with this letter and get it off this Morning so that it will reach you one day after the 4th. I wish you had a lovely time douring the 4th . I cant wish for anything but all the best for you. You know that dont you? I must close as there is something to which I must attend. As for amusement at present I can offer you nothing except a few amusing letters that I always Write purely for my amusement. Be a good girl as you always Have done and don't forget have them to send me the $5.00.

My best dearest love to you and rose. I expect and answer soon as convenient.

And so no more and present. Your good & brother

Haywood Patterson (Im a brother to you) [Reel 5, Box 5, #000331 (folder c55), 1938, ILD]

July 5, 1938
Haywood Patterson
County Jail
Birmingham Ala.

My Dear Anna. I wish you have by his time received my letter in answer to yours. Anna, I am sorry to have to tell you this but you Have got good cause to know everything. See I just learned recently from a white man whom have just came from Atmore Alabama prison. He impart to me that the prison authorities at Atmore beated Ozie Powell unmercial, saying that he insulted a guard which is a deliberately lie. Powell did nothing of the sort. It is just as I have forth told you all that the prison authorities will do these things no matter How good we boys may be they will find fault and do all manner of things, and will say that we gave them trouble. They does this in order to prevent us from getting a pardon or a parole from prison. This added another possible element to be considered, you all should send some one down to see about Powell. To tell the truth I Don't know much more about it than you do, except. I am rather inclined to believe the white fellow statement as truth, because while I were at Atmore I saw him there, we are being punished Horribly without cause. We dont deserve all this! It goes to show what Hate does, it at every Negro within stricking distance.

I sometimes sit and ponder how as a strange wonder, as something so Horribly that had to Happened to me that Had never happened to anyone else in such a terrible way as this before. I don't certainly know, but I do know that I am always grateful to you all only that I am sure that none of the Boys Had ever felt as deeply as I Have towards you my friends, and I do honestly hope that your friends will get me my freedom right now if you can. It is just a waste of time to Hold me waiting to get things fixed for Norris, when you can Have me released.

I consider this an injustice on your all part, when you all saw that you could get the other boys freedom you went ahead & got it so why not do likewise for me? Im Human too, and I have suffered horribly , and each day of my life here is miserable. I gets so sick & tired of these evil minded people of Alabama. Now Anna, I wish you all not refuse my request for the little sun I asked for. I will closing you will send it. I cant seem to think anymore.

Faithfully yours
Haywood Patterson [Reel 5, Box 5, #000336 (folder c55), 1938, ILD]

---

715 Clark Street
Cincinnati, Ohio
July 19, 1938

Dear Rose,

As yet I have not recieved the money order check and today is July 19, 1938, and I know positive the money order have not come. Im asking you if you all have cut me off the relief, why dont you all write and tell me so, so I wont be looking for the check. I also know you all did not send last month's check

June 15, 1938. And you all never write me nothing about the boys case just like you all have over looked me, you all have over looked the other five boys because I never hear nothing about the boys. My mother have worked and made speeches and raised money and what I have learned she made more money than any of the mothers. I do know positive when we was in Chattanooga Tenn. My mother, father, and me have worked and did ever thing we could all the meeting was at our house. You can write and ask Ted Wellman about who did the work there. And since I have been here I have wrote and asked you all about where the I.L.D. office here so I can work here and you failed to do so. I know we have made up enough money and other people have made money more than the boys and prisoner relief will ever use up. know you all have not cut none of the other people off the relief now Iam in need bader than ever the city of Cincinnati Ohio will not help me and I can not find no job, so you all all also forsaken me when Iam in need for some ones help. After mother died Anna Damon and some more wrote and tolded me that they will not forsake me that you all will continue to send the $10. Onetime and you all cut me down to six ($6.) a month and I only received the $6. four time. I say this if you all have cut me off why don't you all write and tell me. I did not received the check for June or July and you all have not sent me nothing an it isn't no sue of writing telling me you all have sent me the check because you didn't or haven't. I can not write every thing I have in my mind. Please write and tell me just whatd you all are going to do or done. You all are glad mother Jane Patterson is died, so you all wouldn't have that money to her she got lesser than any of the mothers yet she done more than any of the mother also the Patterson's family done more than any other family in the case. ask any one that was in Chattanooga as a leader.
Sincerely
Louise Patterson [Reel 6, Box 5, # 000131 (folder c67), 1938, ILD]

---

112 East 19th Street
Room 504
New York City

July 25, 1938
Louise Patterson
715 Clark Street
Cincinnati, Ohio

Dear Louise:

Since Rose is away on her vacation, I am taking this opportunity of writing to you and answering her letter.

I am sure by this time you have already received your relief money order. I am sure that Rose has explained to you how the other one got lost and that as soon as the post office traces it it will be sent on to you.

About your brother's case. I certainly know how much you and your lovely mother did to help in the fight for all the boys but, you must remember that there are long periods of time in which nothing happens. We all wish that this were not so, but unfortunately it is. Right now while I am writing to you, a representative of the Scottsboro Defense Committee is in Alabama presenting to the governor to pardon Haywood and the four boys who are still in jail. While we never count on the outcome of such actions before we see what happens, we hope that the governor will act favorably.

Meetings are going on in many parts of the country, petitions are being signed and there is a great deal of activity. Always remember that no matter how dark everything seems we must never loose hope. I remember the day we spent together, in Chatanooga, Tennessee, and always look back on it with real pleasure. I am sure that if you would think about it calmly, you will realize that all of us were deeply sorry over the death of your brave mother, who never complained and always did whatever she could to help in this great fight. We know what the great loss of her untimely death was. Not only to her family, but to the Scottsboro case.

I hope that you will write to me personally often. I know that it helps a lot to get some things off your chest to a friend and I wish to be your friend if you will consider me one of your friends.

Sincerely,

SASHA SMALL [Reel 6, Box 5, #0000129 (folder c67), 1938, ILD]

---

715 Clark Street
Cincinnati, Ohio
July 29, 1938

Dear Rose,

Your letters which you wrote July 15 and 28, 1938 was received today which came to me with all the pleasure in the world. But first I must say I am not married and never have been engage to any one but I dont see why my cousin Lucile Jones could write such a thing as that to you all, because where I am married I don't understand my cousin writing that to you all. Now I shall but me $6.00 wroth of food until I received another thank you very much God bless you.

Thank you

Louise Patterson [Reel 6, Box 5, #000139 (folder c67), 1938, ILD]

Room 504
112 East 19th Street
New York City

August 1, 1938
Miss Louise Patterson
715 Clark Street
Cincinnati, Ohio

Dear Louise:

I have before me your last two letters, one your note to me and the one you wrote to Rose Baron who is away on her vacation right now. The fact that you are so indignant about your cousin and the stories she told makes me feel that you will understand what I am going to say to you here.

There was one part of your letter to me that really made us feel bad and that is the part in which you say that Rose Baron must have kept the money for herself—for her vaction. That is a very terrible thing to say and a very terrible charge to make against any responsible person in a responsible organization. Particularly against somebody like Rose Baron who has given the best years of her life to the work of relief to prisoners and their families. I am not going to let Rose see that letter because I know how badly it would make her feel. You must be very careful in making such statements against anybody not only in this case.

As you say your moving back to Cincinnati was responsible for the slight mix up that there was about the money and nothing else. I hope you will continue to write to me.
Best wishes,
Fraternally,
SASHA SMALL [Reel 6, Box 5, #000138 (folder c67), 1938, ILD]

9

LETTERS FROM 1939
To Be Free, and Then What

April 12, 1939
Andy Wright
Kilby Prison
Montgomery, Ala.

Dear Andy:

No mail from you for a long time but we trust that you are well. We are enclosing $3 money order. Are you receiving our mail and do you get the money o.k.?

We are very busy with preparations for May Day. This year we hope to have the biggest demonstration of united labor than has ever been seen before in New York City.

Greetings from your many friends and best personal regards from myself. Fraternally.

ROSE BARON [Reel 5, Box 5, #000841 (folder c62), 1939, ILD]

April 26, 1939
Haywood Patterson
Atmore Prison
Atmore, Ala.

Dear Haywood:

We haven't heard from you for a long time and hope that this finds you as well can be expected under the circumstances.

Here in the office we have been very busy preparing for May Day. This year promises to be the biggest in the history of May Day. Not only do we expect hundreds of thousands of people to march in the parade, but New York expects at least a million visitors in town for the opening of the World's Fair and undoubtedly a great number of these will be spectators. Labor's prisoners will not be forgotten in this great worker's holiday and under separate cover we are sending you a number of greeting cards from your many friends all over the United States.

Enclosed is money order for $3. Please write and let us know how you are.

Greetings for everyone in the office here and best personal regards from myself.

205

Fraternally.
Rose Baron [Reel 5, Box 5, #000329 (folder c55), 1939, ILD]

Ozie Powell   May 3, 1939
Atmore Prison
Atmore, Ala.

Dear Ozie:

Again we are enclosing money order for $3. Not having heard from you for quite awhile we are assuming that you are as well as can be expected under the circumstances. Keep well and let us hear how you are getting on.

Very best greetings from everyone in the office here.
Fraternally,
Rose Baron [Reel 5, Box 5, #000609 (folder c58), 1939, ILD]

Montgomery, Ala.
May 14 1939

Dear Rose:

Your letter an also the money was received an I really appreciate it. it found me Ok, only wishing hoping and longing to get out of here.

Rose, im hoping I will receive those things no latter than the 5th of June. Because I am looking for company from Texas on the second sun. in june.

I havent as yet received a letter form mrs. Shapiro but I got one form Dr. Chalmers. I really hope something will be done soon because things are unbearable hoping for much luck.
Andy Wright [Reel 5, Box 5, #000848 (folder c62), 1939, ILD]

Montgomery, Ala.
Kilby Prison
Aug — 6 —1939

Dear Rosa.

i Received your letter and was very glad to hear from you it found me not feeling well though i am in hope these few lines find you well and getting alone fine.

Rosa, I am sure you got my letter and I wants to know why you didn't answer my question — and why you didnt do what I ask you to do. and listen how do you all expect for me to wholed up what do you think I am a iron man. You all is out there where you can dee feen yourself and things done and then have a nerve to write and tell me to cheer up. And knowing to that you havent wrote any thing to cheer me up. i wants to know when is my case coming up Before the pardon Board. and the six month time have all Ready Expired. So if you all are not going to Do any thing i Wants to know and i Will try to Do for my Self that way you all not telling me this and that. i Wants to See Some of it Done and not so much talk about it i done already

got to bee a old man So what you all waiting on waiting until I die So you
can [ ]

Right. Listen Rosa, if you are not going to answer my question dont waist
away your time telling me things i don't care to here. So I guest i will close.
Looking to get these answers in your next letters.

From Andy Wright [Reel 5, Box 5, #000852 (folder c62), 1939, ILD]

August 17, 1939
Mr. Eugene M. Martin, Secretary
Atlanta Life Insurance Company
Atlanta, Georgia

Dear Mr. Martin:

Olen Montgomery, one of the Scottsboro lads who has been in New York
for the past year, left here Tuesday, August 15, to go to live with his mother in
Atlanta. His mother is Mrs. Viola Montgomery, 344 Boliver Street.

The Scottsboro Defense Committee consented with considerable reluctance
to Olen's plan to return to Atlanta because we felt that the situation had certain elements of danger.

Dr. Allan Knight Chalmers, chairman of the committee who is at his summer home in New England, asked that I write you in behalf of the committee
and request that you offer Olen advice and counsel. Dr. Chalmers recalls with
pleasure and appreciation your cooperation of last fall when it seemed that
certain developments might take place.

The first consideration, of course, is that Olen shall have a job. The committee furnished him with railroad fare and some extra money and has agreed
to send him a small stipend for a brief period of time until he can become
adjusted.

It is possible that a situation might arise which would require Olen, for
safety sake, to leave Atlanta on very short notice. If this situation should
develop, the Scottsboro Defense Committee authorizes me to say to you that
we will be responsible for the sum of $25 which you can advance him if it
seems to you that the circumstances he reports to you justify his leaving the
city. We have made clear to Olen that the sum of money (not naming the
sum) which we have authorized you to hold for his use is for emergency travelling expenses only; it is not a fund upon which he can draw for every little
expense which he imagines he must meet. He has been told that he is not to
annoy you with such request.

The committee appreciates that you are a busy executive and we do not
expect that you will be acting as a constant adviser to Olen. We want very
much, however, that he shall have some person to whom he can go for advice
and upon whose judgment, sympathy and interest he can rely. The main point
is that he shall not get into any trouble of any nature so that he shall not be
thrust into the spotlight in any manner, and that he shall have some type of
employment to keep him occupied. The committee trust that this is not placing too great a burden upon you and extends to you in advance its thanks for
your cooperation in this difficult situation.

Very sincerely yours
ROY WILKINS
Assistant Secretary.
Copies to: Dr. Allan Knight Chalmers
            Morris Shapiro
            Anna Damon
            Roger Baldwin
[Reel 5, Box 4, #000009 (folder c51), 1939, ILD]

Detroit, Mich.
11721 Goodwin St.
August 23 — 1939

Dear Richard,

I am not in Atlanta. I had to leave my own Brother tried to start trouble and so I left. I am trying to get me a job here. and if I cant get no job I will be back. I could have stayed in atlanta but my brother aint nothing but a dam drunker and he curses even to my mother and he wanted to start a fuss with me. I written mr. Wilkins last night, and told him to send me some money .

Richard answer rite back address 11721 Goodwin St. give my regards to all.
Lovingly yours

Olen Montgomery [Richard B. Moore Papers, Box 6, folder 2, 1939]

---

344 Oliver St. Apt B.
Atlanta, Ga.
Aug. 27 — 39

My Dear Friend I am riten you a few line to let you here from me. I am Ok in helth as for as I no. Just now But my mine is all upset you no Olin was here with me last week and I was in joying him just fine to see and no my sun was at home with me one more time in life. And you no what happen last Sunday my Sun Frank come over to my home and jump on him you no that all most killed me on of them Boys would Be the last person to jump on. listen I am asking you all for a Favor one morer time. Just help me leve Atlanta be course if my sun will jump on his Brother that Ben in person over six year wae will kill me I wold not leve here for his sake he was here in Atlanta and I hated to leve him I dont wont to see him any more I hope I can see you some day so I can tell you I cant rite it I aint got the hart, I had a letter form Olen yestaday he is in Detroit. I told him when ne left that I would come up there or where so ever he is if he cant stay here I cant ether. I feel that I should be with you all amy way carring on the Fight for the rest of o the Boys Freedom so you take this up with the Committee and see if they will help me out in getting a way from here I am going where Olen is be cause he need me. now you rite me at once what you are gonter do so I can get ready By the 10th of Sep — I dont what to Stay here any longer I ant gonter Stay here I die before I Stay here. my people his killed me I have try to Stay here with them I see I cant so I am giving them all up here I will be crazy if I Stay here so I stop looking for an ancer.

from Viola Montgomery.

PS. When I leve I am going all a lone so I can carrie Olen a round to chirches some Time. [Reel 5, Box 5, #001021 (folder c65), 1939, ILD]

Montgomery, Ala.
Kilby Prison
Sept. 17 —1939

Dear anna,

i am writing to you all in Regar of my self and the promise that Was made to me Bye you all. Now i want you to know that your promise Was. When i Was tried that if i was convicted that i Wouldent have to Serve But two years. So I have did two years and over and I am still in prison.

Listen I Would highly appreciate the information of just what you is going to do and what you all mean to do. i am loosing my health in this place. i have lost twenty two pounds in the past six weeks I cant keep going on like this. you all are just keeping me in prison. Slowly Dying on my feet. Listen When Do my case go up Before the pardon Board and What are you all Waiting on? it to me like you all Would Send Some one Down here to tell me Something I am going crazy, crazy, crazy. Anna please do something I am going crazy.

Closing looking to hear from at once.

Andy Wright [Reel 5, Box 5, #000854 (folder c62), 1939, ILD]

INTERNATIONAL LABOR DEFENSE
112 East 19th Street   New York City
September 26, 1939

Dr. Allan Knight Chalmers
Broadway Tabarnacle,
56th St. & Broadway
New York City.

Dear Dr. Chalmers:

Enclosed is a letter which Haywood asked us to forward to you which speaks for itself. We have received a number of letters from all of the boys indicating a very real, understandable anxiety over the status of their case. They all want to know when it is going before the pardon board.

I am sure that a letter from you with any sort of indication or assurance will make them feel a lot better than they do.

Is there any definite information on about the question of the pardon?

Very Sincerely yours,

SASHA SMALL [AKCP, Box 30, folder 1-11]

September 27, 1939
Andy Wright
Kilby Prison
Montgomery, Ala.

Dear Andy:

I hope by the time this reaches you, you will be feeling much better and will have received a letter from Dr. Chalmers telling you some news about your case. Believe me, Andy, I know how hard it is for you but you have always been very brave and very fine and I am sure that you will continue to be an example of real courage to all of us.

Enclosed you will find your money order, with very best wishes from everyone here. I remain.

Very sincerely yours,
ANNA DAMON [Reel 5, Box 5, #000856 (folder c62), 1939, ILD]

September 29 1939
Miss Sasha Small
International Labor Defense
112 East 19th Street
New York, New York

Dear Sasha Small:

Your recent letter about Haywood did not enclose the letter you referred to which was the particular reason for your writing. Nevertheless I can answer the request you make with this information: that I have written several letters to Haywood in particular and at least one to each of the other boys during the summer. I sent a letter very recently to Haywood. I recognize, because I have had a chance to seem them pretty intimately, how much it helps to keeping up their morale to have some kind of a communication coming to them fairly frequently. I shall be interested in seeing the letter you referred to, if you care to send it, although I imagine it may contain much of the same material he recently wrote to me directly.

The plans are to have a meeting of the committee very shortly. The situation is that the Pardon Board has been authorized but not yet actually created in its personnel. My understanding is that some of the people down south on the committee know the names of the people to be proposed for ratification and knowing that personnel are feeling that we can in all probability work the thing through. They have warned me, however, that until the Board is ratified and we have had a chance to get under way, the insistence upon a hearing might drive the new Board into the position of having to say definitely "No," right now in order to forestall the criticism of their political enemies that they were created solely for the purpose of releasing the Scottsboro boys.

I shall make a fuller report of the opinion of this southern committee at the next committee meeting, where we should discuss the whole matter and decide on policy from our standpoint. I am hoping that that meeting can be called in the near future and I shall see you then.

Sincerely

(This letter was written by Dr. Allan Knight Chalmers.) [AKCP, Box 30, folder 1-11]

Haywood Patterson
R. R. 2 Box 38
Atmore, Ala.
[Date unknown, but sometime within the first two weeks of October, 1939]

My Dear Rose,

Myself and Ozie Powell has been talking things over together about you all and we talked a while longer to day. I don't believe anything we said will go in this letter, but I may as well come out with it since no one is going to read this. You see Rosa I realize that it would be very foolish for me to offer any objection over the way things are going therefore you must overlook any undue answers that I have made. I have always thought you our friend is much too intelligent to attempt or to take [heed] to our saying but you always have let me say whatever comes into my head and that's something I never dared to do before — talked at random just to see how some of my silly ideas sound when put into words as soon as they are out. I know how immature and untrue they are some of them, not many well enough of them to make me seem queer to anyone but you. If I ever expressed myself but if you are shocked you never let me feel that you are and I appreciate that.

I have never had a friend before to whom I could say wild upsetting things without having all the moral platitudes thrown at me. Now in spite of myself I don't mean that I approve or ever condone you all attitude towards me. I have said I did but it was more to shock you than anything else. For yet down inside of me I can't keep feeling grateful for you all broad minded defense of me you see I was a little off when I wrote you last time I should have known better I suppose. I did know that as a rule one cannot place much dependence upon another person but after all I am trusting you to help Anna out in obtaining me a small radio immediately. May I expect an answer from this letter.

Yours Very Sincerely,

Haywood Patterson [Reel 5, Box 5, #000345 (folder c55), 1939, ILD]

---

1 University Place
New York City
Oct. 19, 1939

My Dear Dr. Chalmers —

For two weeks I have been working in the office of the International Labor Defense, answering mail coming from labors' prisoners and their families. I have heard twice from Haywood Patterson who as you know is ever so anxious to have a radio.

Miss Sasha Small told me that you had offered to send him one. Might I suggest that you send one suitable for both direct and alternating current?

Would it be too much trouble for you let me know whether you will be able to send the radio along soon to Haywood, so that I may answer his question?

I am sure my friends in the I.L.D. would wish to be remembered to you if they knew I were writing.

Sincerely,

Hester G. Huntington [AKCP, Box 30, folder 1-11]

October 20 1939

Miss Hester G. Huntington

1 University Place

New York, New York

Dear Miss Huntington:

Thank you for your letter about Haywood Patterson's radio. I received a promise last month that one of the people interested in his case would send him the radio. I supposed it had already been done, since the answering letter form this person was very definite. I happen to know that she is an Alabama woman who returns to Alabama quite frequently, and who has seen Haywood at Atmore on previous visits. She told me in her last letter that she was planning to go down the end of the month; that she was not well but hoped to be better in time to go. If she carried out her plan for the trip, it is quite probable that she decided to take it with her.

I have just written her a letter checking on what she has done. If, for any reason, she has been unable to carry out her promise, I will immediately see what I can do with somebody else. I think it is possible it may have been taken care of already, I'll be glad to have yo let me know if you hear any further news. Thank you for your gracious personal word.

Sincerely,

(Written by Dr. Allan Knight Chalmers) [AKCP, Box 30, folder 1-11]

Mr. Haywood Patterson   October 28 1939

R. R. 2, Box 38

Atmore, Alabama

Dear Haywood:

This is just a brief note to let you know that there will be shipped to you from New York on Monday morning one of the new small radios, which will work on either direct or alternating current, and which has a built-in-antenna. Mrs. Levkoff, who asked me to write you the following message:

> "I do pray that you and the rest of the boys are fine. Please write me a few lines in Dr. Chalmer's next letter — if you do my next note will be longer. Best wishes to all of you."

( ) told me the middle of the summer she was going to send you one, but was unable to do it. This radio comes, therefore, from me, and I'm very happy to send it to you. If it should not get there in a reasonable time, let me know. I'll write more at a later time.

Sincerely,
(Letter was written by Dr. Allan Knight Chalmers) [AKCP, Box 30, folder
1-11]

Haywood Patterson
R. R. 2 Box 38
Atmore, Ala.

My Dear Anna:
    Received your short note enclosed with my monthly allowances. You imagine how glad I was in hearing from you I allways enjoy getting your letters more so than any. So thank a lot for my monthly allowances. Now I must tell you my surprise you know my good friend Mrs. Huntington sent me a nice beautiful radio and the following week I was surprised to receive one from Dr. Chalmers too you see he sent me one too and now that I have two of course I let a friend of mine have the other one. Dr. Chalmers sent me a small majestic one I certainly appreciate all this goodness shown to me by you all. Now think I can get News from everywhere and beautiful music so gives my thanks to mrs. Huntington again for me and tell her that I had some pictures made today and in case they come out well I shall send her one if she likes one. So let me know. Anna please try to mail my monthly allowances or letters exactly this time as I would like to get me some xmas things so send me my extra five dollars along with my regular monthly allowances so that I can use it for getting xmas things. I have been hoping by this xmas that I would be out to enjoy it with you all, well I am disappointed again so I will enjoy my xmas here maybe. Well this is all for now Anna. so write me soon and give my best wishes to all.
Yours very sincerely
Haywood Patterson [Reel 5, Box 5, #000355 (folder c55), ILD]

October 18, 1939
Mr. Haywood Patterson
Atmore Prison
Atmore, Alabama

My dear Haywood:
    Thank you for your letter explaining how Ozie feels. We are returning his money to him hoping he will use it. Can you help me by letting me know from time to time how Ozie is feeling? We are doing everything we can to help him and and all of you get out.
    I am going to remind Dr. Chalmers about the radio. What type of current is your electricity — alternating or direct current?
Sincerely,
Hester G. Huntington [Reel 5, Box 5, #000351 (folder c55), ILD]

Mr. Ozie Powell   October 18, 1939
Atmore Prison
Atmore, Alabama

My dear Ozie:

I am sorry to learn from Haywood that you do not wish to take money from the Scottsboro Defense Committee.

We feel that you are wrong to deny [   ] comforts like smokes and other little things [   ] using this money.

The Committee and the I.L.D. are still trying to use [   ] everything to get you out. I am sending the money back to you, with our money order for October. I hope you will use all of it.
Sincerely,
Hester G. Huntington [Reel 5, Box 5, #000613 (folder c58), ILD]

Montgomery, Ala.
Oct. 29 — 1939
Dear anna,

i received your letter it found me not feeling So Well though i am in hopes these few lines find you well. Listen anna i have asked you this question before and you left it up to Dr. Chalmers and he fail to answer it — So i wants to know When do my case goes up before the pardon Board and just what is you all waiting on. and if you all i sent and not going to do anything please let me know and i will fill out a parole blank and send it up my self because i have got tired of waiting on you all motion and it isent nothing. So if you all dont send in a application by the 6th of Nov., I am going to send in one the 7th of Nov. so that it will be in when the Board Meets on the Second Tuesday in Nov. So you all can Suit yourself Because i am pleasing mine. No one else is doing anything for me I dont have to advertise my case now.

So please answer my question and not yours thoughts.
Truly yours
Andy Wright [Reel 5, Box 5, #000858 (folder c62), ILD]

November 1, 1939
Mr. Andy Wright
Kilby Prison
Montgomery, Ala.

My Dear Andy:

I am writing for Miss Anna Damon who wishes to send you her warm greetings. I have today called Dr. Chalmers to tell him at once what you said to us. Please know that Dr. Chalmers told me that he will write you and do whatever he can on your case.

We have your problem very much in mind.
Sincerely,
HESTER G. HUNTINGTON [Reel 5, Box 5, #000860 (folder c62), ILD]

Atlanta, Ga.
November 13, 1939
(Letter is from Mrs. Josephine Powell, mother of Ozie Powell)
Dear friend anna

I no you have wunders what the matter I am still having an hard time witch I rote you sometime ago to plese send me some shoes I was wearing a pear mens shoes and ask for me a pear lady shoes so for four weeks I Ben in Bed with flue plese excuse me for this note for a am two [   ] I right I am getting my girl to answer it for me.

I do hope next mont I will get me some good coats and warm swettors for me and all so the children for i is going to Be a real Bad Christmas with I dont get any help at all from the relief have three dollars worth washing is all so I am so glat here from my Boy I am so glad he still has a frin in the north so don't for get ne and my Boy I an your truly Josephine
882 Cherry Alley [Reel 6 Box 5, #000210 (folder c68), ILD]

Montgomery, Alabama
December 26, 1939
Miss Anna Damon;

I received your letter and was very glad to get it but it come to me feeling bad and down cast though I hope this one will find you enjoying good health.

You have been often writing asking about my health which has been explained to you time an again. but you or anyone else do not make an effort to see it that any improvements are made. Fact of the matter if you are anyone else were really concerned of my health you all would make some kind of effort to better my condition. You all are nothing but cheap faker and make believers.

If anyone would just listen to you all you would make him believe N.Y. was a big ham and that the Hudson river a bottle of coca cola and you were going to buy them both for him. It seem to one you would find a new story to write about and tire of tell the same one all the time. Closing as ever.
Andy Wright [Reel 5, Box 5, #000862 (folder c62), ILD].

10

LETTERS FROM 1940
Pushed to the Limits

After years of incarceration, the nine Scottsboro defendants, with varying degrees of success, developed an ability to express through the written word their inner thoughts about the trial and their young lives. For example, by 1940, it was quite evident that while Haywood Patterson, Clarence Norris and Andy Wright possessed different writing styles and vernaculars, their ability to verbally transmit highly personalized thoughts and emotions into a letter format was extremely effective in the development of a base of public support. As a result, their written words reveal the emergence of unique and resolute personalities.

At the end of the 1930s one can also easily understand why Alabama state prosecutors were focused upon these nine individuals as examples of an unwanted social element; they were in reality a contradiction to racist characterizations of the African American male. Yet one would not necessarily know this except by reading their written narratives. Despite the fact that these nine men were nearly lynched, tortured, beaten, and shot at, while periodically smelling the nearby burning flesh and hearing the cries of numerous inmates executed at Kilby Prison, they also witnessed an epic struggle between two legal *defense* teams trying to save them from being executed by a third group of Alabama state *prosecutors*. Unquestionably pushed to their emotional and psychological limits, these nine youths managed to describe their horrendous experiences in their own ways. In doing so, they became both symbols of American racial injustice and iconic representations of class disparity, as demonstrated by a series of letters exchanged between Olen Montgomery and NAACP officials, who derided his lifestyle following his parole release from prison on July 24, 1937.

Atmore State Prison
January 1st 1940

Mrs. Hester G. Huntington,
My Dear friend Mrs. Huntington:

I do greatly appreciate your writing me like you did. I received our letter of December 2, 1939 and I found also enclosed my regular Monthly allowance that I appreciate so much and I also appreciate your last letter you send me post marked December 20th 1939. It contained also a gift of two dollars and a Christmas getting card which was so beautiful too. Buying and gretting from you now I don't know how very much to thank you my dear friend, for your kindness and good wishes toward me. Now before I go any farther along the line I want to apologize with you for my long delay writing you. You see I haven't been feeling very good for the last few days. And right at this writing I don't feel so good. But so we must remember, that every word that is being put down on this paper here I am saying them though I am having a friend of mine to put them down for you.

Now I hope you will enjoy reading this letter as much as I enjoy saying the words. Now I am sorry to say that I did not have a good Christmas. Simply because I did not receive a single gift from anyone. Except I receive a box of candy from Mrs. Sadie [Veen?] and I received it today and therefore I didnt get it for Christmas. Now my dear friend I have got myself a Kodak and I would like very much to have you to obtaining me three rolls of films at the price of thirty-five cents each the name of the film is S.S. 620 Bull eye. Now in case you should find the films I promise to send you at least two of the picture when I have them made, and of course I will send the other to friends. All though I realize I promise you a picture of myself before. Of course I didnt like the other ones so good and I thought you would not like it either. Any way I going to send this one to you for the time being and I ask that you will return it to me.

You see I [   ] want you to see this one and in case you send me the films I will have two good ones made and send them to you for keeps by myself. You see I have on this picture with me a little friend of mine Buster Turner. And I would like so much to keep it myself. But I am sending it to you so you can see it. Well this is all for now wishing you had a enjoyable xmas and a happy New Year's so write me soon and try to send me one or two or three rolls of films for my Kodak. Enclosed you will find a picture of me and my friend Buster So please return it and trust me to send you one of me alone.
Sincerely Yours,
Haywood Patterson [Reel 5, Box 5, #000359 (folder c55), ILD]

January 3, 1940
Mr. Andy Wright
Kilby Prison,
Montgomery, Ala.

My dear Andy:

Your letter of December 26th is here on my desk.

I want to tell you that each one of us is sympathetic with you in your illness and confinement. If there were something more we could do for you, we would certainly try. Each one here at the office speaks of you very often, and we keep hoping that you will be better, and out soon.

Sincerely,

(Mrs.) HESTER G. HUNTINGTON [Reel 5, Box 5, #000864 (folder c62), ILD]

The following draft letter was eventually sent to the respective prisoners on January 5, 1940.

Stuyvesant 9-4552

INTERNATIONAL LABOR DEFENSE
National Office

112 East 19th Street   New York City

Hon. Vito Marcantonio, President   Anna Damon, Secretary

William L. Patterson, Vice-President   Robert W. Dunn, Treasurer

January 5 1940

Haywood Patterson
Ozie Powell
Atmore, Alabama

Andy Wright
Charlie Weems
Clarence Norris
Kilby Prison, Montgomery, Ala.

According to the newspapers we learn that the Alabama Parole Board now has your case before them and will render a decision on your case on February 13th.

All of us here earnestly hope that the decision will be favorable.

Sincerely yours,

HGH [Reel 5, Box 5, #000373 (folder c55), ILD]

January 16, 1940
Andy Wright
Kilby Prison
Montgomery, Ala.

Dear Andy:

Enclosed you will find Money Order for $3.00.

Since receiving your last letter we have gotten in touch with Dr. Chalmers who informs us that he has been to see you.

We hope that his visit has put you in better spirits than you were at the time of your last letter to us.

Everyone in the office wishes to be remembered to you.

Sincerely,

HESTER G. HUNTINGTON [Reel 5, Box 5, #000865 (folder c62), ILD]

Montgomery Ala.
Camp Kilby
1–3–40

Mrs Anna Damon

My Dear Mrs Damon I trust the Holidays brought you much happiness and the in New Year hold much success for you and my many friends. Listen Mrs Damon I began to see my Mother & baby Sister. i have been back in 1934 since I had the chance to talk with her. And I would appreciate it very much if you Would fix it one way for them to come down. I am expecting you to do so right away it would mean so much to me to see them after so long of time. I am quite sure you all will do so because you all have help the other boy Mother to come and see them. Here is My Mother Address 3017 E. 30th St [   ] Cleveland, Ohio. I am going to write my mother And tell her that I wrote you all to help her come to see me. I will close with many wishes for a successfully New Year.

Sincerely Yours
Clarence Norris [Reel 5, Box 4, #00111, ILD].

Haywood Patterson
R. R. 2. Box 38
Atmore, Ala.
[Written early February 1940]

My Dear friend Mrs. Hester,

I was sure glad upon receiving your last letter on Jan. 30th 1940 in which I found enclosed my regular monthly allowances That I appreciate so awfully much. Now before I go any further I wish to make an apologize for such long delaying in answering your letter that I received sometime back you must forgive me for that and try to understand the circumstances. You see why didn't answer you more sooner I didn't have the postage stamps and no way of getting them. Now I also received your letter on Jan. 5th 1940 it was just a note telling me the time the pardon board should consider my case. But since that time I have later learned by the Newspaper that my case will be considered Feb. 15th 1940. I am just here hoping for the best my good friend.

Now before I go any further I must admit that I also received three rolls of films that you sent me. I know that you couldn't help but to wonder why I did not answer you promptly after my having received the films. Well my only excuse about it is just as he same mentioned above and I also know that you have been wondering why I haven't sent you the pictures that I promised you faithfully that I would. Well I have a good excuse for that too you see my good friend since and before I got the films the weather have been awfully bad here all last week it was so bad that the Warden didn't check any of the prisoners out to work. And so today I thought would be a nice day which is Sunday but it have been cloudy all day long and right now this afternoon it is raining so you may see by the weather being bad it was impossible for me to make any pictures at all. I regret very much to have disappointed you because you have been so wonderfully kind and a friend like that you is. I always like to be faithful and true to my word although i guess you realize that the world has never been particular kind to me anyway.

My mother was the only real friend I had or known and you remind me of her by being so good and nice to me I can never forget you Mrs. Hester. No matter what happen. Now I must explain to you about my radio that you sent me some time ago it is out of fix now I don't know just what is wrong with it all of a sudden it just quit playing on me and that was very hurtful to me because the thing was most comforting and consoling I dont hardly know what I am going to do you see I sent my other radio home that Dr. Chalmers sent me and so I haven't anything to keep me company now. So I am going to return it to you immediately and suggest that you turn it over to an Emerson dealers for repairs as the instruction tells me that in and everyone cannot fix these sort of radios and that it must be given over to an Emerson dealer only. Although I had a fellow here working on it and from the looks of it he have put it in worse shape, cut the wires and the face came unglued that when you see it you will say or think that I am not taking good care of it but that isn't all together, it the fellow I had working on it has done me damage than good and so I highly appreciate your goodness to have put in good shape for me and send it back right immediately I mean as quickly as possible get it back for me you see I love it and wouldn't take a million dollars for it now. I am going to try to get it off in the mail to you one day this week so you may be looking for it. With very best wishes to you and all and my dearest hope is that you will have my radio fixed up and sent back to me at once. Answer me at once.

Please, yours Sincerely

Haywood Patterson [Reel 5, Box 5, #000366 (folder c55), ILD]

Haywood Patterson
R. R. 2. Box 38
Atmore, Ala.
[Written in early 1940]
My Dear Friend Mrs. Hester:

This comes to imform you that I did sent the radio off to you on Feb. 20, 1940 I hope and trust that-you have received it allright. You see I didn't have any money in which to send it off with. And so I rather had it sent by express so please write me that you have received it and my solely desire is that you will have it put in good shape for me as quick as possible and sent back to me immediately because that is all the comfort I have and I misses it a great deal and would like to have it back right away. Now before I go any farther I must tell you of my health. You see I am very much sick and in hospital for treatments but today I am feeling a little better and one thing I would like you to do and that is to send me Six or eight dollars in which to assist me in gaining my health again you see we have only one doctor here and the rest of them is prison assistance and if a fellow have any money to give them he gets first aid treatment but a fellow without money here he be treated very poorly and by the help of god get on his feet again. You see money got me well before while I was in Kilby hospital for two or three months. Now about

Now about the pictures I promised you of myself. The weather has been so bad here until I couldn't have any made but after [ ] the sun came out one day but yet it was cloudy and so I taken a couple of shots of myself and so they didn't come out well so I am sending you one so you can see for yourself and see that I am truthfully. So please write me right away and don't fail to send me the amount mentioned above in which to help me to get well with . Now I am otherwise slipping this letter out to you and you need not to make mention that you have received it. Write as you allways have done address me Haywood Patterson Route 2 Box 38 Atmore, Ala. In case of Hospital. Yours as ever.

Haywood Patterson

The following notation was made on Patterson's letter by a member of the ILD staff: *"Things so bad that we have to distribute what we have, but we sympathize with your problem."* [Reel 5, Box 5, #000375 (folder c55), ILD]

Haywood Patterson
R.R. 2 Box 38
Atmore, Ala.
[Date unknown, estimated mid–1940]

My Dear Friend Mrs. Huntington

It gives me much pleasure in trying to write you these few lines. Although I haven't any piece of mind for writing at this time you see that I am quite well now and working everyday but somehow I just can't feel right having been in so long and it seems that there is no prospect for my getting out. Now this main thing I wish you to know is that I have received the radio which is a more nicer looking one than the other one I also received this card you sent me in head of the radio. I gladly appreciate the radio Mrs Huntington I shall always be grateful to you for your good kindness unto me. But its one more thing I would like you to do that is to write me some sort of information conserving this case I mean tell me just the reason why the parole board didn't turn me loose now you must overlook this letter and know that my heart and mind wont allow me to do more writing . Best wishes to all. Your friend.

Haywood Patterson [Reel 5, Box 5, #000379 (folder c55), ILD]

Haywood Patterson
RR2 Box 38
Atmore, Ala.
[Written during the last week of February 1940.]

My Dearest Friend Mrs. Hester:

This short note comes to inform you that I have received your letter in which I found enclosed my regular monthly allowances that I do greatly appreciated. Now you can imagine how greatly it moved me to have you to say that you all will continue to fight for my release those words gave me some consolation and a bit of courage to carry on. Yes you can realize that I was very much hurted over the pardon boards decision I do fail to understand. Why they should go on keeping me but still I hope that they will soon change their mind and turn me loose at least give me another chance. Now yes I am very much pleased over my radio it is very comforting because allways do enjoy good music and right at this time I have it on getting music out of Texas the man is playing a fiddle and it sounds very good well this is all for now Mrs Hester you see I have not the mind for writing more so kindest regards and best wishes to you and all.

yours Haywood Patterson [Reel 5, Box 5, #000384 (folder c55), ILD]

March 13, 1940
Andy Wright
Kilby Prison

Dear Andy:
Enclosed you will find the usual money order for $3.00.
We want to assure you that in spite of the fact that the Parole Board has not returned a favorable decision, that we have not stopped, but shall continue to carry on to bring about a reconsideration by the Board.
Keep up your spirits and bear in mind we shall never cease in our efforts to secure your freedom.
Everyone in the office wishes to be remembered.
Sincerely yours,
HESTER G. HUNTINGTON [Reel 5, Box 5, #000866 (folder c62), ILD]

[Letter from Josephine Powell, mother of Ozie Powell]
Atlanta, Ga.
March 19 1940

My Dear frind just a few lines to let you here from me we all are up But not so well lisen i Ben wateing for a hereing it out down here that my Boy is out i Been looking for ancer so i will right and ask plese let me no in your next letter all so rully dose thank you all for my check witch I reeive eatch mont i ruly dose like this kind of wheather it suit my dose all so my close all so my feetz so ancer rat a way plese for I ruly dose want to n if my Boy is out I am still at 882 cherry Alley. Good luck tot all from josphine powell to my dear friend anna. [Reel 6, Box 5, #000220 (folder c68), ILD]

[The following is a draft of a letter that was sent to Haywood Patterson.]

Stuyvesant 9-4552
INTERNATIONAL LABOR DEFENSE
National Office
112 East 19th Street New York City

Hon. Vito Marcantonio, President   Anna Damon, Secretary
William L. Patterson, Vice-President   Robert W. Dunn, Treasurer

March 20, 1940

Mr. Haywood Patterson
Atmore, Alabama

Dear Haywood:

Our letters must have crossed in the mail. I am glad the radio reached you, and that you like it.

I can understand why you feel disappointed after the news that shocked us all. The Parole Board in my opinion denied freedom at this time to you remaining Boys because, united, you have become a symbol of the struggle of the Negro people against oppression. The Parole Board prefers to separate "the Scottsboro Case" into separate consideration now of each boy's case. There is but one way to answer such a decision: to continue the struggle against oppression and to fight for your freedom.

The National Negro Congress will meet next month in Washington and will discuss the Scottsboro case. The Defense Committee has decided to take steps in your behalf. Ben Davis of the Daily Worker has written an editorial asking for letters of protest.

The International Labor Defense will continue to do everything in its power to extend the fight for your release. You can depend upon us.
Sincerely yours,
HGH
(The following sentence was scratched out, i.e., deleted from the draft: "the decision of the Board coincides with a rising tide against trade union leaders which can only be met with solidarity and organization") [Reel 5, Box 5, #000381 (folder c55), ILD]

Haywood Patterson
R.R. 2, Box 38
Atmore, Ala.
[Written between March 20 and 27]

My Dear Mrs. Huntington

This certainly is a great pleasure for me to think that I should write a friend who is dear as you are you are most kind and it always put a warm feeling in my heart upon receiving your letters. I too and very sorry that you was a little late with my monthly allowances I was very much uncomforted about it and then too again I must admit that the little you all send isn't really enough to keep me going I suffer so much.

I am sure sorry for saying this but it is really true. Now I hope you are going to understand me when I explain myself and do be most agreeable with me. You see by you all being a little late in sending me my monthly allowances I put myself in debt. and right now I am in distress and I would like you very much to send me at once my monthly allowances for the coming month and then you wont have to put yourself to any trouble in sending it to me when the time come for you to send it to me again.

I am very glad to learn about you and delegates are taking a trip to Washington to be present to the National Negro Congress in my behalf and the behalf of others I hope you all will makes them realize that I am not really a guilty boy but my carelessness has led me to my present situation for leaving my home but any man that has had my bitter experience in life. But the complete gratification and satisfaction that have been my pleasure in knowing you Mrs. Hester. You have proven yourself to be a good friend and I hate bothering you so much but you must listen this time and don't fail to give me an assisting hand while in distress I need three dollars at once and I hope you will make it possible that I should have it you see Anna Damon used to send us our monthly allowances before hand and you must send me mine this time no sooner than you receive this letter because I am in distress and just got to have it or something bad may happen.

So be sure to send me his amount now and next month you wont have it to do. So I must close for now expecting to hear from you in the earliest possible future so quite forgive my begging you and excuse my bothering you so much but you must grant me this favor this time. So do send me the three dollars so that I may be able to receive it by Monday.

Kindest [Reel 5, Box 5, #000386 (folder c55), ILD]

Montgomery Alabama
March 31, 1940
My Dear Miss Huntington,

I write to express my sincere appreciation for your kindness in complying to my wish. You can rest assured that I will always be thankful to you for making the sacrifer, which serves to show me that I have a true and sympathetic friend who is always rady to lend a helping hand to one who is in my surroundings. It is true friendship that one need in these environments.

I shall always treasure your precious gift and I shall always endeavor to show you that I really appreciate anything you might say or do to give me comfort, chers and encouragement.

This letter leaves me feeling fairly well so to speak, and I hope when it come to you it will find you happy and are enjoying good health

I want you to take the measure of your ring finger and send it to me in your next letter and I hope I get one very soon and I will have you a beautiful novelty ring made and send it to you.

Now let me hear from you soon and tell me what you think the near future will mean to me but remember I like facts of the matter and next be lifting false hopes as I have had so much of that — I do not mean by you. As you know everyone like to know what to expect if there is anything being done. I am wishing and hoping that things will by favorable to me in the near future — say a little prayer for me each night and I shall do the same.

Now my you be successful and happy and enjoy the future. I wish you many blessings.

With fond regards I remain as ever,
Andy Wright [Reel 5, Box 5, #000869 (folder c62), ILD]

Atlanta ga.
Answered at once
April 16 1940

My dear frind just a few lines to let you Here from me i am not feeling so
well hot weather get here with hi Blood presser i dont get much chance to rest
i work. you all plese ad a little more to my check so i can take [shots ?] twice
a mont for it you dont hafter mail it to me you can mail it to my docter if you
can pleas do that for me plese i just live under aspirin trying to keep my head
from Bursting open I reccive the check truly close think you plese dont think
hard of me for not for writing sunner i Ben feeling very bd not much Better to
night so i will close witch Best wishes to all if ou all here any thing form my
Boy plese plese plese let me here how hen gettin a long it Bout to run me
crazy plese let me here from him if you no eneything at all plese ancer rat
back from,
Josephine Powell
882 cherry alley

if you all can help me get my shortz twice a mont plese do so plese i realy
dose kneed it I rully will think you all so much [Reel 6, Box 5, #000221,
(folder c68), ILD].

To my dear frind
Hester Huntery
[Written in mid–May]

lisen i had all ready rote you last night I went to the carnbel olden [court
building] montgomery are making speeks to get ozie Powell a out fittest trable
olden ay my Boy is gone stone Blind say he cant se a Bit. Plese let me go
down to see a Bout him if my poor Boy is Bling [blind] lord what will I do
plese plese at once.
from Josephine Powell [Reel 6, Box 5, #000252 (folder c68), ILD].

Haywood Patterson
R.R. 2 Box 38
Atmore, Ala.
[Written in mid–May]

My Dear Friend Mrs Hester

Although I guess you may no doubt perhaps feel a little ways surprised
upon receiving this letter. But nonetheless I hope that your surprise will be
that of an agreeable kind and after all you must pardon me in my long silence
in not writing you as I have received [   ] one of your letters but somehow of
lately I have been so worried and depressed until I seem to just couldn't get
myself together for writing anyone.

Now I has been wondering whether it is true that Olen Montgomery was in Detroit Michigan and jail for ravishing a Color woman. I read that in a newspaper and I later read where he was released. Now he is making life [   ] miserable for us left behind and also making it more difficult for us in getting freed. I cant imagine that he is guilty of such an act. But if he is really guilty he should be given the hot seat that's the way I feel about it. Those Four 4 boys which were freed has helped us none at all but instead they have made life for us a living hell. I never imagined that a human life was held as cheap as it is here the prisoners here are regarded as animals with-out soul or feeling they does all kind of farm works here I mean the work from six to six and it never rains here why for two weeks straight we were working in mud and water up to our knees. Now if that isn't a slow death to a fellow he will never die. This is a horrible place here our misery and death and all kinds of suffering all the time. why I am always feeling bad with a cold or some other suffering. But the Doctor says you never get sick here unless you die. The public should know about this place.

Now my dear its one more thing. I would like to have you to do for me and that is of course I don't expect you to keep me going in Radio's but I would like you this time to remind some of my good friends about my wants of a small radio this time a R.C.A. Victor Radio that will last the longest. You see I cant seem to go on without one as it brings me all the good music and news of the outside world A radio is all the comfort I have here and it seems to help me to while away the time. So be sure to have my friends including Eugene Williams, Willie Robertson and Roy Wright tell them and my friends to please chip in and get me a small R.C.A. victor Radio immediately and if it be possible I will gladly appreciate it they may be able to get me one costing five or six dollars I would so much appreciate your kindness to see that I have one and I promise you after this one is worn out I shall not wish for another one. You may take a dollar out of my monthly allowances and help my friends to get me another one and just send me two dollars for the month and you can do that until the radio is paid for each month just take two dollars out of my monthly allowance. Now I hope you will see to it that I should have another Radio of my amusement here and I promise you after this one is worn away I will not wish for another one.

So I will close hoping that you will write me in the shortest possible time concerning it. So please do write me at once and let me know is it so about Olen Montgomery. This is all for now will write you again soon.
Yours Haywood Patterson [Reel 5, Box 5, #000391 (folder c55), ILD]

May 29, 1940
Mr. Haywood Patterson
R. R. 2, Box 38
Atmore, Alabama

Dear Haywood:

I have a great deal of sympathy with your feeling of discouragement in heart and mind about yourself and this whole situation. We are doing and shall do the very best we can not only to help on the final result but in making your time in jail as easy for you as we can. You must realize there are still five of you in, as well as four out, in whom we have a real concern, and that the general situation not only of your case but of the world in general makes it very difficult for us to raise money without hurting your cause. The Committee will do the very best it can, and I have told them about recent letter to me. I know it is hard to be patient under the circumstances, but what can not be changed at the moment has to be endured if we are going to work it out at all for you in the end.

Yours sincerely,

(Written by Dr. Allan Knight Chalmers) [AKCP, Box 30, folder 1-11]

Haywood Patterson
R.R.2 Box 38
Atmore, Ala.
[Written most likely on June 1]

My Dear Dr. Chalmers:

Your letter of May 29th has been received and carefully considered. I found pleasure in reading your letter as they doesn't come often from you and I guess that is why it made me feel sort of uplifted after reading. Now that I can understand how things is Doctor but you don't half realize my condition and if things dont soon make a change I am afraid that I will go mad.

You see these people here are driving me crazy and if this thing don't soon come to an end I am going to end it all myself by commiting a suicide as I would rather to be dead than to keep going on suffering under such strain. I have tried so hard to find pleasure in living but life doesn't mean anything to me if I have to go on suffering in prison. And I am going to end it all within the next two months, you can believe it or not but all you have got to do is just wait and see that what I am saying will come true.

You see my dear Doctor I find no sense in suffering all the time and I cant see any other way out except thd one mentioned above. I know you aare going to say that I a am just talking but you wait and see don't something terrible happen. You see this trouble have killed my mother and father and I just can't bear to go on suffering in mind. Now one more thing I would like you to so for me for rhe time being and that is I would like you to get me a carton of Bugler tobacco it will cost you about a dollar at wholesale price. So don't fail me Doctor with all the confidence I have in you.

You see I trust you more so than any so please dont try to make it more harder for me. when I say that I an living a miserable life here. And so if it be possible for you to send me the tobacco, I mean Bugler tobacco at once do so. This all for now and I trust you to keep this letter and saying to yourself for certain reasons you need not tosay anything about it. I am yours most Sincerely.

Haywood Patterson [AKCP, Box 30, folder 1-11]

Montgomery Ala
Camp Kilby
June 3–40

Mrs Anna Damon
Dear Comrade:

I am sure you will be surprise to hear from me but however I trust you are all been served with the very best of health. I have not been doing so well especial in health. My teeth have been causing me much suffing. I have several decaving teeth and I can save them if I start in time I have already save Fifteen dollars $15.00 for that purpose and I need Ten more. I am writing to Mr. Shapiro asking for a little increase in my month allowance. So — want you to increase your as much as Five dollars $5.00 extra for that purpose. I want to have them fix just as soon as I get the money. So I hope you all will not disappoint me. Now I do not want you to send me that amount every month just this month. I would not ask you all for this extra amount if I did not need it. So I will close expecting to hear form you soon.

Respectfully your Clarence Norris [Reel 5, Box 4, #00116 (folder c53), ILD].

Montgomery, Ala.
Kilby Prison
June 9 —1940

Dear Hester,

I Received your letter Was indeed glad to hear from you although it found me not So well at the present. Though I am in great hopes these few lines Will find you Well and in joying a happy life.

Listen Hester I am writing you for the information concerning my case. I would like very much to know just when it will come up before the pardon Board again. Please let me know immediately and listen Hester can I depend upon you to send my mother down to see me. Its been a very long time since I have seen or sit and talk with her thanks I would like to see her on some personal affairs. In doing this Hester please send her enough money so that she will be able to Bring me a nice Box. I am just about gone nuts for Some Real good home cooked food, and please Dont fail to let me know just what Stept is being made in my Behalf.

So i am putting Every inch of my Dependence in you to attend to this for me.

So i guest i might as well come to a close looking forward to hear from you at your Earliest Date. Yours very truly,

Andy Wright [Reel 5, Box 5, #000871, (folder c62), ILD]

Jun 12, 1940
Dr. Chalmers,
Scottsboro Defense Committee

Dear Dr. Chalmers:

I write to ask the committee to help me to get a job and help me along. Write I can get a job since last year Rev. Harten haven't took care of me as he promised I went up to Buffalo a couple of months ago to try to fine work butt I was able only to get a few odd jobs a garage and filling station. When I got back to New York I went to see Rev. Harten and he told me about the man who has been going around to churches as one of the Scottsboro boys taking against us and making it hard for all off us boys. So I went to see Roy Wright an Richard More and now I want the committee to do something to stop this and try to get the other boys out. I am staying with Roy now and I have no room. So I need your help quick. Thank you for what you have done for us boys ad what you will do.
Yours truly
Willie Robinson [Reel 5, Box 5, #(?) (folder c59), ILD]

Montgomery, Ala
August 12, 1940

My Dear Miss Huntington;
    I am at a total loss as to why I did not receive my regular allowance at the usual time which was lose Friday. Is it possible that you made aslight mistake and sens an order to one of the others on the date you should have send mine? I noticed that one of them that usually get his after I do, received his the day I should have received mine. Although this has been done before I do not know what to make of is, as it is. I was put to a bit of inconvience and I am badly in need [   ] now.
    I have written to my mother several times but she has failed to answer. I wonder whether you have heard from her lately. if so please let me know and I would appreciate it very much if you whould write to her and find out why she does not answer my letters. I send my good wishes to you and all. I am as ever,
Clarence Norris [Reel 5, Box 4, #000117, ILD]

Cleveland, O
September 1940
Miss Annie Dammer
    I receive the money order alright try to Send as much as $6.00 next time Because next time it so much the [Carty] don't give i need somme bed lined and [Comear] in my xmas Box the last letter I got from Clarence he was ask me feer money he need it for little thing he need & often think about the draft to all we Can do is pray and trust in the lord
    So all form
    Ida Norris to
    Miss Annie Dammer
Answer soon [Reel 6, Box 5, #000063 (folder c66), ILD]

Haywood Patterson
Atmore State Prisonary
Atmore, Alabama

(two radios were sent: March 1940–Sept. 1940)

My Dear Mrs. Huntington,

I have received your letters but for some Cause, I just couldnt seem to make myself answer them although that's rather difficult to imagine, isn't it? But after all you are not under an — obligation to assist me once. only my wish is that you will response to my request. You see my dear friend, my heart bleed every day from suffering and griefing but you all cant seem to realize my condition why I suffer in need of cigarettes writing material and others little necessary articles that I need most badly for my comfort here. an of course I could obtain them if only I had the cash.

Now I dont deserves all this unnecessary hardship although I am not the best kind of boy, Mrs Hester, but I do tryest so Hard to be everybody friend and am one who ask for nothing of life except to get along and do a good turn for my fellowman whenever the occasion presented itself. And it is inconceivable that anyone should wish to see me continue with suffering unbearable. You see I want more than anything to get this thing completed so that I can be free and want [   ] expect favors from anyone. at least I want to soon get out so that I can get used to the ways of the world & lose some of the mannerisma which mark me as a small boy.

Now my friend, I do not care for any kind of clothing material or anything all I want you to get me is a small cheap radio. You see that is all the consolation hat a man can possibly Have Here and that is a radio to bring him all the out side news. Now I should like nothing better then for you to send me another one. please try to know that to Have a radio is most consoling especially when one gets lonely. I shell come to a close Hoping for a prompt favorable response. And again I Hope I am not due for another disappointment. My best regards to all.

Cordially yours

Haywood Patterson [Reel 5, Box 5, #000410 (folder c55), ILD]

ATLANTA LIFE INSURANCE COMPANY
148 Auburn Avenue, N.E.
Atlanta, Georgia

October 3rd 1940

Mr. Roy Wilkins, Asst. Sec'y
N. A. A. C. P.
New York, N.Y.

Dear Mr. Wilkins:

Olin Montgomery, one of the Scottsboro Boys just left my office. Due to his experience here in Atlanta in August of 1939, I was dumbfounded to see him here again. He stated that he arrived last night and that he wanted to stay, provided he could find work.

He began his conversation by asking me if I had heard of his trouble in Detroit, Michigan and then stated about as follows:

> "I worked, in all, about six weeks since I left Atlanta. The charges made against me by the girl in Detroit were untrue. She was a prostitute and got angry because I could not give her all that she wanted. She cut up two suits of my clothes and my underwear. Atty. Roxborough defended me and the girl would not come into court and swear against me as she knew that the charges were untrue. The judge suggested that I leave Detroit. I decided that I would rather be here in the South with my people. I thought that if I was here, I could always get a meal and a place to sleep."

I gathered from his conversation that his homecoming was not as pleasant as he expected and that he did not receive the welcome that he expected. He rambled on and on and then told the following incident

> "Me and a boy was on the bus. We were sitting on the rear seat. Some soldiers got on the bus and the bus driver, looked around, seeing no vacant seats, said — 'you boys get up and let these people sit down.' I told him that I had come a long way and that I wanted my seat, 'if you are not going to get up, then get off.'"

He stated that he got off of the bus and got a cab and went into Winchester, Virginia. He called the bus company at New York and that the call cost Two Dollars and (2.40) forty cents. The ticket agent there gave him another ticket and told him, among other things, to shut up for they would put you in jail mighty quick in Winchester."

I believe that Olin Montgomery is mentally unbalanced. I do not think that he has a sound mind, by any stretch of imagination. I do not see how he could be otherwise after spending as long as he did in Alabama jails and going through the experiences that he has gone through with. I wonder, after all, if death is not sometime preferable to a long term in some of these southern jails and chaingangs, considering the terrible toll in mind, spirit and body.

I am writing to find out if the Scottsboro Defense Committee is still interested in Olin Montgomery and his future. As I see it, Olin Montgomery is mentally unbalanced and is going to be a ward on society for many years to come and possibly, the balance of his natural life.

I sincerely regret the return of Olin Montgomery to Atlanta, for, I think that any one familiar with Race Relations here in the deep south, will realize that — a State that will elect a man as Governor, whose attitude on Race Problems is like that of governor elect Talmadge, is no place for a Scottsboro boy.

I would appreciate it if you would let me know whether or not the Scottsboro Defense Committee is still interested in Olin Montgomery and to what extent?

> Very sincerely yours,
> E. M. Martin, Secretary,
> Atlanta Life Insurance Co.

[Reel 22, Part 6, #000793, NAACP]

Atmore State Farm
Atmore, Ala.
Oct. 6 1940

Miss Hester G Huntington
112 East 19 Street
N.Y. City, NY

Dear Miss Huntington,

i wrote Miss Damon a couple weeks ago to please send me a Radio, and for some un known reason i have not herd from her, Miss Huntington will you and Miss Damon see to me having a Radio as i would injoy one very much, and i would appreciate it to the highest of corse you all sent my Pal haywood Patterson one, But i don't get to injoy it. Because we are not in the same cell, Miss Huntington this letter leave me well and doing about the same, considering where i am. i Sincere hope you are injoying life greatest Blessing. Please remind me to all of my friends.
Sincerely yours,
Ozie Powell
Atmore State Farm
Atmore, Ala.
(contact: Christina Stead, 212 E. 16th St. NY City) [Reel 5, Box 5, #000618 (folder c58), ILD]

AIR MAIL-SPECIAL DELIVERY

October 9, 1940

Mr. Eugene Martin
Atlanta Life Insurance Company
148 Auburn Avenue, N.E.

Dear Mr. Martin:

I have returned from the Middle west and found your letter of October 3 about Olen Montgomery.

Olen has been a problem to the Scottsboro Defense Committee ever since he came under our care in 1938. When he was released from prison in July 1937, he was offered a job on the very day that he arrived in New York City. I was sitting in the office of Samuel Leibowitdz and by telephone Mr. Leibowitz was attempting to secure jobs for the boys with his friends. One friend was in the clothing businesss and offered Olen a job delivering suits at $17 a week. Olen turned it down. In fact all of othe boys were reluctant to go to work. Someone had made them believe that the famous Scottsboro case had been "a gold mine" to organizations and individuals over a period of years and, as one of them expressed it, "we want to get some of this money for ourselves." Mr. Leibowitz turned them over to a Reverend Thomas Harten, a Baptist minister of Brooklyn, N.Y., who exploited them by taking them for personal appearances before his congregation and other congregations in the New York area. This type of thing soon wore out and the Scottsboro committee took two of the boys on a limited tour over the country with their expenses paid, the understanding being that the money was to go into a defense fund for the liberation of the other boys.

Finally, after all tours were over, Olen decided to come under the wing of the Scottsboro committee. For many months, we paid him $20 a week and indulged him by allowing him to go to school to learn how to play the saxophone. He said that he wanted to be a musician. Finally, we cut his allowance to $15 a week and tried to impress upon him the necessity of his getting a job. He kept saying he was in bad health and could not do much work. All during this time, in spite of this generous allowance, he was coming to us to help him buy an overcoat, or to get his clothes out of pawn. Always there was an excuse to get a few more dollars.

Finally he decided that he wanted to go to Atlanta and, as you know, we arranged for him to go down there and referred him to you for advice. You know what happened. He got into trouble, or thought there would be trouble, within a few days and we immediately sent him money to visit his aunt in Detroit, Mich.

We put him under the care of our Detroit branch, which is the largest in the N.A.A.C.P. and which has the largest treasury. They did everything possible to help him, giving him an allowance at our direction of $10 a week and assisting him in getting employment. After about nine months of this arrangement, our Detroit branch officially threw up its hands and notified us that Olen was "impossible," that they could do nothing more for him, and asked us to send for him.

Before we could send for him, he got into the trouble in Detroit with the woman about which he told you. We then brought him to New York. He had not been here very long before he had an argument with the landlord of the place where he was staying, the results of which was that he was ordered to leave. It was then that he decided that he must go back to his people in Georgia, that he could not get along up here, etc., etc.

I was in the Middlewest when he left, but Mr. Morris Shapiro, secretary of the Scottsboro Defense Committee, tells me that they gave him $25 to go back to Georgia, since he was so insistent that that was the thing he must do. I understand the bus fare was $13 or $14, and he, therefore, had at least $11 extra money above his bus fare.

Mr. Shapiro tells me that he explained to Olen that this was all the money the committee felt it could put up for him and that we expected that he would make every effort to get a job, and since be was living at home, he would not have, for the time being at least, the problem of room rent and food. Mr. Shapiro has asked me to say that the Scottsboro committee feels that it has been very generous financially with Olen and that we cannot be responsible for any further financial outlay. Of course, the committee is interested in his welfare and wants to see him keep out of trouble not only for his own sake, but for the sake of the effect of a scandal on the chances of secuuring the release of the other boys. We believe that the time has come for Olen to get a grip on himself and to realize that the world expects him to make some effort in his own behalf.

The committee will be very happy if you will consent to advise with Olen and to assist him, if it is possible, in getting employment; but the committee does not authorize you to extend any financial aid to him in the expectation that it will be repaid by the Committee.

I wish to express hearty agreement with the sentiment in your letter that the damage which was done to Olen by his imprisonment in Alabama is a great tragedy and one which has already had an effect upon his whole life.

Very sincerely yours
Assistant Secretary

RW:DW [Reel 22, Part 6, #000791, NAACP]

Mr. Olen Montgomery
480 Jones Avenue
Atlanta, Georgia
October 21, 1940

Dear Olen:

I received your letter this morning and will pass on your request to the Scottsboro Defense Committee, but I want to say at once that you cannot hope to make any progress by threatening the people who have done more for you than anybody else in the world.

If for any reason you should make any statements about the Scottsboro Defense Committee or any members of it, you will be harming only yourself.

You see, Olen, there is a great deal about this case which you do not know anything about and do not understand. A record of what the Scottsboro Committee has done is down in black and white over a period of years and that record speaks for itself. From the day you arrived in New York in July 1937, the committee had done everything possible for your welfare, and the record will show that it has been more than generous.

On the day of your arrival, I sat in the office of Mr. Leibowitz and heard him offer you a job paying $17 a week. I heard you say that you did not want to work. Mr. Leibowitz had secured this job for you over the telephone a few hours after you got off the train. It was as a delivery boy for a clothing store.

The committee bought you two complete outfits of clothing from the skin out, arranged for your lodging and provided you with spending money.

Inspite of the fact that you decided to ignore the committee and go on a speaking tour for the purpose of, as you said, "to make yourself some money," the committee stood ready at all times to assist you.

When you returned from the tour after discovering that nobody was "making any money" but that all efforts were for the release of the other boys from prison, you came to the committee and said that you were willing to follow its advice.

The committee made you a generous allowance of $20 a week and paid you that amount for more than a year. All during that time, we tried to get you to go to school and to prepare yourself for a job. But you had many excuses. One of them was that you were "not strong." Another excuse was that you were "very nervous." Another excuse was that your eyes were bad. The committee sent you to an oculist and secured new glasses for you.

Despite the fact that you were getting $20 a week, you made frequent demands on the committee for additional money, you pawned your clothes and demanded that they be redeemed. You bought a guitar. You took a few saxophone lessons, and you bought two overcoats. In the spring of 1939, the committee felt that it would have to cut down on you allowance and it reduced it to $15 a week. You will remember that at that time we talked to you and tried to get you to go to work. We made efforts to assist you in getting a job. You continued to complain and to give excuses, and in the summer of 1939, you said you wanted to go back to your people in Atlanta.

The committee agreed to send you to Atlanta, but before you could leave, you came to see me and said you would have to have a wardrobe suitcase in order to carry all your clothes. You also told me that you had "only eight shirts" and that you would need some more, since you were "almost ragged."

You will remember that we bought you a suitcase, some shirts, socks, ties, underwear, etc.

We sent you to Detroit, and the committee asked Dr. James J. McClendon, president of the Detroit branch of the N.A.A.C.P., to look out for you and to help you get a job. Your allowance was set at $10 a week. The committee understands that you secured one or two jobs in Detroit, but that you could not seem to hold on to them.

In Detroit this last summer you were arrested in some trouble with a woman and the committee agreed to provided lawyers for you. They have just sent us their bill for $160!

After the trouble in Detroit was cleared up, the committee brought you back to New York and tried to secure relief for you with a view to getting some employment later. In the meantime, the committee continued to give you a cash allowance.

You had been back in New York only a few weeks when you got in some trouble at your lodging place and the landlord ordered you out. Here again the committee stepped in and provided you with cash and arranged for you to stay temporaily at the Harlem YMCA. You insisted that you wanted to go back to Atlanta and the committee provided you with bus fare and spending money to go to Atlanta.

On the way to Atlanta you had an argument with a bus driver in Virginia and had to get off the bus to avoid further trouble.

You told us that you were sure you could get along all right in Georgia because your relatives had a farm where you could work. You said you did not want to cause the committee any trouble and that you were going to behave yourself from now on.

Now as soon as you get to Atlanta you write back to New York for more money and when the committee tells you that it gave you $25 and expected you to begin to look after yourself, you write back making threats against the committee and saying you will "talk" in Atlanta and "mess up" the committee.

I am writing you this letter in order to remind you of the record you have made. This record is clear. If you cause any trouble in Atlanta, it will be trouble for yourself and not the committee, because the committee has done more than its share for you and your record of behavior is not the best in the world.

The committee does not want to have any trouble with you, and it does not want to embarrass you before the public. The committee wants to help you and we say now, just as we said two years ago, that you must settle down, get yourself a job, and realize that you must make an effort to support yourself.

If the public knew all the facts in your case, they would blame the committee for being so easy and generous with you.

Most of all, anything you say to cause trouble and publicity will make it hard for the boys who are still in prison and will hurt their chances of being released. The people of Alabama would like nothing better than to point to you as an example of why the other boys should not be released. You can help them and help yourself by trying to get a job and settle down.

I am writing this advice as a friend. This is not an official letter of the committee but a letter from me to you because I do not want to see you hurt yourself.

Very sincerely yours,

Assistant Secretary [Reel 22, Part 6, #000796, NAACP].

Atlanta, Ga.
480 Jones Ave.
Oct. 23 — 1940

Dear Mr. Wilkins,

I received your very kind letter and was more than glad to hear from you. But Mr. Wilkins, let me explain to you, I have already had my trouble. I dont care nothing about the committees record. But I will admitd that they have been nice to me, and I haven't been such a bad fellow. I have did everything I could do, to work along with the committee. When I ought to went out and got money for my self, and went in business.

I wouldn't do it trying to be nice and made a fool out o my damn self. And you and the committee can make all of the excuses you want to, and send them to me. I mean what I say and I am not afraid to speak, and I know what I am talking about. Some people thank I am a fool. But I am not, and I will never forget what has been done to me. Since 1937 I should be rich. I have never wanted to do no body an harm. But deal square with me because I watches everything and I am not a fool, and I dont want to hear about what Leibowitz did, because he aint no damn good. He knew I wasnt able to work, and you to and I dont have to have no excuse about my eyes. Because the doctor know that I cant see much and I am not in good health. And I have did everything I could to geet a job and can prove it. And the committee haven't made one effort to get me a job. Dr. McClendon got me a job in Detroit and I didn't quit the job. And I haven't bought me too over coats either. The committee will have a record, if they haven't got one just because I haven't been lucky enough to get a job, they didn't have to just let me down without any thing. And I dont like it. I still dont have no job. But I am still trying to get one. And ever who say I dont want to work tells a God damn lye, and the truth aint in them. Here is where I spoken to 800 people. Didn't ask for no money. Didn't want any! Just trying my luck out and didn't do any harm.

I herd the meeting and spoken very nice about the committee, and the naacp

yours truly.
Olen Montgomery

[Reel 22, Part 6, #000804, NAACP]

Oct. 27 1940
Miss Damon and Huntington
112 East 19th Street
New York City, N.Y.

Dear Miss Damon and Huntington,

i received My Radio the 18th of this Month, i was so over joyed to receive it until i almost forget my Very surrounding. it is a heart felt Pleasure to Express my thanks and appreciation toward you for your kind Deeds. i consider it a token of Memories and an Emblem of humanity. i injoy 3 are 4 Program very much, such as Amos and Andy, Musical and the war news, although I am hoping that we of the U.S.A. will not have to fight. i have me a guitar too. i practice Music from my radio on it. this leave me feeling fine considering where i am i Sincere hope the [   ] of you are injoying life greatest blessing Please remind me ot all of my good friends.

i remain.
Very Sincerely
Ozie Powell
Atmore State Farm
Atmore Ala.

P S. Miss Huntington and Miss Damon i would enjoy hearing from you all a your most leasured time i injoy reading letter from the out side world as I dont get very many. thinking you in advance.

[Reel 5, Box 5, #000620 (folder c58), ILD]

---

818 West 8th St
Cincinnati, O
12/3/40

Dear Miss Anna

We need some clothes for we need some this year's because it is getten Cold here my size is 34 in the wase, shirt size 16 and socks size 11. my mother some dress size 38 and undereclothes for she are not works and are not able to buy any. I hold you a merry xmas and a happy new year.

Willie Patterson [Reel 6, Box 5, #000147 (folder c67), ILD]

2576 E 40 St.
Cleveland Ohio
Dec. 5 1940

My Dearest Friend I received the package I sure did appreciate it to the highest. I thank you all so much. You all sent it to my old address so send all my other mail and packages to 2576 E. 40st. that is my new address. Please try to send my check so I can get it before Friday.

I wish you all Merry Christmas and a happy New Year.
yours Truly
Ida Norris [Reel 6, Box 5, #000069 (folder c66), 1940, ILD]

11

LETTERS FROM 1941
Dear Miss Hester Huntington

In many ways, the Scottsboro trial became the first criminal justice case in which the defendants who were African Americans attracted international attention. As such, millions of people were exposed not only to arguments for and against racial segregation, but to the willingness of individuals to sacrifice their time and energy in support of judicial justice and human rights. Considering the political developments that were occurring in Europe and in Asia, along with the emergence of racialized political dogma and rallies in major United States cities in support of Nazism, the Scottsboro case became an additional reflection of an evolving international political struggle concerning Colonialism, Fascism and Communism. To a certain extent, these ideological elements were incorporated into the judicial drama of the Scottsboro case, as the prosecution side projected themselves as defending the country against Communist instigations. From this perspective, a racialized segregated judicial system was not only deemed by some to be constitutionally and morally correct in the face of a foreign communist ideology, but needed to forestall the "negro" from being duped or used by foreign political instigators!

By the end of the year, the United States was committed to a two-front war in Europe and the Pacific, and the Scottsboro Defense Committee (SDC), now functioning since 1935 as a judicial alliance between the ILD, NAACP and ACLU, continued the judicial fight to obtain freedom for the remaining five defendants. However, a major interactive component in this process were letters exchanged by the defendants with the SDC members such as Anna Damon, Rose Baron, Hester Huntington, Roy Wilkins, and William Patterson involving requests of money for cigarettes, radios, guitars, and books, that were deemed essential for their psychological and physical survival. This feature of the judicial battle was as critical as were the courtroom attorneys. Notably, the level of communication with SDC members became an essential informational link and psychological release point for both the Scottsboro defendants and their supporters.

Haywood Patterson
Atmore State Farm
Atmore, Ala.

My Dear Mrs. Hester. My desire is to address you more courteously, because you has been most kind & considerate to me. only I wish you could Have seen the relief that crossed my face upon receiving the radio. am glad you have a greater concern for my welfare now that the short days of loneliness and long nights of Terror. May [   ] undoubtly pass a way. Although hopelessness and [   ] regrets one so keen that they paines as might physical hurts. only a brave Heart Have kept me from going mad. Since my mother and father have deceased, I can recall all the anguish & misery and it is not encouraging to consider the vast amount of labor that still comfort me before I can be safe & free to enjoy the rights that is due me. the mere thought of it appalled me, of course with my limited knowledge of practical matters, and with the means at hand I must put the best fight for life & liberty of which I am capable, even though am weak and inexperienced — and unafraid but without a Hope.

Now first of all I must Have you to know that I wrote you a little too quick concerning my having not received the radio because on the same day I mailed it the radio came. I guess I owe you a poligize! So quite forgive my being so anxious. I guess you realize How proud and grateful I am to you Mrs. Hester. Now it may not be any of my business , but perhaps I shell Have to make it so. You see it is rather unusual that I can never learn anything about the other boys and I should prefer being informed. Well Thank you a good deal for the Swell radio & know that I can never forget your Kindness. Best dearest love & good wishes to you & all.
Hopefully yours Haywood Patterson [Reel 5, Box 5, #000423 (folder c56), ILD]

Kilby Prison
Montgomery, Ala.
Jan 7, 1941

Miss Haster Hunt
Dear Miss Haster:

I received your letter today glad was I to received such early reply. yes miss Haster about the radio it is ok to send it the Warden will permitted me to have it so you don't have to worrie about that so please send it as soon as possible I will highly appreciate it.

So please give my best wishes to every one so I will close at this time hoping to hear from you soon.
I remain yours
Charlie Weems [Reel 5, Box 4, #000742 (folder c53), ILD]

STATE DEPARTMENT
of
CORRECTIONS AND INSTITUTIONS
Prison At
KILBY
Montgomery, Alabama
Jan. 10th, 1941

Mrs. Hester G. Huntington
International labor Defense
112 East 19th St.
New York, N.Y.

Dear Madam:

In reply to your inquiry of recent date, relative to sending a slightly used radio to Charlie Weems, inmate, this will advise you that it will be permissible for him to receive this radio, provided that its size conforms to our rules.

We permit the prisoners to have radios, but request that their friends and relatives refrain from sending large radios. Any radio with the over-all dimensions of about 12" × 10" × 15", or less, would be permissible.

Very truly yours,
E. R. Wilson
Senior Prison Warden
of Alabama

ERW/d [Reel 5, Box 4, #000744 (folder c53), ILD]

March 18 1941
Kilby Prison
Montgomery, Ala

Mrs Hester,

Your letter of last month was recid. It found me and also the other two boys that here in good health — and doing the best we can. Mrs Hester I am in debt. I realize its my own fault. I own out more money than I can pay and the fellows that I owe think now that we are liable to be released any day now. So they are pressing me daily for their money. So if you can please send me as much as twenty dollars at once and then you can deduct it from my allowance. for I am sure if I don't soon pay the fellows it will be some serious trouble. and I know of no one to turn too except you all, I will be expect an answer soon.

Your Sincerely
Clarence Norris [Reel 5, Box 4, #000119, ILD]

2576 E. 40th Street
Cleveland Ohio
April 8, 1941

My Dear Friend:

Mrs. Hester G Hungention,

Your letter Found me well and getting alone all right hope these few lines will find you all likewise. We are having some very nice weather it is getting warm. I am sure glad to see it. Tell me in your next letter what is being done on the Scottsburg Boys case. I would also like for you to find out if possible why Clarence don't write me. I haven't had a letter From him in some time. I would like to know if it is that he is or is not allowed to write or if it is his own fault. I am thinking about the parade you all are going to have there in May I sure would like to be there. because I know it is going to be wonderful. listen dear if possible please try to send me as much as $6.00 this time if you can. The baby say please try to send her some dress for the summer. Write and tell me where is angelo [Angelo Herndon] and send me his address. and where is Richard B Moore? Give all of my Friends my Best regards.

I remain your

Truly Ida Norris [Reel 5, Box 4, #000071 (folder c66), ILD]

April 21 1941
Louise Patterson
Mrs. Zierler
6 Pine Street
Woodmere N.Y.

Dear Madam,

I am writing in case you all don't know Haywood Patterson my brother is very sick. I recieved a telegram yesterday Sunday April 20, 1941. I know you all remember him one of the remaining five (5) Scotts B. boys. and he needs one of his sisters down there to see him right away. So my sister that are in Cincinnati Ohio is the closest one to the state of Alabama. I am asking you all to please send her money enought to go down to Atmore Alabama to see what he wonts an the cause of his illness before it is to late talk to him as I understand he is very sick. Please send her enought money to go from Cincinnati Ohio to Atmore Alabama to see Haywood Patterson. If we had the money to go without asking you all for help we would go. She need money to go to Alabama & back to Cincinnati and money to live on while she is there. This case is very important so please dont refuse to take this matter very serious because we are all worried to death. Write me right back leting me know if you all are going to send my sister down tdo see Haywood this is a matter of death or live. The $5.00 I borrowed from you I will pay it as soon as I get a pay, I just got able to go to work I have been sick in Hospital.

Thank you

Louise Patterson [Reel 6, Box 5, #0000156 (folder c67), ILD]

April 22, 1941
Miss Louise Patterson,

c/o Mrs. Zierler,
6 Pine Street,
Woodmere, N.Y.

Dear Louise:

We had a telegram from your sister Mazell yesterday and wrote to her at 715 Clark Street, Cincinnati, Ohio, which I hope is the right address. We told her to ask Dr. Chalmers, the head of the Scottboro Committee for the money. I have just spoken to him and will speak to him again later in the afternoon about what we can do for Haywood. If this address is no longer the right one for Mazell, please send us the right one right away so there will be no delay in getting I touch with her.

I was very sorry to hear that you were sick and hope you are all better now and that your present job is not too hard for you. As soon as I know anything more definite about money for Mazell, to go to see Haywood, I will let you know.

Very sincerely,
SASHA SMALL

P.S. If you can telephone from where you are, call the office tomorrow and give us Mazell's address. Our number is Stuyvesant 9-4552. [Reel 6, Box 5, #000159 (folder c67), ILD]

STATE DEPARTMENT
of
CORRECTIONS AND INSTITUTIONS
Prison at
Atmore

Atmore, Alabama
April 30, 1941

Miss Hester G. Huntington
International Labor Defense
112 East 19th Street,
New York, N. Y.

Dear Miss Huntington:

This will reply to your letter of the 28th instant, inquiring about Haywood Patterson.

Please be advised that at the present time Haywood is not in the hospital, and appears to be in good physical condition. He is working regularly and we have no complaints from him as to the state of his health.

A sister of Haywood's visited him here recently, in the writers absence. Although she appeared on a weekday, which was not a regular visiting day, those in charge in my absence sent out and brought Haywood in from his work, and they had a long conversation.

Trusting that this will answer your questions in full. I am,

Yours truly,

S. W. Hixon, Warden
Atmore State Prison [Reel 5, Box 5, #000447 (folder c56), ILD]

2431 Long St.
Chatt. Tenn.
May 21, 1941.

Mrs. Hester G. Huntington
Dear Mrs. Huntington

I am writing too you about me son Andy Wright. He wrote and told me to write too you about send me down to see him and bring him down a big box. So I am asking you all too please send me down real soon too see him and carry him a big box. He also said he want too see me on some real important bussinas something he want me too do. I would like very much too know what it is. Mrs. Huntington are you on the Scottsboro Defend Committee. I wrote too Mrs. Rosa but she did not ans. My letter. So Andy told me too Write too you. Please get in touch with them and tell them too help you too send me down. It have been over a year. Give all my love. And we all send love.
Love
Mother Wright
Please ans. Right Back [Reel 5, Box 5, #000880 (folder c63), ILD]

Stuyvesant 9-4552
INTERNATIONAL LABOR DEFENSE
National Office

112 East 19th Street   New York City

Hon. Vito Marcantonio, President   Anna Damon, Secretary
William L. Patterson, Vice-President   Robert W. Dunn, Treasurer

May 27, 1941
Mr. Morris Shapiro
225 Broadway
New York City

Dear Mr. Shapiro

I have tried to reach you several times by telephone. Dr. Chalmers has asked me to refer <u>all</u> matters to you, adding that there is no meeting of the Scottsboro Defense Committee scheduled!

I am enclosing a copy of a letter from Mrs. Ada Wright which you will see asks for carfare to go to see Andy, since he is to be considered for parole during August. The round trip rates on this fare from Chattanooga to Montgomery Alabama is only $6.75 will it be possible for you to send Mrs. Wright this amount soon?

During the first week in May we forwarded Haywood Patterson's sister $31.40 in order to send her to see Haywood, who had been injured. Miss Sasha Small received assurance from your office that this amount would be reimbursed, but to date this has not been done. Perhaps it has slipped your mind.

Sincerely

[Editor's note: Original letter was not signed, however the handwriting and context suggest it was written by Hester G. Huntington] [Reel 5, Box 5, #000884 (folder c63), ILD]

Montgomery Ala.
Kilby Prison
Oct. 26. 1941

Mrs. Anna Damon.

Dear Ane.

I am writing a few lines in Regards to let you hear from me. I am Not Doing So well at the time Being though I am in hopes that you are Well and getting along fine. Listen Mrs. Damon I am Need for a little money and I am asking you to Send me much as five Dollars to help me out in getting the things that I Really need. anna it have Been Some time since I wrote you and all so have Been a very good while I asked you for a favor I hate to Worry you or any one Else. But my condition fosted me to call on you for this favor. i Don't Believe that you will for Saken me because you have Been So faitful in helping in my need in the past. anna if is possible that you can Send me five Dollars please Send it Where I can Receive it as Early as possible. Because this money will keep me out of a lots of unessary trouble. i am only asking you for this favor. i am not asking the I.L.D. and Listen Mrs. Damon Even if you cant Send the money I will highly appreciate if you will answer my letter your Self. and please ans Early as possible So I am in hope you don't Deny me of this favor. So I will close,

Sincerely yours.

Clarence Norris [Reel 5, Box 4, #000123, ILD].

Montgomery Ala.
Kilby Prison
Nov. 3, 1941

Mrs. Hester G. Hungenton

My Dear Hester

how are you getting along at this time. Well i am in hopes as these few lines leaves me well i am trusting that they will reach you well and feeling much better than i am. Listen hester i guest you are wondering what kind of fellow i am and just what do i really want. So here it is Mrs. Hungenton. i have did everything that was in my power to prevent asking you all to make any search [ ] or this for me. Listen hester the Radio that you Sent me Before was Really a nice one and was injoyed also appreciated. But now all of my pleasure and injoyment is cut completely off. For like of another one of the same type. Hester the one i had burned completely up. And it coast more to have it repaired than a new one would oast me, so far that reason i am [   ] in every way to call on you to please build my pleasure and happiness back up by sending me a Six tube Radio hester it wont have to be any Special kin just let it Be of Six tubes Because it gives much Better Service so i ask you to give all in office my very best regards to all.

From very truly Yours

Charlie Weems [Reel 5, Box 4, #000747 (folder c60), ILD]

———

Montgomery, Ala.
Kilby Prison
Nov. 12, 1941

Hello Hester.

I Rec your letter of the Nov. 12th. I also Rec the sweater and Really liked it. it is really a Beauty and i certainly appreciate it and hope some Day that I can approve to you all just How much I really appreciate the kindness of every one. Hester in speaking of the cap. Just for get the Big apple part *smile*. And get a cap of the very Latest style and your pick is mine. But please let it be of Dark Brown. Size 7.

and listen hester The information i asked you of here is the name. Mr. George E. hayner. Hester he one time held the same office that Morris Shapiro is holding Now. can you Remember now who i am asking of. then if you Dont please ask Morris and he will tell you. Hayner use to Be secatary of the Scottsboro committee. hester Dear I know that you cant put in all of your time writing and doing for me. But honestly I do appreciate Every Step and Every little turn that you make in my Behalf. and i will approve to you Some day. how much i Really appreciate you. so as it is please give Every one in office my very Best.

Regards. May good luck good Wishes and happiness cooperate with Every one.

Sincerely yours.

Clarence Norris

P.S. Please send two pair of socks [Reel 5, Box 4, #000137, ILD].

———

Montgomery Ala
Camp Kilby
Dec. 28 1941

Dear Ms. Huntington

Dear maden, I am writing you on a very urgent matter. I am a bit worry over my mother. It have been over four years since I have sein her and I would like might well to see her if there is any way possible for you all to send her down I would more than appreciate it. I have been under the Doctor care for about a month now. Therefore I would like to see her more than ever I tried my hardest to put it off until I hear from my cases but my patience have broke And I want you all to send her down as early as you possible can I hope that I am not asking to much of you all. I will depend on you attending to this little matter which would mean a great deal to me. If you all can not send her down please let me know where I will not be expecting her. I hope that I will not be disappointed wishing every one in this struggle for my freedom much success through out the new year.

Sincerely yours

Clarence Norris

My mother address is, 2276 40th St.

Cleveland, Ohio [Reel 5, Box 4, #000139, ILD]

INTERNATIONAL LABOR DEFENSE

National Office

112 East 19th Street   New York City

Hon. Vito Marcantonio, President   Anna Damon, Secretary

William L. Patterson, Vice-President   Robert W. Dunn, Treasurer

Dec. 31st 1941

Mrs. Morris Shapiro

890 West 181st St.

Dear Mrs. Shapiro,

About a week ago I telephoned to Dr. Chalmers, whose secretary suggested that I get into touch with you.

Clarence Norris at Kilby Prison, Montgomery, Alabama has written that he wants so much to have his mother go to see him. He says it is four years since she went to see him. Her address is, 2576 40th Street, Cleveland, Ohio.

He asks to help in sending his Mother.

ARE <u>YOU</u> A MEMBER OF THE I.L.D.? WRITE TODAY FOR INFORMATION [Reel 5, Box 4, #000141 (folder c53), ILD]

12

LETTERS FROM 1942
The ILD Way

The mundane necessities of life are often the essential fibers of being human. For the incarcerated, obtaining these necessities can be painfully protracted, for their supporters, a seemingly irresolvable and unending process. Throughout the remaining years of incarceration, the Scottsboro defendants and their families continued to experience the agonizing truth of being living international symbols of injustice.

Andy Wright's inquiry into the results of his parole hearing ended with the following reply from the Alabama Board of Pardons and Paroles.

STATE OF ALABAMA
BOARD OF PARDONS AND PAROLES
Montgomery

Alex Smith, Chairman   January 22, 1942   Robert Hill
                                                              Edwina Mitchell
                                                              W. P. Shirley
                                                              Secretary

Andy Wright
No. 37,522
Kilby Prison
Montgomery, Alabama

Dear Andy:
   Your letter of January 15 has been received. A number of factors enter into a decision in any case in which parole is applied for. We might call your attention to the heinousness of the crime, the lack of proper parole program, and the short time served.
Yours very truly
Alex Smith
Chairman [Reel 5, Box 5, #000894 (folder c63), ILD]

Kilby Prison
March 9, 1942

Miss Hester Huntington
Dear Miss Hester,

This is to acknowledge your letter of March 5 and the same was much appreciated. I was much afraid I would be imposing on good Nature. How ever — I did not mean that you stop the allowance. I was only offering my months allowance for the articles that I have no other way to get. Nevertheless I am grateful that you will get them. I don't know how to show you just how much I appreciate your kindness. I must confess that I must be a lot of trouble to you, and you seem to have the patience to console us in our present Solitude, you all Kindness is a great example to me, and my destination is; to be able to return this same Kindness to some one of the same Condition that I am in Some day.

I am going to have some pictures made — and if you all wish I will send you Some for your D.W. if it is Convenience, I do wish you could send the articles this weekend, that is — if it is possible, and in case that you have forgotten the articles. I will state them here again; a pair of shoes Color: Black. Size 8. Narrow toe, a Suit of shorts, size 34, and Some Camel Cigarettes. two pair of sox. Soap — and tooth brush and paste. I did not say anything about a shirt on the first letter, but I need one, if you can — please include a white Shirt Size 15, and after I receive these things I will promise to try not to ask for anything out of the ordinary any more. Please pass my best wishes to other members and you have my personal best wishes — with luck and success to you.
yours Sincerely
Clarence Norris (Col.)
Kilby Prison
Montgomery. Ala. [Reel 5, Box 4, #000148, ILD]

Montgomery Ala.
3/15/42

Mrs. Hester G. Huntington

My Dear Mrs. Huntington I takes the advantage of this golden opportunity in addressing you these few lines while sitting here by the window in my little cell inhaling the cool breezes as they slowly pass by and listening to the sweet music as it sofely sing the song of you is my Sunshine. Frankly you is my sunshine of the kind deeds you have enlighten the days of my unhappy life. You have encouraged me at the time I be discouraged you have brought sunshine into my gloomy heart at the much times you have been a God fairy to me of which makes you my Earthly Sunshine (Smile)

Now I must stop to write a line of information of my present health of which is failing me very fast, though I truly hope you is Well blessed with good health and is extremely enjoying life.

Many — many — thanks for the Extra $1.00 it was Very kind of you to remember me at this time, and I highly appreciates your kindness. Well I am certain you is growing tired of reading such horrible writing so I llbring this letter to a conclusion by saying I am patiently waiting a ffew lines of pacification of the outside World concerning yourself and your favorite hobby (etc) extend my best regards to All.

Yours Sincerely

Andy Wright

P.S. Answer Soon [Reel 5, Box 5, #000897 (folder c63), ILD]

Haywood Patterson

Route 2, Box 38

Atmore, Ala.

[Exact date of letter is unknown. Suggested date is June 23, 1942]

Dear Ms. Hester your letter came to me a few days ago and I found it enclosed the usual monthly allowance that I am always grateful for although I am sorry for delaying so long before writing you but you see I has not been feeling so good for some time and then to these are so many things to bother a fellow head until one don't have no piece of mind for writing or anything but I promise to do better in the future.

I has a letter from doctor Chalmers that I intend to answer today. now I has not received my allowance from the N.A.A.C.P. yet. I would be glad if they send it because I need it more than they do. I wish you would send me some books to help me to while away the time. I am sure anyone would be glad to donate me some old books such as detectives and funnies so please do try to send me some in the near future. This is all for the times being so write me soon again with best wishes a much love to you and all hopefully yours.

Haywood Patterson [Reel 5, Box 5, #000431 (folder c56), ILD]

Kilby Prison

Montgomery, Ala.

July 23rd 1942

Mrs. Hester Huntington

Dear Hester,

I received your letter and also the money order which I was indeed glad to receive them both.

Yes you ask me if the four ink spot sing my song yes and i show appreciate them for they kindness and I hope to here them again when they come back off take they vacation although my little radio is in very bad shape but I hope it hold up anyway because it means everything to me.

So please give my best wishes to all. Hope hear from you so

Remaining yours truly

Charlie Weems [Reel 5, Box 4, #000756 (folder c60), ILD]

DAILY WORKER
THIRTY FIVE EAST 12TH ST. N.Y. Algonquin 4-7954.
June 29 1942.
Prisoners Relief Fund,
International Labor Defense,
112 E 19th St.
Dear Friends:
    Please advise whether you want us to continue sending a subscription of the Daily Worker to Andy Wright, Kilby Prison, Montgomery Ala.
Thank you.
Sincerely yours,

DAILY WORKER
Circ. Dept. [Reel 5, Box 5, #000900 (folder c63), ILD]

Montgomery. Ala.
Kilby Prison
Aug. 2. 1942

Dear Ms. Huntington.
    Once again I am Writing to you in all manner of hope. That you will keep out of Search Distress as i am Now in. hester i wrote you to day a week ago. But for Some particular Reason I failed to get any Reply to my letters. So I was forced to write you again. it is not because I can Write. But it is Because i am in a pretty Bad spot Now. i am Still in the hospital. And when i will Be out is unknown. i had Something to grow over my left Eye that caused my whole head to worry me. So I was stop off Duty for a Doctor Examination. And after wards, I was told that it Would have to cut. i stand a chance of losing and Eye. So i Did have it cut. so after Being in hospital for Short period it seems as if every thing is going Bang. Smile. Listen Ms. Huntington, the kindness i mention to you in my Letter a Week ago. please if you can Send it along with the monthly advancement. please for i am completely out of cigarettes, in fact i am out of Every thing such as I am aloued to have them. So the thing that is suit able and a nursing to a Sick person is Not furnished By the State. hester I grant you understand. We Don't get any thing good of course hester I Realize that I am a plumb worry to you. But you have Been so Dear and a mother like to me and seem to be the only one that feel my Sympathy. you Really Seems more like a mother than you Do a friend. So for that Reason I put fourth my fully confidence in you and ask you so Do all thing for me. <u>Smile.</u> So hester please Do your Best for me will you please.
    PS. i haven't heard from the NAACP, that one Reason i have to call on you: a month have past with out any hearing from them, so I will close hopeing that you will continue to stand by me, as you have always.
From Sincerely yours
Clarence Norris
Please answer soon [Reel 5, Box 4, #000159, ILD]

Montgomery Ala.
Aug. 17 1942
Mrs. Hester G. Huntington

My Devotedly Friend. At this present time life affords me the greatest of pleasure to set here and address how these few pen strokes hoping they will find you well and enjoying life to an extreme. I am terrible sorry that you failed to receive my previously letter I often wondered you [   ] Answering because I was asking afavor of you as I havent seen my mother in quite along time and I am real anxious to see her of course I realize it cant be afford often but at this time I am in a low state of mind and health and I needs to see her face to help me endure these unpleasant days here in this confinement and to I dont see no effort being made for my immediately release please be so kind to do all you possibly can to arrange away of my seeing mother of a Early Convenience. I appreciate it Very much.

Many thanks for the $1.00 it was quite a great help, so I'll close. Give me best Regards.
I Remain
Yours Sincerely,
Andy Wright [Reel 5, Box 5, #000903 (folder c63), ILD]

R.R. 2 Box 38
Atmore Ala.
Aug. 24 1942

Dear Mrs. Hester G. Huntington and co workers
yours was rec. by me date Aug 20—.

I was Very glad indeed to hear from you all, and Very, Very glad to hear of you folks are still thinking over me.

Well I am doing pretty good an being in my condition, and I am very sorry that I has not been writing to you folks no More than I have, but from now on I am in hope to let you all here form me as much as once a month. give every body my best wishes and good luck.

From Ozie Powell [Reel 5, Box 5, #000623 (folder c58), ILD].

INTERNATIONAL LABOR DEFENSE

112 East 19th Street	New York City
Hon. Vito Marcantonio	Anna Damon, Secretary
William L. Patterson	Robet W. Dunn Treasurer

[Orignal of this letter was sent to Mr. Roy Wilkens, 69 5th Ave. Copy of this letter was received by the ILD on Sept. 3, 1942, from Miss Mazell Patterson, 648 Rispell St. Detroit, Mich.]

Dear Miss Rose Baron
This leaves me weary till I am most crazy. Know you know if you all will help me I think I can get Haywood out on a parole allright. "If you" write

them it will help me to get him. Please ask the lawyers to do so and write. Tell me just what you are going to do See if you ask the Governor to help him his freedom If I knew how to write the Governor I would and beg him for freedom for my brother. Why they would ot give them that much time if they had killed someone. I know you can get a pardon for him if you all would try. See, you all just dropped the case. Please try to get him out of there. You know you aint fooling me. Make like you all are trying to geet him out. I know better for folks have killed folks and they get out. So I know if you all will try you can get him please sir and ma'am, ask governor to give me my Brother's freedom for he say he wants to get out and fight in the war for his freedom. He wants to help. Send me the Governor's address so I can beg for his freedom and the parole Board. I want to write them maybe they will open wide they heart for it is like a rock in the deep blue sea—

Answer soon as you can. Send me those address. I close with a broken heart Since Mother has been dead you all have forsaken the boys.
Mazell Patterson [Reel 6, Box 5, #000166 (folder c67), ILD]

INTERNATIONAL LABOR DEFENSE

112 East 19th Street   New York City
Hon. Vito Marcantino, President   Anna Damon, Secretary
William L. Patterson   Robert W. Dunn, Treasurer

[Draft of a letter to be sent by Hester Huntington to Mazelle Patterson] September 3 '42

Miss Mazelle Patterson
648 Rispell
Detroit Michigan

Dear Miss Patterson,
I came to work today after being away and found your letter on my desk. Miss Rose Baron is not at this office anymore. I am not sure I have your street number right but hope this reaches you.

We are very anxious for you to do what you can for Haywood. We have not forsaken the boys. I am sending your letter on to Mr. Roy Wilkens, at the N.A.A.C.P., at 69 Fifth Avenue, New York, because the "Scottsboro Committee" is now at that address. I am asking him ot answer your letter, what their lawyers think about your suggestions. I hope he will write you soon. The name and address of the Governor of Alabama is:
    Governor Frank N. Dickson
    Montgomery—Ala.
The name of the Chairman of the Board of Pardons and Paroles is:
    Mr. Alex Smith
    Board of Pardons & Paroles
    Montgomery, Ala.
We had a fine letter from Haywood this week. We send him the usual Moneyorder each month, and books to read. We do not forget him. Greetings and Best Wishes from each one here.

Sincerely
Hester G. Huntington [Reel 6, Box 5, #000161 (folder c67), ILD]

R.R. 2 Box 38
Atmore Ala.
Sept. 21 1942

Dear Miss Hester g. Huntington
    Dear Madam I rec. the money in was very glad to get it. now I wrote to you Some time ago as you asked me to. I am wonding why you did say weather or not you got it. My ideas is I must have insulted you and I was not intent do no Such thing, as that I am asking you to write me if you got it or not.
    Many thanks to you all and many many wishes for good luck.
From Ozie Powell [Reel 5, Box 5, # 000624 (folder c58), ILD]

R.R. 2. Box 38
Atmore Ala.
Oct: 2, 1942

Dear Mrs. Hester g. Huntington
Dear Madam
    if you will allow me please I am applying to you concering a radio to be fix and if it can be fix please replace me one I wont to listing to the war news and I am asking you to see to my radio being fix or please Madam See to me have something to hear the news with. I rec: that dollar that you Sent me for a gift and I Sure did think you so Much for your gift, but I could handly a little more but I dont wont to put you all to any more trouble but I need More. give my very best regards to all in office. Yours truly
Ozie Powell [Reel 5, Box 5, #000625 (folder c58), ILD]

R.R. 2 Box 38
Atmore Ala.
Oct. 21- 1942

Dear Mrs. Hester g. Hunington
    Dear Maam your letter was rec. and I am asking you to please Ma'am just s early as possibility send me on because I am Very Very bad in the need of one I am mighty Sorrow that could not be hep, but I am hoping you to do what So Ever you can for me in replace ing me one, I sure would be mighty glad,
    now if it can be arrainged you can send me a git tere Music box or some-thing or the kind I am so lonesome being of work. I Sure wish that you would Send it Qt and Early date,
give Every body my best regards.
yours truly
Ozie Powell [Reel 5, Box 5, #000627, ILD]

Nov. 13th 1942
Haywood Patterson
Route 2, box 38
Atmore Ala.

My Dear Friend Mrs. Hester.

I cannot wait before writing you another letter you see I wrote you on Monday and Osie received his radio on Tuesday it done my heart good some how I just love a radio it gives a guy great comfort getting all the jass bands and everything I think his swell and I hope how soon you will send mine may I expect it in the near future or I will go crazy I just cannot rest contented without one I guess you know how it is behind prison bars a fellow seems so alone and depressed you see I have so much to contend with but after all I am going on with it trying to make the best I can I am keeping a pretty much clean record here in prison and I hope it will count of course I hav'nt a really bad record but after all I hav'ant been the best kind of boy since I have been here you know how it is write me soon telling me that you will send th radiio, some how I feel good tonight even though if I hav'ant a radio so don't disappoint me only to make me feel sad hopefully your Haywood. [Reel 5, Box 5, #000435 (folder c56), ILD]

Haywood Patterson
Route 2, box 38
Atmore, Alabama
Nov. 14th 1942

My Dear Friend Mrs. Hester.

I have received your letter and its contents and so thanks awfully for that yes I and getting on as best as could be expected under the circumstances, and as usually I am some what bothered. It just that I would like to know what step is being done toward getting me out of this place. I wish a chance to do good like the other four boy now there is one nother thing I would like to remind you of and that is the radio you sent me about a year ago. it fell off the little table I had last week and was jared up pretty bad and so I sent it out to town to have it fix, but the repair man returned it saying that it was beyond repair. I hate that very badly because it was all that I have for comfort, now I don't hardly know how to ask you all to send me another one but I do wonder could you all get me a cheap second had one and send it down now. I do not wish to be of any trouble — experience to you all but after all I am sure that you all do realize that I am unable to assist myself in any way and there for I always have looked forward to you all every thing and so far you all have never disappoint me as this particularly time because some day you and the whole intire committee will be rewarded for every little kind thing that has been done for me during my long stay in prison best regards to you and all and may I expect to hear from you in the earliest possible future giving [The rest of this letter is missing]. [Reel 5, Box 5, #000432 (folder c56), ILD]

Montgomery, Ala
Nov. 23 1942
Miss Hester G. Huntington

Dear Miss Huntington I am writing this letter with a [   ] to good feeling the reason I am not feeling so well is because I am trouble in mind over the debts I owe here so listen I want you to hold up my monthly allowance for this month and send it next month with the other allowance and the extra money witch you all send me for xmas with that all together. I will have that much on the Twenty Five dollars $25.00 that I want for xmas and all that it like I want you to make out the rest because I really need it with out fail. If I don't get these debts off of hand they are going to cause me to get in a world of trouble and I don't want to get hurt or hurt any one over a little money. So I hope you all will understand and send the money right away. Now I will depend on you to send if I will not look for any thing this month. With my best regards to each one in the office.
Sincerely yours.
Clarence Norris [Reel 5, Box 4, #000176, ILD]

Haywood Patterson
Atmore Prison
Atmore, Alabama
[Written sometime in late fall, 1942.]

My Dear Mrs. Hester, I Have received you letter and it contents and I thank you a good deal. Now I am sorry to say that my mind tonight is too much excited to permit me to Write a longer letter at this time. you see the war is on and the outlook appear gloomy for some of us. I am getting all the war news over my radio it is a precious thing. thank you for informing me about the other boys you see I don't ever Hear anything about them. well xmas is almost Here again and I still am in prison. I hope you all will remember me for xmas and send me a nice Box as I am entitled to a letter Happiness I am? Well I guess this is all for now.
Write again soon
yours Sincerely Haywood [Reel 5, Box 5, #000448 (folder c56), 1943, ILD]

LETTERS FROM 1943
Reaching Outward

Montgomery Ala.
Jan 3. 1943
Dear Mrs. Huntington,
  I hope you received my previously letter, you will received a letter from a girl in Mobile Ala. By the name of Ruby B. Jenkins. Please do just as she say and give her an promptly reply By Wire
don't forget to do it. So I Will close
yours truly
Andy Wright [Reel 5, Box 5, #000908 (folder c63), 1943, ILD]

2483 E. 35
Cleveland, Ohio
Feb. 11, 1943

Mrs. Hester G. Huntington
112 E. 19th Street
New York city
Miss Huntington:
  I received your money in the need of time. I was very happy to see it. I was working on W.P.A. when I fell and broke my arm. I'll get compensation but it has not started yet. It seems to be taking quite sometime, all the blanks have been filled and sent in.
  My arm was broken in the wrist the Doctor says it will be a long time before I can work again.
  As soon as you can pleae try and send me $10.00 in this next supply. As I do it very bad.
  Give all my friends my best regards. I am feeling so much better but I go to the doctor every day to get my arm treated.
Write soon
Mrs. Ida. Norris [Reel 5, Box 4, #000179 (folder c53), 1943, ILD]

Montgomery Ala.
3/22/43
Dear Mrs. Huntington
    I write these few lines asking you a speedy and a needy favor of course. I
know how condition is but you must turn me this favor and I wont bother
you no more what so ever but I just got to have $2.50 by Sunday March 28
1943. please don't fail me.
    I made a real bad wish I could explain what I need it for but I cant and I
must have it please send it and Early as possible so I will get it in time.
    Answer Soon
Yours Sincerely,
Andy Wright [Reel 5, Box 5, #000915 (folder c63), 1943, ILD]

Haywood Patterson
Route 2, box 38
Atmore, Ala.
[Exact date of letter is unknown, but probably in the first week of January
1943]

Dear Hester:
    I will take the greatest of pleasure in writing you these lines so as to explain
myself to you I want you to know that I have received all the things that you
sent me for Christmas Candy and the extra Christmas money and also my
monthly allowances I got it for Christmas and also for this month I do highly
appreciate each and all of the things that you have did for me I guess you
know that I don't ever forget you not for a long time that is because you have
been a real friend to me I cannot wish for any better person than you if I were
the kind of person that would pray daily I would often mention you in my
prayers but all I can do for you that is to wish you the best of all good things.
    now my dear friend I guess you no doubt know about my case is suppose to
come up before the board within the next few days and my suggestion to you
is that I would like you all to send some one down to interview me before my
case goes up before the board as there is some things that I would like to say
and do I do believe that it will be of most assistance to me although I do not
wish to undertake to do anything without getting you all consent or wishes. I
hope that you all will be agreeable according to my wishes there is not anything that I should like better than to have my freedom at this time this is all
that I can think of to say at the time being except that I shall be anxiously a
waiting your prompt favorable response.
Sincerely
Haywood Patterson [Reel 5, Box 5, #000442 (folder c56), 1943, ILD]

    "Charlie Weems <u>received</u> Radio 1/6/43 in good condition."
Yours truly
E. R. Wilson, Warden

By M. Suthwhitehead
Mail Censor
Kilby Prison [Reel 5, Box 4, #000767 (folder c60), 1943, ILD]

January 13 '43
Warden Kilby Prison
Montgomery, Ala.

Dear Sir;

    I am writing to ask you if you will kindly give me some information. On or about January 7th 1943 a radio was shipped to Charlie Weems, at Kilby Prison, from a store called the Seymour Shop in New Canaan, Conn. This radio was bought in Connecticut because it is becoming increasingly difficult to find the smaller radios in N.Y. City. Will you please tell me whether the radio arrived in good condition, and if Charlie Weems is now using it?

    If there had been a delay I can ask Mr. Seymour to trace the package.

Very Truly yours.

Hester G. Huntington [Reel 5, Box 4, #000766 (folder c60), 1943, ILD]

Stuyvesant 9-4552

INTERNATIONAL LABOR DEFENSE

112 East 19th Street   New York City

Hon Vito Marcantonio   Anna Damon, Secretary
Doxey A. Wilkerson, Vice-President   Robert W. Dunn, Treasurer

(Copy) Jan. 14 '43

Dear Haywood

    Thank you for your letter which came today. We wish that one of our office staff were able to come to see you, but we are not able to make such a trip. The only advice we can give you now is to do everything possible to make a most favorable impression.

    I just phoned Dr. Chalmers who told us that he has been in constant touch with the Parole Board, and that he has some hope that the Board, when it will meet (in the future) may be more favorable than in the past.

    Each one here, Haywood, wishes you the best of everything. Thank you for writing we are thinking of you. We do not forget.

Sincerely, [Reel 5, Box 5, #000445 (folder c56), 1943, ILD]

Camp Kilby
Jan. 18, 1943

Miss Hester G. Hunington

    I received the Shoes and am very pleased With them. Listen Hester, you Said in your letter for me not to ask for any thing else Soon but I am forced to ask you to do me this favor and then you can rest assured that I Wont ask you for any thing else Soon. I have some Small debts and I'll have to get my

Cigarettes, out of the check you Send. And I need Some Socks and under
wear which I can get here cheap. So I want you to Send me two extra dollars
which will make my check for this month five dollars. If you do this for me I
wont need to ask you for any thing Soon. So please ans Soon.
Respectfully yours
C. Norris [Reel 5, Box 4, #000178, 1943, ILD]

Monroe, Ga.
March 27 1943
Viola Montgomery
[This letter was sent to the *Peoples Voice*.]

   Dear Friend your letter was resend OK found me and my little famley
doing very well much better than I was. when I rote Olen last I told him to
ask you all to send me a small Radio to keep me company when I was sick o
$10.00 to pay the down payment on one. I gess you all like my neve asking for
that much But I taken you all at your word. Some of them told me if I ever
need help of any kind to ask for it so that way I did so. I am thankfull for the
dollar it was over half of my rent. I pay 1.50 a week. I am working now this is
my first week since mas (xmass). I will get a long OK if I dont get sick a gain.
I am sure glad olin is Better I was so in hope that he would keep well and get
a good job and send after me I am still able to get a round and do thing what
I hate I have to work and dont make much here But I gess that all rite we all
cant live in New York some Body got to stay in the south But sure do hate it
me I feel like I Should be still doing something for the ILD. tell all my
Friends I think of them in thear meeing. Ive had a long rest begain to feel like
my self a gain if you all ever need me for any cause how ever just let me no I
will be to glad to come. you rite me and tel me if you all are fighting for the
other 5 boy. I dont here any thing about them. see when I was in atlanta I
could here more rite me send me a good paper ot read. Mary Alice send
regard to you all. she ant for got how we travled a round for the Boy. She is 18
this month look pretty well if I do say so and very smart it just I and her we
got to small room my Boy friend is in the army some where. oh well I will
close rite me often,
Scortsboro Mother [Reel 5, Box 5, #001024 (folder c65), 1943, ILD]

Monroe, Ga.
April 26 — 43

   Olen how come you did not come as you said. I Ben looking for you for
three Week now that why I did not ancer your letter. I thought you wold hve
Ben here be fore you could get my letter so you rite me why you did not
come. I made Sure you would Ben here for Easter. I am a lone. Mary Alice is
in Atlanta again so you come when ever you get ready, dont think I did not
wont you to come. why I did not ancer your letter it just like I say you talk
like you would be here at once and I knew if you did you would not get my

letter. you are welcome to come home when ever you wont to I still here from Tommie he tell me to tell you all hellow. He is over sea some where. well you rite you no I wont to here from you often I a sorrie you all dont love me like some children do. I have three grown up now and no one to give me a dime and I am getting in Bad health it looks pretty Bad some time But I gess it all rite. there are so many mother worst of than I am. I am still able t work for my little Bread and a Place ot lay down when I feel Bad. that pretty good I gess corse I get mity Blue and lonsom. some time I don't gess any one are happy now with this War on like it is and they wont be any more if they dont make up there mine to live for god and lurn to love each other as they should I cant love some people they are so mean. old Grace is Still talking and throwing out hint I do hope I can Stay here this year as I have started my garden and flowers. Well that all I am out of Paper you rite soon.
from your mother Viola [Reel 5, Box 5, #001028 (folder c65), 1943, ILD]

Stuyvesant 9-4552
INTERNATIONAL LABOR DEFENSE
National Office
112 East 19th Street   New York City
Hon, Vito Marcantonio   Anna Damon, Secretary
Doxy A. Wilkerson, Vice-President   Robert W. Dunn. Treasurer

(Copy, letter sent to Answer to one dated April 27, 1943)

Miss Louise Patterson
624 Cumberland St.
Harrisburg, Penn

Dear Friend,

I am writing because Sasha is not here at the office anymore. She is working for the Red Cross now.

We had a letter from Haywood recently written in his own hand, so he must be getting along now. We sympathize so much with you in your anxiety for him. It seems wise if, at this time, Dr. Allan Chalmers go down quickly. He will start within a few days to see him. I do not have you sister Mazelle's present address, so I am enclosing a stamped envelope and a short letter to her. We are not able to send the whole fare for her to go. We are sending along to you ten dollars, as much as we possibly can spare to help out for two in case you decide to go.

Please feel free to write us at any time.

Greeting from each one in the office. [Reel 5, Box 5, #000454 (folder c56), 1943, ILD]

Haywood Patterson
R. R. 2 Box 38
Atmore, Ala.
April 29, 1943

My Dear Mrs. Huntington, It please me a great deal to Have this chance to Write you in regard to my Having Received your letter of April the 27th 1943. My friend, I do feel somewhat since last I wrote you, say I do Honestly trust that you all will fulfill my wishes as Have been a mention. Yes there is some little gift that you can send me I would like a couple pr. of underclothing. I mean shorts, pants size 30, shirts size 40, and a cheap pr. of no. 9 shoes something that I can rest my feet in after my day work is done.

Now I am really sorry to have to tell that I sold my radio. I regret it very much because I miss it more than you would imagine, wish I could have another one of some kind. they gives me so much pleasure and comfort. All for now and do keep remembering me

yours Sincerely

Haywood Patterson [Reel 5, Box 5, #000451 (folder c56), 1943, ILD]

Louise Patterson
624 Cumberland St.
Harrisburg, Pa.
May 2, 1943.

Dear Sir,

Your letter off April 29, 1943 was recieved a few days ago, very glad to know that you all are sending a doctor down to see my poor brother, that are very generous off you all, God Bless you all. In your letter you said you all was not able to send all off my sister's fair down to see my brother and you said you didn't have my sister's address have she wrote to you now? You said that you was sending me $10.00 to help me go down o see my brother but I didn't see any thing for my sister. But I wrote my sister and told her that she could get the $10 that you send me to help me if I decide to go down, but as it is I am working on a defense job and just can't get off as I would like too. But you know just how those conditions are on Defense jobs. That is very nice off Sarah to be a Red Cross Nurse. Pleases keep informed about my brother's condition every thing that you all learn and hear because I don't know nothing only what I hear from my sisters.

Love to all in the office.

Mazell Patterson
648 Riopelle
Detroit Michigan

Thank you Louise [Reel 6, Box 5, #000170 (folder c67), 1943, ILD]

Monroe Ga.
May 3 —1943

My Dear Friend your Card was reseived OK found me well hope when this reach you it will fine you the same. thank so much for the dollar. It sure did make me feel Glad in my hart when I open it and Seen the dollar. it was the inty Card I reseived from any one I dont know what to thank a bout Olen I cont here from him. I rote him a letter and it come Back so I am Sending it to

him will you see that he get it if he is there I had a letter from him some time
a go telling me that he would be home the next week and he did not ccome
and has not rote why I reseived the Paper OK and in joy reading it I ment to
have rote you be fore now But just haden. I am pretty Bizy now day in my
Garden and I cook out to, and just dident take time and a gain Ive ben had a
Bad finger the nail is cocming off now so you now could not rite so well and
it being my four finger and my rite hand But it better now. well I will close
you all rite me, I am all ways glad to here from my Friends. give all my regard
from a Friend
Viola Montgomery
Monroe, GA. [Reel 5, Box 5, #001032 (folder c65), 1943, ILD]

Atmore Ala.
5–18–43
Miss Hester G. Huntington

I received your nice box of candy and I want you to know that I appreci-
ated it very much. I am getting along alright, and I hope that you all are in
the best of health. the weather is very hot down here. I Send my best wishes
to all I will close resp:.
Ozie Powell
R. B-38
Atmore Ala.
P.S, Tell Miss Rose hello, and I think about her very often.
(Note on letter: Ozie Powell now in Kilby Prison Montgomery) [Reel 5, Box
5, #000631 (folder c58), 1943, ILD]

Montgomery Ala.
May 23, 1943

My Dearest Friend,
    your most kind and welcome letter was mine to read you really Cannot
imagins how proud I was to receive your encouraging letter I must say it
found me feeling better and it needless to say how your Devotion letters do
uplifts me I am always happy to receivers your letters and I hope you will
continue to Write me frequently.
    Now I hope when these few lines reaches your precious hands they will find
you Well and enjoying life to an Extreme. Roy Wilkens turned the matter
over to Dr. Chalmers and he wrote and explained the whole situation to me
and I was forced to agree. Many Thanks for showing me your interest it was
very Sweet, I mean nice of you for doing such your loyal will never be forgotten by me, and some day I hope to be able to show my Sincere appreciation,
so I'll close with my best regards to All.
Yours Sincerely
Andy Wright
P.S. Answer Soon [Reel 5, Box 5, #000920 (folder c63), 1943, ILD]

Montgomery. Ala
Kilby Prison
Sept. 13 —1943.
Dear Mrs. Huntington.

just a few Lines in Regard to let you hear from me. i am Not Doing So well in my health. though i am in all manner of good hopes that when my letter Reaches the hand of you. it will find all in the Best of health also in joying a happy life.

Listen hester I Really thought that i would have Been in the present of you all By this time. But as my mind have Lead me to Believe that my chance of Being paroled have been Denied i am asking a Little kindness of you Which will Be very favorable to my health. hester i am confined to a very warm job, that causes me to be wet at all times and it is getting very cool now. So i am asking you with my Best confidence to forward to me this small article, which is a white Sweater, to relieve my self of other clothing whild going to and from my job, to avoid any further Exposing.

hester the Sweater will cost $4.60 and i truly hopes will not Be Denied of [ ] kindness of you, for Every pinch of your time and Every Stept that you make in my Behalf will never be forgottin.
Sincerely yours.
Andy Wright
Please answer in Reply [Reel 5, Box 5, #000927 (folder c63), 1943, ILD]

AMERICAN COMMUNICATION ASSOCIATION
327 South LaSalle Street   *Room* 527–528   Chicago, Illinois
Phone Harrison 3759

Anna Damon, Secy,   Chicago, Ill.
Intl Labor Defense   June 28, 1943
112 East 19th St.,
New York, N. Y.

Dear Madam:

Sometime ago I received a rather nice letter from Ozzie Powell, one of the Scottsboro boys in Kilby Prison.

I replied to his letter thanking him for writing and wishing him luck and pledging all the help we could muster in their fight.

Several days ago I received another letter from Kilby Prison this time from a chap named Haywood Patterson asking for financial assistance. Apparently from his letter treatment in Kilby Prison is not too good which of course we can readily believe.

The purpose in writing you is to get some information on this chap. Is Haywood Patterson one of the Scottsboro boys? If we hear favorably from you we will make a small contribution but I am wondering whether we should send it to you or to the boy direct.

Will appreciate a prompt reply.
Sincerely yours,

Dick Cardamone
(This correspondence was answered July 1st.) [Reel 5, Box 5, #000458 (folder c56), 1943, ILD]

STATE DEPARTMENT
of
CORRECTIONS AND INSTITUTIONS
Montgomery, Alabama
Prison at
KILBY
July 3, 1943

Mr. Hester G. Huntington
International Labor Defense
112 East 19th Street
New York City

Dear Sir:

This will acknowledge receipt of you inquiry of July 1, 1943, relative to one Haywood Patterson, Negro male.

We have one Haywood Patterson confined in this institution who was sentenced from Morgan County, Alabama, for Rape. This negro was sentenced on June 14, 1937 and has a term of 75 years.

Yours very truly,
R. P. Williams
Senior Prison Warden [Reel 5, Box 5, #000460 (folder c56), 1943, ILD]

Haywood Patterson
Route 3, Box 115
Montgomery, Ala.
(Letter and money sent August 26th 1943)

My Dear, Hester, this comes to inform you that I have certainly Received your letter that was forward to me from Atmore Ala. Now of course I Havent my own self personally written you since I have Been transferred from atmore State farm. you see why I Havent written you all is because you failed to carry my Wishes out you were very well understand what I mean. as I don't want to go on to describe everything because — no it doesn't matter now its of no importance, you see I am a forsaken, friendless, fellow nobody have loved me [or] wish to help me while in distress.

I feel now that I have no friends to turn to in a fix like this. and you see I am always un happy boy who have never able to adjust myself to the vicissitudes of a World in which I Have always been Denied the love & advise of a real friend. Now I want you to know that life to me seem Hollow and existence but a burden.

Now Hester I was just wondering Could you send me $2.00 that I really need at once. this courtesy I will so appreciate and be sure to address all your

mail to me in the future to Kilby prison Montgomery Ala. And have the N.A.A.C.P. to do likewise as I am now in Kilby Prison with the other boys so is ozie Powell. My best wishes yours
Haywood Patterson [Reel 5, Box 5, #000467 (folder c56), 1943, ILD]

60th Bedachl /Builders Birthday Committee
80 Fifth Avenue, New York 11, N. Y.   *Algonquin 4-7733*
September 14, 1943

<u>Committee Members</u>

Rockwell Kent,
   Honorary Chairman
Rubin Saltzman
   Chairman
Peter Shipka
   Treasurer
Ernest N. Rymer
   Secretary
Mario D'inzillo
   President, Italian-American
   Section
Boleslaw Gebert
   Presdient, Polish-American
   Section
Ben Gordon
   Organization Director
Daniel Kasustchik
   Secretary, Russian-American
   Section
Eugene Konecky
   Managing Editor
   Fraternal Outlook
John E. Middleton
   Executive Secretary
   New York District
Sam Milgram
   Mid-West Regional
   Director
Walter Ribak
   Secretary, Ukranian-
   American Section
George Sandler
   Assistant Secretary
   Jewish-American Section

International Labor Defense
112 East 19th Street
New York, 11, New York

Dear Friends:

We are herewith enclosing a letter received from Haywood Patterson, one of the Scottsboro Boys, addressed to our Lodge #607. Since the Order does not have facilities for aiding such individuals cases, we are forwarding this letter to you and know that you will give it the deserved attention.
Sincerely yours,
International Workers Order, Inc.
Peter Shipka
Treasurer

[Reel 5, Box 5, #000465 (folder c56), 1943, ILD]

International Workers Order
Lodge 607
Woodside, New York
August 27, 1943

Haywood Patterson
Kilby Prison
Montgomery, Ala.

My Dear Friends and Fellow Workers it have pleased me a good deal to have this privilege to write you all but not knowing exactly how to proceed have made it difficult for me although I guess you are to be surprised upon receiving this Communication from me you will pardon this communication when I tell you that a member informed me to write you all for some assistant although I have realized that you all have put forth greatest degree of corporation and I do feel that you all are still making every possible effort to obtain my liberty but you must realize my dear friends that we need help on the inside as well as out if only you understood my poor condition it would be enough to arouse pity in the coldest hearts.

Now I hope you all will pay particular attention to this pathetic you see we suffer most of the time for prison comforts and not having the money to obtain some of the things that we so desire to have make life seem hollow and existence but a burden. Now I wish to ask as a special favor from you all to please send me about 25 dollars so that we can have a little money to spend for comforts. I say 25 dollars but anything you send I will be happy to accept every cent is so necessary send me at once what you can anything I will appreciate it so could I ask you to reply the earliest moment his courtesy I will so appreciate. you see I have often been required by you all to make a good faith but how can I when everything seems so disappointing now I must tell you all a little something about myself.

I was always unhappy boy who have never been able to adjust myself to the vicissitudes of the world in which I have always been denied the love and advice of good friends. You see my parents though were poor before they deceased had instilled in me the Code of honesty and clean living but I was young practically uneducated wholly ignorant of the way of the world and existence have always been a poor struggle for me. I am afraid that must insist that you all send me the money by a post office money order are a check to be Certain now I hope I can persuade you all to be reasonable. I don't want you to feel any other way. I want you all to be my friends if you will I am sure you haven't any real objection to this now that you see that I really am in distress so may I expect a prompt favorable response from you all with my whole heart respect and good wishes to you all.

I remain from one of the Scottsboro boys who was left behind.
Haywood Patterson
Kilby Prison Montgomery, Ala. [Reel 5, Box 5, #000461 (folder c56), 1943, ILD]

Haywood Patterson
Route 3 Box 115
Montgomery Ala.
[Letter was sent on September 10, 1943]

My Dear Mrs. Hester,

Thank you kindly for your letter and the enclosed $5.00 now that is a help I can use every cent of it. this is Monday morning and it found me miserable. Monday morning always found me so because it began another week's slow suffering. I generally began that day with wishing I had had no intervening Holiday. it makes the going into captivity again so much more odious. but all trials bring their compensation. now am sorry to say but I must make this letter short as it is time for me to go on the job. Promise to Write you more in the future so thank again for the Money

Hopefully yours

Haywood Patterson [Reel 5, Box 5, # 000469 (folder c56), 1943, ILD]

Sept 17 1943

Dear Sir

I am write you a few ask you for more [   ] help un till I get able to work I broke the Big Bone in my arm and cant work an please try an help me until I get able to do something.

Very sincerely

Josephine Powell [Reel 5, Box 5, # 000472 (folder c58), 1943, ILD]

Haywood Patterson

Route 3 Box 15

Montgomery Ala.

[Letter sent on September 21, 1943]

My Dear Mrs. Huntington, this come to advise you once again about mail. You see I noticed again that you addressed my Mail to atmore State prison farm you see I advised you to address me now at Kilby Prison same that you use in writing the other boys. you see that we are all together now. so try to think of us all being together when you Write Charlie, or andy or Clarence think of me as Being with them.

Best wishes and Dont forget.

Haywood Patterson [Reel 5, Box 5, # 000471 (folder c56), 1943, ILD]

Kilby Prison
Montgomery, Ala.
Oct 12 1943

Mrs. Haster G. Hunington

I received your letter also the money glad indeed was I to hear from you. by the way I will have to ask you to forgive me for o writing you an soon yet I am sure you will smile yes I received four flat fifty of cigarettes and I appreciated them.

Yes, I to wish to hear some good news soon. so I will close hoping to hear from you soon. give my best wishes to all.

So I remain
Yours truly
Charlie Weems [Reel 5, Box 4, #000777 (folder c60), 1943, ILD]

Haywood Patterson
Route 3 Box 115
Montgomery Ala.
[Letter sent out October 18, 1943]

My Mrs. Hester, I was glad to get both of your letters that reached me some while ago. and may I assure you of my deepest appreciation for the little extra kindness you Have shown me that I can never forget Mrs. Hester please I am sure sorry to learn about you not being in a position to obtain me the shoes now I need them most of all. I can no doubt obtain some that have been used for four or five dollars so you just send me the money and I will take care of the rest.

now I saw in papers where some of the boys was to be free shortly now with the other Boys getting out have gave me strength and Determination because I needed both. now dont you think that I am not beginning to be thankful for any Help the people give although the paper speak against me no more than I expected. now that I have to stay on in prison But believe me when I say that I have struggle Hard to make a clean record while in atmore but to no avail. I wish I could explain all that happened to me but well that would be a rather long story and I wont go into it right now But I can say am not responsible for things happen in Atmore. one thing was certain the load was more on my shoulders all the time many things Have been placed against me that I wasn't no way involved of course I resisted.

All fights brought to me without a just cause although I was peacefully so long as on one battered. now I am not trying to establish an alibi for getting out but I do wish to establish the true facts and soon I am going to make it clear to the world. I have some white boys friends who was office boy there in atmore could be of considerable Help to that effect. Now I wont write you much this time so please do send me the money request for the shoes my best wishes.

Most Sincerely yours
Haywood Patterson [Reel 5, Box 5, #000475 (folder c56), 1943, ILD]

November 17, 1943: Charlie Weems is paroled from the Alabama State prison system.

Atlanta, Ga.
Dec. 17 1943

Haster G. Hunington

Dear Haster,

I received your letter some time ago and also the five dollars which I was I indeed glad to get it by the way Haster you will have to for give me for not writing you any sooner but you know first how it is I be working hard every

day and I tell you it is a shame for a man to be working for such little pay altho I will have to stay until the out come of the other boys because I wants to see them free and do not wish to do anything that would harm them ok yet you ask about my street address this is all of it.
142 Hilltop Circle apt 481
atlanta, Ga.
give my best wishes
to all answer soon
yours truly
Charlie Weems [Reel 5, Box 4, #000779 (folder c60), 1943, ILD]

2483 E. 35th St.
Cleveland, Ohio
Dec. 28: 43

Mrs. Hester Huntington
Dear Friend:
 In close you will find a letter I rec today. And I want you ot look it over and tell me what is best to do. I also rec this card I want you to look it over and tell me just what to do. I did go to see him. I rec the box and thanks a lots give all my love.
Merry xmas.
Happy new year
Looking for an early reply
Sincerely
Ida Norris [Reel 6, Box 5, #000087 (folder c66), 1943, ILD]

14

LETTERS FROM 1944
To Be Paroled or Not

On January 8 Andy Wright and Clarence Norris were released on parole under the conditions that they would work and stay within the state of Alabama. Haywood Patterson's response to their release was strained due to years of fighting between him and Norris, some of which ended up with Patterson being stabbed by Norris. Many such conflicts occurred as a result of gambling debts acquired and not repaid, as well as the extent of their personal interaction and struggle for domination over other inmates. Some supporters even suggested that a psychiatrist would define Patterson's growing anxiety as a natural development of a "persecution complex" after years of incarceration. Nevertheless, Patterson's volume of letters to a variety of supporters continued to expand and was remarkable considering his limited lines of communication with the outside world.

Recently paroled Norris and Wright faced another set of problems. Endeavoring to negotiate their way through a society that had rapidly evolved during their 13 years of incarceration into a war economy mode while sustaining traditional racial and class mores, they now had to shoulder the Alabamian stigma of being "Scottsboro Niggers." By September 27, both Norris and Wright would violate their parole terms and leave Alabama.

INTERNATIONAL LABOR DEFENSE
112 East 19th Street   New York City
Hon. Vito Marcantonio   Anna Damon, Secretary
Doxey A. Wilkerson, Vice-President   Robert W. Dunn, Treasurer

Jan 4th 1944
To Mrs. Norris

    Answer the Reverend Chalmers and thank him for his letter, telling him that anything that you can do to do help have Clarence paroled, you certainly will be glad to do. So send him word, and he will go ahead with the Board after hearing from you.

Now about the enclosed card. We suggest that you take it to the Cleveland Branch of the N.A.A.C.P. [Reel 6, Box 5, #000086 (folder c66), 1944, ILD]

Haywood Patterson
Rt. 3, Box 115
Montgomery, Ala.
January 7, 1944

I was heartily glad to get your last letter and it was a great comfort to found enclosed the regular monthly allowance for which I thank you. Now I hardly know just what to write about tonight. You see I am serious — very serious — and nothing can pacifice my mind at present. I want you know that Andy and Clarence went free this morning to where I can not say definitely. But there wasn't much for them to choose from under the circumstances, if I recollect rightly; not it do not impress me very favorably. Somehow I am licked, now that it is plain to see. Of course my record though they say is bad or have been bad. It a serious situation and I would like to give an account of what had to happen to me in Atmore, and maybe that would open the door leading to a complete solution of the Scottsboro case. Now there was nothing serious that the warden and my superiors done to me there in fact the warden were my friend, but still I had some very treacherous enemies there in Atmore, who pester me all the time, and therefore I should not be held responsible.

Now I can not say anymore. But I do wish you friends would send me a little more money that what you are sending because I don't get on so well with you now send. Although am thankful for it even if it so little.

Best wishes to everyone,
Yours truly
Haywood Patterson [Reel 5, Box 5, #000466 (folder c56), ILD]

January 8, 1944: Clarence Norris and Andy Wright are paroled and acquire jobs at a lumber factory [Fosher Lumber Co.] outside of Montgomery, Alabama.

[The first part of the following letter is missing. It was written either in late fall 1943 or the first week in January 1944]

...to send me Some money. to help me out & getting the things that I need. I am quite Shore that you will do what you can for me because you have been so Dear to me in the pass. Listen Hester I need as much as $30.00 but if you are not able to send me that remand send me as much as you can of Course I relize that I am working but this job that I am on dont pay all that much but I can make out with what I am making until I get to Cleveland I hope it wont be so offer long before I be there. As I was telling you I am going to get married I think that I will fare more better by getting married to the one that I really love and I just need enough money to furnish of me a room. I have a lilter but not enough to furnish of me a room with.

From Yours sincerely
Clarence Norris [Reel 5, Box 4, #000199, ILD]

Montgomery. Ala
Route 2, Box 130

(Written in the second week of January 1944)
Dear Miss Huntington
   We have been paroled here in Montgomery and will go to work at Fosher
Lumber Co, of course you know we was Penniless and needs clothes and
When We go to Work we wont be making no fortune and our Board is $7 per
week and if it possible send us some money at once to Buy clothes, shoes and
hat as you know everything is very high Please send cash money and as much
as possible we only asks you all for a start in life and here after I am confi-
dently we can carry on ourselves. Please send it at once the Weather is very-
very bad
Yours Truly
Andy Wright c/o Fosher Lumber Co.
Route 2, Box 130
Clarence Norris, c/o Fosher Lumber Co.
Route 2, Box 130
Montgomery, Ala. [Reel 5, Box 4, #000194, ILD]

BROADWAY TABERBACLE CHURCH
Broadway and Fifty-Sixth Street
New York 19, N.Y.
Dr. Allan Knight Chalmers
Minister

Rev. Cyrus R. Pangborn   January 14th 1944
   Assistant Minister
Miss Roberta Northrup
   Counselor in Religion
Mrs. Harry S. Martin
   Parish Visitor
Miss Frances M. Chamberlain
   Minister's Secretary

Dear Mrs. Huntington:

   I was glad to see the letter which Haywood sent to you and I am returning
it as you requested. In the letter to me he dwells at great length upon the
quite natural feeling of "treacherous enemies." It is what the psychiatrists
would consider an evidence of a persecution complex. I do not feel it, myself,
to be necessarily so dangerous that he could not be rehabilitated very successfully on release. I am much more worried about the other psychological and
physical baits which are so natural to prisoners that they call them "prison
psychoses."

If it were not for the fact that a proper psychiatric examination would be helpful in our attempt to get his release, I would not, of course, adopt that method, although I do think, in any case, we have to be realistic enough to face the situation as it is, even though we agree, as you and I do, that he is not responsible for the condition but is a victim of it.

I note in your letter that you speak of a successful hearing of his case in April. I want to make it clear that I have no hope for such a successful outcome as of that date. What I hope to do in April is to get some indication from the Board on when they will give it serious considerations. I doubt very much if there is any chance at all of its happening this spring, although I shall make every effort to bring that happy result. What I said to the Committee was that I expect when I saw them in April, to be able to judge whether we had real hope of some immediate action in the not too distant future; or if they were adamant on the 1948 date and we should then consider different tactics.

It has been a difficult maneuver, at best, and is not at all a satisfactory outcome of a case of great injustice. When I think how poor Andy and Clarence, the last two to come out, were boys in their 'teens when they went in, and who seemed almost like old men the last time I saw them, I realize what a terrible thing society has done to them. While I am pleased at the recent result, I have no complacent feeling of satisfaction but rather one of great regret that the stubborn prejudices and fears of people have delayed so long something which should have been done in the last decade instead of this.

With all good wishes to you,
Sincerely,
Allan Chalmers [Reel 5, Box 5, #000482 (folder c57), ILD]

Haywood Patterson
Route 3 Box 115
Montgomery Ala.
(Approximate date: January 16, 1944)

My Dear Hester thank you for your charitable attitude as I Have just received your letter and founded five dollars in cash so thank awfully. Now I am very gloomy tonight, although I Have found a little measure of comfort in the knowledge that you dear friends will continue to carry on the struggle until I am freed too, an I Hope this change of event will give you all immediate leads to begin work on, now the release of the other boys didnt provide a sensation or so it seemed everything were quite.

well Hester I was just turned out to be the goat, but to me I have done everything I could to obtain my freedom and success seems as far from me now as before, despite the fact that I Have been into a thing since I was transferred that should establish the fact that I Have tried very hard to be good but there were those who had personal grude against me. I have bent over backward to be Decent to everyone, now this certainly is the absolute truth, now it is you all duty to exert every effort to get me release at once because I can not endure the suspense much longer my long confinement in prison. Have treacherous enemies there in atmore who pester me all the time and therefore I should not be Held responsible now I can not say anymore But I do Wish you friends would send me a little more money than what you one sending because I dont get on so well with you now send.

Although am thankful for it even if it so little.

Best wishes to everyone

Yours truly Haywood Patterson [Reel 5, Box 5, #000489 (folder c57), ILD]

C/O Foshee Lumber Co
Route 2 Box 130
Montgomery Ala.
(possible date: January 17, 1944)

Dear Mrs Huntington

I received your letter and was very glad to hear from you at the present I am not feeling so well I am so sore and my Back is hurting me so until I couldnt work today maybe it wont go so hard with me after I get use to out of three days I have worked here 40 hours and it was a killing to me as I havent did no hard work in 13 years. so far the farmer seems to be a very nice guy the job aint all that hard But I have bad kidneys and they are giving me a plenty trouble.

We stays about 6½ mile from town in a very small room and everything is so inconvience and I will never be happy not until I am out of the state of Alabama. I dont feel safe here I cant knowing how I am hated here and every body acts a towards us ase we are in human and Board is $7 per week and we are not making anything an we are complete nake and need shoes, hat and heavy clothes. We got a outside job and it is cold

and if the ILD will help give us a start I believe we can carry on ourselves. we need about $35 to help us in our need and need it bad at once Because they hold back 2 days and we just make enough to pay Board if it were be enough to please send it at once.

Thanks for Roy address. I do wish that I was in some other state. Clarence will write Immediately.

Answer Soon.

Yours Truly

Andy Wright [Reel 5, Box 5, #000930 (folder c63), ILD]

Montgomery Ala.
Route 2 Box 130
(About January 22, 1944)

Dear Mrs. Huntington

I received the letter also the Money in each letter. Foshee is starting to Work 6 hours a day at 35c hour and we have to pay $7 per Week for Board and I really dont see how we are going to Make it But the main thing I wants out from down here the Colored people is Worse as the White and they are

Working me harder than they do the rest and they makes the same [   ]
Women Works her and I I don't do their Wash and mine to they tells the
farmer I aint doing Nothing the farmer didnt get funny until the Parole officer
come out here Tuesday. I dont know what she told him but they have framed
up something and their work is killing me. I [   ] out Wednesday and felled
and hurted my right leg cant hardly Walk. Continue to send the cash money
we received it alright.
Yours Truly
Andy Wright [Reel 5, Box 5, #000933 (folder c63), ILD]

Haywood Patterson
Route 3 Box 115
Montgomery Ala.
(Written sometime in late January 1944)

My Dear Mrs. Huntington, I am justly proud to have your beautiful letter.
I get a lot of enjoyment out of them. My thanks to you for helping to consoling me, now I Had hoped to write you a longer letter tonight But for some
cause I am feeling pretty blue. Now I want you to know that I am full of thanks
for the $15.00 money order that I found enclosed, by I was disturbed by the
thought that you all did not send me the full amount in which to get the
radio. Now May I assure you that this have proveded to be completely dissat-
isfying under these aspects. You know that I stand well in the cause, and the
outcome of this thing have left me blank minded. and another thing is that I
have been getting a rotten deal out of the whole thing and that is because of
my belief in you all and therefore I should not be neglected at any time.

you undoubtedly Have found by now that this is true. I know the people
have given you reason to think me disrespectful and rough, an of course I
Have suffered tenfold in the recollection of such. now I can not describe it
justly to you now, but I will do my endeavour to prove out different someday.
Then I would appreciate the privilege of meeting you someday in the earliest
future I hope.

Now understand me clearly, yes I have of course made know my wants and
suffering to those who write me which are few not more than 2 or 3 goods
friends an of course it hasnt appeared in public, and I can assure those who
may Write me that it is a much easier & less distressing thing to send me
whatever little money they have tdo give in for my comfort Here. However
although they seem to Have little feeling for the poor and distressed ones
because they adds not a little to my difficulties and distress. Now that is my
special reason for troubling you all for assistance often times and I would prefer you to please send me the five more dollars in which to obtain the radio.
you see I can not talk the fellow out the other five dollars. He says $20.00 or
nothing and if you all dont send me the other five at once, why I dont get the
radio that I so desire to Have for my comfort. Nobody Hardly ever send me
anything except you all now several years ago I used to Have lot of friends
who would send me a little money and things but for particular reason they all
have ceased writing me.

Of course I regret very much to keep bothering you all because you have cared for me so nicely in the past now I hope this come to your attention at least I hope This letter will be carefully consider, but please judge of my feeling.

My best personal love & good wishes to you and if you can please send me the Five dollars move at once, and just leave the usual $3.00 off. I remain hoping for a early reply.

Haywood Patterson [Reel 5, Box 5, #000492 (folder c57), ILD]

Haywood Patterson
Kilby Prison
Montgomery, Ala.
(Letter was possibly sent on February 1, 1944)

My Dear Miss Maria Sulek, and to all whom this may concern. Now I am writing Miss Sulek because she have seemed so willing to cooperate with me to the fullest extent, and what more she understand the situation, and may I now express my belief and confidence that I have in her.

Now I am most certain that you all know about all the boys getting released except myself and Powell. of course it was Hardly fair to see the boys go and I Remain on incarceration well Dear friends I was just turned out to be the goat. but to me I have done everything I could to obtain my freedom. And success seems as far from me now as before. Some how the people says my prison record wasn't good enough But I have tried very Hard to be good but there were those who had personal grudge against me. Why I have bent over backwards to decent to everyone. now my main reason for writing you dear workers at this time you see it have come a time that I should ask for some very needed assistance.

you see dear workers I have consult a lawyer of this State and He have assured me that He could get me released too for the amount of $500. Now my sister who is poor recently sent me 200 and $50 and I now need 200 and 50 more dollars Before the lawyer can act. Now He do not wish the money until He have done the work. Now I do Hope and trust you all will raise whatever you can of this amount. Your friends can give from one cent up because every cent would be necessary. So please send me whatever you all can possibly raise within the next 3 weeks to come. Now it is you all duty my friends to exert every effort to get me released at once because I can not endure the suspense much longer. My long confinement in prison have done a lot to my nervous system and Health condition and if I dont soon get out of this climate I am to Die a slow Nouseous death.

Now I can never forget the ones who Have vouched for me and I only Hope now that I could succeed in obtaining the amount preferable now you dear workers can send whatever you possibly can raise for a Helpout, so May I expect to Hear good news from you all in the shortest possible future.

Haywood Patterson
Kilby Prison
Montgomery Ala [Reel 5, Box 5, #000498 (folder c57), ILD]

Atlanta, Ga.
Feb. 5 1944
Mrs. Haster G. Huntgtion,
Dear Haster

I received your letter glad indeed was I to hear from you to know that you all are well by the way you ask me if I was getting the messages that you sent me? Yes, I do get me it oh well you know that I am a very poor writer — smile. Oh yes, I went down for the exam to go in the army I don't know how long they will Let me stay out but I will write you if I have to go back but I hope that I don't have to go back.

yes I written to Andy but have not get any answer.
So I must close.
Charlie Weems [Reel 5, Box 4, #000781 (folder c60), ILD]

Foshee Lumber Co.
Route 2 Box 130
Montgomery Ala.
(Possibly written February 7, 1944)

Dear Mrs. Huntington

I received your letter a few days ago and Was very glad to hear from you at the time. I am not feeling so Well I asked the Parole officer for permission to visit my Mother. he granted it so I am asking you to help me with my fare Because I Want to see my Mother real Bad and to she is Sick. plea

Please send it at once so I can go I only makes enough here to pay my Board cigarettes and laundry Bill. Please dont fail me.

I received the $1 you sent me many Thanks.
yours Sincerely,
Andy Wright [Reel 5, Box 5, #000936 (folder c63), ILD]

INTERNATIONAL WORKERS ORDER

Midwest District　　316 N. Michigan Ave.　　Chicago, Ill.　　Randolph 0545
Louise Thompson, President　　　　　　　Irwin J. Stein, Executive Secretary
February 18 1944

International Labor Defense.
112 East 19th Street,
New York, N. Y.

Dear Friends:

I am herewith enclosing a letter received by one of our members from Haywood Patterson, one of the Scottsboro boys.

This Sister Sulek has been raising some monies in the past and sending them on to Haywood Patterson for his personal use.

In view of his request, we have notified our members not to do anything about any defense measures, and are sending on the letter to you.

Fraternally yours,

Louise Thompson
District President [Reel 5, Box 5, #000497 (folder c57), ILD]

Route 2 Box 130
Montgomery Ala.
(Possibly written February 21, 1944)

My Dear Friend!

I received your letter today and Was indeed glad to hear from you and am proud that you are Will and getting along fine. at the present I am very well in health but Worried in mine the Parole officer Waited until time for me to go and Visit my mother and denied me with the alibi the government advise them to use the train least as possible and they Want to cooperate and for me to wait until mother day which is in May. my Mother is Sick Now and I feel that I shouldnt be denied the privilege to visitd her I sent his letter to Dr. Chalmers asking him to contact the Board Mr. Alex Smith the Chairman and I Wish you would do likewise.

This Parole officer dont like me because of Roy in 1934 he tried to Whip Roy and I wouldnt let him and he is determinded to get even with me and is working against me in every respect.

I received the $10. Many thanks will wait to see if I succeded in making my trip. Will notify you the minute I [arrier] if I be permitted to go. give my Best regards to all.

yours affectionatedly
Andy Wright [Reel 5, Box 5, #000938 (folder c63), ILD]

Montgomery Ala.
Feb 25, 1944
Route 2, Box 130

Dear Hester.

I am Droping you a few lines just to let you hear from me at this time. I am well & at the present & Do hope when this letter reaches you it will fine you OK.

Listen Hester yes I receive everything that you send me. And it is always best to Send Cash money because Money orders & Checks is to much trouble to get cash here. Hester I am Fixing to get married & I am asking you & the rest of my friends (editor's note: page missing from letter probably sent by Clarence Norris). [Reel 6, Box 5, #000088 (folder c66), ILD]

Montgomery Ala.
Route 2. Box 130
Mar. 10 '44

Dear Friend

I received your letter and was very glad to know from you, my kidneys is giving me particularly trouble I have not been able to Work in five days and I Want you all to contact some doctor down here and have him to give me an Ex ray picture and see what the matter with me. I am losing too much blood and am just as weak as water.

please do this at once by telegram because I am Bad shape and I got to Work or go back to Prison and I really dont want to go Back there. Please explain the matter to Dr. Chalmers. I have Wrote him three letters and no answer as yet.

Clarence received his leter But it Wasn't no Money in it. he said you must to have forgot to put it in the envelope ans said please send it as Early as possible, so I will close answer at once.
Yours truly
Andy Wright [Reel 5, Box 5, #000941 (folder c63), ILD]

March 13, 1944
Rev. Allen Chalmers
Broadway Tabernacle Church
New York, N. Y.

Dear Dr. Chalmers:

I have at hand a letter from Andy Wright telling us that his health is not good. He says his kidneys are in bad shape and that he is losing blood.

Do you suggest sending a doctor to visit Andy from the Scottsboro Committee? If this is not possible, shall we take steps to send a doctor to treat Andy from the I.L.D.? Please let us hear from you so that we know what you suggest.

With best wishes for yourself from Mr. Colson and myself,
Sincerely,
Hester G. Huntington [Reel 5, Box 5, #000943 (folder c63), ILD]

BROADWAY TABERNACLE CHURCH
Broadway and Fifty Sixth Street
New York 19, N.Y.
Dr. Alan Knight Chalmers
Minister

March 15, 1944

Dear Mrs. Huntington:

As Dr. Chalmers will be away until Tuesday, March 21st, I thought I would let you know that I shall bring your letter of the 13th to his attention as soon he returns.

I knew you would wonder why there was no answer to your letter.
Sincerely,
Frances Chamberlin
Minister's Secretary
Mrs. Hester G. Huntington

International Labor Defense
112 East 19th Street
New York 3, N.Y. [Reel 5, Box 5, #000944 (folder c63), ILD]

March 17 '44
Route 2 Box 130
Montgomery Ala.

Dear Friend

I received your letter today and was very glad to hear from you it found me just about the same of course I should Back to work Monday. have to or else go Back to Prison and that I do not Wish to ever return. I have Wrote Dr. Chalmers three letters and have failed to receive a answer I dont know what the trouble

I think you Better send Money order in the future in case of Misplaced. I certainly appreciate tha you are doing for me. give my Best regards to all so I will close.

Yours affectionatedly
Andy Wright [Reel 5, Box 5, #000945 (folder c63), ILD]

BROADWAY TABERNACLE CHURCH
Broadway and Fifty Sixth Street
New York 19, N.Y.
Dr. Allan Knight Chalmers
Minister

March 21, 1944

Dear Mrs. Huntington:

On returning to New York, I find you wrote about Andy. We have received similar letters from him, of course, in the past, as you have, and while he was in prison, the official reports of the doctors were furnished to me and there seemed nothing physically that was as bad as he felt. He is, as you know, one of the boys who is most worried about himself, differing quite a bit from Clarence, for example.

I have, however, immediately gotten in touch with a minister in Montgomery who has already made a contact with Andy just for pure friendliness, and have asked him to see to it that Andy is attended to by a doctor. The committee will bear the expenses of it. I am quite sure that whatever needs to be done will thus be taken care of.

I'll be glad to let you hear about it when I know more.

As ever,
Allan Chalmers
Mrs. Hester Huntington
International Labor Defense
112 East 19th Street
New York, New York [Reel 5, Box 5, #000947 (folder c63), ILD]

Route 2 Box 130
Montgomery Ala.
(Possibly written on March 26, 1944)

Dear Friend:

I received your letter and Was Very glad to hear from you. at the present I am Very Well only still have kidney trouble. I am trying to get transferred to Mobile Ala Better job and pay more Work is lighter and Everything is more conviences.

I aint doing so Well here on this job. Work is straining. I Want to make a nice upright and decent living Without the aid of some one else But I cant do it here. today is raining No work today nor Tomorrow and room and Board and laundry Bill insurance Bill got to be paid and no money to pay it With. I received the Money thanks use so much Wish it had Been More.
Yours Sincerely
Andy Wright [Reel 5, Box 5, #000949 (folder c63), ILD]

Montgomery. Ala.
[   ] Box 115
April 2, 1944.

Dear hester,

just a few lines as to let you hear from me as these few lines leave me. Well i certainly hope When you Rec my letter the Same can Be Said of you. Hester i Recd the amount of three Dollars for the begining, and highly appreciated it. So its my own Desires to write in Regard of the kindness of Every one in office, and it have Been quiet a while Since i have written to you all so in my spair time I will try to write more often. So dont think Bad of me for delaying your letter. So long for i guess you understand how it is with any one in Prison.

So as i must come to a close. Give my very Best Regards to all.
From your as Ever,
Ozie Powell [Reel 5, Box 5, #000640 (folder c58), ILD]

Route 2 Box 130
Montgomery Ala.
(Possibly written on April 3, 1944)

Dear Friend

just a few lines to let you hear from me at the present I am not feeling none the best it have been raining here every since Sunday Morning and No Work We can do so the Monthly allowance you been sending us please double it april and Miss May please send it in time for Easter send Money order so I'll close
yours truly
Andy Wright [Reel 5, Box 5, #000950 (folder c63), ILD]

Atlanta, Ga.
April 6 1944
Mrs. Hester G. Huntgun
   I the money that you sent to me glad indeed was to get it by the way you
can send me money order it will be alright it much better [   ] thank you.
   Oh yes, where is Roy Wright, Eugene, [   ] and Willie. How are they get-
ting along oh by the way please find out how long that I will have to go on
under their parole? I would like for you to find out for me please.
Yours truly
Charlie Weems [Reel 5, Box 4, #000784 (folder c60), ILD]

                                              Atlanta, Ga.
                                              April 1944
                                              (Specific date unknown)

Hello Hester,
   by the way I know you ar some what surprise to receive this letter from me
but in the meantime I hope that you will give me an answer right a way
because I need some one to tell me something bad for you do not under stand
Hester since I went to prison and came out I has gain a mean and uncontrol-
lable temper which I cant do something with for it cause me to do something
to day that I regret but I could not help it and it hurted me so bad until I had
to leave my job an d come home and here is what I did. I hit the girl that I
am in love with please tell all the young men to try hard and not go to prison
for my sakes.
So long for this time
yours truly
Charlie Weems [Reel 5, Box 4, #000786 (folder c60), ILD]

Montgomery Ala.
April 12, 1944

Dear Mrs. Huntington
   I received you letter and Was Very glad to know from you. sorry you are
Sick hope you are Better by now.
   Many thanks for the $10 it certainly helped alots and I appreciate it to the
highest.
   the Doctor that Dr. Chalmers promised to send haven't arrived as yete.
Yours Truly
Andy Wright [Reel 5, Box 5, #000951 (folder c63), ILD]

Montgomery Ala.
April 22, 1944

Dear Mrs. Huntington:
   Dr. Chalmers was here to Visit Me Wednesday he gave me $10 Wedding
present and I also expect a present from you all to help me get straighten and

he saw how things Was Situated here With me and Suggest that it Would be better for me to marry so I am going to Marry Sunday Evening so please send me What Money you possible can right Back,
Yours Sincerely
Andy Wright [Reel 5, Box 5, #000952 (folder c63), ILD]

Haywood Patterson
Route 3 Box 115
Montgomery Ala.
(This letter was written sometime in mid–May, 1944.)

My Dear Mrs. Huntington I Have Received your most disheartened letter with telling me of death of our dear beloved friend miss Anna Damon. now I can assure you that to me is one of the sorryhest blows any man can possibly stand. you see Miss Damon was to visit me twice and I promised her that I would some day meet her a free man But what a disappointment god have made between us. Now I feel Heartbroken and my grief is to great to express. I feel as if I had lost a Brother or Sister Because Miss Damon was Very dear to me all the while she gave of her best assistance toward Helping we boys. I can never forget Miss Damon and she must live again in our Hearts & Minds. we must speak of her often. now my friend Ozie says that He regret the death of Miss Damon. Now my Heart is too full to put into words on paper my regret over miss Damons death.
Yours Sincerely
Haywood Patterson and
Ozie Powell
P.S. tell Mr. Marcantonio I appreciated his letter [Reel 5, Box 5, #000518 (folder c57), ILD]

139½ Oak St
Montgomery Ala.
(Possibly written May 1, 1944)
Dear Mrs. Huntington:

I received your letter todeay and Was Very glad to hear from you. at the present I am Very Well I have already married. I Married Saturday April 22 and have Move so my address is 139½ Oak St. many thanks for the $10 it certainly helped alots. The parole officers said she is going to get me a better job in about Month. I need one I havent worked But 18 days out of this whole month. the weather wont Permit it.
Yours Sincerely
Andy Wright [Reel 5, Box 5, #000954 (folder c63), ILD]

Montgomery Ala.
24 Davidson St.
May 1, 1944

Dear Hester

Just a few lines to let you hear from me. I am well at this time & truly hope when these few remarks come to your hand they will find you enjoying the very best of life. Listen Hester I got married on the 27 of April & now I am living at 24 Davidson St. So from now on Send all my mail to this address. Listen I am in need for much as ten Dollars. I wont ask you to give it to me but I will you to send my little money that I received monthly. Send it for this month & also rent month. Hester please send it By in time enough where I can receive it Friday I am sending this letter By air & I hope you will get it in time enough to do this for me. so this is all at this time. Mrs Dora Lee Norris Sending her Best regards to you From Yours

Sincerely

Clarence Norris [Reel 5, Box 4, #000204 (folder c53), 1944, ILD]

> Montgomery Ala.
> 145 Oak Street
> June 15, 1944

Dear Hester

This is to say I am Doin fine and working every Day & I am so proud of that well hester hope when these few lines come to you it will find you the best of life. hester hope you Don't think I am hurring you but I haven't got my money for this month & Andy have been got his so now other wise I am Fine so far well guess you will notice My address is now change. hester I will be so glad when I can Do Something for Myself but I will have to be out of this part hester you no I cant Do much making from 18 to 20 Dollars a week & sometime less then that if it rain. Never nothing left after I pay board & buy Grocery I am Digusted but have to wait till my time come hop that wont by very long. Guess I have said enough.

From yours Sincerely Clarence Norris to a True Friend Hester GH. [Reel 5. Box 4, #000207, ILD]

139½ Oak St.

Montgomery Ala.

My Dear Mrs. Huntington:

I received your letter and Was Very glad to hear from you at the present I am very Well But Clarence is Bid Sick. had the doctor With him twice this Week and he dont seem to be getting No better.

My Wife name Ruby [Billie] Wright she sends her heartiest regards. many thanks for the three dollars I appreciate them Very much [   ] if I did had to borred them. give my Best regards to all so I'll close. Answer Soon

yours Sincerely

Andy Wright

139½ Oak St.

Montgomery Ala. [Reel 5, Box 5, #000953 (folder c63), ILD]

2483 E. 35th St.
Cleveland. O
May 23, 1944
Miss Hester Huntington

rec your letter and was very glad to hear f rom you. We all are well and hope you all are the same. I am so sorry Miss Anna Damon pass away. She was a grand person. We all must go some day, her family has our sympathy. She will be miss by all who knew her.

in your next letter please send me Mr. Richard Moore address, and I will write him. I had a letter from Clarence he isnt so well. had hurt him self on the job. He married now. in your next letter tell me when Clarence will get a proal from the State of Ala. I would have liked to have been there for May Day I know you all had a nice time. send me Mother Wright address. give all my best regards I will close with lots of love Sincerely
Ida Norris [Reel 5, Box 4, #000195 (folder c67), ILD]

Haywood Patterson
Camp Kilby Prison
Montgomery Ala.
September 15, 1944

My Dear Mr. Coleman on this particular evening. However I have decided to write you once again. now that I must confess that each one of your letters has been received. However, although my mental & physical conditions hasn't been at all good, under the circumstance and at this present time I don't feel at all good something Have got to be done for me & done at once. for a lately I found ever greater difficulty in getting on in life. There is nothing to console me. now I am eternally grateful for the monthly allowance even though it did me very little good as I owed it all out by making debts But now that I can smoke for a while & be relieve of some of my daily worries. Now Mr. Coleman I only wish to suggest a small favor of you all & that is I am in dire need of five dollars for a special purpose and I Hope my wishes will not be a sure sign of Bad luck to me.

while I understand your deepest Sympathies are with me still it seems only right for you all to not to let me suffer too much now in your leisure [   ] please spare a few moments to response to this. and know that I can not Hide my grief and my broken heart
Most Sincerely yours
Haywood Patterson
P. S. Write me information [Reel 5, Box 5, #000538 (folder c57), ILD]

WESTERN
UNION
NBM 29   29=BX DETROIT MICH 17 124OP   1944 OCT 17   PM 1 24
LOUIS COLEMAN=
112 EAST 19=

PLEASE SEND HAYWARD PATTERSON A DOCTOR RIGHT AWAY HE HAS GOT HURT THIS IS NOT TO BE KNOWN HE SLIPPED A LITTLE OUT AND ITS NOT TO BE KNOWN=

MAZELL PATTERSON HAYWARD MAZELL [Reel 5, Box 5, #000541 (folder c57), 1944, ILD].

October 18: Clarence Norris returns to Alabama after his attorney, Dr. Allan Knight Chalmers, convinces him that no punitive actions by the Alabama Parole Board will occur. The Board quickly sends Norris to Kilby State Prison.

Louis Coleman
112 East 19th St.
New York, NY
Dec. 12, 1944

My Dear Mr Coleman. I have received each one of your letters to me but it was therefore perfectly clear to you the reason for my long silence. why I wrote you is because I thought that you would give immediate assistance. but I was greatly disappointed wasnt I? now that I have been given the privilege to Write again and it would be cruel to Have you wait still longer on a letter from me. of course now I realize that I haven't any real good friends since my mother and father died in 1939. you see that I some time feel no regret and no fear because life Have left me nothing more to wish, and soon I Hope to be deliver from the Burden of such existence.

the future some time seems to have nothing more to offer me so why keep long for a life which can be for me now only an isolated, isolate and gloomy one? I am a poor boy mr. coleman without a prospect of the freedom I disevern. of course I Have I Have never learned to know what is usually called misfortune, but is there a greater misfortune then not to Be happy, than to sigh trough a life without comfort or Hope; to wear a way the endless weary days of an existence without delight. Now you can comprehend that the situation isnt at all favorable to me. now yous is almost Here again & we would be Happy at this time If all all would let us know the little service that you all can show now please don't forget our candy as it some extra. and our extra [ ] money. now I still be waiting in dreadful suspense and expectation, or may I say that I trust you will not darken my future any more than what It is. But to fulfill my wishes this time will light up my future perhaps with bright flowers, I must not go talking so therefore Wish you a good night.

yours truly,
Haywood Patterson [Reel 5, Box 5, #000545 (folder c55), ILD]

15

LETTERS FROM 1945
Patterson's Burden

BROADWAY TABERNACLE CHURCH
Broadway and Fifty Sixth Street
New York 19, N.Y.
Dr. Allan Knight Chalmers

February 2, 1945
Dear Mr. Coleman:

The enclosed is a copy of my letter to Andy. I have had a letter from the Parole Board this week which is a little more encouraging than I have had in the recent past. I plan to be down there, as I indicate, in the spring.

It might interest you to know that I have written seven other letters this week on general Scottsboro business. It may seem almost a closed issue with some people, but certainly it is not with us.

With cordial personal greetings,
Sincerely
Allan Chalmers

Enclosure
Mr. Louis Coleman
International Labor Defense
112 East 19th Street
New York 3, New York [Reel 5, Box 5, #000958 (folder c63), 1945, ILD]

BROADWAY TABERNACLE CHURCH
211 West 56th Street
New York 19, N.Y.

February 2, 1945
Dear Andy:

Your letter that came to me through Mr. Coleman is one that he felt that I ought to answer. He may have told you that already.

I do not know the length of time that your parole was to run. I was not one of those who told you that it was to be only for a year. I think I did say that when the parole had run for a while, I would make the effort to get you a full pardon; but that has to wait until we have worked it our for Clarence as well.

I am at the present moment trying hard to get a job offer for you and Clarence so that you can be shifted out of the state. Our major difficulty has been that the parole boards of outside states have not been willing to accept jurisdication. I am trying hard to get it worked out, with some hope of success, and may have some news for you before long. Do realize, however, that these things unfortunately take time. There is a lot of red tape involved, and it's almost impossible to cut it and hard to follow it out. I am working on it.

In any case, I expect to be down in Alabama again the first week in April. Meantime keep in touch with me as you want to, but plan to see me then if meantime we haven't been able to work it out. I have a constant concern about your interests and only wish I could move in this matter as rapidly as I want to. We are up against the difficulties of the rules and regulations on the one hand, and the inertia on the other of public officials.
Remember me, please, to your wife.
As ever,
Allan Knight Chalmers [Reel 5, Box 5, #000959 (folder c63), ILD]

Mr. Louis E. Burnham, Secretary   February 6, 1945
Southern Negro Youth Congress
526 Masonic Temple
Birmingham 3, Alabama

Dear Louis:
   I am enclosing a copy of a letter from Haywood Paterson. Is it possible for someone to go to see him and reassure him that everything possible is being done — preferably a white person but I suppose not necessarily.
Best regards,
Sincerely,
Louis Coleman [Reel 5, Box 5, #000552 (folder c57), ILD]

February 6, 1945
Dr. Allan Chalmers
Broadway Tabernacle Church
Broadway & 56th Street
New York 19, N.Y.

Dear Dr. Chalmers:
   Thank you very much for your note of February 2 and a copy of you letter to Andy Wright.
   I am sending to your attention a copy of a letter which we have received form Haywood Patterson. You will know best what the situation is in connection with that and whether you should communicate with him.
Sincerely yours,
Louis Coleman [Reel 5, Box 5, #000957 (folder c63), ILD]

Haywood Patterson
Kilby Prison
Montgomery, Ala
2–7–45

Dear Mr. Coleman,

I Have been trusting and prayin that you have Received my former letter in which I was suggesting that you send some one to my rescue, but so far I Have been greatly disappointed. you see the people Here are continual mistreating me without a cause that it is hard to conceive of it. of course I would be in much more comfortable circumstances than I am now if doctor Chalmers should come. I shell, However, say nothing to the doctor respecting the new attack which Have been made upon me until I see him.

I have been compelled to bear a many unjustice things. you see the people sought to make me sick; they sought to wound me, and I have no way of giving back the sickness & the wounds which they Have inflicted upon me will not so soon Heal. I am only a poor, powerless being & seem to Have no friends to come to my rescue at a time I most need some one so to disburden myself of a load. So may I say again please provide a way for Dr. to come down at once. I remain a friend.

Haywood Patterson [Reel 5, Box 5, #000553 (folder c57), ILD]

February 19, 1945
Miss Louise Patterson
632 Riopelle
Detroit 7, Michigan

Dear Miss Patterson

We have been hearing from Haywood. He is in good health but naturally not happy over his situation. I want to ensure you that we have not given up the case but as a matter of fact new efforts are being made to help him get out. Someone is going down to Alabama in a few weeks to try once more. Don't expect anything to quickly. It is a very difficult job to overcome the prejudices of the Alabama authorities but you may rest assured that everything possible is being done and will continue to be done to get him out as quickly as possible.

Very sincerely yours,

Louis Coleman [Reel 6, Box 5, #000179 (folder c67), ILD]

BROADWAY TABERNACLE CHURCH
Broadway and Fifty-Sixth Street
New York 19, N.Y.
Dr. Allan Knight Chalmers
Minister

Rev. Cyrus R. Pangborn   211 West 56th Street
Assistant Minister

Rev. Roberta N. Pangborn
  Counselor In Religion
Miss Frances M. Chamberlin
  Minister Secretary   February 20, 1945

Dear Mr. Coleman:

I had a letter this [   ] from Haywood which goes through the routine that
I know so well from long experience with him, in which he gives me up — and
he adds you in at the present time — and does not want to have anything to
do with either of us again. I don't need to tell you that this is a perfectly natural reaction of his present depression of spirit.

I rather suspect that he may not be getting my letters. I have written him
several times in the last month and one-half, and the replies I have had from
him, some of which have apparently been sneaked out of the prison, have
given no indication of his having received my letters at all. I wrote him again
today and said in the letter that I was checking with the Parole Board about
whether he was receiving my letters and have, of course, done that with them.
If I hear more about it, I'll let you know. I assume you are too experienced
with these things to let his recent attitude make any difference to you personally. We will remain his friends and do everything we can to effect his release.
[Reel 5, Box 5, #000556 (folder c57), ILD]

---

5. 9. 1945
648 Riopelle
Detroit 7, Mich.

Mr. Louis,

Dear's am write you ask you is' get worry one to help me is get my Brother
freedom this year for he have put up 15 years in there and look like with
someone can hup me is get him freedom pleases' am all mose crazy for he
write me and said me his his heath is gone Bad on him and he my never get
freedom for worry one have turn thy back on him sohupme pleas is suth for
me am write Ala. the Pardon and know they are not gone to hup me for they
are so dirty that they wont answard my letters write them mean my Brother
Haywood Patterson.

Well close please answard soon well wrote to Mr. [   ] Knight is in NY.
[Reel 6, Box 5, #000185 (folder c67), ILD]

Haywood Patterson
Camp Kilby Prison
Montgomery Ala.
June 25 1945

My Dear Coleman, I am bitter and Sad, and you understand it, for the
Horizon is dark for me and offers me no cheerful prospect. Now I Hope you
Have received my former letter in which I was giving you the true facts. Now
I posses secure means in which to prove that my conduct isnt what they make

out like. O posses them by Both white and Black inmates they have punished me terribly for No cause at all. that I can prove by the inmates they have held me in a dark dungeon for days and night without food or water. they Have whipped me more than once and Now I am placed in a solitary cell where all the inmates can come by and see me but they are not allowed to say anything at all to me without Being subject to a punishment. But in reality I am being used as a warning example to the whole herd of inmates but still I can get Mail out by a white trusty who Have no fear.

Now I say again that I am wearied of being perpetually threatened and punished by these criminal minded people and it is time that you all should Hunt down the chief facts concerning my conduct which they say are keeping me held a prisoner.

Now it isnt a day pass that they don't beat on some Black person only in this way to intimidate them & inspiring them with hate for me. it is High time now to make an example and shoe these people at last that I claim the right of freedom. you see that these old people are always egging or trying to egg some one upon me they appear to Have no other aim than to get rid of me an of course wearied with their aims and counter-parts because of their own persons who are prisoners and those of their Hightest helpers always remain friendly to me. these old people sometimes tells me, why dont you hurry up and die. You will never get free, and seem like they arrange their plans always at a safe distance between the time they thinks I should get some consideration from the parole Board to frame me in class C as a rule Violator. the parole Board people will make an outcry about my conduct.

now I want you to appeal to the public by using all means to regain Their confidence and re establish the true fact concerning my conduct and Have them to know that I will no longer serve as a slave but to be a Burden to the state of Alabama. I promise no longer work on this fame up charge. So please Write me through by Clarence Norris and be sure to send me a little money in his name that I will get also through him.

Yours truly Haywood Patterson

(please I Hope you can read this I am shake) [Reel 5, Box 5, #000562 (folder c57), ILD]

Haywood Patterson
Camp Kilby Prison
Montgomery Ala.
July 19 1945

My Dear Mr. Coleman and to all whom are concerned. I Have just a few days been released from the dog House after serving 14th days and nights there in on Bread & water. I mean one Biscuit a day and one cup of water for 14th days. laying on the hard floor, I nearly went under from such cruel treatment spent 3 days in Hospital and still I Havent got straight yet. the Doctor says that my Heart is Bad, my feets are right now swelling my condition are getting worst each day. They Have impaired my Health.

You see as I told you before that I am constantly surrounded by enemies who watch me with an evil eye and misrepresent every step I take. it Have always been Like this an will remain so until I die or become a decrepit old man whose arms is no longer useful to himself. Now that I am young they wish me labor as long as I will give it freely, But some How I believe that the time has arrived where that you all may recover my liberty. But you must first get some of the most influential and respectable citizens of this state to assist you all. fortunately it is not too late.

Now take such a resolution for if we allow this to pass too all is lost not only the freedom I wish but also you all Honors. Now this opportunity must not pass as many a brave friends we Have that is eager for a war with Alabama and other southern places for their inhuman treatment to Black people. the I.L.D. has friends and a faithful intrepid people which is sincerely devoted to its country and the rights there in for the unfortunate.

You know as a fact that they Havent give me an opportunity to distinguish myself and gain a popular name. You see these people are in error about my conduct for show little interest in what goes on here and appear numb and stupid. But when even I planned a pitful attempt to make a clear record I am not permitted to carry it into effect. When ever with my good efforts I might Have exerted a decision influence upon the parole Board I am ordered to be put in class C for something of no importance what ever, and when I remonstrated they charge me with rebelling against the authorities. I have suffered a great deal and the wounds which my heart Have received from their hands are bleeding yet and swelling me up. Something Have got to be Done at once. You all must send some one down to see bout me at once because my condition is serious each day. I am swelling and Nothing is being done for me.

Yours truly Haywood Patterson [Reel 5, Box 5, #000567 (folder c57), ILD]

Haywood Patterson
Camp Kilby Prison
Montgomery Ala.
July 27–1945

My Dear Mr. Coleman. I am unwell and very feeble to day However, though I am afraid that my health are impaired But still I must say a few additional words. Now that through Clarence Norris I Have enjoyed a letter from my sister Sebell. So I Have advised her to Write you my condition. So be good as to send my monthly allowance to her instead of me. you see that I am punctual and I must tell you that I Have been almost too impatient to wait no I Hope you all do not regret your promise to assist me while am need and so I trust that you mean to give me the noble assistance that you once promised me and I now has pressing need of money.

you see that my one desire of my soul in this Life is I want to be independent and not to ask favors of others prisoners. Now you will be gracious enough to give at least my monthly allowance to my sister and she will see that I gets it. now mr. Coleman I only trust that you have by this time gotten my former letters to you and doctor chalmers in which I open my heart to you all and layed my innermost thoughts at your feet. as fate is willing to give us another opportunity to repair and show that we are worthy of the rights, and if my cause are present before the highest court these people will no longer succeed in their mischief and frame up lies and it is owning to the efforts of you & the I.L.D. that it is so of course we are indebted to the I.L.D. for their zeal, energy & struggling for the good cause which is now no longer of yours but that of Alabama and their cause will succumb. god will not allow a great & noble people like you all to be trampled under foot by a few alabama tyrants who Bids injustice & unrighteousness to the black race.

now this can be related out the History according to what the U. S. constitu says who promised to protect our rights. God may not decree this But He may perhaps allow it if the I.L.D. and commetter should not be strong enough to set Bounds to such Mischief. as I am so unable to defend for my rights But god Have appointed a many Noble men to defend them for me but they seem to have lost faith in themselves & in their Honors & now all my rights & struggling for liberty are being taken that I can prove & we are still Temporizing & Hesitating to do anything about it. why we are not courageous enough to strike back when that you all can deliver me form the hateful yoke of these people for they are the meanest people I ever saw.

So again I say that I believe that the time has arrived where that you may recover my liberty. But you must first get some of the most influential & respectable citizens of Alabama to cooperate with you. Now Mr. Coleman I implore you to not to refuse to carry my wishes out and be reasonable sure to send my sister some money at once. She will get it to me through Clarence Norris.

Yours very Truly Haywood Patterson [Reel 5, Box 5, #000572 (folder c57), ILD]

Haywood Patterson
Route 3 Box 115
Montgomery Ala.
Oct. 9 — 1945

My Dear Mr. Coleman it an Honor to have your letter which I accepted with gratitude altho It almost crushed me at present time. but permit me now to open my heart to you & to lay my innermost thoughts at your feet. So I implore you to believe me.

you see now that I feel very much discouraged after the way you all have treated me. I know that you all have received the letters I wrote you while in trouble and you refused to give me any consideration at all. please Don't ever treat me like that How do you expect me to use controlled language when there this awful trouble staring me in the face all the time. Now I Have Been without money for four months and so I Have had to Borrow and in my borrowing I Have played myself way in debt so now I am asking you all for a Helping hand, so as to avoid anything that might give me Trouble. So I wish you all to send me at once $20.00 to clear up my debts with. Although it is almost too much to hope for that of course but I will be specially pleased for this valuable assistance for really and Truly I now needs Help more so than ever before so please do not Delay me for any great length of time as I would call this favor a most wonderful event of my life.

Now I taken advantage of this occasion in order to Have you know in advance my trouble is that I am in debt so be as good as to send me the requested amount you see that I am punctual & I must tell you that I have been almost too impatient to wait. Now I Hope you all do not regret your promise to assist me & that you mean to give me the Noble assistance your promised now you have the power over me to cause the future to appear not gloomy but full of promise and to allow me to Hope if not for happiness at least for rest and enjoyment. I Havent forgot I can yet realize that you are ardently Devoted to our cause and love the I.L.D. and none of us will ever forget what you have done in the past. So in patience & trust I will wait your return answer & Hope for favorable result know that I am still bounded to you all in gratitude.

Yours truly

Haywood Patterson [Reel 5, Box 5, #000578 (folder c57), ILD]

La Crosse, Wisconsin.

29 September 45

Dear Mrs. Huntington: I am troubled about our friend Haywood Patterson and hope you won't mind my turning to you for help. He implores me for a sum of money with which to secure his freedom.

He doesn't make clear to me how this is to be accomplished and I feel too uncertain of the matter to go ahead. In his latest letter he says you have sent him $100 to be used in this purpose and he begs me for $75 more. I am far from being wealthy, but would scrape up this amount for him if convinced it would bring him his release. Unfortunately, I've already tried to help other prisoners with cash and in both cases my aid turned out ill advised. These men took advantage of my interest and deceived me.

I don't understand, if Haywood's letters are censored at the prison, how he can write as openly as he does; and at that I cannot always be sure of his meanings. I keep sending him money — usually $5 — every month, but now he wants far more.

Anything you will say to me about this case will be kept a confidence, I assure you. I only want to do the best thing for Patterson, as you do.

Very best wishes,

Don Jonson

1147 Main

La Crosse

Wisconsin [Reel 5, Box 5, #000582 (folder c57), 1945, ILD]

October 9, 1945

Mr. Don Jonson

1147 Main St.

La Crosse, Wisc.

Dear Mr. Jonson:

Thank you for your letter addressed to Mrs. Huntington, who is now living in Connecticut and is no longer connected with our office.

I am afraid that Haywood is not informing you exactly of the situation. We have not sent him any sum of $100, and have no intention of doing so. We send him $5 a month, which is about all he is able to spend for legitimate purposes in prison.

Unfortunately he has been able to secure considerable other sums through a well-organized campaign of letter writing, and as a result has gotten himself into trouble over and over again in the prison. There is no doubt that the scrapes he gets into in the prison through such spending have contributed to the difficulty of obtaining his release.

You are correct in saying that it is ill-advised to send him any large sums of money.

Please consider the contents of this letter confidential, as Haywood's prison psychoses make it difficult for him to understand why people should not send him, money.

Very sincerely,

Louis Coleman

Secretary [Reel 5, Box 5, #000583 (folder c57), ILD]

16

LETTERS FROM 1946
Andy Wright's Return

Haywood Patterson
Route 3, Box 115
Montgomery Ala.
Jan 3 1946

Mr. Louis Coleman

My Dear Mr. Coleman. It an Honor to have your letter which I accepted with gratitude although it almost crushes me at present. But permit me now to open my heart to you and to lay my innermost thoughts at your feet. I implore you to think that I haven't any friends at all and my heart is wearies with so much false Hopes, and the Bitter disappointments I have been Receiving from you all in recent years. I can realize that you all good spirits and good will toward me Have died a way or disappeared and I have found no trustworthy companions among my so called friends to bear my secrets. I now mistrust every one. I have been treated so unfair by everyone until I doubt everything. I mistrust everybody and consider everybody my enemy. Now under the present circumstances my requestes you all has been refused you see now under the circumstances. Therefore I considered it good policy to pay my debts in order to avoid anything that might cause my trouble now the reason I wrote you for some assistance in order that it would resulted in the Betterment of my own good. you see right at the present I suffer in need of smokes Because every cent I Have gotten went on a debt. I must close.

Yours truly,

Haywood Patterson [Reel 5, Box 5, #000584 (folder c57), ILD]

Following the advice of Dr. Chalmers, in October 1946 Andy Wright returned to Kilby Prison, expecting some leniency after breaking parole by leaving Alabama, having his driver's license confiscated by a police officer and getting into a verbal dispute with a "white man" in Chicago. He would spend the next four years in and out of Alabama's prison system before his final parole in June 1950.

38 West Garfield Blvd
Chicago, Illinois
October 22, 1946

Mr. Roy Wilkins
409 Edgecomb Ave.
New York City. N.Y.

Dear Mr. Wilkins

Enclosed please find signed statement by Andy Wright requesting that he be sent to Alabama. We are also sending you itemized statement for living expenses and transportation incurred by us.

Very truly yours,

Henry W. McGee [Reel 22, Group 11, Box A514, #000341, NAACP]

October 25, 1946
Dear Mr. McGee:

I have your letter of October 22 with enclosures and I wish to thank you for taking care of this emergency job in such an excellent manner.

You may be interested to learn that the man was arrested and returned to prison when he got back home. All of us regret it very much but it is a thing he should have expected after what he called his "little trouble" with a white man, plus his leaving the state, that was the reason we felt he might be able to get away with staying in Chicago. We felt that the state might have just given up going after him and let him alone. However, since he insisted on returning we will now have to start on the whole weary business of getting him released on parole again. Under the circumstances you did exactly right and we are grateful for your cooperation.

A check is enclosed, made out to you personally, with the idea that you will reimburse the Chicago branch. We do not wish the check to bear the endorsement of the branch.

Very sincerely yours,

Assistant Secretary

Mr. Henry W. McGee
38 West Garfield Blvd.
Chicago, Illinois [Reel 22, Group 11, Box A514, #000346, NAACP]

[From Roy Wilkins, Asst. Secretary, NAACP]
November 4, 1946

MEMORANDUM TO MRS. WARING FROM MR. WILKINS:

Andy Wright was returned to prison about November 1 and should begin receiving once more our monthly check for $3 charged to the Scottsboro Defense Committee. [Reel 22, Group 11, Box A514. #000348. NAACP]

(From Roy Wilkins)
December 24th 1946
Dear Andy Wright:

All of us here are delighted to know that you are again a free man and we trust that nothing will happen in the future to interfere with your being with your wife and family.

The enclosed check was sent to you, but was returned with the information that you had been released. We are very glad to send it to you again with our best wishes of the Holiday season.

Very sincerely yours,
Assistant Secretary
Mr. Andy Wright
12 Winifred Street
Montgomery, Ala.
Enclosure: CHECK
RW: ELJ [Reel 22, Group 11, Box A514, #000352, NAACP]

LETTERS FROM 1947
The Cost of Parole

September 1947
Montgomery, Alabama
Kilby Prison

Dear Sir

I have written you one letter August 30 and no reply as yet concerning a copy of some Driver license I purchased there in October 1946 for the following year 1947 I purchased them in the name of James A Wright [   ] of Chattanooga Tenn. 2421 Long St. age 35, hgt 6ft, 2½, Wt. 184 Complexion dark brown, eyes light Brown and the alicense was taken by officer of State of Alabama Montgomery County and it cause me to be back in Prison of a Broken Parole unless I can get a copy of the License to Prove to the Pardon Board that I did have driver license I shall remain in Prison serving time for a crime that Wasn't committed and I cant make no 99 years. and I extremely appreciate it if you will write to Mr. Howell Turner, Chairman, c/o State Board of Pardon & Parole, Montgomery Ala. notifying him that I did get license there so that I may unite with my Wife and two Small children one 4 months and the other one 18 months. Enclose you will find $11 for the license I copy. Thanking you in Advance.
Respectfully
James A Wright
Kilby Prison
Montgomery Ala.
P.S. hope a promptly reply [Reel 22, Group 11, Box A514, #000367, NAACP]

Oct 30th 1947
Montgomery Ala.
Kilby Prison
Mr. Roy Wilkins

Dear Sir!

I have written you two letters and no reply from you as yet. I am beginning to wonder whether or not ou received them as it was some important things I asked you to do, and did you do it? another thing I have been here going on five months and have received only $6 from you, I noticed Haywood received his every month. the Pardon Board set me back until May 1949 unjustified decision, have Dr. Chalmers come back to New York? Please answer soon. and send me some money. I haven't got a cigarette.

So I will close.

Yours truly

Andy Wright [Reel 22, Group 11, Box A514, #000370, NAACP]

LETTERS FROM 1948
Patterson's Guile

Montgomery, Ala.
Friday, the 13th
(Feb. 13, 1948)

Dear Walter & Roy.

This is for your confidential eyes only.

Your tongue would do well to keep it close as well. I am off for South America very soon until after Easter and I want news as to how's the dope.

The main "dope"—and I do mean dope is Andy Wright. He tried to make a "deal" with the Parole Board—his liberty for information on the where abouts of Clarence Norris who has jumped parole. "They" claim that Clarence is in New York and harbored by Sam Leibowitz (which may mean am explosion for not telling me that they thought I was doing it.) I told them that it was fantastic to think that a judge would "harbor" an escaped prisoner; and that I did not know where he was. But isn't that stupid of Andy. This attempt has set back his parole until early 1949.

In spite of that, I've gotten them to agree that if we can get up a Parole Program in Chattanooga and the Tennessee Board will accept him they will advance his luck of landing parole. The stupid oaf. Hasn't he more sense than to try to make a "deal" with this gang.

Haywood is in bad shape. A homosexual fight in Kilby in Oct. has set his case back—indefinite. But we'll try again after we get Andy out.

My job was complicated by the Board now having two new members whom I had to "soften up" before I could even get them to agree to discuss it.

Roy, could you write Attorney George Chamlee in Chattanooga asking him to write out that parole set up. He wrote me he thought he could arrange.

Also—Can the office send Money Orders instead of Checks? The prison had clamped down on personal checks.

Finally Brethern, how can any decent man black or white—bear it to live in the "South." "I'm telling you" as the saying goes,

I'll see you North in April.

Allan [Reel 22, Group 11, Box-A514, #000394, NAACP]

MEMO...
To Mrs. Waring
March 11, 1948
From Roy Wilkins

Dr. Chalmers has advised us that there has been a change at Kilby prison in the handling of checks to prisoners and he asks therefore that our Scottsboro checks, which we send each month to Andy Wright and Haywood Patterson, be money orders or postal notes instead of checks.

RW [Reel 22, Group 11, Box-A514, #000391, NAACP]

March 11th 1948
My dear Mr. Chamlee:

We have a letter from Dr. Allan Knight Chalmers stating that the Alabama Parole Board has just about agreed that if a parole program can be set up in Chattanooga and if the Tennessee board will accept him, they will advance the date of Andy Wrights's parole. Wright you will remember, I am sure, is one of the Scottsboro defendants.

Dr. Chalmers, who is now in South America, wrote me asking if I would write you to find out if you could do anything on the parole set up. He says you wrote him that you thought you could arrange it.

I will appreciate hearing from you at you convenience.

Very sincerely yours,
Assistant Secretary.
Roy Wilkins
Attorney George W. Chamlee
212–213 Times Bldg.
Chattanooga, Tenn. [Reel 22, Group 11, Box A-514, #000392, NAACP]

Law Offices
GEORGE W. CHAMLEE
Attorney at Law
122½ East Seventy Street
Chattanooga 2, Tennessee

3–17–48
Mr. Roy Wilkins, Asst. Sec'y.,
20 West 40th Street,
New York 18, N.Y.

Dear Mr. Wilkins:

I am in receipt of your letter in reference to Andy Wright's parole in the State of Alabama.

Dr. Chalmers wrote me some time ago and I have some petitions with a few names on them addressed to the Alabama authorities requesting his parole and I will try to contact the Tennessee parole Officer for Chattanooga, and I think I can get him to agree to take Andy in charge and let him report to him at Chattanooga, or get arrangements for him to go North to seek employment.

He was here once but the prejudice was strong against him he said he did not want to stay here and I tried to prevail upon him to stay here anyway but he returned to Alabama and I think his parole was cancelled because of some dispute he had or was said to have had, with a hot-headed white man.

I will see if I can help this boy because I have always helped him and when they were looking right up at the gallows I found a legal chance in Scottsboro where the court had failed to sign an order overruling all motions for a new trial but had failed to sign the order and I was permitted to amend the motions and got into the record the fact that they were inadequately represented by council which resulted in a reversal of the cases in Washington, D.C.

With best wishes and kindest regards, I beg to remain,
Yours truly,
/s/ G.W. CHAMLEE
G.W. Chamlee [Reel 22, Group 11, Box-A514, #000389, NAACP]

Goal this year 2500 Members
MONTGOMERY BRANCH NATIONAL ASSOCIATION
FOR ADVANCEMENT OF COLORED PEOPLE
123½ Monroe St. — Third Floor — Telephone 3-8005 — 3-4824
Membership Drive Now On — "Join To-Day,
You May Need NAACP To-Morrow"

MONTGOMERY, ALABAMA

E.D. NIXON
Pres. State Conference of Branches

MRS. ROSA L. PARKS
Secretary of Branch

REV. H.H. HUBBARD
Campaign Chairman

MARION O. BOND
Campaign Director
National Office

June 14, 1948
Dr. Allan Knight Chalmers
Treasurer of NAACP
20 West 40th Street
New York 18, N.Y.

Dear Dr. Chalmers:

Inclosed you will find check for $10.00 for Alabama Conferences of NAACP Branches, National/Convention Tax. Dr. W. P itts of Montgomery, Alabama was kind enough to give me your message concerning Andy Wright. I regret to say, but it seems as if Wright has made it hard for parole for quite sometime. This last incident, I talked to Wright about it in the City jail, and he admitted that he did not have Drivers License to operate the Car. But if there is anything that I can do to help him, I will be glad to render my assistance.

Yours truly,
E.D. Nixon, Pres.

Montgomery Branch
NAACP [Reel 22, Group 11, Box A-514, #000387, NAACP]

On July 20 the Scottsboro Defense Committee, along with thousands of supporters around the world as well as their protagonists, were shocked to learn through newspaper accounts that Haywood Patterson had apparently successfully escaped from prison. An article from the *Birmingham News*, posted out of Montgomery, Alabama, and titled "Scottsboro Felon Escapes," described the event:

> Haywood Patterson, one of the defendants in the famed Scottsboro criminal attack case in the early 1930's escaped from Kilby Prison late today along with eight other Negro convicts.
> Patterson, now 35 years old, was serving a 75-year term. He was convicted in 1937 and had escaped once before tonight. That was in 1943 when he got away and was recaptured two days later.
> Five of the nine Negroes who fled today were taken into custody a few hours later but Patterson and three others were still at large.
> Patterson's escape brought a promise of an investigation by State Prison Director Frank Boswell.
> "That Negro had no business working on the farm. Boswell declared, "He should have been kept inside the prison. I don't know how he got out on the farm but I'm going to find out."

In the story, Boswell went on to describe the prisoners' escape from a work truck, with Patterson "the first to run," and the guard firing upon the fleeing men, without effect.

Haywood Patterson, who escaped on July 17, 1948, from Kilby State Prison Farm, wrote the following undated letter. Though the intended receiver is unknown and possibly the first part of the letter is missing, its intent is clear and direct. Titled by an archivist as "Yes, I am the Scottsboro Boy," the brief letter is an attempt by Patterson to vindicate himself.

Yes I am the Scottsboro boy namely Haywood Patterson, and am not a refugee from justice. I am only a victim of circumstances over which I have had no control. and I do want the people of American to realize that I am not trying to hide from justice, but what I have done was just & right. the only unjust thing I have did in Alabama that is I killed two state dogs in order to make my escape clear....
Save me from my personal enemy. I would be very glad you know,
Haywood Patterson

Of the nine Scottsboro defendants only two, Clarence Norris and Haywood Patterson, managed to escape from Alabama state prison authorities. Though both defendants failed on their first attempt (Patterson on April 12, 1943, and Norris by violating the terms of his parole in 1944, only to be sent back in October 1944), they were not discouraged from making another escape attempt.

When again paroled in 1946, Norris successfully skipped parole after serving fifteen years. He assumed his brother's name, Willie Norris, and eventually arrived in New York City. He found a job working as a maintenance man for New York City and raised a family. Norris was eventually pardoned by Alabama Governor George Wallace on October 25, 1976. On January 23, 1989, Clarence Norris died at the age of 76 in New York City. He was the last surviving defendant of the Scottsboro case.

Patterson's successful escape from the Kilby Prison State Farm on July 17, 1948, represented a monumental demonstration of fortitude, guile and rational thinking. Patterson spent nearly two years planning the escape. Once beyond the limits of the prison, he utilized his previous years of experience as a hobo, traveling the intricate southern railroad system, and reaching Atlanta, Georgia, within a few days of his escape. Throughout this harrowing trek, Patterson befriended both black and white farmers and railroad workers who knew of or otherwise sympathized with his escape. He described one encounter with a friendly family of railroad workers, at whose house he stopped in search of a meal. After broaching the subject of the Scottsboro trial and determining that his hosts were sympathetic to his cause, Patterson identified himself and asked for food:

> "I tell you, I am a little hungry. You can help me a great deal if you would give me a little something to eat."
>
> She said sure, she'd give me a much a she had. She ran right into the kitchen.
>
> "That good enough," I said.
>
> She had some green peas, pork chopped up in it, corn muffins. She brought it out. Fed me.
>
> Expressed her sympathy. Made me feel like I had friends [Patterson/Conrad, 237–238].

In another instance, Patterson recalled that a black fireman on a freight train in Valedocia, Georgia, saw him hiding on the train and exclaimed:

> "They arrest you and put you in jail and give you six months for riding trains here."
>
> "Do they have anyone around now going to arrest me?" You not going to say anything, are you?"
>
> "No, I'm not going to say nothing. You stay there and I'll protect you. I'll

ride the train down to the crossing in order to block you — put the look on me instead of you."

He stayed on and jumped off as the train picked up speed and I got through there.

I rode on to Collegeville, Georgia, about ten or eleven miles outside of Atlanta. I got off there. I began walking, headed toward Atlanta [Patterson and Conrad, 242].

Once Patterson reached his destination of Detroit, he quickly made contact with his sister and began an attempt to assimilate into a lifestyle that had changed considerably over the last eighteen years. He made contact with sup-

"Yes I am the Scottsboro Boy," letter written by Haywood Patterson after his escape from Kilby State Prison Farm, July 1948. The specific date is unknown (courtesy the Daily Worker/Daily World Photographs Collection, Tamiment Library, New York University).

porters of the Scottsboro defendants and novelist I.F. Stone, who put him in contact with author Earl Conrad, who assisted Patterson in publishing an autobiography in June 1950, *Scottsboro Boy*. By the fall of 1950 Patterson was arrested by the FBI and faced extradition to Alabama; however, Michigan Governor G. Mennen Williams refused to obey the extradition order amid a growing campaign by Patterson's supporters. In December of that year, Patterson was involved in a barroom brawl that ended with a stabbing death. He was charged with manslaughter and eventually went to trial which ended with a hung jury. His second trial was ruled a mistrial, and after a third trial he was found guilty and sentenced to serve six to fifteen years. Patterson served only one year before he died in jail, reportedly of lung cancer, on August 24, 1952.

LETTERS FROM 1950
Andy's Walk

Joseph B. Robinson, M.D.
57 South hawk Street
Albany 6, N.Y.

January 31, 1950

Mr. Thurgood Marshall
Ass't Chief Special Counsel
N.A.A.C.P.
20 West 40 Street
New York, New York

Dear Thurgood:

I am sorry to have taken so long to accomplish a small task, but I feel that we should be able to settle Andy Wright in Albany. I have secured a nice room for him at the home of Mrs. Johnnie Hamilton, 187 First Street, Albany. Board can be arranged either there or at some nearby convenient place. The room rent alone is $6.00 per week.

I have secured a promise from the Director of Personnel at the Albany Hospital that he will hire Andy as either kitchen boy, porter, or possibly as an orderly after he arrives in Albany, providing he is able to pass a routine physical examination which would include an X-ray of the chest. The Personnel Director is Mr. R.A. Brunner.

Let me know if this is satisfactory or if any further details are necessary. In the event that Andy comes to Albany, I will be glad to keep an eye on him and help him in any way possible.

Sincerely yours,

(signed)

Joseph B. Robinson, M.D. [Reel 22, Group 11, Box A-514, #000418, NAACP]

WESTERN UNION

NA307 RX PD=ATLANTA GA   552P=
ALLEN KNIGHT THLOMAS=

CARE NACP=DLR 20 WEST 40 ST

ANDY WILL ARRIVE PENN STATION 11AM TUESDAY=
GENE=

> Telegram
> Received by _____ *MS* _____
> Time _____ *9:AM* _____
> Date _____ *6/13/50* _____
> Referred to _____ *WPO* _____
> PC THLOMAS [Reel 22, Group 11, Box A-514. #000425. NAACP]

6/17/50
Afro American (Newspaper)

**Scottsboro
Case Near End
Andy Wright Last
to Leave Prison**
MONTGOMERY, Ala.—

After 19 years all of the details of the famed "Scottsboro Case" seem to be ended. The last of the nine defendants in the case has been ordered to be paroled. He is Andy Wright, 38, who has spent about 19 years in prison.

Wright was paroled in 1944 after having served seven years of a 99 year sentence. His parole was revoked in 1947 when he was convicted of reckless driving and driving without a license.

To Work in N.Y.

According to the State Pardon-Parole Board, Wright will work as a porter in a hospital in New York State. He will leave Kilby prison on Friday.

The nine Scottsboro boys in March 1931, were jailed and tried on charges of criminally attacking two white women while on a freight train in Paint Rock, Ala.

* * *

POSTSCRIPT

Throughout the forty-five years of judicial ignominy known as the Scottsboro rape case, literally millions of people worldwide became familiar with the public criminalization and humiliation of nine African American migrant youths. They were subject matter for newspapers, plays, books, and pamphlets; massive rallies were held on their behalf; radio programs and newsreel film documented their trials; even an international spectacle such as the 1939 New York World's Fair reportedly displayed depictions of the Scottsboro defendants as wax figures (Dixon, 1980). None of the nine youths were executed by the State of Alabama; all but one were eventually released, paroled or pardoned. One defendant, Haywood Patterson, utilizing guile and ingenuity, successfully escaped from Alabama's notorious Kilby State Prison in 1948. All of these men suffered a variety of debilitating chronic disabilities as a result of their incarceration. Unfortunately, their letters about this experience, though available in a number of archives, were originally poorly photocopied, and due to the defendants' illiteracy and poor grammar were also marginalized as insignificant data on the African American fight against repression.

It is now evident that letters written by and to the Scottsboro defendants contained not only indispensable information about the trial's progression, but strategies utilized by the defendants in hopefully ensuring their survival under a brutal justice system regime perpetrated by prison guards, white prisoners and conspiring prison superintendants. Within this cauldron of hate, symptoms of madness appeared often in letters sent to supporters, yet madness never took control of their lives. What is indicated was their expressed opinions and concerns over the legal and ideological battles being waged for control of their case by the ILD and NAACP.

As the legal battle between these two contentious defense teams intensified, an often confusing fog of who represented whom in court was disseminated through newspapers, magazines and radio reports into the public arena. What now appears to be evident is that letters written by the defendants or composed by others were critical in the legal jostling beween the two defense teams. At stake were a number of political issues, some of which were mired in traditional white American racial and class biases, made more difficult at the time by an economic depression. For some, the Scottsboro youths were problematic in that they presented a racial imagery dilemma due to their rural southern and mostly illiterate backgrounds. Portrayed often as the political pawns of one defense team or another, the Scottsboro defendants' personalities, intelligence and desires were often diminished by unsympathetic media reports or slighted by internal organizational memorandums. As a consequence they were viewed either as heroes or villains by a public that had little knowledge of the defendants' personal thoughts and perspectives on their trial.

In today's world, as in the 1930s, access to information is critical to the public's understanding of issues concening civil rights and human justice. With continual developments in the field of information transmission and knowledge sharing, municipalities are systematically bombarded with related issues such as data collection, its analysis and use. An ever-increasing number of incidents similar to the Scottsboro case are now questioned and adjudicated in the public eye, but often at the expense of in-depth analysis.

The importance of these issues is paramount in understanding the Scottsboro letters as written narratives that required of their authors an ability to write reflectively and purposefully about a fleeting moment while being subjected to a brutal real-time existence. In today's world filled with a whirlwind of newly experienced events, such reflections are often perilously left for others to decide what is of historic importance. Fortunately, most of the Scottsboro defendants found the means by which to document their own thoughts, concerns, ambitions, loves and fears in the most available format at the time — the letter. Without their labor in this regard, efforts to interpret the Scottsboro defendants' concerns, whether complex or seemingly trivial, would have been left in the often uncaring hands of others.

As an unfortunate corollary, letters written by the Scottsboro defendants were often utilized by social scientists in a manner that sadly minimized their visceral quality and, by inference, their emotional and racial significance. As a consequence, studies on the Scottsboro case have generally exhibited a deference to trial correspondence, court room proceedings and support committees that skewed our understanding of the Scottsboro trial's most important aspect, its defendants.

Though the attorneys for the Scottsboro defendants eventually prevailed in the court room, within the walls of Kilby and Atmore prisons and Birmingham's jail they were only minimally effective in lessening the brutality.

Material support in most instances was brought about by support committees' ability to document and to internationally publicize their clients' plight. Conversely, the defendants' ongoing written contact with various members of support committees, both national and internationally, provides the contemporary reader with an understanding of the differences and similarities in the defendants' historical narratives.

However, these letters in themselves do not provide the reader with a total understanding of the Scottsboro defendants' subjective experiences. It should also be noted the reader's *real time* awareness of state terror and judicial racism, then and now, is often cerebral rather than intuitive, unless supported by previous experiences. That is to say, for the oppressed and incarcerated African Americans during this era, terror was innately perceived before it was manifested, not the reverse.

* * *

At the end of the day, one must keep in mind that the selected Scottsboro letters in this volume are responses and reactions by the writers to their reality. They were composed with all of the emotion and passion that the surrounding social context would force upon their authors. Understandably, the letters offer the reader an opportunity to identify with, begin to recognize and possibly empathize with the young men, their parents and supporters as they engaged in a monumental struggle against the state of Alabama.

Finally, the selected letters by the Scottsboro defendants illuminate their troubled existence of almost two decades, an exisence filled with shackles, stone walls, beatings, and witnessed executions, along with the continual expectation of further psychological and physical violence. These letters underline a fundamental reality for millions of Americans: what it meant to be an enemy of the state in the country of their birth. These defendants understood this not only in the sense of wanting to be respected, but in a comportment that emphasized their own dignity, virtue and most important, social distance from their tormentors. This is revealed when their letters increasingly began to indicate that they viewed themselves not simply as victims, but as protagonists in an honorable cause, their freedom.

* * *

April 19, 2013, was a cool morning in Scottsboro, Alabama, as the editor of this volume witnessed the official signing of two documents: Senate Bill 97, which allows for future posthumous pardons in the state of Alabama; and House Resolution 20, which exonerated the Scottsboro defendants of any criminal charges. This task was performed by Alabama Governor Robert Bentley in the nave of the oldest standing African American Church in Jackson County, dating back to 1878. Though the approximately 200 people attending this historic ceremony were acutely aware that this exoneration after 82 years was long overdue, the weight of an infamous judicial process and the accompanying terrors of incarceration lay heavily on everyone inside the church's sanctuary. In this fashion American judicial justice was ostensibly rendered.

— KMK

APPENDICES

A. Report of the "Traveling Salesman"

In the early days of what would become known as the "Scottsboro Boys" case, Alabama newspapers such as the *Huntsville Daily Times* relied primarily upon local white residents from Paint Rock and Scottsboro to assess what occurred on March 25, 1931. However, published observations by a "traveling salesman" in the *Times* alerted local residents, both white and black, that two deeply held southern white rules had been violated, in the physical assault by blacks upon whites, and sexual assault by black males upon white females. For many whites, the incendiary nature of such alleged violations provided a level of credence where evidence was lacking. In an article published just a day after the events on the train, the following observations were made:

> A traveling salesman passing through Paint Rock, Alabama in the afternoon of March 25th 1931 recalled seeing some "hundred men standing grimly about and that the nine negroes were lined up against the wall of a brick store, in charge of a deputy sheriff who happened to be in Paint Rock on some county business." However, he also discerned that "the crowd of men was orderly, though it would have taken just a little leading for a wholesale lynching" [ADAH Digital Archives: *The Huntsville Daily Times*, March 26 1931].

B. Kilby State Prison

Built in 1923 at a cost of $2,250,000, the Kilby State Prison complex was situated on 2,550 acres some four miles outside of Montgomery, the state capital of Alabama. A main building held approximately 900 prisoners, and the complex also included a cotton mill and shirt factory, both of which used the labor of the convicts to produce 105,000 yards per week of "the highest grade chambray cloth." Two-thirds of the chambray produced was used by the Kilby shirt factory, which assigned some 350 convicts in the manufacture of 12,000 blue work shirts per month. The rest of the chambray was sold on the open market. Kilby Prison also maintained a dairy farm consisting of one hundred cows to produce milk and butter. A large portion of the land, some 1,500 acres, was devoted to garden and farm crops for the prisoners; however the vast majority of the surplus was sold on the open market (Chazzman 34). Kilby prison was known as Alabama's "Death House." One of the Scottsboro defendants, Clarence Norris, recalled that the execution rate was so high that "while I was on death row at Kilby I've seen some seventeen or eighteen people going to the electric chair, or what we would call doing 'walk-bys.' In fact, back there in February 9, 1934, I saw five men walk past my cell on their way to the electric chair. In one night, right behind each other, just like hogs going to the slaughter, they killed Ernest Walker, Solomon Roper, Harie White, John Thompson and Bennie Foster. I'm not sure why all of them was put to death, but I do know you could actually smell burning flesh all up and down death row after they was executed" (Kinshasa 2003, p. 54).

C. The Death of Janie Patterson

Daily World Newspaper
December 25, 1937

Mother of Scottsboro Boy Dies In Cincinnati of Paralytic Stroke

Cincinnati, Ohio. Dec. 24 —

Janie Patterson, mother of Haywood Patterson, one of the five Scottsboro boys still imprisoned died of a paralytic stroke here this morning. Her death came in the midst of six years of suffering and grief over the frame-up of her son and other Negro youths more than seven years ago.

Mrs. Patterson died at the home of her daughter Louise at 1037 Cutter St. Cincinnati. Anna Damon, national secretary of the International Labor Defense, Louis Coleman, Sasha Small, and Rose Baron, all leading members of the I.L.D. staff in New York City, immediately sent a wire to Mrs. Patterson's family expressing the "profoundest sympathy" and pledging to redouble the fight for the freedom of the five boys still in Alabama jails. The I.L.D. is a member of the Scottsboro Defense Committee which has charge of the defense of the imprisoned youths.

Mrs. Patterson, who was one of the most widely known of the Scottsboro mothers, has travelled throughout the country in the interest of the movement to free the boys. She was stricken with paralysis early this year when she went to Alabama to see her son. Her family had to assist her return to Cincinnati.

Her whole right side became paralyzed and her condition became more and more critical until she passed away today.

The death of Mrs. Patterson made Haywood an orphan. His father, Claude, died last March 25, the very day that the Scottsboro boys were framed in 1931.

D. Death Warrant of Haywood Patterson

<u>DEATH WARRANT</u>
THE STATE OF ALABAMA
CIRCUIT COURT, SPECIAL SESSION, APRIL, 1931.
JACKSON COUNTY
No. 2404. THE STATE vs Haywood Patterson
INDICTMENT for Rape
TO THE WARDEN OF KILBY PRISON GREETINGS:
    WHEREAS, on the 7th day of April, 1931 came H.G. Bailey Solicitor, who prosecutes for the State of Alabama, and also came the said defendant and the said Haywood Patterson in his own person and by his attorneys, and the said defendant the said Haywood Patterson being duly arraigned upon said Indictment for Rape, for his plea thereto says that he is not guilty.
    Thereupon came a jury of good and lawful men to-wit; George R. Joyner and eleven others, who being empanelled and sworn, according to law, upon their oaths to say "We the jury find the defendant guilty of Rape as charged in the indictment and fix his punishment at death."
                            (Signed) George R. Joyner, Foreman.
    And the said defendant the said Haywood Patterson being in open Court on the 9th day of April, 1931 and being asked by the Court if he had anything to say why the sentence of the law should not now be pronounced upon him and he says nothing. It is therefore considered by the Court and it is the judgement of the Court and the sentence of the law that the said defendant the said Haywood Patterson be sentenced to death by electrocution at Kilby Prison in the City of Montgomery, Montgomery County, Alabama, on Friday on the 10th day of July, 1931, as provided by law.
    NOW, therefore you are hereby commanded in keeping with the law and the verdict of the jury and order of the Court as aforesaid, that you take charge of the said defendant the said Haywood Patterson and execute said sentence at Kilby Prison on the 10th day of July, 1931.
    Herein fail not and make due return of how and when you have executed this writ.
    In Witness whereof I have hereunto set my hand and affixed the Official Seal of this Court on this the 18th day of April, 1931.
    <u>C.A. Wann</u>
    Clerk of the Circuit Court
[Scottsboro Boys Museum & Cultural Center. Scottsboro, Alabama].

REFERENCES

Sources

Alabama Department of Archival History (ADAH). Montgomery, Alabama.
Allan Knight Chalmers Center/Howard Gotlieb Archival Research Center. Boston University, Massachusetts.
Beinecke Rare Books and Manuscript Library. Yale University.
Bobst Library/Tamiment Library, New York University.
Cornell University Law Library and Collections, Cornell, New York.
Harry Ransom Center. University of Texas at Austin.
Henry Wadsworth Longfellow Dana Collection, 1932–1938. Manuscript, Archives and Rare Book Library. Emory University.
Instituur Voor Sociale Geschiedenis (International Institute for Social History). Amsterdam, Holland.
John Jay College of Criminal Justice, CUNY/PSC-CUNY Sponsored Research and Award Program.
Manuscripts, Archives and Rare Books Division, Schomburg Center for Research in Black Culture. The New York Public Library, Astor, Lenox and Tildew Foundations.
National Association for the Advancement of Colored People (NAACP). Baltimore, Maryland.
Schomburg Center for Research in Black Culture (SCRBC). New York Public Library.
Scottsboro Boys Museum. Scottsboro, Alabama.

Works Cited

Acker, James R. *Scottsboro and Its Legacy: The Cases That Challenged American Legal and Social Justice*, New York: Praeger, 2007.
Burns, Haywood. Foreword, *The Man from Scottsboro: Clarence Norris and the Infamous 1931 Alabama Rape Trial, in His Own Words*. Kwando M. Kinshasa. Jefferson, NC: McFarland, 2003.
Carter, Dan T. *Scottsboro: A Tragedy of the American South*. Baton Rouge: Louisiana State University Press, 1979.
Chamlee, George W. *Papers of the International Labor Defense: National Office File-Records*. University Publications of America. SC Micro R-981. Schomburg Center on Black Culture and Research 1931.

Conrad, Earl. *Scottsboro Boy.* Garden City, NY: Doubleday, 1950.

Dixon, Mamie. The editor's 1980 interview with Ms. Mamie Dixon indicated the existence of wax figures of the nine "Scottsboro Boys" at the 1939 World's Fair in New York City. Subsequent inquiries have not indicated that these wax figures were preserved.

Herdon, Angelo (1934). "Indict the Social System!" in *Socialism and Liberation*, 1934. http://socialismandliberation.org/mag/index.psp/aid=163.

Kennedy, Randall. *Race, Crime and the Law.* New York: Vintage Books/Random House, 1997.

Kinshasa, Kwando. *The Man from Scottsboro: Clarence Norris in His Own Words.* Jefferson, NC: McFarland, 2003.

Linder, Doug. "Retrial by Judge Callahan" http://www.law.umkc.edu/faculty/projects/FTrials/scottsboro/SB_bCalla.html. Retrieved 2009-09-20.

Linder, Douglas O. "Without Fear or Favor: Judge James Edwin Horton and the Trial of the 'Scottsboro Boys.'" *UMKC Law Review* 68 (2000), pp. 549–583.

Norris v. Alabama (No. 534 April 1935). www.law.umkc.edu/faculty/projects/ftrials/scottsboro/SB_norus.html.

Papers of the International Labor Defense. *Scottsboro Case.* Frederick, MD: University Publications of America, Inc., N.D.

Papers of the NAACP. Part 6. *The Scottsboro Case,* 1931–1950. Frederick, MD: University Publications of America, Inc., N.D.

Rampersad, Arnold. *The Life of Langston Hughes: I, Too, Sing America.* Volume 1: 1902–1941. New York: Oxford University Press, 2002.

Ransdell, Hollace. *Report on the Scottsboro, Alabama Case.* New York: American Civil Liberties Union, 1931.

Scottsboro Trial Homepage: Biographies Page, *Victoria Price.* www.law.umkc.edu/faculty/projects/Ftrials/scottsboro/SB_Bpric.html.

_____. http://law2.umkc.edu/faculty/projects/FTrials/scottsboro/SB_bPATT.html.

INDEX